ABOUT THE AUTHOR

THEODORE BRAMELD, a pioneer in culture-and-education interdisciplinary studies, is Professor of Educational Foundations at Boston University. He has lectured widely in universities beyond his home campus, including those of Japan, Korea, and the Philippines, under the auspices of the United States Department of State. His field work in Japan was carried out as a Fulbright research scholar with the cooperation of the Wenner-Gren Foundation for Anthropological Research.

Dr. Brameld's long involvement in anthropology, philosophy, and education is exemplified by several previous books, notably *Cultural Foundations of Education: An Interdisciplinary Exploration* (1957), *The Remaking of a Culture: Life and Education in Puerto Rico* (1959), and *The Use of Explosive Ideas in Education: Culture, Class, and Evolution* (1965). The present work, *Japan: Culture, Education, and Change in Two Communities*, is an application and elaboration of the theoretical position presented in his earlier works.

JAPAN
Culture,
Education,
and Change in
Two Communities

Books by Theodore Brameld

*The Remaking of a Culture: Life and Education in
Puerto Rico*

Cultural Foundations of Education

The Use of Explosive Ideas in Education

Education as Power

Values in American Education (coeditor and coauthor)

Education for the Emerging Age

Patterns of Educational Philosophy
(revised and published in two volumes):
*Philosophies of Education in Cultural Perspective
Toward a Reconstructed Philosophy of Education*

Ends and Means in Education

Minority Problems in the Public Schools

Design for America

Workers' Education in the United States   (editor and coauthor)

A Philosophic Approach to Communism

JAPAN

Culture, Education, and Change in Two Communities

Theodore Brameld
Boston University

Holt, Rinehart and Winston
*New York   Chicago   San Francisco   Atlanta
Dallas   Montreal   Toronto   London*

Copyright © 1968 by Holt, Rinehart and Winston, Inc.
All rights reserved
Library of Congress Catalog Card Number: 69–12561

2730901

Printed in the United States of America

1   2   3   4   5   6   7   8   9

To Shigeharu Matsuura

FOREWORD

This is a comparative study of culture and education in two small communities in the setting of their larger municipalities and still wider cultural environments. Since comparison is one of the trademarks of an anthropological approach, and for other reasons, this is a book with an anthropological orientation. Professor Brameld is not a formally trained anthropologist but he has assimilated anthropological concepts and methods and modified them to his own purposes. The influence of his background in education, and particularly in ethics and social philosophy, is clear in that unlike most anthropologists he takes a value-oriented position in the interpretation of his evidence. He sees the major relationships among subcultures and institutions in the ways in which they conflict, reinforce each other, or are congruent with certain goals, rather than in the functional interdependency of these groupings and patterns within a cultural system. Nevertheless, he is committed to the principle that all learning and teaching must be understood in cultural and social context, so these functional interdependencies are not neglected.

His interpretation is based upon substantial evidence, and he makes the procedures for the collection of this evidence clear. He utilizes objective techniques such as random sampling in his study of value orientations but, like most anthropologists, depends heavily upon interviews and contact in depth with a number of key informants. He makes the basis for the selection of these informants clear. His data also demonstrate that he spent, as he states, countless hours in social interaction as a participant observer.

Because he has substantial data, collected systematically and under conditions as controlled as possible in the field as well as from his participant observation, he is able to accept the reality of the wide dispersion of characteristics and responses in all dimensions of his inquiry. Though his interpretation is value-oriented and though he sees connections between parts of a culture system more in goal-directed than functional terms, he meticulously avoids underplaying conflicts and differences that could otherwise lead to premature closure in his interpretation.

The study is comparative. It is also inductive. Professor Brameld does not begin with generalizations, then document them. He describes and interprets and comes to generalizations, in normative terms, as a result of an immersion in the situations he is studying. This, too, except for the explicit normative strain, is in the anthropological tradition. Because he proceeds inductively and because he uses both wide-ranging observation and explicit, semicontrolled research procedures, he is able to make definitive statements about teacher attitudes, educational goals, administrative policies, and community receptivity or rejection of policies in their actual settings. He does not confuse the particular and local with the general and universal, a fatal mistake in any study, but particularly where a normative analysis is the aim.

Anthropologists and other social scientists who do field studies should take heed of Professor Brameld's procedures for relating his research to the communities in which it was done. He sought the active participation of the members of the community in the study and attempted to share the results so that they might be of some benefit to the people. In this way he avoided the all too familiar situation where the researcher mines the area for information relevant to his unshared, and sometimes undeclared, purposes, then leaves without submitting any of his results to public discussion and criticism.

The author's treatment of education is an integral part of his inductive comparative analysis. Evidence concerning various aspects of educational process therefore appears long before the final chapter, which is devoted to a consideration of educational goals in the social and cultural context described.

Professor Brameld's study is made especially relevant not only because it is about two rapidly changing communities, with an additional comparative perspective provided by his regional leader panel, but because it is a study of prejudice and segregation that reaches deep into cultural life and into the educational process. This applies both to the community of fishermen, *gyomin*, and to the pariah community of *burakumin*, but even more acutely to the latter—a population who bear no visible stigmata of race or creed, but who suffer discrimination in nearly every social form. The special situation of the *burakumin* and the consequences of this situation in the schools are described. Americans reading this analysis will see mirrored the treatment of minorities in American society. Because neither *burakumin* nor *gyomin* are physically distinguishable from the rest of the population, the social and psychological foundations of prejudice and discrimination become dramatically clear.

George D. Spindler
Professor of Anthropology and
 Education
Stanford University

ACKNOWLEDGMENTS

The generous cooperation received from many friends and colleagues in both Japan and the United States is more deeply appreciated than any formal acknowledgment can possibly convey. It is to be regretted that the names of primary informants cannot be included; they have been assured of anonymity. It is with a sense of pride and satisfaction, however, that others who also befriended, advised, and otherwise assisted at various stages in the planning and execution of this work are presented, in alphabetical order:

Tsugio Ajisaka, Genji Akie, Shoko Akie, Tomi Akie, Kinji Ando, Mitsuru Aoki, Tsuneo Ayabe, Glenn Bowersox, John F. Bridgman, Freeman Butts, Jack Childress, Kyoko C. Cho, John B. Cornell, Merle Curti, Kazukimi Ebuchi, Munenori Enjoji, Charles B. Fahs, Edward J. Findlay, Toshio Fujitani, Martha G. Geesa, Jiro Hane, Keiko Hani, Toshiyuki Hara, Masao Hattori, Kiyoomi Hirata, Masunori Hiratsuka, David Hitchcock, Kazuyoshi Ikeda, Susumu Ikeda, Eijiro Inatomi, Tsugio Ishida, Jiro Ishii, Kikuji Ito, Ryoji Ito, Jinichiro Jinriki, Tokiomi Kaigo, Zenji Kajiura, Masanori Kaneko, Jintaro Kataoka, Shuichi Katsuta, Victor Kobayashi, Yoichi Kodama, Gunzo Kojima, Hiroji Kuriya, Masami Maki, Yukiko Maki, Shigeo Masui, Yoshiaki Matsuda, Kyoichi Matsuoka, Charles L. Medd, Hiroshi Miyazaki, Yasuko Mizoue, Akira Mori, Seiya Munakata, Kiyoshi Murayama, Monkichi Nanba, Iwao Nishimura, Nobusada Nishitakatsuji, Matao Noda, Nobukiyo Nomura, Edward Norbeck, Yoshio Nozu, Kuniyoshi Obara, Tetsuro Obara, Katsumi C. Okuza, Kazuo Onga, Morris E. Opler, Lita Osmundsen, Juichi Oyabu, John E. Reinhardt, Takeo Saito, Nigi Sato, Takakatsu Sekiguchi, Arashi Shigyo, Robert J. Smith, George Spindler, Shido Sumeragi, Nobuya Takagi,

Masao Takahashi, Kazuo Takeda, Susumu Takumura, Takeo Taura, A. B.
Taylor, Margaret V. Taylor, Shintaro Tokunaga, Nobushige Ukai, Satoru
Umene, Yoshitomo Ushijima, Jisho Usui, Akira Watanabe, Yoji Watanabe,
William P. Woodard, Tatsuo Yamada, Iwao Yamanaka, Tsuraki Yano,
Kiyoshi Yokoi, Teigo Yoshida.

In addition to the above, gratitude is expressed to the Committee on
International Exchange of Persons and the United States Educational Commission in Japan which authorized an appointment as Fulbright Research
Scholar; to the Wenner-Gren Foundation for Anthropological Research for
its consistently encouraging support of this as well as preceding studies;
to Boston University for providing a sabbatical leave and its Graduate School
for grants aiding in completion of the manuscript; to the Asia Foundation
for an assisting grant through the Research Institute of Comparative Education and Culture at Kyushu University; and to the latter for officially and
courteously sponsoring this study in Japan. It should be emphasized that
neither this institute nor any of the persons or institutions listed can be held
responsible for the descriptions and interpretations contained herein.

Four persons deserve a special word of deep appreciation for their
participation in this work as a research team, as well as for their careful attention to the manuscript, from inception to virtual completion: Miss Midori
Matsuyama, research assistant; Dr. Nobuo Shimahara, interpreter and adviser; Professor Hirokichi Inai, collaborator; and Professor Shigeharu Matsuura, interpreter, adviser, and collaborator, to whom this book is dedicated
with affection and admiration.

                                                                    T. B.

Boston
November 1968

CONTENTS

Appendix

INTRODUCTION

It was just a century ago, in 1868, that the period known as the Meiji Restoration opened in Japan. With it began one of the most turbulent and remarkable eras in the history of any nation. The privilege of publishing this work during the Meiji Centennial therefore affords the author and his research associates special satisfaction. It does so, however, not merely because of this happy coincidence, but also because one of our principal tasks has been to describe and assess crucial features of Japanese life as these appear to us in the perspective of the period for which 1968 becomes a special landmark.

We have been primarily interested, that is to say, in the dynamics of recent cultural change. For, as everyone should be aware, contemporary Japan has literally risen from ashes. Less than a quarter century ago, with the atomic bombing of Hiroshima and Nagasaki and the fire bombing of most other important cities, defeat and destruction were perhaps as total as that ever suffered by any great nation.

Today Hiroshima and Nagasaki, Nagoya and Osaka, indeed cities everywhere in the land, have been rebuilt on a much more handsome and modern scale than before, and the whole country bursts with exuberance. Economically, Japan has emerged in less than a century from its feudal heritage to become one of the three top industrial nations of the world, surpassed only by the United States and the Soviet Union. The transformation is no less incredible in other less measurable ways: in the profusion of esthetic creations, many of them ultramodern; in the high health and low mortality rates; in the control of population growth; and surely in the educational program.

Simultaneously, and largely because of these same events, Japan is a troubled nation. Tensions and conflicts, both covert and overt, both psychological and social, beset the culture on every side. The fact that despite industrial strength the standard of living is lower than that of some twenty other countries is not the least of its negative conditions.

We have been fascinated by all such conditions, certainly by the positive as well as negative. But since our special concern is the theory and practice of education, it is here that this study comes into sharpest focus—a focus, however, that immediately diffuses outward to encompass much more than education per se. Indeed, we find it necessary to give the paradoxical impression of seeming at times to neglect education. For if we are to examine and appraise this complex institution in an effective way, we are compelled to perceive it constantly in the matrix of other institutions. Japanese education, like that of any other culture, by no means exists as an enterprise sufficient unto itself. Rather, it becomes interwoven with a thousand and one threads into a total way of life. As in the case of any culture, the design that one eventually detects may be distinctive enough. Yet no matter which culture one may choose, education is an inextricable part of that way of life. Culture, in short, remains education's senior partner.

This observation is not a novel one. That culture and education, broadly rather than narrowly understood, constitute a partnership has long been recognized as an indubitable fact of human evolution. But recognition can hardly be regarded as equivalent to searching penetration. Neither theoretical formulations nor research studies that could contribute fundamentally to the meaning and practical relevance of this partnership are as yet plentiful. Anthropology, the science of culture, has more often than not circumvented systematic treatments of education, while education, in turn, has been derelict in its concern for the significance of culture. To be sure, educational anthropology has begun to emerge as a new specialization, but it is rarely regarded as respectable by the typical anthropologist. As for the typical educationist, he has yet to make its acquaintance.

The present volume is the third in which the author has undertaken to explore relationships between culture and education, with due regard for some of the philosophic dimensions of both fields. Therefore, like its predecessors, this study may be regarded as a "triadic interpretation" in which the primary disciplines of anthropology, education, and philosophy are treated in mutual relationship. At the same time anthropology is the most utilized discipline, incorporating the other two in much the same way that cultures incorporate them into their everyday habits and beliefs.

We have sought, accordingly, to utilize important features of the models and techniques of our two previous studies. The interested reader is invited to consult Appendix I primarily and Appendixes II and III secondarily, where our method of approach and something of our underlying theory are reviewed.

But this work also differs from the previous ones. Most conspicuous, of course, is the great and complex culture chosen for investigation. Japan is very different indeed from Puerto Rico—the subject of our preceding research work. For example, it is Oriental; it is much larger; it is an independent nation; and it has a far older, richer, more complex history. But one is struck, too, by astonishing similarities—above all, by the breath-taking rapidity of cultural changes in both cultures. These changes appear most dramatically in the swift transition from a predominantly rural and agricultural to an increasingly urban and industrial order. Recently, too, the United States has had a prodigious influence in both cultures—an influence, moreover, that extends far beyond industrialization. Witness only the present organization of school programs in Puerto Rico and Japan, each of which, superficially at any rate, is much more similar to, than different from, American programs.

Since, however, we are concerned mainly with the distinctive features of this work, let us turn to our plan of investigation. Everyone who has ever tackled cultural research in the field is confronted at the outset with problems of selectivity—what to concentrate on as well as what to exclude. In our case, we have tried to solve this problem by limiting ourselves primarily to two small subcultural communities at the grassroots (or as someone has suggested, perhaps we should say "rice roots"). These communities, to which we have given the names of Ebibara and Kawabara, are comparable especially in the fact that they consist largely of citizens on socially low levels of affluence and status. That they are comparable in numerous other ways as well should gradually become apparent. But they differ, too, particularly in one graphic regard: the first is a community of fishermen (*gyomin*), the second a community of pariahs (*burakumin*).

Thus the question can legitimately be raised as to whether these choices are too atypical to justify the general title of this book. Our answer is severalfold. First, no community is ever perfectly typical of any culture made up of many or even a few communities, although (depending on one's measure of typicality) some are bound to be more so than others. At any rate, in the case of Japan we are aided by the extreme density of population—estimated as the third highest in the world—one consequence of which is not only that virtually every community exists in close proximity to others but that even so-called segregated communities are in almost constant communication and other forms of contact with those surrounding them. This observation applies to Ebibara and Kawabara equally well.

Second, at the same time it cannot be denied that *gyomin* and *bura-kumin* belong to "minority groups." Indeed, one reason for choosing them was, we confess, our long interest in the problems of somewhat similar groups elsewhere in the world. But it has also been hypothesized that if even *gyomin* and *burakumin* are found to manifest important characteristics similar to those of "majority groups," then still stronger grounds may be provided for any generalizations concerning Japanese culture and education than could be derived from more "typical" communities. To anticipate for a moment, this is exactly what we do find: Ebibara and Kawabara, although certainly different from many communities in some important respects, are also strikingly similar to them in other important respects.

Third, it should be noted that while these communities have been studied most intensively, they by no means constitute our exclusive interest. Not only did our research schedule at times carry us to quite distant parts of the country—to Tokyo, for example—but it required prolonged attention to two other primary sources: (1) to each of the small cities (we call them Utsumi-shi and Yamada-shi) with which Ebibara and Kawabara are officially connected; and (2) to a panel of regional leaders, a majority of whom maintained headquarters in the capital city (we call it Hiroi-shi) of the prefecture within which Utsumi-shi and Yamada-shi are located. This prefecture, somewhat comparable to an American state, shall be named Yoneshima-ken. The central purpose of our close association with both the smaller cities and the prefectural leader panel was to include a broader range for comparison and to achieve a wider perspective than would be possible from a study of Ebibara and Kawabara alone.

Fourth, let us emphasize that although important generalizations concerning the whole of Japanese culture and education are, we think, justifiable, arriving at such generalizations is not our principal objective. Actually, we are not deliberately concerned with them at all until the concluding chapters, and even then only in qualified respects. We wish, rather, to throw whatever light is afforded us upon the life of two communities undergoing fast and often painful flux—always with special concern for the roles that education plays in accelerating or retarding an extraordinary period of change.

But here too our interpretation is selective. We have not attempted to encircle the whole educational program even on a local scale; rather concentration has been chiefly upon those features of most direct importance to Ebibara and Kawabara—the elementary and junior high schools. The question of the extent to which this selective approach has relevance for wider circumferences not only of the Japanese but of other cultures and other educational practices, Western as well as Eastern, must be left as much to any inferences readers may wish to draw as to those we ourselves shall venture.

Meanwhile, we urge the reader to note that Ebibara and Kawabara are both interpreted in a parallel sequence of three chapters. In Part I and again in Part II the first chapter concerns itself with what we prefer to call the *order* of both subcultural communities; that is, their respective overall structures in terms of such characteristics as occupation, class, family, politics, religion, and education. The second chapter deals with *process:* the ways that each community actively functions both internally and in relation to its surrounding ecological and cultural environment. The third chapter focuses chiefly upon *goals*—our inclusive term for cultural values, directions, and purposes. The two chapters on process are in a sense the heart of our study; they aim to expose the pulsating life of Ebibara and Kawabara and thereby to trace relations back to the order and forward to the goals of both communities.

Part III develops perspectives on the very specific and empirical portrayals that are the intention of Parts I and II. It too occupies three chapters, treating successively: a comparison of Ebibara and Kawabara both in themselves and with their two surrounding municipalities of Utsumi-shi and Yamada-shi; the contributions to perspective provided by our panel of regional leaders; and the attempt to channel our most relevant evidence through the institution of education, defined as a major agency of Japanese culture. In the latter, the concluding chapter, we evaluate our findings more explicitly and critically than in preceding ones.

For it becomes our obligation, we believe, to make entirely clear that this volume does not pretend to conform merely to the canons either of orthodox social science in general or of anthropology in particular. While the author owes a great deal to these canons—particularly to those most directly concerned with the tasks and duties of "objectivity"—he is concerned even more with the practical applications of theory and research to the human struggle for a life of abundance and well-being. Accordingly, while objectivity is surely a necessary criterion in obtaining defensible results from, say, anthropological research, it is not a sufficient criterion. As the reader may wish to discover by turning to Appendix IV, Bibliographical Notes, these applications are grounded in a philosophy of education and they emerge from it. In this sense, the two preceding volumes referred to, although they are directly foundational to the present one, themselves belong to a continuum of philosophic efforts imbued with a common theme— the potential power of education to bring about, in concert with other powers, the renewal of cultures on a planetary scale.

A few practical comments may prove useful to the reader. Occasional Japanese terms have been introduced because they add a certain flavor to the presentation. These are always translated—often several times—but a glossary is also provided in Appendix V.

Some of the specific figures cited at various points, as well as other precise data, have been modified by the lapse of time between field research
and publication. This is inevitable, but it does not alter essential characterizations. In any case, since we have chosen to conceal actual locations, we
are concerned less about the exactitude of many of these figures and other
data than about relevant and relative proportions.

Pseudonyms as a rule are substituted for real names. Not only are the
names of our focal communities, the two small cities, and the prefecture
pseudonymous but so too are all other names of places, institutions, and
persons directly involved in the content of this study. The reason is familiar:
to encourage as much frankness and openness as possible among all those
from whom we have learned. It is our hope that this safeguard has been sufficiently successful to neutralize any sense of frustrated curiosity that readers
may otherwise experience. At the same time, because the need to visualize
at least approximate positions and relations may be felt by some readers, we
present herewith a somewhat fictionized map of the territory we are now
ready to explore.

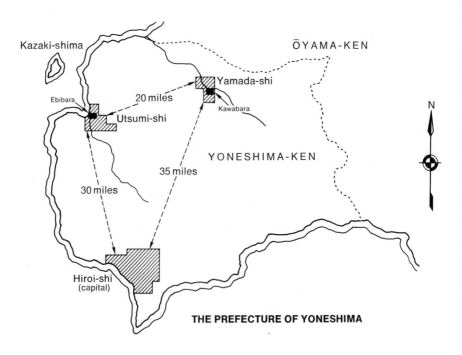

THE PREFECTURE OF YONESHIMA

Part I

A Community of Fishing People

1

PROFILE
OF EBIBARA

I

As you drive along the perilously narrow curving main street through the heart of Utsumi-shi, dodging bicycles and pedestrians, maneuvering past monstrous trucks by a straw's width, and avoiding perilous ditches, you soon suspect you are in the fishing section of the city. A smell pervades the air. It is faint at first but after a minute or two it is very strong indeed—not of fish, exactly, but of an oily pungency. Then you see the little open factories on both sides of the street where young women, mostly, are sorting packages, carrying huge boxes, and operating machines obscured by clouds of steam. These are the *kamaboko* factories where fish paste is made into pink or gray sausagelike links, a favorite food of the Japanese and famous for the distinctive flavor of the Utsumi-shi brand.

In another moment you must stop, for the road ends near the little harbor. Before you, scarcely 25 feet from the wharf's edge, is the fishing fleet of Ebibara. Five o'clock in the afternoon is approaching, and on every boat men are chatting and calling to one another as they prepare for the night's work. Nets fastened high on the single masts slope gracefully downward to the deck, and as you gaze upon the orderly platoons of some 80 boats, the white nets form a kind of rhythmic pattern set against the bright blue sky and the darker blue water, with the orange sun descending behind them.

Nearly all the boats weigh between 3 and 5 tons, and average some 35 feet in length and 8 or so feet in width. Each is unpainted except for a

3

small ornamental design of brightly painted curlicues on both sides of the prow. Near the middle of the boat is a small cabin just large enough to house the diesel engine set below deck level. Besides the nets, which the men are now lowering and folding, very little is on deck except a few poles, wires for an electric light or two, coils of rope, and baskets for the newly caught fish.

While you are watching, one of the engines begins to putt-putt. Soon a boat moves cautiously backward out of its platoon until it is free enough to turn in a slow circle toward the opening in the breakwater, the outer edge of the harbor, several hundred yards away. Almost simultaneously dozens of other engines awaken, and in the course of a mere 15 or 20 minutes nearly all the boats are, as if by common consent, moving out to sea in uneven lines. As they pass the breakwater, they at once begin to fan out in order to cover the fishing grounds allocated to them. Then, as darkness descends, you are finally able to discern only their blinking lights, like hundreds of drifting fireflies.

On the wharf, activity continues. A boat perhaps three times as large as those of the fleet is unloading scores of wooden boxes of small fish, each box sprinkled liberally with chopped ice. These boxes contain fish soon to be decapitated by women workers, then ground and cooked into *kamaboko*. A hundred feet away, two men are breaking up scrap iron with hammers and blow torches, preparing to load it on a freighter. No one pays the least attention or stops to chat with them. For they are *burakumin*, members of the "outcaste" Japanese minority, and although they work on the wharf daily almost side by side with *gyomin* (fishermen), the nearest anyone comes to socializing with them is to exchange a word of greeting. Otherwise they are usually ignored.

Facing the harbor is the fishermen's co-operative, the economic heart of Ebibara. Here is the market which, by six-thirty in the morning when the fleet returns, is crowded with chattering men and women, from the very young to the very old. When the boats are anchored, the men remain on board briefly to hoist nets and tend to their engines; then they go home to bed. Meanwhile, their wives, older daughters, or sometimes their mothers or mothers-in-law, complete sorting and rinsing the catch, often rowing to their family boats, and then watch over the business of selling at the co-operative auction that begins almost the moment the boats return. The buyers, owners of little retail shops, larger wholesalers, and men and women fish peddlers, have all appeared promptly. Some have traveled many miles and arrived with small three-wheeled trucks, bicycles with carriers, and push-carts. Some even come by train from nearby towns with only straw hampers. The fish, most of them small (shrimp are by far the most numerous, but octopus, squid, and mackerel are among the other varieties), are placed on

the floor wherever there is room. There are so many little piles that it is difficult to avoid stepping into them. During the procedure the noise often approaches bedlam, with everyone chattering or arguing, hoses spraying,
pushcarts clattering, and the deep rasping voice of the auctioneer calling
over it all. He presides majestically from a kind of rostrum where he detects
mysterious signals from the crowd of buyers as he shouts a jargon completely
meaningless to uninitiated visitors.

Gradually the market empties. By eight o'clock only two or three men
remain to wash the littered floor, or to fill boxes with fish for transportation
to the cooperatively owned refrigerator next door. The women, too, have
left the market. Some have returned home to help with their husbands'
breakfasts if they are not too late; others have gone directly to their jobs in
kamaboko or other factories nearby. As a rule, their children have already
departed before they are back, for the nearest elementary school is a mile
away and the junior and senior high schools are a good deal farther. By the
time school is out and the children have returned by foot or bicycle, their
fathers have probably left again for the harbor and their mothers are still
working. Ordinarily, the fishermen in Ebibara awaken before three in the
afternoon, eat an early supper, perhaps chat with a neighbor or two over a
glass of *sake*, and then return to their boats to prepare for another night's
work.

But while the market is quiet and the fishermen sleep, the co-operative
headquarters is active indeed. The director, Oka-san, and the assistant director, Sato-san, appear constantly harassed with duties, although their staff
of three young women secretaries and three men assistants usually seem
more relaxed. Every afternoon, money must be ready to pay each fishing
boat for its morning sale. Piles of *yen*, one for each boat, are laid out on a
large desk awaiting collection. Perhaps the boatowner himself comes to the
paying office on his way to the wharf, or his wife or daughter may represent
him. Meanwhile, since plans are always afoot to expand or improve co-operative facilities, meetings are constantly being held with co-op committees,
officials from the city hall, or experts from the prefectural Department of
Fisheries. Seaweed farming, which will be of particular interest to us later,
occupies a good deal of the directors' time. Further responsibilities include
the sale of engine fuel and other supplies to members for their boats, pro-
tecting the rights of members in disputes with nearby co-ops over alleged
trespassings on assigned fishing grounds, and preparing for meetings of the
board of directors.

Most of this activity occurs in a shabby, rather dark and grimy building
behind the co-op market. This building houses the paying room, four small
fishy-smelling offices (one has a safe, another an adding machine but no
typewriter, and still another an electric fan, a forlorn plant, and marine

scenes on the wall), and an upstairs meeting room large enough to accommodate perhaps 40 persons seated on *tatami* (straw mats). Rows of framed
photographs, some fading from age, of founders and leaders of the Ebibara
co-op are the only adornment.

II

Ebibara is a crowded section of Utsumi-shi, a city of about 50,000 citizens.
It is the oldest section, but no one knows how old it is. The earliest map,
dated 1700, already shows a fair-sized village. Utsumi-shi was incorporated
as a city only a little over a decade ago; before that time, there were several
loosely connected neighborhoods and outlying villages. The total area of
Utsumi-shi is close to 4 square miles, not including an island 7 miles off the
coast which we shall call Kazaki-shima and which contains another community of fishermen. Such a small incorporated city is usually quite different
in structure from cities of America and Europe; particularly the little farms,
which are scattered all about, are different. They are very small: the average
size in Utsumi-shi is approximately 1¼ acres, as compared to the national
average of slightly less than 2½ acres per household. (The average farm in
the United States is nearly 300 acres in size, and the smallest farms in Europe, those of Italy, average over 12 acres.) Except for the heart of Utsumi-
shi, where dwellings are packed together in almost solid rows of houses and
shops, the visitor receives an impression of spaciousness. At one point, the
view resembles a green-yellow checkerboard some 2 miles wide, where the
farmhouses are separated from one another by tiny plots of rice or vegetables. Intermittently one also discerns clusters of buildings consisting of
two or three shops and several homes for nonagricultural citizens who work
in factories, offices, stores, or at other jobs.

Utsumi-shi is indeed economically diversified to a remarkable degree.
Farmers, for example, are almost seven times more numerous than all fishermen and marine workers combined. Persons engaged in manufacturing are
about four times more numerous; those in retail, and wholesale enterprises,
also about four times more numerous. Actually, only about 1200 persons out
of the 50,000 in Utsumi-shi are directly engaged in fishing or in work resulting from it. Still more graphically, only about 400 of the 10,000 households
in the city consist of full-time fishing families, and less than another 200 of
part-time. Nevertheless, the long history of Utsumi-shi, it seems safe to say,
has been more profoundly affected by its fishing culture than by any other
influence; after all, fishing was the original occupation, and to this day it is a
major concern of the city government. In the entire Prefecture of Yoneshima

the single largest fishing co-operative, with over 300 members, is still in Ebibara.

An understanding of the network of relations of Ebibara with the wider circumference of culture is essential to an understanding of the fishing community itself. Let us consider a little further, then, the nature of the city. Politically, the Liberal Democratic party, the conservative and dominant party in Japan, is decidedly in control. Twenty-seven of the 30 members of the city council are Liberal Democrats either in allegiance or in formal affiliation. Only two are Socialists, and only one is a member of the Kōmeitō (Clean Government party), the political arm of the militant Buddhist Sōkagakkai movement of which we shall learn more. Miyakawa-san, one of our informants and the only mayor that the city has had since its incorporation, is a Liberal Democrat, as are the elected representatives from Utsumi-shi to the prefectural and national legislatures. It is even said that Kasuga-san, the one member of the House of Representatives in the national Diet who comes from Utsumi-shi and who is strongly supported by most Ebibara citizens, is a more powerful Liberal Democrat than *shichō-san* (Mr. Mayor), as he is often addressed. In short, Utsumi-shi appears to be politically conservative—a not surprising discovery in view of the proportionately large number of farmers and fishermen who, as in many cultures, are considered less amenable to innovation than urban populations. Yet easy generalizations about conservatism in Utsumi-shi cannot be sustained. On the contrary, the current of cultural change is quickly reaching far into this fairly remote area of the country.

Urban patterns of industrialization are already conspicuous. Utsumi-shi has several branch factories of large companies; the most impressive are those for farm implements, marine products, and textiles. A few of the workers are unionized; for example, another of our informants, Tsuji-san, belongs to a national union of implement workers, as do the more than 400 others in his factory. But this is the only union local of any size. The 600 textile and clothing workers, mostly young women, are not yet unionized, nor are any of the single largest group of workers, that is, the thousand or so men and women in the *kamaboko*, shrimp, and other fish processing factories. In any case, and again this is especially true of small cities, most of the factories are very small and of local ownership. It is not astonishing, at least to a Japanese, to find that Utsumi-shi's 4000 factory workers are distributed among nearly 300 companies.

Even the unionized minority, however, are not necessarily supporters of the Socialist or Communist parties—another differentiation from the larger cities where support of these parties is heavily concentrated among industrial workers. Tsuji-san himself supports the Liberal Democratic party.

True, he knows a considerable number of fellow workers who favor the two major left parties, but he cannot think of a single one who belongs to the third and weakest of the left parties, the Democratic Socialist party. It goes almost without saying that none of the fishermen are unionized, not even those who are employed by fishing-boat owners. Most fishermen are as conservative politically as their farming neighbors.

Residential patterns of Utsumi-shi mirror the diversity of occupations. With one exception, people do not sharply divide themselves into neighborhood groupings according to what they do for a living or how high or low they are in the class structure. The exception is the *burakumin* community in the very center of the city; here about 70 households are completely segregated. Even fishermen do not necessarily live in homogeneous neighborhoods. Although it is true that there are nearly 200 households dependent wholly or partly on fishing in the Ebibara section of the city nearest the harbor (the rest in Utsumi-shi live either on Kazaki Island or in another village on the edge of the city), people of almost every economic occupation, chiefly shopkeepers, small manufacturers, wholesalers, industrial workers, and white-collar workers (*sarariiman* is the Westernized word), also live here.

Even an occasional farmer may be found in the most congested sections of Utsumi-shi. Thus, another of our informants, Soma-san, is a full-time farmer, although his land is a quarter of a mile away from his home. Soma-san is relatively well-to-do by community standards. He owns 2½ acres, but his two-story house stands side by side with much poorer ones. Indeed, economic status rarely coincides with place of residence. One affluent friend in Utsumi-shi, a wholesale oil distributor, has a fine home on land he inherited as the oldest son, and he keeps the ancestral one as a kind of storage house. Even so, he lives in the middle of a neighborhood that approaches a slum.

Our mayor informant, Miyakawa-san, offered one explanation for such heterogeneity. Like nearly all very old communities, the feudal order of landlord relationships required close proximity of all residents within a narrow area for self-protection against marauders and for efficiency. Thus, the paternalistic reponsibility of the feudal owner to his dependents in return for their allegiance and service to him is still apparent in rural residential patterns. In such Japanese metropolises as Osaka, Kobe, and Tokyo, however, such patterns have now almost totally disappeared.

This is not to suggest that a vertical order of classes does not prevail in Utsumi-shi. Mayor Miyakawa, for example, is the son of the biggest pre-World War II landlord in the Utsumi-shi area. Indeed, much of the land that *shichō-san* can view from the windows of his magnificent third-floor office in the finest building in town, the new city hall, once belonged to his family.

Miyakawa-san was doubtless right in classifying himself as a member of the "upper-upper" stratum, although he recognized that "newly rich" upper-class people are now blurring this aristocratic but less affluent image. At any rate, he was most reluctant to locate himself on the class ladder according to criteria such as W. Lloyd Warner's, with which we acquainted him. He reminded us not only that the huge land holdings of landlords like his father were confiscated after World War II, but that no one has ever received more than a small fraction of their worth in compensation for them. He also reminded us that the biggest most powerful capitalists of prewar Japan were likewise greatly weakened by the MacArthur occupation, while at the same time the lower levels of economic life have slowly been rising.

The fact remains, nevertheless, that people in Utsumi-shi do judge each other according to class and status. Traditionally fishermen are often placed near the lowest level, although not as low as *burakumin*. (Perhaps it is not surprising, then, that prejudice toward *burakumin* by Ebibara people is exceptionally strong, compounded as it is by their own invidious position and by the familiar need for some other group to look down upon.) Within communities of *gyomin*, however, class distinctions likewise operate. Certain families on Ebibara unquestionably hold more status than others. The same four or five family names are mentioned when one asks who are the most influential people. These are usually the ones with long histories and numerous members. Sometimes they also own the largest boats.

In between the base and the aristocratic peak of the social pyramid one detects other class levels. One of our teacher informants, Shinohara-san, a native-born resident, viewed the Utsumi-shi structure rather uniquely. He placed the "commercial classes" at the top. He pointed out that two or three merchants in the city, one a druggist-cosmetician, do an annual business grossing many thousands of dollars, which is higher than that of most local manufacturers. Below the commercial classes he placed land-owning farmers, below farmers the fishermen, and below the fishermen the "day laborers." In not relegating fishermen to the bottom rung, he tended to agree with Masumi-san, another teacher informant who lives in the Ebibara area. But Masumi-san distinguished between fishermen who own boats and those who do not. The former he grouped rather generously with the *sarariiman* and petty shopkeepers, the latter with little wholesalers of *kamaboko*. The "poor working people" he placed lowest of all.

Although the class structure is not always perceived similarly by our informants, no one would be likely to deny that the middle and upper-middle strata include very few, if any, fishing people. Most of the marine processing factories in Ebibara consist of personnel usually related to fishermen, and the owners themselves seem more often to belong on the "lower-middle" level than on higher ones. One *kamaboko* manufacturer who lives in an attractive apartment with a lovely rear garden attached to his factory could be ranked, to be sure, above the halfway point. But the relatively few Utsumi-shi citizens who belong on higher levels are the kind one meets, not in Ebibara, but at weekly luncheons of the local Rotary and Lions Clubs, at the office of the chamber of commerce, or at meetings of local school administrators and high-ranking city officials. Utsumi-shi teachers seem generally classifiable as lower-middle class, although a few who have inherited property or hold a second position besides that of teacher might be considered upper-middle. Masumi-san, who heads a prosperous tutoring school attended by many children of *gyomin*, is one such person; whereas he would probably be regarded in, say, Kyoto as of lower-middle status, in Ebibara he is a little higher than that.

The overall social structure of Utsumi-shi may also be perceived by means of an organization called *jichikai* (literally, self-governing meeting). It is an extraordinary invention by which, formally, every citizen has a voice in affairs of the community. Actually, some citizens never participate, but the organization is still open to them. *Jichikai* is not unique to Utsumi-shi. As we shall see later, it is also very active in Yamada-shi and has spread all over Japan. Its historic roots are deep, at least as far in the past as the feudal Tokugawa Era (1603–1867). The *kumi,* originally a neighborhood group of about five families, is the key to *jichikai.* Traditionally, each *kumi* chose a leader who joined with five other leaders, who in turn selected one of their members to serve on a higher level with four other leaders, who again selected two of their members as chiefs of the village. This rather complicated system was strictly hierarchical, and it remains so to this day.

But the purposes and to some extent the methods of operation are different than they were in the premodern era. The feudal *kumi* system was designed to systematize control over the people by the *samurai* (lords), an intention carried to its extreme during the militarist-nationalist period of the 1930s when membership was made compulsory. Today, the federal government has no authority over *jichikai,* and each community is free to develop its particular structure and program according to its own needs. The *kumi* still remains the key, but it deals with its special problems, whether or not these are related to problems of the city, prefecture, or the country as a whole. For example, during one of our visits, Soma-san, our farmer informant who happens to be leader of his *kumi* of 13 households (the number varies somewhat), met with other *kumi* leaders in his section of Ebibara. The problem before them was whether or not to recommend moving the house of a fellow resident out of the way of a sanitation ditch then under construction. (The house was moved.)

All *kumi* leaders are, like Soma-san, affiliated with about a dozen others to form a sectional *jichikai.* This group is presided over by a leader chosen by his fellow *kumi* leaders, and he in turn meets on the next higher level with other sectional leaders, of whom Ebibara has five. Finally, these five leaders belong to a city-wide organization of 50 sectional leaders. Only rarely, however, do the household members of any *kumi* hold a "town meeting" with those of other *kumi*. Tsuji-san, our industrial worker informant and a sectional *jichikai* leader, remembered only one occasion in 20 years when his rank-and-file members joined with those of another section to discuss a common problem. (Incidentally, the problem was that of the same sanitation ditch mentioned above.) But let us note that Wada-san, a fisherman sectional leader and also an informant, saw no need for such meetings; he felt the important thing is that the leaders meet.

Thus, most activities of *jichikai* are concentrated in the leadership. Each *kumi* leader, after meeting with other *kumi* leaders in his section, is expected to report back to his dozen or so households, often by door-to-door calls, and to receive directives from them as to how they wish him to represent their interests. At other times his mission is to collect Red Cross or other donations, to facilitate tax collections, and in other ways to keep lines of communication open between city hall and his neighborhood. As is to be expected in an entirely voluntary organization, the quality and quantity of *kumi* participation varies a great deal. Some *kumi* in Utsumi-shi seem to be almost wholly moribund. But active ones, too, have trouble in gathering representatives of more than half or so of their household members to any *kumi* meeting.

Even so, Tsuji-san estimated that, in his own sectional *jichikai*, perhaps 100 *kumi* gatherings are held in the course of a year. They are almost always held in the home of one of the members. If all five of the sectional *jichikai* in Ebibara were equally active, this would bring the total to over 500 meetings. But since other sections are not always so active, perhaps a safe estimate is that something less than half of all households in the Ebibara *jichikai* participate in any one year.

III

In viewing Ebibara within the larger order of Utsumi-shi, an important fact is that our fishing community, far from being self-contained or unified, becomes intermeshed with countless strands both internally and in its relations to communities surrounding and permeating it. Let us imagine a series of concentric circles: the most inclusive is, of course, the entire world of interconnected national cultures, Oriental and Occidental alike; next within this widest circle is the Japanese culture as a whole; then the four major islands of Japan, which are themselves distinguishable regions of the national culture; then the Prefecture of Yoneshima; then Utsumi-shi; then the loosely connected "towns" within the city (about 20 in all); then the most concentrated area where nearly half the city's population lives; then Ebibara itself, which overlaps with this area and, as we have seen, is subdivided into five sections; then the *kumi*, the neighborhood grouping of about a dozen households; and, finally, in the center, the nuclear family, the single household.

Weaving back and forth across these concentric circles in myriad ways are the great institutions common to cultures everywhere—the most obvious being the political, economic, religious, recreational, and educational. Utsumi-shi, hardly surprisingly, embraces all of these institutions, as does Ebibara. Our preliminary sketch of two of them, the political and economic, may now be supplemented by similar sketches of the other three.

Beginning with religion, Utsumi-shi has 25 Buddhist temples, each with its own priest, but none are in Ebibara proper. Nearly half of the citizenry is affiliated with a single sect, Shingonshū. The most prominent temple, which is visited by hundreds of pilgrims each year and is said to have been founded over a thousand years ago, lists on its roster such venerable and distinguished families as Mayor Miyakawa's. The rest of the citizens belong to several other sects, such as Tendaishū, Jōdoshinshū, Nichirenshū, and Zenshū. Curiously, Zenshū, often regarded as the most philosophically profound of the Buddhist sects, appears to include the largest number of fishermen members, with Shingonshū next. One Zenshū temple, in particular, claims more fishermen than any other subcultural group. More than half of its 300 believers are fishermen.

Nichirenshū, although its fishermen members are relatively few in number, attracts disproportionate attention because of its aggressive and often noisy rituals. Soma-san, the fisherman informant mentioned earlier and a devout worshipper, sometimes joins others on marches through Utsumi-shi streets on cold days (to strengthen one's spiritual character, so we were told) to the sound of drums and chants. Nichirenshū should not, however, be confused with Nichirenshōshū, the Buddhist sect of the militant Sōkagakkai movement. Actually, according to the priest of Soma-san's temple, there are nine subsects of Nichiren Buddhism, and eight of them are bitterly hostile to the "heresies" of the ninth—Nichirenshōshū itself. This priest told us, for example, that he would refuse to officiate at the funeral of any Sōkagakkai member.

No Nichirenshōshū temple can be found in Utsumi-shi, but the priest of one about 4 miles outside the city claims several thousand household members and says the temple is the largest in the area. The few hundred Sōkagakkai members in Utsumi-shi attend this temple, but no fisherman whom we met belongs. The vast majority of households in Utsumi-shi are formally affiliated, however, with one Buddhist sect or another, even though participation may be nominal.

There is also a small Christian church in the city that claims over 100 members, but only a single person in any Ebibara family with which we associated had ever been converted to Christianity. And even this person, the wife of an ex-fisherman informant, Nakayama-san, joined her husband's Nichirenshū after her marriage. She had been a Christian for about five years.

Along with the Buddhist, the most important religious institution is, of course, Shintō. There are about as many major shrines as temples in Utsumi-shi, but by far the most important in the area is the huge shrine dedicated to the supreme god of fishermen located several miles distant from Utsumi-shi. It is one of many honoring him in Japan and is visited at least once a year by nearly all fishing households.

Two shrines may be found within Ebibara itself, but only one, at the very edge of the harbor, is central to the life of the people. This venerable weather-beaten shrine contains the sacred symbols of two male deities (Ryūōjin, the god of the sea, and Ebisu, the god of riches) and one female deity (Benzaiten, a beautiful goddess who, by making musical sounds, is said to enable fishermen to predict the weather). These deities, among others frequently referred to in Japanese folklore, are obscure to the average citizen, and few realize that they are said to derive originally from India by way of China.[1]

A much larger shrine, also facing the harbor, is located on a high hill outside Ebibara overlooking the city and sea. This shrine was supposedly first constructed in the fifteenth century, and a myth has ground up around it, repeated in very old books owned by the city, whereby the people of Utsumi-shi are assured of special protection. Unlike other Shintō shrines in the city, this one is so important that it is able to maintain a full-time priest who lives in his own attached house on the top of the hill. Many fishermen climb to the top intermittently.

In addition to Buddhism and Shintoism, we must note one other religious institution, a cult that specializes in magical rites. Its priest (known locally as *gyōja*) and his wife, both aged, have conducted these rites in Utsumi-shi for 40 years. Their son is also a priest of the cult, and has his own establishment in another city. The old priest's ceremonial quarters are a part of his home and are called a *kyōkai* (church). Although Shintō and Buddhist elements permeate the cult in rather obscure ways (a phenomenon not unusual if its claim is true that it was established as far back as the tenth

[1] The terms "deity" and "god" are not strictly accurate translations from Shintō, but are often loosely utilized. The preferable Japanese term is *kami*.

century A.D.), fortune-telling and other occult rituals are most frequently practiced (for a fee, of course). The wife of *gyōja*, who is decidedly more articulate than her husband, insists that their supreme purpose is to help believers discover "peace of mind." In any case, the exact line between superstitious customs and religious rituals is as difficult to fix in the religious patterns of Utsumi-shi as it would be almost anywhere in Japan. Later we shall pay more attention to both kinds of practice.

IV

If the religious life of this community is anything but uniform, even less so is its sociable life. Recreation takes many forms; some are not at all unique (television viewing is the most ubiquitous and popular of all), whereas others are more expressive of the local culture.

In Ebibara proper, by far the most colorful and characteristic event is the Shintō festival in July of the fishing people. Almost every fishing household in Ebibara takes the day off, and Shintō ceremonies that begin in late afternoon are performed before the altar of the harborside shrine by the priest from the much larger hilltop shrine, aided by two secondary priests. Important leaders in Ebibara, such as Oka-san, the co-op director, are privileged to sit inside the shrine opposite the priests, together with a few guests such as the Diet Representative, Kasuga-san. Other citizens, all men likewise, take turns stepping up to the altar, bowing, clapping their hands, and receiving sips of *sake* blessed by the priest. Many people mill about the grounds and talk and laugh so loudly that it is difficult to hear the priestly chants. Finally, as the devout bow low, the priest quickly carries the sacred symbol of Ryūōjin, the most important of the three enshrined *kami* ("gods"), from the rear where it has been concealed (no one actually sees it) and places it in a small enclosed portable shrine (*mikoshi*) held upon the shoulders of eight young men costumed in white cloaks and head bands.

Now the procession begins to move through the main street, led by a white-cloaked figure wearing the mask of a goblinlike face with a very long nose. Carnival stands that sell such tempting novelties as cotton candy, balloons, cakes, drinks, and gold fish line the street. The young porters followed by 20 or 30 local dignitaries and co-op officials make up the entire procession. But the few followers are, in any case, largely ignored. Everyone is watching with obvious delight the antics of the *mikoshi* porters. Instead of carrying it with solemn and cautious concern for its sacred content, they do their best to tip and push the *mikoshi* from one side of the street to the other, as they shout boisterously and crowd into the lines of spectators. The *mikoshi* seems imperiled, but it is never dropped. When the porters were asked why they treat their beloved *kami* in so violent a fashion, one answer was that Ryūōjin enjoys this activity. The occasion is, after all, a happy one, and he is a virile *kami*.

The procession turns around after a brief stop at another small shrine near the boundary of Ebibara. Fishermen's wives, most of whom have stayed at home, hold a kind of open house. Friends sometimes leave the procession, enter a house for a few minutes, and drink a glass of *amazake*, a thick, sweet homemade brew of rice especially prepared for the festival day.

As evening approaches, the procession returns to Ebibara harbor, where a crowd of men, women, and children have already gathered. Two of the fishing boats have been roped together next to the wharf. They are gaily decorated with flags and Shintō symbols, and are crowded with the children of fishermen. The porters place the *mikoshi* on deck and all of them, along with the masked leader of the procession and as many other men as can find room, climb into the boats. Soon they move out into the harbor. A great deal of beer and *sake* have been brought on board, and the children seem to enjoy the gaiety as they watch their fathers and other relatives become more and more convivial. The porters, despite their earlier exertions, now seem even more exuberant. As drinks are passed back and forth, the twin boats travel in great circles outside the breakwater, then again inside, and at last return to the dock where many spectators still watch. But as soon as the *mikoshi* has been lifted ashore and carried back to the shrine, everyone goes home. The harbor festival is over for another year.

We have described only one festival in Utsumi-shi; a city document lists over 75 in a single year! Most of these occur only at small humble shrines; often the occasion is not much more than a neighborhood gathering, embellished by a few rituals. One event, however, is gigantic. It is sponsored by the dominating hilltop shrine, occurs in mid-October, lasts three days, and, like hundreds of others during the same month in Japan, is a time of thanksgiving; it is a harvest festival. Then there are other special festivals; for example, the more than 100 farmers near Soma-san's section of Ebibara take one day off late in March to herald the new planting season. Households rotate in serving as host for a party at which a Shintō priest officiates. Fishermen and farmers do not participate in each others' festivals, but they may sometimes observe them. Money-raising festivals often take place on the grounds of Buddhist temples, although the sacred ceremonies of a particular event, such as Bon (ancestor commemoration), occur only within the sacred precincts of the temple altar.

Money-making is, in any event, a primary incentive in much of the sociable life, religious or otherwise, of Utsumi-shi. Many small bars two or three with bar girls, a few hotels which cooperate with more or less authentic *geisha* girls, three movie theaters, and the inevitable *pachinko* parlors (containing rows and rows of pinball gambling machines) which usually seem crowded with both men and women from morning to night—all are as typical of Utsumi-shi as they are of much larger cities. Even the ever-popular pastime of "cherry-blossom watching" (*hanami*) in early April is now sponsored by the chamber of commerce.

The only widely popular commercial amusements that are not provided by Utsumi-shi are the gaudy neon-flashing cabarets with their array of always zealous hostesses, the Turkish (*toruko*) baths with their scantily clad masseuses, and the resorts with their often artificial "hot springs." Utsumi-shi is not quite large enough to sustain such luxuries as these, and in any case few resident are affluent enough to afford them. Those who can are able to reach them within an hour or less. There are even several strip-tease (*storippu*) joints at the foot of the great shrine a few miles away.

Whether or not residents of Utsumi-shi travel to enjoy these particular indulgences—and many do not—certainly they travel wherever and whenever they can find the time and cash. The chief delight of Ebibara fishermen, for example, is to form a group of friends and travel all day or night by bus to a nearby prefecture in order to share in some special ceremony of a principal temple. Equally intriguing is a pilgrimage led by *gyōja* to a mountaintop retreat of his diviner's sect. Once a year or so, women of the Ebibara fishing co-op raise enough money to visit a hot-spring resort for one or two days. And student groups, a familiar sight all over Japan, are constantly traveling to historic spots.

If these leisure-time activities are in no way peculiar to Utsumi-shi (nor are popular Westernized sports, particularly baseball), three instances may be noted that are somewhat more distinctive. One is the vast popularity of the large sandy beach, especially in the uncomfortably hot summer months of July and August. Not only do Utsumi-shi boys and girls congregate there in uncountable numbers, but so do thousands of adults who often come from considerable distances. One may, as at most large beaches in Japan, rent a shaded cubicle 10 or 20 feet square, order drinks and food, and sprawl on the straw mat to one's heart's content. Few Ebibara parents or children enjoy this luxury; instead little boys, especially, spend hours splashing in the water and staring at families on the sand or in the dozens of cubicles.

The bicycle races of Utsumi-shi are the second unusual form of recreation. Other cities have these, too, but none nearer than Hiroi-shi, the capital of Yoneshima-ken. Bicycle racing is thoroughly commercialized. The vice-mayor is officially in charge, for the city government sponsors the races, hires athletes, maintains the track and grandstands, enforces rules, and uses the substantial profits to improve city services such as public roads. About 2000 citizens attend the two races held each month, always on a Sunday. Most spectators come, however, not for the pleasure of the sport itself but primarily to gamble. In the most recent year for which figures are available the profit to Utsumi-shi was $40,000, about 15 percent of the entire city budget.

The third instance is likewise gambling, but this form of recreation is scarcely a public enterprise. Informants often told us that many fishermen love to gamble, too much so for the good of their meager pocketbooks. One of the most popular games is said to be *hanafuda* (flower cards), a game usually played by four or five persons. Fishermen sometimes sacrifice sleep on working days in order to gamble surreptitiously (the game, strictly speaking, is illegal) or do so on their two free days per month. On several occasions we observed fishermen or other Ebibara citizens (the auctioneer of the morning market was one) playing a kind of Japanese chess. Tossing coins toward a target (*hōbiki*) is equally popular, and not infrequently we saw a group of urchins playing with whatever *yen* they were able to garner.

V

Education, the fifth institution criss-crossing Utsumi-shi and Ebibara, is by no means least in importance to the people of this typically education-conscious city. True, families of *gyomin* have traditionally been viewed as less concerned than most other families, but even this assertion must be qualified. If past generations of *gyomin* were inclined to regard any more education than the required minimum as a luxury unnecessary to their occupation, more and more members of the present generation do not so regard it. For example, a substantial proportion of children of high school age from Kazakishima travel by sea ferry to and from home in order to attend the Utsumi-shi senior high schools. This trip from island to school and back requires some three hours every day.

Ebibara itself maintains no regular public schools, but in the city of Utsumi-shi as a whole there are nine elementary schools, three junior high schools, three senior high schools (one general, one commercial, and one part-time), eight kindergartens, five nursery schools, and a very modest public library. There are also 16 part-time private schools, among them one nursery school and others specializing in tutoring, dressmaking, knitting, abacus, and other skills. A public department of social (adult) education offers courses and institutes of various kinds. A junior college is just getting started. Altogether, about 15,000, nearly one-third of the city's population, attend school on one level or another. No four-year college operates in Utsumi-shi, but some students do attend the public university at the prefectural capital, others go to Yamada College less than an hour away, and a tiny number are enrolled in universities of higher learning as far away as Tokyo.

In Ebibara (which it must be remembered includes a mixture of both fishermen and nonfishermen) only about 7 percent of the adults have graduated from secondary high school since World War II, but even this is 3 percent higher than before the war. Attendance through junior high school, nine years altogether, has been required since the war. Nursery school and kindergarten are not compulsory, but increasing numbers of children, especially of working parents, attend them. A comparison of figures for Ebibara with those for Utsumi-shi as a whole indicates that over twice as large a proportion of the total population graduated from high school, both before and after the war, as graduated in Ebibara proper. A still sharper way of highlighting this distinction is to note that whereas three-fourths of Utsumi-shi junior high school graduates now go on to senior high school, less than half of the children of fishing families do so. The rest take jobs.

The organization of the school system of Utsumi-shi is strictly comparable to communities throughout Japan. It is a line-staff structure, with all basic policies established by the national Ministry of Education (Monbushō). These policies are handed down to the prefectural administration, and from there to each municipality. Both Yoneshima-ken and Utsumi-shi are required to maintain boards of education—the former appointed by the governor, the latter by the mayor—subject to approval by their elected assemblies. The prefectural board in turn selects, with Monbushō's approval, the school superintendent of Yoneshima-ken. The superintendent in Utsumi-shi is chosen by the mayor from the members of the local board, with the consent of the prefectural board. Principals of individual schools are chosen in turn by the superintendent and the municipal board which, on the recommendation of principals, also choose, assign, promote, and dismiss teachers.

Financial support is markedly different from that in the United States. Only about one-fourth of the budget comes from the Utsumi-shi treasury; over one-third comes from the prefecture, and the remainder chiefly from national revenues. Because compulsory education ceases after the ninth year of schooling, Yoneshima-ken must assume by far the largest share, over three-fourths, of the cost of its senior high schools. Social (adult) education is also a heavy prefectural responsibility. All told, Utsumi-shi spends 15 percent of its budget or about $2,000,000 on education—roughly the same percentage earned from the bicycle races. The budget, incidentally, is rigidly controlled by the mayor, to whom the superintendent must go even for petty appropriations.

The curriculum is largely prescribed by Monbushō. Nursery school and kindergarten programs understandably are the most flexible. But in elementary schools, beginning with the first grade and continuing through the sixth, the curriculum is divided into specific numbers of hours for each of the following subjects: language, social studies, arithmetic, science, music, arts and handcrafts, homemaking, physical education, and moral education, with two or three additional hours per week for extracurricular activities. Language and arithmetic receive the largest proportion of time. In junior high schools, the same areas are continued, with equally precise allocations of time, and English is added. A number of electives are now available. Senior high school curricula proliferate even more: all the subjects already noted are subdivided into more specialized areas, and there is even greater stress on language, mathematics, and science. At this level, however, a student chooses either a comprehensive program, which may lead to higher education, or a terminal program in vocational education.

A good deal of emphasis is placed on testing. Arduous and frequent examinations for admission to senior high school and college, the so-called National Achievement Tests (NAT), and a host of other checks are of as anxious concern to teachers and students in Utsumi-shi as they are throughout the country. In one way, the examinations are of even more than usual concern: a situation has arisen in Yoneshima-ken and particularly in Utsumi-shi which once again sets off these larger and smaller "subcultures" from Japanese culture viewed in macrocosm. Yoneshima-ken has achieved a reputation for the extraordinary record of its schools in National Achievement Tests promoted by Monbushō. A previous prefectural superintendent of schools was largely responsible for this reputation. Year after year he insisted that schools under his jurisdiction drill their students to pass its own achievement tests with the highest possible scores. All local schools in Utsumi-shi of course responded. Whether teachers liked the tests or not, they were under orders, and the effort paid off. Yoneshima-ken ranked high among all prefectures in NAT scores.

But not without objections. In Utsumi-shi, almost alone among the communities of Yoneshima-ken, an organization of teachers continues to function which is, to say the least, opposed to the NAT program. The Japan Teachers' Union (Nikkyōso) dislikes the program because, the organization contends, students benefit from it very little while it greatly increases the teachers' burden. Even in Utsumi-shi, however, Nikkyōso membership has dwindled to a fraction of the 500 or so teachers. Indeed, unlike the majority of prefectures where the union is by far the largest and most powerful teachers' organization, Nikkyōso can now claim less than 15 percent of all Yoneshima-ken teachers—a figure considered still too high by its critics. But no one denies that the heaviest concentration of Nikkyōso teachers in the prefecture is to be found in or near Utsumi-shi itself.

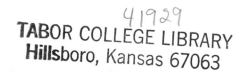

Another organization, the Japan Teachers' Association (Kyōshikai), not only favors the NAT program but, unlike Nikkyōso, usually endorses the policies of Monbushō. The total membership of Kyōshikai in Yoneshima-ken is also comparatively small, but in Utsumi-shi, under the energetic leadership of Yoshida-san (principal of the junior high school with, incidentally, the largest percentage of *gyomin* children), the membership is estimated by its friends to be more than half of all teachers in the city.

The conflict between Nikkyōso and Kyōshikai, which is more acute in Utsumi-shi than in any other part of Yoneshima-ken, deserves additional discussion. Here we wish only to note two other important groups within the educational structure. One is the PTA (*pii-chii-ei*), which is active in every school but is also organized on the neighborhood level, the city level, and finally on both the prefectural and national levels. The other is the various organizations of students; these include student governments, children's clubs, sports teams, Boy Scouts and Girl Scouts, and a host of others. Ebibara parents belong to the PTA as a matter of course, but only a minority participate faithfully. Ebibara children are active in organizations although we shall find that their behavior patterns, if they are from fishing families, are often noticeably different from those of children from other sections of Utsumi-shi.

VI

The family is at the core of our simple model of concentric circles. As we have moved back and forth between the outer and inner circles, however, we have thus far only touched upon it. Let us complete our profile of Ebibara by describing some of its features.

Perhaps the most impressive is the persistence with which the Ebibara family retains its customary structure, a fact by no means equally true of Japanese families in general. There appear to be two main reasons for this. The first is the location of Utsumi-shi, separated as it is from the main arteries of industrial and urban reconstruction. The second is the comparative resilience with which the Ebibara subculture accommodates itself to change while retaining much of its traditional order. This is not to say that customary forms of family life are not to be found elsewhere in the country. Of course, they are—very widely so. What strikes the visiting observer, nevertheless, is the remarkable sturdiness of Ebibara family patterns in spite of heavy pressures to alter their character—pressures which are certainly having an effect in this community, but which so far have not been nearly powerful enough to shatter them.

The practice of primogeniture is an important instance. This practice, which ordains that the eldest son shall inherit the primary family property, is still almost universal not only in Ebibara but in the whole of Utsumi-shi. The eldest son in turn assumes full responsibility for the care of his parents, who usually reside in the same household with him and his own family throughout the remainder of their lives. Occasionally we have even found a family with four generations living under the same roof, although in many other families the eldest son has not yet married, or there are no sons at all so that only two generations, the property-owning parents and their children, live together. At any one time about one-fifth of all households in Ebibara and Utsumi-shi consist of two couples living in the same house—the eldest son and his wife, and his parents. But almost all households maintain this two-couple arrangement at some period in the span of a generation, most certainly if they are fishing or farming families. During this period, the older couple often assumes a major part of the care of their grandchildren while the parents are at work.

Another deeply ingrained custom sanctions a family's adopting a son if it has only daughters. He then takes the family name, breaks off completely from his original family, and marries the eldest daughter. Thereby the family line remains unbroken, and the main household is again perpetuated through primogeniture. Among our informants, two had been the bridegrooms of eldest daughters: one a junior high school teacher, Yamamoto-san; the other our factory union member, Tsuji-san. They are called *muko-yōshi* and both know several similar families in their neighborhoods. Adopted sons usually come from another community since in-group fishing families would like to avoid the custom; not only is it considered a necessary evil, but it deprives the family from which the son comes both of a potential money-earner and of further identification with his own kin. Neither Yamamoto-san nor Tsuji-san was born in Ebibara, though their birthplaces were nearby. Even so, *muko-yōshi* has if anything increased in recent years. Fewer children are being born (the average family now includes three children or less, a sharp decline from previous generations) and therefore fewer sons. Sometimes, too, a *muko-yōshi* family is set up with the second or third daughter as the wife. Occasionally, where there are no children at all, a son is legally adopted who eventually marries and thereby continues the family name. In such cases, the kinship line of descent through blood relationship prescribed by traditional primogeniture is, of course, broken, although it should also be noted that many marriages in Ebibara are between first, second, or third cousins. Thus, another of our informants, Muta-san, the wife of a fisherman, is married to her first cousin. They have four children. Her husband is not a *muko-yōshi*, however.

Another system of adoption, now fading, may be considered as rather unique to Ebibara, if Oka-san, the co-op director, is correct. It is called, in local dialect, *yoboshigo* and still includes many citizens of middle age or older. *Yoboshigo* provides for a kind of ritualistic adoption, or "fictive kinship," by a father of "sons" and sometimes "daughters" from other families. Oka-san himself has seven *yoboshigo* "relatives," five "brothers" and two "sisters," each from a different family. In each case, moreover, his own father felt a strong bond of friendship with the father of the adopted relative. Although Oka-san is not, unless remotely, related by blood to any of the seven, he continues to feel close loyalty and affection toward them. One original purpose of *yoboshigo*, he pointed out, was to strengthen a family, especially if one or more of its children were physically rather weak. By joining one's own home with the name of the "father" by whom one is being adopted, it was expected that some of the health of the "father" and his family would permeate the weaker adopted "son." Thus, it is still common for older men in Ebibara to have two names, their own legal name and one by adoption. In addition to this purpose, *yoboshigo* strengthens economic and political ties between the connected families. At one time, children so adopted were utilized, according to one informant, as a source of free labor. Even today, *yoboshigo* "relatives" join together to back a candidate for some local position (Oka-san admits such personal benefit as co-op director), and in time of death, marriage, or crises such as may arise, for example, from storms at sea, they often come to one another's support.

Although *yoboshigo* might be regarded as one form of "extended family," and is even reminiscent of the godfather-godchild syndrome prevalent in cultures such as the Hispanic, it is not to be confused with the more legal and systematic form of family, known as the main family (*honke*) and branch or satellite family (*bunke*), which remains today as the dominant pattern in Ebibara. Here the network of kinship connections between *honke* and *bunke* is extremely complex, chiefly because of the great extent to which so many families have continued for generations to live in the same community and to marry among themselves. To take a striking example, we found that seven fishing women with whom we met one afternoon were all born in Ebibara; so were all of their husbands, parents, parents-in-law, grandparents, and grandparents-in-law—a total of 98 persons embracing three generations. In the fishing co-operative the largest extended family group consists of 13 households, the second largest of 10. We shall find that this phenomenon is of major importance in shaping the pattern of control. Only within recent years, indeed, has intermarriage between farmers and fishermen within Ebibara itself begun to occur with some frequency.

The *honke* family consists typically of the eldest son as house master, together with his wife, children, and often his parents. The *bunke* families consist of the second and successive sons and daughters, unless for some reason the eldest son prefers not to continue in the same household. In this case, the next son (Nakayama-san is one example) inherits the family property including, in the case of *gyomin*, the most valuable property of all, the family fishing boat. Often a second or third son may become a partner or assistant to the eldest son, and work with him for years on the same boat. Often, too, *bunke* couples may live for a period of time after marriage in the *honke* household before moving into their own house. Then, since they can seldom afford a boat of their own, they may become workers in another occupation such as fish processing. In a few recent cases, even the first son has changed from fishing to a more lucrative field while continuing to occupy the ancestral home.

Whenever a master of the *honke* can afford to do so, he assists the *bunke* families in various ways. Take the case of our informant Wada-san, a retired fisherman and *jichikai* leader. He has five sons (one adopted) and three daughters; all are grown. Seven live in Ebibara and the eighth, the wife of a farmer, lives within the city limits of Utsumi-shi. Four of Wada-san's five sons are fishermen, and all but the youngest daughter (a textile worker) and one son (a fisherman) are married. The two unmarried children plus the eldest son and wife and three grandchildren all live together with Wada-san and his wife. His aged mother lives three doors away in the house where he was born, so that four generations are together every day. Moreover, Wada-san built houses and provided land for his second and third sons; otherwise, he said, he would have felt compelled to rent houses for them.

Our farmer informant Soma-san offers a comparable example. He has six sons (one adopted) and two daughters. His eldest son and daughter-in-law and their four children live with him and his wife. Five of his six sons still live in Ebibara, but none except the beneficiary of primogeniture are farmers. The others hold diverse jobs. One is a junior high school teacher, a second a school janitor, a third the owner of a grocery store, a fourth a tax accountant. This diversity doubtless resulted largely from the difficulty of subdividing into smaller parcels the limited and very costly acreage belonging to Soma-san. No similar economic obstacle confronts fishermen, since the sea is public property. Soma-san, incidentally, built branch houses for all six of his sons on land that he owned.

One other feature of the family structure, especially among fishermen, is, like *yoboshigo*, rather unusual although by no means limited to Ebibara. (It is often known in other communities as *wakashūgumi*, group of young people.) At any rate, in accordance with time-worn practice, teen-age boys form small informal clubs of close friends while in elementary or junior high school, and then after graduation regularly sleep together in a single room. The son of Nakayama-san, the ex-fisherman and marine processor, exemplifies this tradition. Three others besides the son, only one not involved in some form of fishing occupation, occupy the upstairs room of Nakayama-san's two-centuries-old house. There is no rental, although an occasional gift may be offered to the host. Thus far the four have been together for three years, but Nakayama-san himself belonged to his club for 12, from his thirteenth to his twenty-fifth year. His father, before him, also belonged to a young men's club, and all three generations have successively occupied the same sleeping room. The club members, we were told, become "like brothers" to one another, often more so than to their own kin. Only marriage, death, or departure can dissolve a club. If a member leaves to be married, his fellows offer him a farewell gift. One can understand, then, why group loyalty would be strong, so strong that it was common in the Ebibara of Nakayama-san's boyhood for clubs often to fight one another. Indeed, the familiar reputation that fishermen have acquired of being pugnacious may well derive in considerable part from these precursors of the "gang wars" of today.

Meanwhile, it is still routine for members to take their meals in their own homes and keep their belongings there, but to come together in the evening to talk and sleep. Or on stormy days when they cannot go to sea, they may spend their time chatting and drinking. According to Nakayama-san, the custom has no common name in Ebibara, although *neyado* ("dormitory" is one of several translations) is sometimes heard. This little group simply calls itself *Nakayama-no-wakashū* (young men of Nakayama's house). In preceding generations, the strong devotion of group members to one another also frequently resulted in *yoboshigo* relationships, but even today many young unmarried fishermen are bound in lifelong allegiance to their sleeping clubs.

Nevertheless, *neyado* is beginning to decline. Senior high school graduates, though still few, are not enthusiastic about it largely because they seldom remain in the family occupation. Their work schedules differ from those of fishermen, so their sleeping hours do not coincide. Actually another custom, *hiyori-moshi*, remains stronger than *neyado*. *Hiyori-moshi*, meaning literally "talk about weather," involves topics of conversation without limit. Groups of perhaps eight young men gather at two or three regular spots on the river banks, presumably to decide if the weather is propitious for fishing, but preferably to chat for as much as two or three hours about sports, fishing successes or failures, and, above all, girls. Rumor-mongering, according to several informants, is a chronic indulgence among Ebibara people.

2

CONFLICT
AND COOPERATION
IN EBIBARA

I

Ebibara is a community of disturbing problems. It is an exemplar of Japanese culture not only in this respect but, even more dramatically, in the ways that it has struggled valiantly to face up to them.

By far the most serious of these problems has been the threat to perpetuation of Ebibara as an exceptionally old and proudly indigenous community. The cause is chiefly technological: fishing is no longer the relatively uncomplicated occupation that it once was; on the contrary, increasingly efficient techniques are being introduced, making possible larger and larger catches and therefore, *other things being equal*, greater compensation. The powerful diesel engine with which every boat in the regular Ebibara fleet is now equipped was first installed here in 1932, but was not legalized by the government for another five years for fear over-fishing would result, and it did not become common for over a decade. Even so, this was the single most important of all technological changes.

But other things are *not* equal. With the diesel engine, boats not only are able to move faster and farther but can utilize new methods of catching many more fish in briefer periods of time than ever before in marine history. Nylon nets have also reduced wear and tear. Precise methods differ, to be sure, but common to most of them is the trawl—the slow, steady, forward motion of the boat as it pulls the large weighted nets sweeping deep in the sea behind it.

Less than a quarter of a century ago the vast success of such innova-

25

tions was so substantial that it resulted not only in better family income but also in more fishermen and more boats. In numerous fishing villages, these were both controlled by only one or two men often called *amimoto* (net-owners). For example, in Kazaki-shima, the offshore island which we remember as part of the Utsumi-shi municipality, this system of centralized ownership is still a dominant one, in contrast with that of Ebibara where each boat almost invariably belongs to a single family. Yet, whatever the system of ownership, the increase of powered craft and of fishing population was not a serious problem—for a while. Boats could easily travel a hundred or more miles away and thus expand their fishing fields several times over. According to Co-op Director Oka, the 20 or so years after 1932 were, in strictly relative terms, prosperous ones. He, like a majority of other Ebibara fishermen, spent five months a year away from the home port and the other seven near enough to it so that he could usually return after each day's labor. All of this could be accomplished, moreover, with substantially reduced manpower: not only does a diesel engine require no stoking or other care to the extent that earlier steam engines did, but its power can easily be used to pull nets aboard and for other heavy work.

But the new system could not last. Many other seashore communities besides Ebibara were likewise developing their powered fleets, so competition for the larger rewards assured by larger catches was soon overtaking and reducing these rewards. Only one remedy seemed practicable—to demarcate all fishing areas according to the location of communities. By 1950, federal and prefectural laws were adopted to restore a degree of order to an occupation that was bent on ruining itself. Thereafter the Ebibara fleet was confined, as were all others, to the waters adjacent to its port. From that day none of its boats has traveled much farther out to sea than 2 or 3 miles.

The familiar irony of technological progress was far from dispelled, however, by new restrictions. On the contrary, with only small fields of operation now available for a large number of boats, the quantity of fish that could be caught with modernized equipment was almost invariably less than actual capacity. This was chiefly due, of course, to a contradiction everywhere familiar in the modern history of natural resources: the efficiency with which fish could now be caught was considerably greater than the rapidity with which they could reproduce and grow. As long as *gyomin* could move about freely, the contradiction was not so acute, but the moment that their range of endeavor was radically narrowed it became acute indeed. Thus, almost simultaneously with the new laws of demarcation, the imbalance between technological capacity and natural supply began to be felt, and family incomes, however lucrative at best, began to shrink alarmingly. Ebibara was faced with disintegration of its way of life.

II

The story of the struggle to overcome the powerful forces aligned against Ebibara's security and character is many faceted. Today victory is far from complete and problems continue to multiply. Nevertheless, by comparison with many another Japanese society of fishermen, Ebibara has managed much more successfully to continue on its rugged course. It has done so, however, not so much by any single momentous accomplishment as by a number of interlocking strategies of change that are conspicuous in the ways that they have generated both conflict and cooperation.

This is not to imply that changes are always deliberately planned. Much of the stability that Ebibara is able to maintain is due to hard and long hours of work which compensate in part for often meager hauls. Unlike factory labor, which is governed more strictly by legal regulation of work schedules and which organized labor constantly presses to improve, the typical fisherman like the typical farmer in Ebibara thinks of himself as his own boss and sets as many of his own rules as possible. For example, in less than a decade, the number of days per year devoted to fishing has increased by 20 percent—whereas industrial work schedules have decreased. When a fisherman is working (there are many days when the fleet does not go out at all because of poor weather or scanty catches), he averages over 12 hours per day in preparation and at sea. Thus, even if the total catch of the fleet increases substantially, as it has recently, this is hardly proof of replenishment of the sea's natural resources but rather of heavier labor as well as of more efficiency. Equally important is the fact that boats are frequently manned by two members of the same family, who thereby avoid the necessity of hiring outside labor but who, because they must also divide the income from their catch, are compelled to intensify their efforts that much more.

Moreover, not all Ebibara fishermen are able to find places in the fleet. A few join the crews of large ships that travel to the far north or south for salmon, tuna, and occasionally whales. Others who belong to families unable to afford a large motored craft (over 10 percent of all boats in Ebibara have only outboard motors or no motors at all) fish by themselves near the shore part time and supplement their income with additional jobs. Still others are employed by propertied fishermen. Nor should it be forgotten that one or more members of the typical Ebibara family may work at a job not related to fishing, especially in the branch factories of national industries. Finally, a few members simply follow the migratory trend from rural to urban areas and move to big cities where wages may be higher and jobs easier.

Yet, with due regard for all of these conditions, none is sufficient to account for the dynamics of Ebibara life. Several other conditions are more crucial, and it is these that may be viewed as strategies of planned change. None, to be sure, is the invention of this community, for all of them have been introduced partly or wholly from outside. Even so, the complex of relationships that results from the mutual and constant reinforcement of these strategies is, we think, distinctive. They may be grouped as six: (1) the fishing co-operative; (2) the frequent use of illegal fishing practices; (3) the Department of Fisheries—national, prefectural, and local; (4) the systematic cultivation of sea foods, most notably seaweed, which earlier had been regarded as a trivial source of income or simply ignored; (5) marine processing factories; and finally (6) education.

III

The co-op, of course, both affects and is affected by all of these forces. Let us describe it more carefully. Producer co-operatives in agriculture and fishing were established throughout Japan with strong federal enouragement shortly after World War II, but some, including the Ebibara co-op, developed well before the war years. Today, it is one of some 6000 in the nation devoted to helping fishermen improve their economy. Two smaller co-ops— one on Kazaki-shima, the other on the outskirts of the city—function within Utsumi-shi, but plans are under way to integrate all three into one association.

To belong to the Ebibara co-operative, one must devote at least 90 days per year to fishing; own five or more shares of stock, each valued at $5.60; and agree to the rules of fishing established by the membership. (The largest number of shares owned by any one officer is 23, the smallest 9.) Although, since these requirements were adopted, membership has decreased by over 100 members unable to meet them, the co-op itself is considered stronger. Today it consists of over 300 members for whom fishing or allied endeavors are their chief occupation. Oka-san is the seventh director.

The co-op is governed by a central board of directors consisting of 12 members and 5 financial officers, all of whom are elected at an annual general meeting of about two-thirds of the membership. In addition, 3 representatives are elected by each of 5 grassroots subdivisions of Ebibara so that the full board consists of 32 persons. The election itself is by secret ballot, but this is for the benefit of "good human relations," we were told, rather than because there are competing candidates: most if not all have already been handpicked by the leadership. The full board of 32 meets about 20 times each year; in addition, there are many smaller meetings by the sectional representatives or the central board. Members of the latter receive

$28 per year for their services, the others about $10. None of the board members, according to the data mentioned earlier, has continued formal education beyond junior high school. All but two were born in Ebibara, as were their fathers and grandfathers.

A women's auxiliary is led by an executive board of 17 members, elected by the same five community subdivisions, who in turn choose the president and vice-president. The executive committee meets about once per month. Women are never elected to the co-op board of directors itself, and the auxiliary has no official power. Nevertheless, it has contributed significantly to the stamina of Ebibara both by the enthusiasm of its leaders and by the attractiveness of its program. Since about 10 percent of the 300 or so auxiliary members are not from fishing families, there are more opportunities for women of disparate backgrounds to mingle socially than was once the case.

Still another adjunct of the co-op is the youth division of about 35 male members. Another dozen young fishermen would belong if they were not away on long expeditions to the Antarctic Ocean or near the northern island of Hokkaidō. The president, the son of our informant Wada-san, describes the program as a mixture of recreation and service.

One other organization, related unofficially to the co-op, is called *kogi kumiai* (the term *kogi* derives from old-time net fishing by rowboat; *kumiai* means union, or co-op). It is really a kind of local pressure group organized by the owners of the fleet of powered trawlers, although recently several other fishing fleets in Yoneshima-ken have on occasion joined forces with it. *Kogi kumiai* aims to strengthen the rights of the fleet to engage in its search for fish without so many restrictions. Even more, it seeks to protect its own members by collective action whenever they engage in the illegal practices that we are about to describe.

Oka-san, interestingly enough, has become not only director of the official co-op but, reportedly without authorization by the board of directors, also heads *kogi kumiai*. Otherwise it would have broken up, he says, for no one else wants a position fraught with so much conflict. Somehow Oka-san adroitly manages to serve both groups at the same time, apparently with little doubt that the one is necessary to the welfare of the other.

IV

To appreciate more graphically why illegal methods are so difficult to avoid, we join one of the Ebibara trawlers on a chilly February day. Manned by a crew of two brothers, our boat chugs out of the harbor at midmorning. The day schedule has been in effect since early December and will continue until April, but very few boats are out today: the sea is a little rough, and the catch has been paltry. Many members of the fleet are working temporarily at other jobs in Utsumi-shi or harvesting the last of their seaweed crop.

A mile or so from shore the partners prepare to set their *senshakogi*, a name commonly used for this form of trawling. It is now a legal technique although some years ago it was not; only persistent petitioning to government officials finally resulted in reluctant authorization. As the engine slows, two nets are lowered by pulley from thick bamboo arms that extend horizontally at an angle from each side of the boat. An iron rake a yard or so wide with curved teeth about 2 feet long follows each net. The two identical contraptions sink to the floor of the sea. Then the engine is throttled gently upward and the trawling begins. For a while the brothers have little to do except to steer or occasionally check their engine as we move through choppy water. Finally, as the boat slows again, the pulley begins to draw the rakes and nets up toward the back of the boat, where they are lifted on deck.

The nets are spread out, and the catch is quickly sorted by hand into baskets. The most impressive fruits of the haul, however, are not the quart or so of tiny shrimp, several clams, two octopuses, three 15-inch sea eels, and a few other small miscellaneous fish, but the debris. The rakes, stirring the bottom as they scratch into the mud, have loosened several tin cans, an old shoe, a rusted iron bar, muddy boards, tangled weeds, and sundry unnamable objects. All of the litter is tossed back into the sea, probably for some later trawler to dredge to the surface again. A few of the smaller fish are also redeposited. Then the deck is swabbed down with pails of water and, 20 minutes after they emerged, the nets and rakes are once more in position.

This is the routine of *senshakogi* trawling, a term that originally suggests "rowing a tank." If the catches are worthwhile, the nets may be lowered and raised several times in the course of one trip. Today, the catches are even smaller than usual, so we do not remain at sea more than a few hours. Halfway through the trip, however, our hosts prepare lunch for us. They light a cozy charcoal brazier near the stern, fix a kettle of tea, and skillfully clean and broil several of the newly caught fish. One of the octopuses is cut open and several hundred eggs that look very much like cooked rice except for their yellowish color are removed. These, along with slices of its tentacles, are boiled. The eggs are considered a special delicacy, and soon one of the partners, grinning proudly, offers them to us with the single English word: "Babies!"

Senshakogi is a technique used by most of the fleet especially in the late fall but often into the winter as well. At other times it is prohibited, although not very strictly. Ebibara, we were told, was the original community in this part of Japan to adopt *senshakogi* (it was first observed near Nagoya) and soon fishermen traveled from considerable distances to watch its operation by the Ebibara fleet. The principal importance of this technique is that it is able, because of the rakes, to disturb and then ensnare shrimp and other small fish that normally remain in a semidormant state at the bottom of the sea when the weather turns cold. At times the catch is substantial; unfortunately, however, *senshakogi* does not discriminate between fish that are marketable and those that are not. Department of Fisheries experts as well as Ebibara *gyomin* disagree about the extent to which agitation caused by the rakes destroys fish that are too small to be caught in the nets. They also disagree about the extent to which the rake performs a beneficial role by destroying marine enemies of edible fish and by "cultivating" the bottom. Both experts and *gyomin* do completely agree, because this is no longer a matter of debate, that regardless of technique the average catch is lessening.

This brings us to discussion of the common practice of illegal fishing methods which are resorted to because legal ones provide insufficient income. There are several variations. One, called *soroban-geta*, a modification of *senshakogi*, is utilized at certain times by most members of the fleet because they consider it more effective than the net-and-rake technique. *Soroban*, incidentally, is the Japanese term for abacus, the ancient counting-figuring apparatus that all Japanese school children learn to manipulate, and *geta* is the word for a familiar style of wooden clogs. Thus, *soroban-geta* is a colloquial term; it suggests a kind of walking on the floor of the sea by nets fastened with rounded stones resembling the beads of an abacus. Although this technique is said to disturb the sea bottom substantially more than the fairly narrow rakes utilized by *senshakogi*, and thus to eliminate a greater quantity of infant shrimp and other fish before they are ready for consumption, Director Oka as well as apparently most of the membership of *kogi kumiai* regard it as an effective method of fishing that should be legalized. That many law enforcement officers and marine experts in Yoneshima-ken may tacitly agree is probable, as they rarely interfere when *soroban-geta* is at work. Most of the time, they look the other way.

But they are not so tolerant of a second illegal technique called *ichijōkogi*, roughly defined as "one-net fishing." Although some leaders such as Wada-san would like to see even *ichijōkogi* legalized, Oka-san and others would not. The reason in this case is not only that it, too, destroys tiny fish but more seriously that it catches so many marketable ones (twice as many as by standard techniques, if Oka-san is correct) that it depletes the resources of the sea much more ruthlessly than other techniques do. The principle of *ichijōkogi* is the use of two long, heavy planks called *kaikōban*, which are tied to a large net in such a way that, as the boat moves forward, the net fans open much more widely than in the case of smaller nets used in legal trawling.

The interesting fact about *ichijōkogi* is that it is adopted in spring and fall by at least four-fifths of the Ebibara fleet despite the fact that police patrol boats are constantly on the alert, particularly during the spring season. It is safer, of course, to utilize *ichijōkogi* at night, but some fishermen dare to even during the day. The only period when no one is likely to do so is during the warmest season of the year, from mid-June through September, when shrimp and other fish ascend into warmer water and are attracted by the strong electric lights. During these four months, most fishermen restrict themselves to the primary legal method called *sokobiki*, which is the standard type of open-net trawling to which no rakes, *soroban* weights, planks, or other ingenious paraphernalia are fastened. *Sokobiki* becomes illegal only when attempted in shallow offshore waters; there it is out of bounds because it disturbs the life cycle of fish much as do the other methods.

When asked why illegal methods are not usually used during the summer months, the reply was always similar. Because fish are more abundant during these months (although by no means abundant enough), it is not so essential to run the constant risk of being discovered by police patrols. But at other times of the year the risk must be taken; without *soroban-geta* and especially *ichijōkogi*, the fleet would not be able to support itself at all during the poorer months.

What happens when a boat is caught? The punishment varies. Equipment may be confiscated, but more often only the catch is. In addition, a fine of at least $14 is usually imposed on each arrested boat, which *kogi kumiai* may help to pay. The fine is hardly stiff enough to discourage typical *gyomin* from trying again, yet it is serious enough to worry about. Enough recurrences may even lead to revocation of a fishing license, although this has not yet happened to anyone here.

To reduce the dangers of discovery, the Ebibara fleet has adopted a routine which Watanabe-san's wife termed *mōshi-awase* (reaching agreement). Almost every midafternoon during the *ichijōkogi* season, fleet fishermen gather at the wharf to learn whether patrols have been sighted during the day. Ebibara boats of other types that were out for different kinds of fish in the morning or afternoon often return to port before the fleet is ready to leave; it is they who bring back reports of patrols on the prowl. Discussion among the 150 or so fishermen is led informally by various spokesmen for *kogi kumiai*, who also sometimes recommend that the fleet stay home on a particular night, not because of patrols, but because the weather looks threatening. This recommendation is especially welcome by younger apprentice fishermen. After perhaps 15 minutes of lively discussion, agreement is reached, and only then do all boats either leave together or decide to stay home. Whatever the agreement may be, it is invariably unanimous; no boat ever departs by itself. If the decision is to remain ashore, the session often turns into a prolonged free-for-all gossip session similar to the custom of *hiyori-moshi.*

Illegal practices among our fishermen are by no means limited, however, to *soroban-geta* and *ichijōkogi.* In the course of a year a fairly large part of Oka-san's time (let us recall that he is director of both the official co-op and *kogi kumiai*) may be devoted to coping with conflicts that arise from poaching in areas of the sea that are off-limits to the Ebibara fleet. There are two kinds of poaching: (1) simple trespassing beyond the boundaries established by law (Oka-san estimates 25 or more instances in a single year, although only a fraction are ever detected); and (2) less common but more serious, breaking into traps set by fishermen of other co-ops for the purpose of capturing certain types of fish, primarily octopuses and cuttle fish.

Although they are few, it is extremely difficult to recognize the invaders because they operate at night with their lights extinguished. The result is that whenever it becomes known that traps were invaded and broken, the entire *kogi kumiai* must share responsibility, because no individual member ever admits that he is the guilty party. Several times a year cases of poaching and invading reach the stage where *kogi kumiai* officers must meet with their accusers, usually the officers of a neighboring co-op, to work out a settlement of damages. This is not easily accomplished, and both sides in the dispute often compromise between what the offended parties demand at the outset and what *kogi kumiai* offers to pay. The victimized co-op might demand as much as $300, but settlement is likely to be closer to $50 or even as little as $14. In one recent case, however, the amount agreed upon was $180—a sum which must have strained the treasury of *kogi kumiai,* to which each member contributes a little more than fifty cents per month.

That poaching is not carried on exclusively by Ebibara fishermen makes negotiation somewhat easier. Other co-ops have been known to trespass on Ebibara territory as well, although much less frequently. At the same time, it is usually difficult to deny guilty practices once they are detected, for Ebibara boats have distinctive markings.

When boats are observed out of bounds they are reported either to police patrols by telephone or, more often, to leaders of the offending co-op. Only once, so far as we could learn from our informants, did actual violence occur on the sea between boats from different communities; that was in 1952. It is much more likely for both sides to take conciliatory attitudes, since neither side may be innocent. Some spokesmen contended, nevertheless, that Ebibara is more notorious for its poaching practices than any other community in this section of Japan.

The exact conditions under which patrols decide to "crack down" on suspected violators remain ambiguous. Federal boats seem to be stricter than prefectural boats, one reason perhaps being that the latter tend to be more sympathetic with the plight of people in their own territory. In one respect, however, there is little ambiguity; boats that *both* trespass and resort to illegal fishing techniques at the same time are in real danger of trouble.

A case in point was the arrest during our study of some 10 members of the fleet on a single spring night. All of them were utilizing the *ichijōkogi* method in an area of the sea across the line from their own. Watanabe-san, the husband of one of our informants, told us that he pleaded with the officers not to confiscate their nets or other valuable equipment since he and his fellow fishermen had to make a living. Evidently the officers were partially persuaded, because they released the entire group after confiscating their night's catch, imposing a fine of $14 on each boat, and, most crucially, removing their *kaikōban*, the illegal structure of planks that has already been described. Fisherman Watanabe planned, he said, to build another *kaikōban* as soon as possible. But when he, his wife, and brother later invited us to join them on an all-night summer trip, only their *sokobiki* was operating. During this period of the year, there seemed to be almost no poaching. When we asked why, the wife of Watanabe-san answered that it was only because catches were then too poor to justify the risk of being caught. Were fish plentiful enough, she said, poachings would be continuing as frequently as ever.

V

That the Department of Fisheries on all levels of the government is quite aware of illegal practices is evident, because no one, official or fisherman, tries to deny them. Rather, as we have shown, officials are often remarkably temperate in their own reactions.

The arduous life that *gyomin* endure is a matter of at least moderate concern to all political parties. Certainly the ruling Liberal Democratic party, which we remember the vast majority of fishermen support, has by no means entirely ignored their problems. The government has sought solutions that will enable the half million Japanese fishmen and their families to share in the benefits of an increasingly technologized economy rather than to be penalized because they, too, have inevitably become more and more technologized. Thus, much of the change that has been occurring in Ebibara is the direct result of governmental efforts, especially of the Department of Fisheries working hand-in-hand with the co-operative movement. Certainly the cure for chronic illegal practices has not appeared to be a policy of stern and costly law enforcement, but instead a program of multilateral development for the community as a whole.

The principal features of this program are included within an ambitious five-year plan which Utsumi-shi (one of four cities in Yoneshima-ken with a staffed planning office) has well under way. For example, a storage warehouse for tiny sardinelike dried fish is to be built by the co-op, and 75 percent of the cost is to be met with outright federal and prefectural grants. This new facility will be used by the two other fishing co-ops of Utsumi-shi, and will unite them for the first time in a common attempt to stabilize financial returns at a higher level than is possible when produce is sold quickly at fluctuating prices. For similar reasons, presently limited refrigeration facilities will be enlarged and utilized jointly. New gasoline tanks to fuel the diesel engines of the fleet are to be rebuilt near the wharf below ground (at present the exposed tanks are a constant danger to crowded Ebibara), and this cost, too, will be met largely by grants. By far the most extensive project, however, is the construction of a new breakwater which we shall describe. Its cost will be shared by all governmental levels.

Meanwhile, a five-year plan, loosely related to a federal five-year plan, is under way in Yoneshima-ken to double the income of the marine economy. For example, we were told by Adachi-san, one of our panel of leaders and the head of the prefectural credit union of the fishing co-operative, that a principal objective of the Yoneshima-ken plan is to divert almost one-third of the fishing population of 8000 households into different occupations on the ground that there are simply too many fishermen in proportion to the amount of natural resources now available. At the same time, subsistence-level fishing with small boats will be discouraged. To make the changes feasible, nearly a million dollars will be granted outright to individual households in order to cushion the inevitable disruptions of such a change, and another million dollars will be lent to them by the credit union at a much lower than average rate of interest: 3.5 percent. Thus in Kazaki-shima, if Adachi-san is correct, the proportion of households that have already moved elsewhere is nearly half of the total—although this migration occurred even before the government offered much help. But in Ebibara, largely because of its planning strategies, almost none have done so.

The credit union of the Ebibara co-op is important for different reasons. It is one of the strongest affiliates of the prefectural credit union, and many of its members save regularly in it at an interest rate of 6 percent. Some are also able to borrow, at 9 percent interest, over $1000 toward repairs of their boats or for equipment (although they may borrow up to 80 percent of the cost of a new boat directly from the government). The Ebibara credit union itself already has capital approaching $150,000, whereas the capital of the prefectural credit union has tripled in four years, to a total of well over $3,-000,000. Frequently we were told that this growth could not have occurred without a slowly growing trust by fishermen in their co-op.

Nevertheless, many loans are still negotiated privately at a higher rate of interest, presumably by fishermen who cannot obtain the necessary two co-signers even among close relatives because credit is too weak (defaults are rather frequent), or because some members do not wish others to know their income. However, every member, whether he likes to or not, must deposit 20 percent of his monthly income in the co-op so that it can maintain daily operations. This deposit is not a savings account; it is returned without interest at the New Year, when everywhere in Japan it is the custom to settle all small or large accounts. At other times during the year, especially in the slack winter season, many fishermen also draw upon savings that they managed to accumulate when the catch was good.

The fishing co-op as a producer is far stronger than is its related consumer co-op. Yet the latter does a fairly substantial business in products needed by fishermen for their occupation, all of them sold under the universal co-op principle of one vote per member regardless of the number of shares that any member owns, with some saving to purchasers. Gasoline, oil, nets, and other boat equipment are the principal commodities, for which about 30 percent of the gross income of fishermen is expended. In addition, the women's auxiliary sometimes sells small amounts of such daily necessities as blankets, winter clothing, charcoal, insect spray, soap, paper, and toothbrushes, and uses the profit for a spring recreational trip to the cherry-blossom park in Utsumi-shi or occasionally for longer trips. But such activities are intermittent and are apparently not carried on according to the strict rules of a genuine consumer co-op.

When informants were asked why the latter has not been well developed in Ebibara, we were given two reasons. One was that the development of fishing co-ops lags far behind farming co-ops ("by at least 65 percent," Director Oka believes), some of which do have fairly large consumer stores. Even in the several Yoneshima-ken communities where fishing and farming occupations are combined in a single household—and far more engage in this combination than in one or the other exclusively—consumer co-ops that unite the two occupations rarely if ever exist. The second reason was that Ebibara fishing households are so frequently related to people who run small retail shops in the Ebibara section of Utsumi-shi that they are unable to establish a consumer co-op without straining kinship ties.

Nevertheless, leaders of the women's auxiliary seemed to agree that a consumer co-op would be desirable, and there was even talk of visiting one community some distance away where an impressive beginning has already been made. Both Director Oka and his assistant Sato-san hoped also that such extensions of their program will be possible. A plant for processing seaweed was actually built by the co-op with federal help, but the building was closed because of disputes among members who had objected to rental fees. Even so, Sato-san contended vigorously that a plant could still succeed if well managed. He was also eager that his co-op become a pioneer among fishermen in establishing an eight-hour work day, and Oka-san has even dreamed of providing a co-op barber and other personal services. Because such innovations are less urgent, they have not yet been discussed with the board of directors.

VI

Meanwhile, much more audacious innovations have been acted upon with remarkable vigor. Easily the most far-reaching is the experiment in seaweed cultivation, first tested in the early 1950s. Now, under co-op supervision, it is an established and expanding enterprise. Ebibara is one of only two communities in Yoneshima-ken that combine fish and seaweed as their two chief resources.

Seaweed cultivation began at the instigation of the prefectural Department of Fisheries, which has on its staff experts who have studied at Tokyo Marine University. In Utsumi-shi, seaweed pilot projects became the direct responsibility of Ogawa-san, a largely self-educated young man hired by the city office. He had been a fisherman himself and came from a family of fishermen—doubtless an important factor in the success with which Ebibara households slowly decided to modify the single pattern of occupation that stemmed from a time-worn past.

This decision was by no means an easy one. Resistance, skepticism, and caution were far more common than zealous support. Ogawa-san found, indeed, that problems of human relations were often more serious than technical ones. But, with ever more threatening economic deprivation, seven households were at last prevailed upon to risk the new venture. Before long the total grew to 20, most of whom were more desperate than usual and had relatively less to lose. Both the co-op and the prefecture, but not the city, helped to provide necessary funds for the first equipment, and results became gradually impressive. By the late 1950s, a majority of families were ready to join the project.

At that point, unfortunately, a conflict arose which split the co-op into two warring factions. The pioneer group of 20 insisted that, because they had been there first, they should have priority in the shallow waters off the Utsumi-shi beach—the same beach, we remember, which is teeming in summer with swimmers. In 1960, the situation had reached such an impasse that, when a general meeting of the co-op voted to allow equal space and equal rights to all members, the group of 20 not only resigned en masse but considered erecting barriers to keep the rest out. Oka-san was brought in as director about this time, apparently as a trouble shooter, but the board itself was changed three times during the crisis. At last, the patriarchal prestige of the elder co-op members (and age is perhaps as powerful an influence in Ebibara as it is anywhere in Japan) was apparently sufficient to win the rebels back.

The hostility generated by the conflict has now largely disappeared, certainly on the surface, and almost 200 household members of the co-op presently share in the seaweed enterprise. Each of the five community divisions of the co-op has its own section of the shore, the only exception to equal allocation being a few members who devote most of their time to this occupation. The rest, of course, continue with the Ebibara fleet.

The process by which seaweed is grown is a fascinating one. The season runs from October to February, which is lucky in one sense: this is also the poorest time for fishing. The first step in cultivation is to drive hundreds of bamboo poles in orderly rows into the sandy sea bottom, after which special nets (averaging about 15 for each household) are fastened to the poles. The annual rental space for each net costs about fifty cents per year, paid to the proprietary federal government. Because the beach is next to a tidal river, Asa-kawa, a certain amount of fresh water is carried along the shore by currents and mixes in a salutary way with the salty sea water.

The seaweed is formed from spores of a species of red algae which fasten themselves to the nets and multiply during the late fall months at a prodigious rate. Whenever the growth appears to be substantial enough, the crop is scraped off during low tide, for at this period the nets are above water and caretakers can walk among them. The number of such harvestings varies from season to season, as does the quantity thus obtained. In a good season four scrapings are likely, but in others only one or two. Income from a single net varies accordingly. When the project was in its early stages the amount was about $2, whereas in 1961 it was over 20 times as much, so that by 1963 the community income from seaweed approached $60,000—about one-fourth the total income, as compared with about one-half from trawling and another one-fourth from deep-sea fishing. During our field work, unfortunately, it had dropped far down again, and in a season when the harvest was unusually good elsewhere in Japan.

This drop, according to such informants as Nakayama-san, was the result of waste pouring into Asa-kawa from factories in Utsumi-shi, a problem considered by two or three informants as the single most serious one now confronting the co-op. Seaweed nets placed near the mouth of the river that had been previously generous in their crop suddenly yielded virtually nothing, and even those farther away became badly "infected." Thus, still another worrisome conflict has begun to emerge, this time between industrial establishments in Utsumi-shi and many Ebibara people. Marine experts have been brought in from Kyushu University to study the problem, but it is not yet clear precisely what caused the crop to shrink so alarmingly. Perhaps, however, this difficulty is already on the way to being corrected: a late report from Ebibara indicates that the crop following the near failure has been the most abundant thus far and that the total fishing income of the community is rising again.

In any case, even if it were proved that industrial wastes are the chief culprit, how could they be controlled? The government of Utsumi-shi is itself caught in a dilemma. It wants industry to develop rapidly because in this way the slump in population, which began some years ago but has now leveled off, can be prevented from recurring. Yet it also wants to see Ebibara prosper. A paper manufacturing plant highlights the dilemma. It has seemed to resist all efforts to prevent it from polluting the river with chemicals, which also contaminate drinking water, even going so far at times as to empty its used acids at night, so that when the water is tested in the daytime it is pronounced "safe." A diversionary ditch through part of Ebibara has been proposed, but opposition to this is also powerful, from many ordinary citizens including fishermen. To be sure, a fine may be levied under the present law if pollution is proved, but the penalty is much too small, perhaps $150, to deter industrial offenders like the paper plant, itself a branch of a powerful national company. In any case, is this plant the only one to blame? What of a company that deposits an oily film on the surface of Asa-kawa? What of the *kamaboko* and other small processors of marine products within Ebibara itself?

Still, one would misrepresent the situation to imply that the mayor and other political leaders of Utsumi-shi are willing to let industrial expansion dominate completely. This is by no means the case. Although, to quote the mayor, business pressures are "very difficult" to resist, we have already seen that the city government does offer frequent support to *gyomin*. Ogawa-san, the municipal employee, gives full time to fishery problems and projects. Only recently he has helped persuade the seaweed cultivators to improve their technique in a radical way. Instead of merely waiting (as was earlier the case) for spores of the red algae to attach themselves to the fastened nets as they circulate freely in the offshore waters, the spores are now grown artificially in covered shallow tanks within the same building which was to have been used for the now defunct seaweed processing project. Hundreds of empty inch-long shells hang suspended in sea water already rich in microscopic spores. This process of "germination" continues for several months prior to the fall season. Then the infant seaweed is transplanted to the outdoor fields of submerged nets along the mile or more of beach, where it continues to grow for additional weeks. For a time, the transplantings were purchased from a nearby co-op; now, with its own "germinating" plant, the cost to the co-op membership is slowly going down. Meanwhile, the Ebibara co-op benefits from use of its own building and the only expense to growers themselves is the labor involved. During our study, three different types of algae were being tested for maximum yield.

The city government, it will be remembered, has also approved the plan for a costly new breakwater. Its principal purpose, as developed first by the co-op, is to extend further into the sea the long narrow strip of shallow water adjacent to the beach. Since Ebibara seaweed farming cannot be stretched farther in either direction along the shore (on one side of the port a dike has been under construction for several years to provide additional land to Utsumi-shi farmers by holding back the sea; on the other side the beach is controlled by another co-op), only one recourse remains. This is to increase the space where seaweed can grow by reducing the height of tides. The new great venture requires six years to complete, for the breakwater will extend the full length of the present seaweed fields. Well before construction is finished, co-op members will already have begun to enlarge their allocated spaces, which are planned to extend over 1500 feet out into the sea; these spaces will be rotated each year among members until the breakwater reaches all the way. Behind the investment is, of course, an expectation that the contamination problem will be permanently solved. The goal, at any rate, is to expand seaweed farming by some 250 percent.

Three other activities that help to increase income from the sea deserve brief mention. Very minor is the growing of an inch-size clam that propagates rapidly and is popularly used in soup. It is dug from the muddy bottom of Asa-kawa during low tide, and is largely the monopoly of the processor, Nakayama-san, who rents this river space from the federal government.

Another is the summer occupation of sardine catching. This miniscule fish, after being boiled and dried on mats in the hot sun, is eventually consumed in many kinds of soup. Two of our informants, Nakayama-san and Wada-san, are among five or so household masters who engage in this occupation (on Kazaki-shima the number is much larger, and the income from sardines is several times that of Ebibara). In addition, some 30 households process dried sardines on whatever open ground the crowded quarters of Ebibara afford. The sardine boats, which may make as many as three round trips in a day if the catch is large, testify even more dramatically to the age of technology than do those of the trawler fleet. For they are equipped with a radar system by means of which they are able to detect the whereabouts of schools of sardines. Nakayama-san also operates a shortwave two-way radio. His boat does not actually catch sardines; rather it purchases them from other fishermen, with whom he has an agreement, and the radio serves to direct his representative at sea in negotiating purchases.

The sardine economy, although far less important than that of shrimp or seaweed, has been another source of friction among Ebibara citizens. The attempt of the co-op to control prices to wholesalers has not yet succeeded fully, nor is there thus far any co-op management of the boiling-drying process. The result is that households engaged in catching or preparing sardines are often at the mercy of competitive maneuverings. Shortly after he became director, Oka-san did attempt to stabilize prices by preventing some members from selling in *laissez-faire* style; at one point he even arranged for other co-op members to keep watch over competitive wholesale establishments while he rushed from one to the other on his motorcycle to supervise the "blockade." Yet even now only a little more than half of the total sardine catch is handled through the co-op, for at least two of the nine wholesalers are often able to obtain the product at lower than co-op prices by such lures as interest-free loans, easy rules of repayment, and even occasional pseudo-*geisha* parties. The projected integrated storehouse, we were told, should finally resolve this troublesome situation, although we were also told that most household sardine processors who cannot qualify as co-op members are frequently more supportive of the co-op's struggle to stabilize the market than are many bonafide members.

Clams and sardines can hardly be regarded as venturesome projects; unlike seaweed, both have long been minor products of hard Ebibara labor. One other project is, however, somewhat more venturesome. The Department of Fisheries is encouraging in Ebibara, as in other places, the construction of "fish apartments." These are, in fact, hollow concrete blocks a little over 3 feet square which are dropped into 35 feet of water at 10-foot intervals. In 1963, 500 such apartments (*apaato*) were placed some 300 feet out from the shore, and the number is soon to be increased substantially if the co-op approves. Being stationary protuberances they encourage the growth of plankton as food for small shell fish, which in turn become food for larger fish. Trawlers obviously cannot move through the *apaato* areas, so fishermen with smaller boats and engines benefit by dropping lines and small nets over them.

This project is the only significant one in Ebibara, with the exception of seaweed, that pays direct attention to the urgent problem of replenishment. It is true that some other fishing communities are engaged in replenishment projects (shrimp and pearl growing, perhaps most notably); it is also true that the youth division of the Ebibara co-op once attempted a small octopus-growing project. But the latter failed, and others have not as yet received serious consideration.

The *apaato* project has one additional and surprising feature. Fishermen are encouraged to sell their worn-out boats to the government; these are then sunk to become *apaato*. While interviewing a fisherman living in quite a different region of Japan, we were once told that boat sinking is really another means of encouraging *gyomin* to change occupations. But this purpose is denied both by Adachi-san, the credit union head, and by Mayor Miyakawa. Even so, the fact is that Utsumi-shi does invite the purchase of venerable boats. With 85 percent of the cost once more borne by the prefectural and federal treasuries, nearly $6000 worth were sunk into the sea off Ebibara in one recent year alone.

VII

Marine processing factories, we have said, are another of the chief generators of economic development in Ebibara. Through them, perhaps as much as through such impressive ventures as seaweed farming, the standard of living has recently remained on an even keel, and so in turn has the community itself. Trawling, indeed, has decreased to the stage where less than 20 percent of all fishing families depend entirely upon it for their incomes.

Our description above of sardine and seaweed production already reveals a range of processing activities that cannot, except by considerable stretching of terms, be called actual "factories." Thus the 30 or so families engaged in sardine boiling and drying usually own little more equipment than a large iron vat and enough straw mats to expose the myriads of spread-out sardines to the rays of the sun. Similarly, since no co-op plant is operating to dry and cut seaweed into wafers, the usual practice is for several families to purchase a drying machine cooperatively. This means that all of the Ebibara seaweed growers are also small processors; in fact, the number may increase as new fields are made wider by the projected breakwater.

Nakayama-san, whom we have already met a number of times, is a striking example of how a fisherman can transform his traditional calling more and more completely into a factory owner-manager-worker. Besides having a boat with its shortwave radio, he processes exceptionally large quantities of sardines (hundreds of square feet around his factory are covered with the tiny drying fish during the busy season). He is the chief grower of the soup clam. He is a pioneer in the seaweed enterprise and also supervises the "germinating" plant. In addition, he purchases chunks of large frozen fish brought by big boats from Africa; these he broils and refreezes. Processor Nakayama, his wife, son, brother, sister-in-law, two or three irregular workers who are also relatives, and on particularly busy weekends his two daughters (ages ten and twelve), all work together in his factory near the beach. It is a very busy place, so much so that in the hot months of July and August when the sardine run is at its height, the owner, his wife, and his daughters move into a corner of the factory with the barest essentials of living, embellished only by their television set and occasional breezes from the summer sea.

There are, to be sure, several much larger factories in Ebibara itself; almost none are any longer owned exclusively by fishermen. No other fishing community in the whole prefecture boasts as many female workers either in piece-work or as full-time employees of these factories. In the latter they work eight hours daily, with two free days per month. One estimate has it that less than 20 of all employable Ebibara women confine their activities merely to housekeeping. True, only one wife regularly accompanies her husband as "second mate" on his daily trip with the trawler fleet. Quite a number, moreover, do not work in factories; they are door-to-door peddlers of fish and fish products and have their own organization, a kind of guild that demarcates peddling territories, regulates retail prices, and discourages intruders. A few others work at dressmaking and knitting at home for firms that employ them on piece-work contracts. As one teacher informant who lives in Ebibara emphasized, however diverse the ways in which women now occupy their time, the pattern has altered radically from a quarter of a century ago. Then, as he recalled, fishing women seemed to spend hours of each day chattering across their back alleys.

Neither of the two principal products of Ebibara marine factories are processed by Nakayama-san, probably because most machines are too costly for a petty manufacturer. These two products are, as we might now anticipate, shrimp and *kamaboko*. Both types of factories employ hundreds, including a minority of men. The largest shrimp factory is owned by the Utsumi-shi councilman and Ebibara patriarch, Kita-san, who has been a processor for over 40 years and has invented a machine for shelling dried shrimp. Now he finds time for politics because his eldest son has taken over supervision of 20 workers and the several departments of the business itself: a retail shop near the railroad station; refrigeration of shrimp for shipment by air as far away as the United States; transportation of live shrimp, also by air, to nearby cities; and the manufacture of hors d'oeuvres in the form of boiled and fried shrimp or pressed wafers sold in cellophane packages. The tiny red shrimp, scarcely an inch long after cooking, that are caught by the Ebibara fleet are widely adjudged to be exceptionally tasty (as indeed they are), so Ebibara is the largest shrimp center in this area of Japan. Kita-san, apparently, exercises a good deal of authority in negotiating wholesale prices with the Ebibara co-op, but he also buys from several other co-ops.

Four smaller factories feature the special native variety, but at least two others, one a branch of a national concern, purchase a larger species caught in distant waters. In one factory you may often observe 35 or more women ranging in age from perhaps 17 to 60 doing nothing but shelling shrimp by hand. In another, an equally large number are dipping and rolling the shelled shrimp in a batter prior to freezing and eventual sale as tempura, the delicious deep-fried dish that is one of Japan's famed culinary specialties.

The wife of Watanabe-san, one of our informants along with her fisherman husband, has a more or less typical working pattern. She rises at 5:30 A.M. and retires at about 11 P.M. In addition to doing the housework, preparing meals, caring for her high school–age son, selling each night's catch at the early-morning auction, and being a supervisor-worker of the family seaweed plot, she is a factory piece-worker—reputedly the fastest sheller of shrimp in the community. She makes about $1.50 per day for eight hours of labor, which is nearly one-third more than the average full-time sheller. For a full month, with two Sundays off, the pay for most factory women is about $30, but Watanabe-san averages only 20 days per month because of her other responsibilities. Men workers earn more during the same total of time, the most experienced ones nearly twice as much as women. Watanabe-san, like her friends, does not seem to resent any inequity; rather, they agree that their own jobs are "lighter" than most men's.

Next to shrimp shelling, the most common routine is cutting off the heads of a herringlike fish that is shipped in for kamaboko. (A mixture of other fish, including sharks, is also ground into the paste.) Women may repeat this operation thousands of times in a single day. None of them, or for that matter none who work in Ebibara, are unionized, and none of the many piece-workers receive pensions, bonuses, or other benefits. Competition between factories and demand for jobs seem so acute that any collective demand for higher wages or better conditions of work rarely if ever occurs. The point is underscored, not only by the frequent failure of many little independent factories (there are now only about 25 members of the "Utsumi-shi marine products association" as against three times as many ten years ago), but also by evidence from our own value study, to which we will return later.[1] According to this evidence, the great majority of Ebibara respondents disapprove of any attempt to unionize for better wages; the most common attitude is one of congenial subservience to employer control. The Socialist Party, we may remember, is very weak among gyomin, and of course the fleet is not unionized at all.

Child labor in Ebibara is also perhaps as frequent as in farming areas, where it is taken for granted especially during such busy seasons as planting and harvesting. Children are not kept out of school, to be sure, and are usually paid even by their parents for whatever hours they work at shrimp shelling or other temporary tasks. Processor Nakayama's daughters, for

[1] Cf. pp. 175–188.

example, receive about eight cents an hour, or half the pay of an adult. Incidentally, our informant, the tutoring school director, Masumi-san, approved of this kind of work, since otherwise many children would only be "wasting time." The extent to which such practices approach serious exploitation cannot be determined from our evidence; no one seemed concerned enough to treat it as a problem.

One further revealing observation. Official records disclose that about 20 families in the whole of Ebibara receive public aid from Utsumi-shi welfare funds because they are unable to support themselves adequately. In the more concentrated fishing section, however, only two families receive such aid, although a few children also obtain modest financial help from their school for such necessities as lunches and book supplies. Traditional pride is too strong among these people, if Etō-san, the principal of the closest elementary school, is correct, to permit more public help than is unavoidable.

VIII

Does the dynamic character of Ebibara life manifest itself also in education? If one is willing to regard education not merely as a distinct institution but as the total cultural process by which any community discovers how to perpetuate and modify itself through the ubiquitous ability of human beings to learn and to teach, then the answer is clearly affirmative. The grassroots organization of *jichikai*, for example, encourages a greater or lesser proportion of citizens to participate in community affairs and thereby to learn something of how democracy functions.

But the single most powerful "teachers" in the Ebibara of recent years undoubtedly have been the staff of experts in the prefectural Department of Fisheries. It was this agency which, far more than any other, instigated the most direct and radical change in the traditional pattern of life by means of the crucial seaweed project. The Ebibara co-op, equally a nonformal agency of education, has been almost as influential because it is the chief implementer of this project. Without its persistent efforts to achieve cooperation among its members and to resolve the resistances and conflicts which the venture generated in its early years, one cannot conceive how so many families would now be working amicably side by side in their allocated plots. Neither can one conceive how it would otherwise be possible for such complete blueprinting to have been drawn and accepted for the doubling of space in the shallow waters of the seaweed field.

True, neither the Department of Fisheries nor the Yoneshima-ken co-op headquarters has any program that can be called educational in a formal sense. In this respect neither organization can be considered as ad-

vanced as, say, the agricultural co-ops. But education culturally understood
is never merely formal. The persistence of Ogawa-san, the young ex-fisherman appointed by the government of Utsumi-shi to promote the seaweed
project; the backing of such top officials of the prefectural fishing co-op as
Adachi-san; the patient and often trying efforts of Oka-san and Sato-san,
the two directors of the Ebibara co-op—these men are "teachers," and are
at least as influential as Principal Etō of the elementary school in which
most children of fishermen are enrolled. Equally so, the families who are
learning to modify their ways of life are as effective learners, again in the
cultural sense, as their children in the classrooms.

Although the department of social education, which we remember is
the adult section of the Utsumi-shi school system, has not been directly
connected with any of the innovations thus far described, it has at times
attempted to involve Ebibara men and women in other ways. For example,
according to Tsuda-san, director of this department, a city-wide organization
of Utsumi-shi young people has been more active until recently than any
other comparable organization in Yoneshima-ken. The highlight of its annual program is a public induction ceremony for those who have reached
the voting age of 20, a ceremony widely celebrated in Japan.

The vigor of the Utsumi-shi group has been largely due, Tsuda-san admits, to the enthusiastic leadership of several young Socialist members.
Unfortunately or not, however, depending on one's politics, such enthusiasm
has not seemed sufficiently contagious to sustain the interest of youthful
fishermen, even though originally some 50 young adults of both sexes in
Ebibara not only joined in a meeting or two with persons from other sections of Utsumi-shi, but even in "lamp light" reading and study groups. Also,
there were special programs to provide instruction in current methods of
marine cultivation and new techniques of fishing.

A spokesman for the youth division of the co-op recalls rather wryly
how these ventures culminated. Ebibara officers of *jichikai* decided to award
three large bottles of *sake* to the local youth group in appreciation for its
participation in the city program. But when the young men members consumed all three bottles, apparently at a single fête, the young women members resigned indignantly. Only long after have they consented to rejoin.
Meanwhile, the Utsumi-shi organization has itself shrunk in membership to
about one-third of its original size.

The co-op auxiliary has been much more zealous in its educational endeavors than the youth division. We have already mentioned the women's
overnight excursions to shrines and resorts. We have not mentioned that
occasionally they conduct their own cooking and sewing classes, that they
sometimes hold a kind of Oriental equivalent to the old New England "quilt-
ing bee" (*futon* is the name for Japanese quilts), and that they have even

sponsored a few *ikebana* (flower arrangement) and *sadō* (tea ceremony) demonstrations. The latter two are, of course, deeply traditional arts, but they have so often been the prerogative of the middle and upper classes that they may imply a half-expressed urge on the part of fishing ladies to join in the currently rather frantic climb up the status ladder of Japanese society.

The social education department likewise includes programs for Utsumi-shi women's organizations. According to Social Director Tsuda, however, there has been a decline in their activities, just as among the younger folk. In any case, it is not apparent that his department has exercised conspicuous initiative in sponsoring events such as those of the co-op auxiliary which have just been mentioned. In fact, the latter withdrew from the Utsumi-shi organization several years ago from lack of interest in its programs. Much exuberance in Ebibara seems rather to stem from the women themselves, so often, indeed, that one can hardly help being reminded of a "matriarchy."

Not only has the auxiliary begun to discuss the establishment of a strong consumer co-op—a start, we recall, has already been made. With the money earned from selling simple commodities it has even gone into the business of renting gorgeous bridal costumes (costing the auxiliary over $200 for each of two) at about $17 per wedding, a charge of less than half, incidentally, of a professional costumer. Also, it has campaigned vigorously to reduce the burdensome expense of ceremonials by the menfolk traditional to boat launchings. Historically, as many as 20 fishermen would present large expensive flags with family symbols as gifts to decorate new boats, and a Shintō priest always performed the correct rituals. Nowadays, not only are priests rarely engaged, but a mere three or four flags may be flown from the mast, all of which could have been rented for the occasion through the auxiliary. (Here, however, we must record that these simplifying and economizing innovations are not easy to maintain. Several informants were worried over what they detected as a relaxation of the newer ways in favor again of the older. Perhaps such setbacks are one reason it is difficult to find women willing to serve as auxiliary officers.)

At any rate, whereas these activities are surely educational in the pervasive sense, two further auxiliary activities more closely approach the stricter meaning of that term. One is the opportunity of Ebibara women to associate in educational and social meetings with auxiliary members of other communities. Most of the women belong to local co-ops under the sponsorship of the prefectural fishing co-op but a few belong to women's groups of agricultural co-ops—a feat that the male co-op members of Ebibara have never attempted. Whether, indeed, inter–co-op gatherings could become significant by encouraging a rapprochement between communities that, historically, have frequently held aloof from one another is not yet discernible. Still, within the prefectural fishing co-op itself, meetings of both men and women do occur two or three times yearly; these meetings feature lectures on changing aspects of the Japanese fishing economy and a wide range of other topics.

The other educative opportunity is an entirely new venture in Ebibara. At our suggestion, the auxiliary decided to organize a study group on the theme of child rearing. Several meetings have already been held in the upstairs hall of the co-op headquarters. Although Social Director Tsuda seems to be involved marginally, it is Principal Kurata of a second junior high school in Utsumi-shi who has been the chief resource person, so much so that women who attended the initial meetings appeared to accept him as the supreme authority. Nearly 40 women belong to the study group, for many of them recognize that children of fishing families are sometimes confronted with serious problems of healthy development—of proper nutrition, for example, or proper care, difficult for working mothers to provide. One result is that juvenile delinquency, as more than one nonfisherman informant mentioned, is higher than average among Ebibara teenagers.

On the elementary and secondary levels, meager attention is given to Ebibara as a community with a character of its own. Repeatedly, the point was made by informants connected with Utsumi-shi schools that courses of study, strict schedules of National Achievement Tests, constant examinations, and other prescribed duties allow little or no time for attention to the idiosyncracies of any one cultural group. A pilot project in two or three schools is underway with PTA cooperation dealing with problems of family development, but very few fishing people seem to be included. Similarly, children's groups have recreational and other programs for out-of-school hours, but again these lack perceptible concern for the special needs of fishermen's children. There is no kindergarten, no playground, and no community center in Ebibara, despite such crowded living quarters that some three-fourths of all households have no garden space to enjoy, compared with about two-thirds of all Utsumi-shi households which do.

Nor are the two teachers' organizations, Nikkyōso and Kyōshikai, noticeably interested in local community affairs. At most, a few individual teachers, including one or two of our own informants, seem to be concerned seriously with studying educational problems peculiar to Ebibara. No such study has yet been made by any school. But as Principal Yoshida, the leader of Kyōshikai whom we met earlier, pointed out, his junior high school enrolls children from various occupational groups other than fishing—farming, commerce, and *sarariiman*, among others—so it is quite impracticable to pay special attention to any one of them. This position was supported by Principal Etō, who reiterated that courses of study are already overcrowded with required subjects.

In at least one major respect, nevertheless, Utsumi-shi public schools are involved in cultural innovation. This is because of the privilege they afford children of continuing their education beyond the level of most parents. As one 75-year-old informant reminded us, many children when he was a boy were compelled to go to work well before completing even elementary school. Today, all typical Ebibara children not only finish junior high school, a total of nine years, but increasing proportions are encouraged by their parents to go on to senior high school. The change from the earlier quite anti-education attitude of many *gyomin* is nowhere more clearly exemplified than by the fact that today about half of the 300 children whom Masumi-san's private school tutors in their free hours are from fishing families. Granting that this proportion is well above the average of all Utsumi-shi tutoring schools, it is still impressive. Masumi-san, incidentally, disagreed with our teacher-informant, Shinohara-san, who believed that Ebibara children are of lower than average intelligence; all they need, Masumi-san insisted, is encouragement, kindness, and an attitude on the part of teachers that it is not the subject to be learned that is of first importance, but the joy of learning itself.

Yet, in an ironic way, the gradual lengthening of the educational span mitigates against the success of Ebibara's struggles. Those who continue well into senior high school rarely wish to become fishermen. Not only is this fact true but often they expect to qualify for jobs as technicians or as *sarariiman* in the vast ever-beckoning cities that lie only a few hours distant from Utsumi-shi. Thus the question of how long or in what ways Ebibara can maintain its historic continuity is impossible to answer. As we proceed to the next chapter, the concomitant question of evolving goals and values comes into sharper focus. Meanwhile, Ebibara remains very much a valiant Japanese community.

3

VALUE PATTERNS
IN EBIBARA

I

What beliefs about the good life, what hopes, what expectations, what goals do the people of Ebibara cherish? Since these questions permeate every facet of Ebibara life they have already permeated the two preceding chapters on patterns of order and cultural processes. Likewise, the question of goals has already reached far beyond this community itself—into Utsumi-shi, into Yoneshima-ken, and at least as far as the outermost boundaries of the Japanese nation.

How may we hope to weave together the delicate, elusive threads that constitute such values as the good and right of a community which, although in some ways remote and insignificant, has been shown also to be distinctive and complex? Our evidence is chiefly of two kinds. First, that of a modest investigation of value orientations. Second, that of prolonged interviews and other kinds of direct involvement in the life of these fishing people. Neither by itself, nor both together, can claim to have penetrated as deeply as one could wish into Ebibara values. Even so they provide, we hope, enough familiarity with them to justify our exploration.

The instrument constructed for the purpose of investigating value orientation, as well as the methodology by which it was utilized, are described in detail in Appendix II, and reported in Chapters 7 and 8,[1] where we treat the data comparatively. In this chapter, we confine ourselves entirely to the second kind of evidence.

---

[1] Cf. pp. 175–188 and 190–193.

II

Reflected throughout both kinds, nevertheless, is what may be regarded as a common denominator of values prevailing in the community; that is, the "modal personality" approximating a kind of archetype of individual traits. As anthropologists remind us, modal personality is an abstraction; no particular person is ever identical with it because every person is in various ways different from any other. Nevertheless, the concept has often proved fruitful in personality-and-culture studies even though it has seldom been as deliberately utilized in the context of value orientations as we shall attempt. Please remember, meanwhile, that not all of our informants are members of fishing households; one is a farmer, another a factory worker, several are active in education. Yet almost all have lived in Ebibara for many years. The image that emerges is an amalgam of qualities as perceived both by fishermen of themselves and by their next-door neighbors.

Ebibara *gyomin*, we find from our impressionistic evidence, may be described in terms (as can modal personalities in many cultures) that are by no means always harmonious. As noted in the preceding chapter, *gyomin* are strongly cooperative in some respects, yet strongly competitive in others. They readily unite for protection of their own interests; they quickly come to one another's aid in such emergencies as illness, accident, or death (a traditional name for neighborhood mutual-aid groups is *kōju*, and apparently every family belongs to at least one); they continue the venerable custom sometimes called *neyado*, the young men's sleeping clubs that often develop bonds of lifelong fraternity; they engage in Quaker-like "sense of the meeting" decision-making through the practice of *mōshi-awase*; they support an extralegal association (*kogi kumiai*) to protect themselves collectively against just or unjust complaints of illegitimate fishing practices. Most important, they have maintained a fishing co-operative for many years through which they are able by unified agreement and action to reduce exploitative pricing of marine products by wholesalers, to develop the remarkable venture in seaweed farming, and to promote a number of other beneficial economic ventures such as the construction of a new storehouse.

At the same time, members of the Ebibara fleet rarely hesitate to trespass upon the fishing domains of the same neighboring co-operatives which come to their aid if a boat is missing or in similar cases of trouble. The minority who raid and damage out-of-bounds fish traps never reveal themselves voluntarily. Hence *kogi kumiai* is compelled resentfully to meet the costs of retribution, although not without widespread suspicion as to the identity of the guilty parties as revealed by abnormally large catches. Within the official co-operative, disputes have also frequently become so bitter (for example, in the early stages of the seaweed project) that feuding among members has threatened the survival of the co-op itself. Even during less critical periods some members continue more or less secretly to sell to wholesalers, despite contrary co-op policies.

Several informants pointed to a psychological corollary of such conflicting behavior. Fishermen are often so intensely jealous of any kind of success (large catches, most of all) by their fellow fishermen that they are willing to risk defiance of federal and prefectural laws and even, on occasion, of co-op rules in their zeal to prove that they, too, can be successful. Jealousy also accounts in considerable measure, we were told, for a habit mentioned earlier: rumor-mongering and gossip. A principal reason, indeed, why a fisherman dislikes borrowing from the co-op credit union, however legitimate his need, is that people will spread the rumor that he must be in financial straits. According to the wife of Watanabe-san, jealousy (in local dialect, *serai konjō*) may also be vented by gossiping about a prosperous politician, a well-dressed woman (no doubt she is having an affair!), or even a young couple seen strolling amiably along the street. All such rumor-mongering, she said, is carried on very surreptitiously, since people keep in mind that they must not make enemies if they are to expect mutual aid in emergencies. Even jealousy is not an entirely negative value, or so Co-op Director Oka contended, for it does incite fishermen to greater exertion and higher returns. Still it must be admitted that the distinction between the "good side" and "bad side" of jealousy is sometimes "paper thin."

One explanation offered for such antisocial values is the largely solitary nature of fishing as an occupation—an occupation that encourages a sturdy sense of individual self-reliance and rugged endurance. The difficulty, as Sato-san, the co-op assistant director, expressed it sharply, is that Ebibara *gyomin* seem to be far more concerned with their individual rights than with community duties and responsibilities. Indeed, individualism is a major obstacle to innovations involving joint endeavor. This characteristic also helps to account for the strong resistance encountered in launching the seaweed project and, long before that, in organizing the co-operative itself.

Symptoms of ambivalence in personality structure were indicated in still further ways. Often, for example, fishermen were characterized as outreaching, warm, volatile, congenial. Another fisherman's wife, Muta-san, suggested that such qualities were conducive to open and frank marital relations. Several spoke of the "loud voices": thus our mayor informant Miyakawa-san mentioned that the two ex-fishermen who are members of his city council in Utsumi-shi can usually be heard in the din of a spirited session above everyone else. His own conjecture was that this mannerism is the effect of long years on the sea where winds often howl and storms are thunderous.

Yet we were also told that the blustering of fishermen is largely a façade, concealing feelings of insecurity and inferiority—characteristics also attributed to the erratic, unpredictable natural environment upon which they depend for a living. So aware are they, moreover, of the poor esteem in which they have been held habitually by other sections of the population that by no means are they always eager to disclose to strangers their residence in a fishing community: the name Ebibara itself has long carried the stigma of lowly social status and slum housing. (Thus the mayor would hesitate to refer to a friend of his as an *Ebibara mono*—"man of Ebibara.") As a consequence, fishermen are all too easily browbeaten; even when they are able to form a sufficiently united front on some issue to pay a visit to the city hall, they are much more easily persuaded to yield or compromise than, for example, farmers. Indeed, only after imbibing substantial draughts of *sake* do they seem fortified enough to become belligerent, so that the term "violent" which nonfisherman informants sometimes ascribed to the behavior of fishermen seems farfetched.

Other valuative terms recorded in our quest for an image of the Ebibara modal personality reveal equally diversified perceptions. With only occasional dissent, the same characterizations were, nevertheless, reiterated almost as often by fishermen as by others on our grassroots panel. Let us recapitulate with no particular order a number of additional traits. The Ebibara fisherman is said to be:

rough-mannered	authoritarian	envious
respectful (of elders)	complacent	outreaching
simple-minded	loyal	recalcitrant
risk-taking	cautious	status-minded
promiscuous	loud-voiced	group-centered
violent	anxious	generous
erratic	quick-tempered	law-breaking
present-oriented	skillful (at games)	shortsighted
cordial	shame-laden	custom-bound
face-saving	selfish	careless
insecure	shy	courageous
ill-informed	conciliatory	convivial
superstitious	untidy	blustering
indulgent	individualistic	evasive

These interesting attributes deserve further discussion. Repeatedly the allegation that fishermen are "present-oriented" and "shortsighted" was illustrated by their habit of hoping for good luck at the bicycle races, at the pinball game of *pachinko*, or still more frequently at such illegal card gambling games as *hanafuda*. Likewise, heavy borrowing from marine whole-salers or other willing lenders, and overspending when times are good with little concern for planning of family budgets, were emphasized several times. The leader of the fishing youth group made the perceptive point, however, that as fishermen become successful seaweed farmers they may learn to plan as land farmers do—for example, by preparing "seed" for their next year's crop.

Equally emphasized was the habit of "face-saving." Fishermen appear to be even more inordinately anxious than many Japanese, including farm-ers, about the extent to which they are respected by the rest of the com-munity. Here is the principal reason, we were told, why Ebibara weddings are often so lavish that years of indebtedness may easily accrue as the result of a day or two of celebration—an indebtedness, by the way, from which the more frugal farmers of Utsumi-shi suffer much less often. No wonder that Oka-san, father of three daughters and no sons, returned to the worrisome subject on more than one occasion. He quoted an Ebibara saying: "If a man has three daughters he is bound to go bankrupt!" Although varying somewhat according to community status, his estimate was that the cost to the bride's parents of a typical fishing family wedding is about $1500, more than a year of average income, and the cost to the groom's parents is about half this amount. Indeed, the famous term of Thorstein Veblen, "conspicuous con-sumption," seems peculiarly apt. The more purchases a bride can display before her wedding, such as a clothing chest, another chest full of new shoes, a washing machine, a bicycle, an electric rice cooker, even a new television set, the more deluxe the social prestige she attains not only for herself but for her whole family.

Ebibara families privately grumble over such costliness but almost no one does anything about it. Perhaps the only important economy, mentioned earlier, is the rental of bridal costumes by the co-op auxiliary. At the two Ebibara weddings that we attended, food, drink, and a small gift for each guest were so abundant that most attendants wrapped up a goodly portion of their meals to take home—a familiar practice at affluent Japanese parties. At one wedding, pseudo-*geisha* entertainers also appeared; at the other, a special hall in an Utsumi-shi Shintō shrine was rented by the groom for a banquet and speeches by honored guests. The professional photographer's bill alone must have been substantial, although modest financial relief was perhaps afforded by the gifts of money that some guests brought to the feast in special ceremonial envelopes.

Nor is this all. Oka-san, only one of whose daughters is married thus far, bemoaned the cost of his new status as a grandfather. It is an Ebibarian custom, he said, to provide a gift of money as high as $300 at the birth of at least the first grandchild. He estimated, in fact, that 50 to 60 percent of the entire income of an average Ebibara fishing family is expended for what he himself termed face-saving obligations. These obligations Shinohara-san (he will be remembered as one of our teacher informants living in the community) traced chiefly to the "inferiority complex" that he detects in the *gyomin* personality type. It is this, he contended, that induces indulgence in such extravaganzas as wedding parties and even funerals. Emotionally, such events compensate for what he described as the fishermen's chronic "sense of shame" conditioned by lowly status and precarious occupation.

A comparable kind of behavior appears in co-operative meetings when few members are willing to disagree openly or to propose too novel a departure from routine practices for fear that others, especially relatives, will frown upon them for any sign of nonconformity. Such reluctance seems to some observers to be especially pronounced among younger co-op members who have long been taught to respect the judgment of their elders. In recent years, to be sure, deliberate effort has been made to increase the involvement of younger men in co-op affairs which for decades have been controlled by men in their sixties and seventies. Nevertheless, the innovations described in Chapter 2 were not, it was insisted, so much the consequence of youthful audacity as of ordinations by Ebibara patriarchs who still continue frequently to dominate the board of directors.

Subtle connections undoubtedly exist between hierarchical relations of this kind and the whole ancient tradition of *oya kōkō*, itself one of the central values of Confucianist ethics. Although we could not hope to trace these connections in detail, it is revealing to note how often informants referred to the paternalistic authoritarianism to which they themselves had been subjected as children in the name of "filial piety." Thus, one of our teacher informants, although perhaps this was an extreme case, described his father as a "fearful being" who often whipped him and dominated all family affairs. Another, a fisherman's wife, recalled how little affection she felt between herself and her father, even though this was partly due to his night schedule of fishing or long absences which provided only rare opportunities for close relationship. Several others spoke of the rule that no one could touch his food during mealtime until the father began, a rule still frequently followed, as is the rule that the father bathes first in the family tub. Nevertheless, it should be emphasized that all members of our Ebibara panel agreed that the patriarchal family pattern is now changing—far too rapidly, according to several—in the direction of greater equalitarianism. At least one of our informants, a mother, said that no corporal punishment is ever practiced against her children. And an anecdote is told of how, at one vituperative session of the co-op, a son actually told his father to leave the meeting.

III

If the picture that begins to emerge is sometimes blurred by apparently incongruent value orientations, perhaps it will seem less so if we consider the term "obligations" already mentioned in connection with face-saving behavior. This term brings us directly to the high priority attached to the cluster of values related to *on*, values which Ruth Benedict first made familiar to Western students of Japanese culture.[2] Our own attempt to understand the value patterns of Ebibara as reflected in its personality profile is aided most, however, by more recent and perhaps less controversial treatments, such as that of the anthropologist, Richard K. Beardsley. *On*, Beardsley says, is "a beneficence handed down from one's superior. It institutes an obligation (*ongaeshi*) to the superior on the part of the person who receives it or enjoys its benefits." The "superior" may be a higher-class person, such as a house master; an age-status individual, such as a teacher; one's kin, such as an older brother or father; or a person in a "limited situation," such as a go-between in marriage.[3]

Giri, another pervasive value, carries somewhat dissimilar meanings among the Japanese. It too, however, is often imperative in its demands; it connotes a whole range of reciprocal obligations, whether status or hierarchy is involved or not. To clarify the distinction, *oya kōkō* may be an expression of *ongaeshi* when regarded as a hierarchical relationship, whereas *giri* may be regarded as the more inclusive value of mutual obligation between parents and children.

The effect of both *on* and *giri* upon the Ebibara modal personality is indicated by our evidence. For, to violate or ignore one's individual and group obligations is a virtually certain road to ostracism by the community—not always overtly, to be sure, but in the form of covert disapproval so severe as to cause more anguish than most citizens are willing to risk. Actually more than one informant contended that the elaborateness with which obligations are fulfilled is expanding today rather than contracting, particularly when measured by the affluence of weddings. We remember, too, that despite the struggles of the women's auxiliary to reduce the financial burden of ceremonial boat launchings, concern was also expressed that the recent trend is again toward the more costly traditional affair.

At the same time, regret was expressed repeatedly, especially by older

---

[2] Cf. Ruth Benedict, *The Chrysanthemum and the Sword* (Boston: Houghton-Mifflin Company, 1946).

[3] Cf. John Whitney Hall and Richard K. Beardsley, *Twelve Doors to Japan* (New York: McGraw-Hill, Inc., 1965), p. 94.

informants, that the ancient virtues of *on* and *giri* are gradually weakening. True, these virtues have continuing practical value in the *honke-bunke* (main-branch family) system; for example, relatives often join as partners in fishing operations. True, too, they play an important role in perpetuating the practice of fisherman-wholesaler "deals" at the expense of co-operative policies. Nevertheless, children are growing up with less and less of the old-time sense of family and community loyalty that was so pronounced before the second World War. Youngsters today are "selfish," and seldom help regularly with chores like carrying water or painting. Indeed, parents themselves are often indifferent as to how children spend their spare time. Such laments were echoed by educators, too. Principal Etō, for example, insisted that *on* and *giri*, granting their feudal roots, are by no means wholly outmoded if correctly understood. On the contrary, because they often strengthen human ties, they ought to be encouraged.

Miyakawa-san also regarded *on* and *giri* with abiding respect. As mayor of Utsumi-shi, he has quite deliberately and consciously encouraged *ongaeshi* toward him but without any more reciprocal obligations toward others than he can avoid. The fact, moreover, that his father and grandfather were wealthy landlords and private bankers is remembered today by older tenants, who cannot forgo the attitude of *on* simply because landlordism is no longer the power that it once was in Japan.

Even so, if Processor Nakayama is correct, the diminishing influence of *on* and *giri* remains a major source of weakness in the fishing co-op. Leadership today is often ineffective because, to succeed, it must command strong feelings of obligation and respect on the part of rank-and-file members, especially of younger ones, and such feelings today are much more feeble than used to be the case. Processor Nakayama himself, on the contrary, repeatedly depends upon the virtues of *on* and *giri* not only in his own efforts to build good business connections but in the *honke-bunke* obligations that undergird his six-man working force.

IV

The extent to which *on* and *giri* do or do not influence the dominant value orientations and the concomitant modal personality of Ebibara may be tested by further attention to courtship and marriage. The continuing custom of primogeniture is itself, of course, deeply affected by *giri*—both in the obligation of the eldest son to perpetuate his father's household, and in the obligation of the father to perpetuate the family property by deeding it to his oldest son. *Giri* is also exemplified by the continuing practice of *muko-*

yōshi (son adoption) as well as by the now fading tradition of *yoboshigo*, ritualistic adoptions among neighboring families. Both have had the practical effect of strengthening family obligations and responsibilities.

Thus far, however, another relevant marriage custom has not been considered. This is the custom, still influential throughout Japan, known as *mi-ai kekkon* (arranged marriage) as compared with *ren-ai kekkon* (love marriage). Almost all of our informants seemed eager to discuss the two practices, but they could hardly agree as to which is preferable. What did emerge was a strong consensus that in Ebibara, quite contrary to the national trend, *mi-ai* marriages are now increasing more rapidly than *ren-ai* marriages. In other words, although love marriages are becoming more and more popular especially in the great urban areas of Japan, in Ebibara arranged marriages have certain advantages, according to our informants, that love marriages do not.

To appreciate what may appear to be an incongruity one must first understand that Ebibara has experienced a long history of relatively permissive sexual relations. Although practiced less openly and less commonly today than a generation or two ago, the custom of nocturnal visits by young men to the homes of neighborly young women[4] as well as to homes of mutual friends, or conversely to young men's "dormitories" (*neyado*) by young women, has been a familiar one. Moreover, this has often happened with the cognizance of parents who may conveniently absent themselves during courting visits. *Ren-ai* marriages have resulted frequently, of course, from these liaisons, some induced by premarital pregnancies, but others simply from the abundant romantic and erotic opportunities that they easily afford. The wife of Watanabe-san, for example, told us that she had known her prospective husband as a friend and playmate since both were children, but that she had never known other boy friends. Another informant who is married to her first cousin knew her husband an equally long time.

Today, despite the longevity of this endogamous custom, *mi-ai* marriage is said to be usually preferred especially by the typical young Ebibara woman. She would like if possible to marry a man from outside of the community because, as we have found, being the wife of a fisherman promises anything but a secure or abundant life. Moreover, it often carries less community approval than marriage to a *sarariiman* or even to a farmer. Thus exogamous marriages are now increasingly frequent—one informant estimated 40 percent—and whereas some of these marriages result from per-

---

[4] The old Ebibara tradition of "house visiting," sometimes called *musume yado* on Kazaki-shima, is not to be confused with another tradition that is now virtually defunct in rural Japan. This is called *yobai* (literally, night-crawling) in which a young man would dare to creep into the bed of a girl whom he had admired but perhaps never previously met, while fellow members of his "gang" kept watch nearby.

sonal contacts that develop in factories or offices and thereby lead to *ren-ai* marriages, many others are prearranged. True, a *nakōdo* (go-between) is traditional to both *mi-ai* and *ren-ai* marriages. His role in the latter is more or less a formality, however, whereas in the former he deliberately seeks eligible marriage partners, investigates their family backgrounds, and if satisfied that they are suitable not only brings the young couple together but usually takes chief responsibility for details of the marriage party. In these numerous cases, love is likely to be of secondary value. Both the young man and woman, and probably even more their closest relatives, are often most concerned with finding a partner who hopefully will assure modest upward mobility.

But the weakening of *ren-ai* as compared to *mi-ai* marriages in Ebibara (although it must be emphasized that both kinds have always existed) is also due to other factors. For one thing, prejudice against fishermen by other groups in the area has been diminishing; indeed farm girls sometimes move to Ebibara as the wives of fishermen, a phenomenon described as "unthinkable" hardly a generation ago. For another thing, it seems reasonable to suppose that *ren-ai* marriages could easily conflict with the ethics of *on:* to marry someone because of personal desire may strain one's sense of obligation to marry in accordance with parental preference. (To cite an example: one of our teacher informants recalled how his father, appealing to *oya kōkō*, "forced" him to marry a girl he did not even know and to reject another girl with whom he was in love.) Again, the premarital pregnancies and consequent marriages that sometimes resulted from the easy liaisons of earlier times are now quite rare. Almost everyone, no matter of how little education, is familiar not only with birth control practices but with the routine for obtaining an abortion. Finally, sexual laxity seems to be frowned upon more than it once was perhaps in part because, by comparison with the rest of Utsumi-shi, Ebibara's moral reputation has been a source of embarrassment to its inhabitants. As our farmer informant, Soma-san, expressed it, there was "too much indulgence" in Ebibara during his youthful years, whether one was a fisherman or not. Almost every young man and many a young women had, he contended, one and perhaps several sexual experiences before marriage. Not that Soma-san completely favors the *mi-ai* alternative; prospective marriage partners should become acquainted, to be sure, but not to the extent of sexual intimacy or loss of virginity.

This attitude was endorsed by several others, but how qualified our panel of informants were to clarify the issue of *mi-ai* versus *ren-ai* remains a question. It does appear clear to us that economic influences are more primary than, say, moral ones, although any one causal explanation is always dubious in such complex patterns. At any rate, one can justifiably contend that *mi-ai* has again become even more predominant in Ebibara than in earlier days because it assures greater stability than does *ren-ai*. In fact, all but two or three of our informants are themselves the product of *mi-ai* arrangements. Several married virtual strangers, as did many of their closest relatives. Only one informant, Masumi-san, who married during our field work in Ebibara, could be regarded as consistent in his support of the *ren-ai* preference. Yet he, too, felt it essential to bow to the custom of a *nakōdo* at his elaborate wedding party, even though the proud go-between's responsibilities (those of the present author) were perfunctory indeed. The decision to marry had already been reached between Masumi-san and his charming fiancée, with parental blessings on both sides.

Although sexual standards have tightened somewhat, our Ebibara informants on the whole were tolerant in their attitudes toward sexual morality. True, teen-age dating, including teashop meetings and movie-going, is still frowned upon by many parents. Nevertheless it occurs quite often, surreptitiously or not, and some young couples most of whom have finished school visit local dance halls. But other practices that would trouble many Westerners are widely approved. Sterilization, for example, is considered proper especially for women whenever a couple decides that they have produced enough children—typically, two or three. Abortion is disliked and sometimes feared because of postoperational complications, but no one on our Ebibara panel wished to see the practice outlawed. In fact, unmarried girls who become pregnant are considered better off as a rule if abortions are performed. No one with whom we talked seemed to regard masturbation by either boys or girls as unnatural or wrong, although one father said, without indicating why, that he might try to discourage his son from the practice if he detected him. The same father, our industrial worker Tsuji-san, also would not approve of his high school–age daughter going to movies with a boy friend, and he was sure that she had never done so. On sex education he was equally cautious, and believed it better for his wife to inform his daughter and he his sons about sex rather than to have the schools attempt to do so. It had apparently not occurred either to him or to most Ebibara informants that sex education might become a part of the school curriculum. Yet Tsuji-san was more moderate otherwise: like Processor Nakayama and several others, he has no objection to *ren-ai* marriage for his own children since he feels their own happiness is, after all, the primary concern.

Perhaps the single most insightful interpretation of marriage and family values in Ebibara was offered by the Utsumi-shi superintendent of schools, Fuji-san. After World War II most Japanese tended, he said, to swing from one extreme to the other—from the feudally influenced value orientation of *on* and *giri* to the individualistic, even anarchistic, opposite that justifies personal freedom with slim regard for familial or group responsibilities. Today, however, a greater harmony is being sought between both extreme attitudes. Thus *ren-ai* and *mi-ai* marriage are not so often regarded as conflicting choices; rather they provide counterbalancing values. *Mi-ai* marriage by itself is too feudalistic, too dominated by *honke-bunke* and *nakōdo* authority. But a purely *ren-ai* marriage may be too democratic; it seems to repudiate all sense of loyalty and obligation to the family itself. A synthesis of both practices recognizes the need of young couples to approve of their own marriage by sufficient opportunity to know each other well beforehand, and an equal need to be guided by the greater experience and perspicacity of elders in judging the qualifications of prospective mates.

V

Frequently the fishing people of the offshore community, Kazaki-shima, are compared with those of Ebibara. Despite only a few miles of sea separating them from the municipality proper, several real or imagined differences were mentioned such as dialect, clothing, and even facial structure. One informant spoke of the muscularity of Kazaki women, a result of their constant need to carry loads up the steep slopes; of the exceptional young swimmers who find little space on the island for other sports; and of the alleged "immoralities" that result from confinement to an area scarcely half of a mile across.

Kazaki-shima *gyomin* are most noteworthy, however, for special provisions in times of pregnancy. A separate community center attended by midwives accomodates expectant mothers who enter a week or two prior to childbirth and remain a week or two after. This custom is the consequence of an ancient taboo, by no means unique to Kazaki-shima or to Japanese culture, which regards childbirth as a polluting experience. If a husband comes into contact with his wife during the taboo period, this is sure to produce a bad effect upon the size of his catch or otherwise to bring misfortune. The fact that fishermen, at least in earlier days, were often away for many days or even months makes it all the more necessary to discourage them from sexual temptation should they return home during the immediately dangerous pre- or post-natal stage. Ebibara, for reasons unknown to us, has no such institution for pregnant women, and even in Kazaki-shima the establishment appears to be less uniformly patronized than it was a generation ago. Nevertheless, the custom is still influential; it dramatizes the power of folk beliefs in both communities and thus one of the characteristics attributed to the local fisherman's modal personality—that he tends to be "superstitious." Accordingly, we turn next to those Ebibara patterns of value that become discernible through a number of other folk beliefs and religious practices.

Although all of those explained to us cannot be included, one of the most intriguing customs is called *yakudoshi* (bad-luck year) and is associated primarily with the male ages of 42 and 61. No man who reaches these milestones of life would think of ignoring proper safeguards against dangers that threaten him during either perilous year. In Ebibara, unlike many communities (although the custom is otherwise widely followed in Japan with some variations), the ceremony must be held on the thirteenth or twenty-third of January, or the first of February, according to the lunar calendar (which fishing folk invariably follow since it correlates with the tides).

The experience of Fisherman Watanabe, age 42, is probably typical. An *odō* (miniature Shintō shrine) was burned along with all other objects on the *kamidana* (shelf containing offerings to Shintō gods). The act of burning is a purifying rite intended to exorcise the evils that Shintō "devils" could otherwise inflict. Well before dark, he and his wife also climbed the long high hill to the main Shintō shrine in Utsumi-shi, dropping 43 small coins on the path to the top which were promptly pocketed by the child of a relative following close behind. The coins were said to hurry the arrival of his forty-third year when life would be safer again. Meanwhile, the Shintō priest, who had previously reminded them by mail (it is his business to follow the city hall records) of the necessity of holding a *yakudoshi* ceremonial, was awaiting them in his robes at the summit shrine. In return for an offering of a thousand *yen*, he prayed for Watanabe-san, entered his name anew in the shrine roster, then provided him with a new *ofuda*, a sacred strip of paper on which the name of a *kami* ("god") is written, to be placed on the family *kamidana* with fresh offerings. The couple then descended to their home, where a dozen close relatives and friends awaited them. A special bag of ceremonial rice and abundant *sake* were presented as gifts, and the climax of the evening was a drinking party.

The sixty-first year follows much the same ritual, except that 62 coins instead of 43 are dropped on the way to the shrine, with another inevitable urchin in the wake of the pilgrims. Usually the party is smaller than the earlier one, since by that age younger relatives may be preoccupied with their own *yakudoshi*. In the case of women, the age of 33 is widely considered the most dangerous year, so the Watanabe couple also visited the shrine on that occasion with a trail of 34 coins. No party was held afterward, and only fresh offerings for the *kamidana* completed the event.

Farmer Soma, now 72, clearly recalls his own forty-second and sixty-first *yakudoshi*, although at those times guests were prohibited from bringing any gifts of rice because of a national shortage. Now perhaps he is looking forward to the third and final perilous year—88.

The extent to which these and other ceremonials are believed to manifest supernatural power in behalf of Ebibarian well-being is difficult to estimate. Both Farmer Soma and Fisherman Watanabe confessed that they did not take the supernatural motivations of *yakudoshi* very seriously, although their wives were more inclined to do so. Such ceremonials are performed mainly because friends and neighbors expect them to be. Several other Ebibara informants shared similar views. Their children and grandchildren, moreover, are largely indifferent to any religion, they confessed, and only the old are likely to be devout supporters of temples and shrines. Certainly it is also obvious that such an important summer festival as we earlier described, which honors the venerated community *kami*, Ryūōjin, appears to be conducted at least as much for recreational as for sacred reasons. So, too, are such major Buddhist holidays as Bon that likewise occur each summer.

Yet the values of Ebibara people are by no means wholly secular. As the priest of the Zenshū temple attended by more fishermen than any others contended to us, the Ebibara section of Utsumi-shi is more religious than other sections of the city. Recently, to be sure, Shintō or other folk priests are no longer invited to the venerable ritual of boat launchings. Nevertheless, every new boat is abundantly decorated with Shintō symbols. Intermittently, too, the Shintō priest is asked, especially when catches are poor, to come to the Ryūōjin shrine and pray with groups of fishermen. Still more impressively, every *honke* (main family) that we were able to visit contains its own *butsudan* (Buddhist family altar), often several generations old. Some *bunke* (branch family) households do not have a *butsudan*, not only because a new one may cost many thousands of *yen*, but because until members of their own families die it is customary to keep family tablets commemorating the dead in the *honke* household. Virtually every household, however poor, also displays its *kamidana* with daily offerings of rice, flowers, or fruit to a favorite *kami*. In fishing households there are usually several, such as the supreme *kami* of fishermen, together with a household *kami*, marriage *kami*, and one or two others. One school girl of a *gyomin* family also mentioned how an electric light is kept on over the *kamidana* whenever her father is out to sea.

Almost all our informants, moreover, spoke of participation in the *hōji* ceremonial, which commemorates at precisely stipulated intervals the death of close kin. This ceremonial is attended not only by relatives but by one or more Buddhist priests who officiate for a fee, usually before the *butsudan* of the *honke* family, and share in a generous repast after the service. Soma-san, for example, recalled that the last *hōji* held in his home commemorated the centennial of the death of his great-grandfather. Nakayama-san held a *hōji* recently to revere four dead kin at one time—his father and mother, a sister, and a lost child of his own. His wife prays daily at the *butsudan* for the "peace of the family." Yet he does not consider himself really religious: "My conscience is my guide," he said.

Tsuji-san was planning a *hōji* during our field work to honor the memory of the father who had adopted him. Yet he too insisted that he is at best vaguely religious: thus he does not think that the spirits of dead kin return at a *hōji;* its purpose is purely to honor their memory. At the same time, he, his wife, and stepmother (but not their children) pray before the *butsudan* every morning and evening, and five times a year they also visit the cemetery because kin are "sleeping there." His *yakudoshi* ritual, soon to occur, will vary from Watanabe-san's. He and his wife will drop the necessary coins but, instead of holding an evening party, will take a short vacation trip that should also have the effect of warding off misfortune.

The most zealous Buddhist and Shintoist among our informants, Fisherman Wada, admitted that only six or seven Ebibara citizens, all of them retired or near retirement, are as devoted to religion as he. His own devotion, he says, was deepened because of vows he took when his wife once became desperately ill. He poured cold water over himself each day for 50 days and performed other ascetic rituals while beseeching Buddha to save her, which He did. Religious faith has helped in other ways, too, both in Wada-san's own recovery from illness and in finding strength to rebuild his occupation even after his boat had been wrecked. No wonder, then, that he proudly displayed the many religious tokens, some faded with age, that bedeck his walls and surround his *butsudan.* As one of the head sponsors not only of the Ryūōjin shrine in Ebibara but of the greatest one in Utsumi-shi, and as a faithful officer of his own Buddhist sect, Nichirenshū, Wada-san has received various scrolls and gifts lauding his services in collecting money for festivals, marching through the streets in winter, and contributing to the rebuilding of his priest's house.

In addition, he and groups of others, sometimes 50 or more, make several pilgrimages a year to important shrine and temple ceremonials in adjoining prefectures. Along with almost all fishing families, he visits the great shrine of fishermen once or more yearly. Finally, every morning he spends about half an hour chanting sacred words from *kyō,* the huge collection of sacred Nichiren scriptures. One phrase, *nam myōhō renge kyō,* is repeated endlessly; its meaning evades Wada-san but is sometimes interpreted as "Honor the Lotus Sutra." It assures him of Saint Nichiren's blessing and thus of Buddha's as well.

Our earlier sketch of religion as an Ebibara institution included the local folk priest or *gyōja* and his "church"—an eclectic religion featuring fortune-telling and other occult practices. That his influence is considerably weaker today than it was in previous generations was nowhere disputed by informants. As Processor Nakayama put it, only people whose "minds are confused" still resort to the *gyōja.* Nevertheless, the mother of one of our more sophisticated Ebibara informants, Masumi-san, director of his tutoring school, is probably more typical than not, at least of older citizens, in her attitude toward folk beliefs. At 70 years of age, she had gone to the *gyōja* to learn whether or not her son would marry a certain girl of his acquaintance. Likewise, she is always careful to respect various taboos; for example, when her son's wedding day fell on the seventeenth, a day when east is always a threatening direction, the eastern door to her house was kept carefully locked so that neither bride nor groom would suffer by passing through it. Her son, however, scoffed at such "superstitions." Much like Tsuji-san, he thinks of his late father not as an immortal soul but as a personality whom he reveres in memory and associates with small precious moments, such as the taste of a cake that his father had found delicious.

Not all middle-aged or younger people are as secular-minded as Masumi-san. The wife of Watanabe-san, for one, wanted to have the *gyōja* predict how soon her husband would recover from a serious illness, but her husband forbade her from doing so. Yet even he did not stop her from seeking help from the same venerable *gyōja* when her seaweed nets once disappeared—an event which, incidentally, we have included in our value instrument as item 29.[5] As she told this anecdote, the *gyōja* first prayed at length and then consulted esoteric documents before informing her that the nets had been stolen so that there was no use hunting any further. Help is also obtained in deciding the proper direction a new house must face, including the location of the toilet, since this is the most defiling spot possible. Even Tsuji-san admitted that he would "feel better" were he to consult the *gyōja* about such a matter: after all, when a child is accidentally injured or killed the cause is often attributed by the priest to the evil influence of a wrongly placed toilet.

According to one estimate, some 70 percent of Ebibara families still resort to the *gyōja* in critical times. He has been engaged also for *yakudoshi* ceremonials; by waving his wand with its streamers over the household *kamidana* he helps block the disasters that hover about anyone unfortunate enough to reach the age of 42, 61, or even 88. Yet, for over two years, another custom has not been followed at all, that of a blessing by the *gyōja* administered to the fleet when a major change in fishing routine is imminent.

One further comment on the religious dimension of Ebibara value patterns concerns the Buddhist movement of the Sōkagakkai referred to in Chapter 1. Although it is true that we met no Sōkagakkai member within the fishing community as such, we were told that a few, usually people without their own boats but with abundant insecurity, do apparently belong. According to one fisherwoman, Sōkagakkai members here must be very lonely and unhappy despite their effort to appear otherwise, because Ebibarians tend to isolate them for their nonconformist behavior.

[5] Cf. p. 290.

At any rate, most illuminative for our own study was the privilege of attending the large funeral of a woman member in an adjacent section of Utsumi-shi. Interestingly, Fisherman Watanabe belonged to the identical *kōju* (neighborhood mutual-aid group) as the deceased, and seemed to be chief arranger of the funeral itself. The event took place in a large tent in midafternoon at the burial grounds. Since the dead woman had been the wife of Toda-san, the lone Sōkagakkai councilman in the city, several hundred persons were present, including such dignitaries as Mayor Miyakawa. A great semicircle of gaudy artificial flower wreaths, rented at a thousand *yen* each from a funeral shop and labeled with the names of friends, politicians, businesses, and civic organizations surrounded the tent. Almost everyone at the funeral received a gift, a package of three stamped postcards costing five *yen* each. Earlier, many in attendance had sent gift envelopes of money or baskets of fruit. That *on* and *giri* were quite as influential on this occasion as they are at Ebibara weddings goes without saying.

One extraordinary feature, however, was the involvement of four priests representing four different Buddhist sects. Watanabe-san informed us that only one priest represented Nichirenshōshū, the official sect of the Sōkagakkai, but at a *kōju* meeting lasting far into the previous night relatives who were members of other sects had violently opposed an exclusively Sōkagakkai funeral. They had also exacted a promise from Councilman Toda that he would not, as is usually the case, turn over money gifts to the Sōkagakkai treasury. Even so, about 50 Sōkagakkai members living in Utsumi-shi had earlier visited the home of the deceased, beating drums as they prayed. Almost as many members occupied prominent places in the tent next to the bereaved relatives and the candle-lighted altar, where the simple wooden coffin rested above a large framed picture of the departed.

Sharp hostility toward this "new religion," revealed by the funeral arrangements, was often expressed by our Ebibara panel. One fisherwoman said that Sōkagakkai members become so fanatical that they neglect their regular jobs. Co-op Director Oka reported how Councilman Toda, before he had become a widower, had tried to "pressure" him into joining the movement. Toda-san's tactics are known as *shakubuku*, a persistent, aggressive effort to proselytize especially associated with the Sōkagakkai. But Oka-san had resisted on the ground, he said, that traditional Buddhism is good enough for him. This attitude is shared equally by Fisherman Watanabe, who quoted himself in responding to Councilman Toda's *shakubuku* exerted against him: "Each person must have his own God and express his own conscience in his own way." Hostility was most often expressed, however, against the requirement of Nichirenshōshū not only that the family *kamidana* but the Buddhist *ihai* (memorial plaques to departed relatives) must be destroyed as sacrilegious. The sect is simply too dogmatic and too exclusive, several spokesmen felt.

Perhaps the harshest criticism of the Sōkagakkai was delivered by Masumi-san, newly wed director of the tutoring school. Not only, he said, are Sōkagakkai members "blindly" lacking in critical-mindedness, but the way the organization rigidly disciplines its membership in political matters reminded him all too painfully of the fascist movements of prewar Europe and Japan.

VI

Masumi-san's comments are in one sense hardly typical. Ebibara people are not nearly as vocal about explicit political values as they are about religion or family relations. Indeed, our conversations failed to generate keen interest concerning politics. It is not surprising, then, that *gyomin* voters seem to take for granted in even larger numbers than other Utsumi-shi voters most policies of the ruling conservative Liberal Democratic party. Nor is it surprising that in a campaign for national senator that occurred during our involvement, the Socialist candidate lost in Utsumi-shi although he won in the prefecture and was elected.

True, a handful of Socialists and even a Communist or two reside in the vicinity of Ebibara. These political deviates seem to be regarded with good-natured toleration. However, when Fisherman Wada, our religious enthusiast, candidly admitted that he had little knowledge of several political issues we raised, he may have been more or less representative of many citizens. For example, he did not know that Red China was not a member of the United Nations; he had not heard of Kōmeitō; he assumed that all unions were run by Communists; and he regarded the problem of the right to strike as too far removed from his own experience to warrant an opinion.

This is certainly not to imply that political values in Ebibara are of no importance, but rather that the prevailing ones tend to be supported more or less by default. Just as *gyomin* seem to indulge quite amorally in illegal fishing techniques, so apparently many of them are hardly averse to accepting "favors" from a politician in exchange for their votes. Bribery in the city, we were often told, is commonplace during most political campaigns—not always in the form of cash (police are increasingly on the alert) but at least in gifts, such as *sake*, which are paid out of funds allocated to local campaign managers from prefectural and national party treasuries. (Tsuji-san estimated that about $1.40 or its equivalent is roughly the cost of a single vote.) Such illegal tactics, so Oka-san among others averred, are much less common in the Socialist and other minority parties than they are in the controlling party. Yet it is by no means only the greater financial allurements that hold most fishermen on the Liberal Democratic line; it is still more the personal connections, often with strong *on* and *giri* overtones, that a politician such as the local Diet representative and ex-fisherman, Kasuga-san, is able to establish with his constituents.

Something of the amoralism common to local politics may have been revealed by two incidents reported to us. One concerns a local councilman who, having lost his house and gone bankrupt because of a love affair with a local *geisha*, pocketed the money he had collected as a sectional *jichikai* chairman. Nevertheless, although he never returned the money, he has been re-elected to his office. Whether the councilman's salary, said to be his only current source of income, may have stimulated his many relatives to campaign for him with extraordinary vigor was never made clear. The other incident involves two leading politicians of Utsumi-shi. According to the story told us by one of our leader informants, both men had been found guilty of mishandling funds raised at the bicycle races. Meanwhile, they continued to perform their official duties, although only at a later date were they legally authorized to do so.

In our attempt to obtain a more focused image of Ebibara political values, we asked about a dozen informants several parallel questions. Their answers indicate that, although the Liberal Democratic party which most of them support reflects much more of a conservative than either a liberal or radical ideology, their attitudes hardly seemed in strict accord with that ideology. An impressive minority, for example, would like to see increasing public ownership of industry. The group was sharply divided over whether the United States should withdraw from Vietnam; a majority was opposed to changing Article 9 of the Japanese Constitution, which prohibits an armed force; and several favored world government rather than national sovereignty, although several others considered such a goal too difficult to realize. The strongest consensus, however, emerged on two further issues: only one informant opposed admission of Red China to the United Nations, and only one wanted to see the Japan Communist party outlawed. On the latter point it is noteworthy that Liberal Democratic supporters as far removed from one another on the class ladder as Mayor Miyakawa and Processor Nakayama totally agreed that the Communist party serves as a "watchdog." Indeed, *shichō-san* went a good deal further: had the Communist party among other critical voices not been silenced before the war, Pearl Harbor never would have happened. For the values of freedom of speech and thought, he argued, are indispensable to healthy politics.

VII

The value patterns of Ebibara education are our concluding concern. They may be approached, no less in the case of this institution than of others, on two levels—the implicit and the explicit. On the former, it is imbued with more or less nonverbalized and unformalized values; on the latter, it is the level of consciously articulated values.

Something of the implicit level has been detected in the kinds of values typical of the Ebibara modal personality. It would be unusual, then, if the children of fishing families were not regarded by teachers, administrators, and fellow students in terms rather similar to those with which their parents are regarded. Thus in Utsumi Junior High School, which enrolls more Ebibara adolescents than any other school in the city, the characterization reiterated most often was that of ingroup, clique-forming behavior. As Yamamoto-san, a teacher related to many fishermen, explained it, a "psychological distance" separates Ebibara and non-Ebibara students. He attributed this phenomenon to "feelings of inferiority" on the part of fishermen's children, with a strong correlative need for reinforcement of morale by their own subcultural group.

This behavior pattern is more conspicuous among Ebibara boys than girls, Teacher Yamamoto contended. Even so, it is true of both sexes and still truer of Kazaki-shima students, who commute to the senior high school daily by boat. Yet, whatever the residence, their ingroups are easily detected. Yamamoto-san singled out characteristics such as aggressiveness, loyalty to group leaders, loud talk, rebelliousness, clumsy ways of verbalizing, amiability toward strangers, lower than average learning ability, lower educational ambition, less willingness to abide by school rules, and a higher than average tendency toward delinquency.

One strapping young 15-year-old, leader of an Ebibara ingroup, was described as a case in point. He delights in such mischief as jumping through school windows, writing "official" notices on blackboards to confuse students, and trying in every way to call attention to his own deviations. His mother, a fish peddler, has had little time to devote to him, and his fisherman father was once arrested for illegal gambling, an incident which the boy loudly proclaimed to his fellow students.

Teacher Yamamoto's profile of Ebibara teen-agers was sharpened by that of several other teachers in the same institution. Indeed, they agreed that especially during the third and final year these children, along with children of the *burakumin* section, constitute the "biggest problem" confronting the faculty. Still, no plan has been developed, they said, for dealing with it; rather, each case is treated sporadically and haphazardly. That parents living elsewhere in Utsumi-shi may also discourage their own children from mingling with children of fishermen seems implied in a proposal made some years ago by non-Ebibara parents to build a separate elementary school to accommodate Ebibara children. The school was never built. In any case, no systematic attempt to deal with possible or actual prejudice either in parents or children has been made. On the contrary, according to Yamamoto-san, the attitude of many teachers, particularly the older ones, is that problems of this kind are quite insoluble.

A boy and a girl informant in the same junior high school, neither one of whom lives in Ebibara itself, corroborated such reactions of their teachers. Although conceding that a few Ebibara students are highly intelligent, negative value terms like "rough" (arai) were reiterated more often than positive ones. This particular term, incidentally, was emphasized also by Superintendent Fuji. It is perhaps revealing that neither student had apparently made friends with any child of a fishing family. According to our girl informant, Suzuki-san, her own peer group would disapprove if she tried to associate with Ebibara girls. For one thing, she said, they talk about sex more freely than other students, even more freely than Ebibara boys; also, more secret dating and movie-going occurs among them than among other groups of girls in the school.

On the elementary level, the image of Ebibara children is more opaque than on upper levels. Nevertheless, self-created ingroups, some of them including "problem children," were said to begin forming in the early grades, an observation supported by a sociogram of fourth-grade children. It revealed that a group of seven Ebibara boys all liked each other, but disliked all boys from other parts of Utsumi-shi. Almost as revealing was the evidence that seven out of ten Ebibara girls had no friends among non-Ebibara girls and that one group of three girls seemed completely isolated. Three non-Ebibara boys did, however, like one Ebibara boy.

According to Teacher Shinohara, a higher ratio of below-average ability also prevails among fishermen's children, due, he thought, to lack of discipline at home. The term "key children" (kagikko) is attached, as it often is in the United States, to those who presumably carry keys to enable them to unlock the doors of their homes while both parents are away at work. This neglect is illustrated, Shinohara-san maintained, by a recent community survey of home lighting intended to help children study more efficiently: only two out of 70 Ebibara households were sufficiently interested to pay the modest fee requested. Such critical judgments were partially contradicted by the head of a kindergarten in Utsumi-shi; she finds Ebibara children no less intelligent at this age than other children, and equally well disciplined. Yet on one point she was in agreement with several others: Ebibara parents, often being "thriftless," give their children too much spending money. Two girls in the sixth grade whom we came to know seemed to support this opinion; both receive money almost every day to spend as they wish on candy or other pleasures. Neither, incidentally, wants to marry a fisherman when she grows up.

Somewhere between the more or less implicit values revealed by the personality profile of Ebibara school children, and the explicit values illustrated by official pronouncements of the board of education, are those patterns of values that permeate the everyday work of education, such as the curriculum, testing procedures, and teacher organizations. We cannot hope to disentangle all of the complexities that appear in this intermediate sphere of partially implicit and partially explicit values, although we shall return to them. In any case, with one partial exception, they are hardly distinctive of Utsumi-shi, much less of Ebibara.

This exception is the status of teacher organizations. As we discovered earlier, Nikkyōso (Japan Teachers' Union) has maintained a greater degree of strength in this municipality than elsewhere in Yoneshima-ken. It happens, moreover, that the disputes that are constantly arising between Nikkyōso and its chief rival organization, Kyōshikai (Japan Teachers' Association), center in Utsumi Junior High School itself. This is because, we may recall, Principal Yoshida is a leader of Kyōshikai; simultaneously, one of the single most influential Nikkyōso veterans in the prefecture is Tamura-san, a long-time teacher and former Nikkyōso officer stationed in the same school. The elementary school enrolling most children of fishermen also includes some members of both organizations on its faculty.

Vehemence of feelings has been so acute, so Teacher Shinohara informed us, that on one occasion early in the conflict Nikkyōso teachers besieged Kyōshikai meetings, and on others picketed school administration headquarters with the militant support of several other unions. A substantial number of teachers in the area belong to neither organization, however, quite possibly because they do not wish to be embroiled.

Conflicts between Nikkyōso and Kyōshikai in Utsumi-shi have deep ideological roots; therefore they inevitably reflect differing values regarding the means and ends of education and its network of relations to Japanese culture. Unquestionably, the former of the two organizations has been and remains heavily influenced by the Marxian philosophy; leaders both locally and nationally have usually been Socialists and in some cases Communists. They conceive of education as involved everywhere in the class struggle, and they regard Monbushō, the Ministry of Education, as the pawn of the dominant power structure embodied in the Liberal Democratic party. They are constantly agitating for higher salaries, shorter work weeks, and many curriculum changes.

Kyōshikai, on the contrary, repudiates the conception of the teacher as a member of the working class. It claims to be "neutral" politically, to concern itself entirely with professional education, and to oppose collective bargaining on the ground that teaching is not to be compared with other occupations. Official pronouncements of Kyōshikai speak of the need to study "right" and "proper" educational problems, and to investigate such matters as teachers' salaries and working conditions. Control of Kyōshikai rests in the hands of school administrators, whereas in Nikkyōso it appears that rank-and-file teachers often on leave from their classrooms occupy many of the important leadership posts, although principals being regarded as employees are also eligible for membership.

Explicitly, to be sure, both movements ardently favor "democracy." According to Principal Yoshida, Kyōshikai rests upon a philosophy of "democratic humanism," which he locates somewhere between socialist and capitalist democracies. He admitted, however, that most members are Liberal Democrats, even if he himself is personally sympathetic with the gradualist policies of the Democratic Socialist party. Although Tamura-san did not indicate to us his party affiliation, he reflects in his values the general policies of the political left in Japan.

This is by no means to contend that all Nikkyōso members in Utsumi-shi are equally radical, any more than that all Kyōshikai members are equally conservative; many are doubtless typical of thousands of Japanese teachers and are not committed to any one political ideology. Nevertheless, it does remain true that Nikkyōso's values are openly identified with the international struggle of working people for full democratic participation in political, economic, social, and educational life; therefore it opposes every attempt to weaken or divert the role of education interpreted as one important agent of that struggle. Kyōshikai, on the other hand, assiduously avoiding any such "revolutionary" doctrine, receives the blessing of many more school board members, superintendents, and Monbushō officials than Nikkyōso receives.

Even if we assume with Superintendent Fuji that the two organizations are "completely opposite," it is only fair to point out that teachers of both organizations, at least in the Utsumi Junior High School, tend to show more conciliatory attitudes in daily practice than they do in theory. This is partly due, it would appear, to the rather liberal stance noted in Principal Yoshida. Indeed, he himself admitted to us that two teachers' organizations are better than one, because each forces the other toward more satisfactory policies. Thus, during one of our visits to his school, both groups on the faculty found a way to avoid an open clash over a new schedule delegating the student-body to clean all halls and classrooms (a common practice in Japanese schools). The schedule, they agreed, should first be submitted for consideration to *seitokai*, the student council, rather than be determined by fiat of the faculty.

This example suggests that although the Nikkyōso-Kyōshikai issue does not bear directly upon Ebibara value patterns, it does at least indirectly affect them because it affects Ebibara children. A similar generalization applies to *seitokai* itself. Few Ebibara children are conspicuous in student government activities; yet the influence that this organization exerts upon the shaping of their youthful values may be considerable. *Seitokai* is headed by a board of directors elected by the entire student body of Utsumi-shi Junior High School, and consists of representatives from each homeroom and a series of student committees concerned with such matters as the library, discipline, publications, health, and athletics.

Our own interest must be confined to a single question: Does the primary purpose of *seitokai*, that of advancing democratic participation by students in school affairs, appear to be carried out in practice? The answer is clear from our evidence: just as in the case of Utsumi-shi teacher organizations, disparity prevails between this explicit purpose and such implicit values that may be observed in daily behavior. The not unfamiliar complaint was heard, for example, that relatively few students are directly involved in *seitokai* activities, rather that officers and committees once they are elected not only assume most responsibilities, but that some programs they sponsor (baseball is one) benefit relatively few of the total student body. Still more seriously, two of our informants, one a *seitokai* officer, Suzuki-san, the other the teacher, Yamamoto-san, both protested at the total faculty control that they said prevails over *seitokai* financial affairs. They maintained that students have little voice in deciding how the relatively large annual sum of $1000, mostly from student fees, should be spent for athletic meets or other affairs.

On other matters, however, Student Suzuki considered *seitokai* admirably democratic, more so than did Teacher Yamamoto. Boys and girls, she said, are quite evenly chosen as officers; school-wide campaigns for election are spirited; teachers serve mainly as advisers; officers evaluate all student tasks such as cleaning, then share their evaluations over the loudspeaker system; and each week the executive committee meets for several hours to plan its program for the following week. Parents, in fact, sometimes complain loudly because *seitokai* activities interfere with preparation for examinations—a complaint which, according to Teacher Yamamoto, has been known in turn to generate disturbances in children themselves.

In addition to *seitokai*, four other "self-governing" student organizations function under the sponsorship of the Utsumi-shi school system. The first, *kodomokai*, consists of some 160 neighborhood groups, and is usually

supported by *jichikai*, the PTAs, and the coordinating social education department. Its program is largely recreational: field trips, sports, swimming,
but also occasional study groups, are intended to develop cooperative behavior in children and thereby to reduce the incidence of juvenile delinquency. Officers are again elected by the children who likewise share in
program planning. According to Tsuji-san, the industrial worker, *kodomokai*
groups in the Ebibara district have been an important factor in breaking
down barriers between *gyomin* and other occupational groups; parents are
able to find a mutual ground of interest in their children regardless of other
real or imagined hostilities.

A second organization is called *jidōkai*, which is partially modeled after
seitokai but functions in the elementary school, with children of the upper
three grades serving as officers. The third, also in the elementary school,
was just getting started during our research; it is called *oyakokai*, consists of
both children and parents, and aims to develop the value of cooperation in
Utsumi-shi by drawing disparate ages closer together. The fourth organization functions at least nominally in both elementary and secondary schools
throughout Japan: each homeroom (*hōmuruumu*) has its own class organization and meetings are frequently held involving problems like cleaning
responsibilities.

Thus far we have been trying to move upward, as it were, from the
lower, more implicit patterns of values encompassed by education, through
layers that are a mixture of the implicit and the explicit, until now we arrive
at a frankly explicit attempt to deal with values through formal instruction.
This attempt, so far as our study of Ebibara is concerned, is confined to two
ventures; neither is limited to fishermen's children but both must include
them.

One is the project in family education mentioned in Chapter 2. Groups
of parents have been selected for special guidance, with modest grants provided by Monbushō and administered by the social education department.
The pilot groups, initially four schools but presently increased to eleven,
have been studying problems of changing patterns of family life in the
community and reporting back at intervals to large PTA meetings. Superintendent Fuji, who has already been cited for his concern over the rapid
shift from the authoritarian-paternalistic to a more libertarian-equalitarian
family ethics, considered the project of such crucial importance that he
hopes to see it widened.

Another junior high school in Utsumi-shi has been the center of a
project where 300 parents applied and 50 were selected for admission to
the first study group. This group held 22 meetings in its first year and has
published a series of reports on its deliberations to be shared with other

parents. One such report, called *Mutsumi* (mutual friendship) and written by selected participants, illustrates the kind of topics discussed: parents must find ways to re-establish their "prestige," too much of which deteriorated after the war; the "self-determining spirit" of children is the chief goal of education, but it also requires parental discipline; home tasks compensated by modest allowances are good family practices; it is necessary to treat household maids as members of the family if they are to have a wholesome influence on children; religious meetings in the home, sometimes with a priest present, have been beneficial in solving family problems; the adolescent period of maturation is especially difficult, yet too many parents have been ill-prepared to cope with it.

Our young *seitokai* officer, Student Suzuki, felt that at least in her own junior high school the changing order and goals of the Japanese family are given too casual attention. On this point she disagreed again with her teacher, Yamamoto-san; his judgment was that the total of several hours already provided in the social studies curriculum over a three-year span are quite adequate.

Principal Etō, of the elementary school that we came to know best, made a relevant point in discussing the parent project. With the gradual weakening of ancient customs such as *hōji* (ceremonial of commemoration) which once helped so much to knit families closely together, the school today confronts an unprecedented task, that of guiding families toward discovering new ways to maintain their internal solidarity. From this viewpoint the *gyomin* of Ebibara might be said to be more fortunate than many "modernized" families; to a striking extent, as we have found, traditional family customs continue to be faithfully observed.

A number of educational informants insisted, nevertheless, that good family relations are more difficult to achieve among fishermen than among other groups in Utsumi-shi. Some of the causes are by now familiar, but one, Ebibara's crowded living quarters, was re-emphasized. The study circle on problems of family relations initiated during our visit by the women's co-op auxiliary is the first organized attempt in Ebibara to do something about this situation.

The second explicit approach to matters of value within the school program is called *dōtoku kyōiku* (moral education). This program has such a long and disturbing history in Japan that we shall give it additional attention. In Utsumi-shi itself, *dōtoku kyōiku*, like every other feature of the school curriculum, is prescribed by Monbushō. Since 1958, all Japanese children from the first grade through junior high school are expected to study the subject for one hour per week, although we have been told of exceptions. In senior high school where a course has been in effect only since 1964–1965 it is limited to the second year, for one hour per week also.

The precise contents and methods of instruction are somewhat flexible. Monbushō, to be sure, has managed to encompass elementary moral education in 36 principles, beginning with the goal of "respect for life" and concluding with "love of mankind." It provides sample outlines and source books for both elementary and junior high schools. It also suggests how to use slides, tapes, and discussion methods. But each school and each teacher are expected, theoretically, to develop a particular program of study designed to meet the needs of each group of children. On the senior high school level, 16 different textbooks in "modern ethics" were published within a year or so of the new requirement.

In Utsumi-shi, Principal Etō has been particularly interested in this subject. His elementary school has been host to a prefecture-wide conference on problems of *dōtoku kyōiku,* and he himself was one of the first educators in Yoneshima-ken to devise a course of study for use in his own school. Nevertheless, Nikkyōso leaders such as Tamura-san have opposed compulsory moral education from the beginning, contending that it can easily degenerate as it did before the war into indoctrination for extreme nationalism or some other ideology anathema to democracy as Nikkyōso conceives of it.

Mifune-san, PTA leader in Principal Etō's school, did not agree with Tamura-san. He contended that when *dōtoku kyōiku* is developed in terms of the child's own experience and personality, indoctrination need not occur. Although patriotism has a place in the program, "personal happiness" is the primary goal.

Mayor Miyakawa found himself somewhere between Mifune-san and Tamura-san in this dispute. Children, he thought, require some "frame of devotion." True, the Imperial Rescript on Education (1890), which was the foundation of all moral education before World War II, is no longer suitable. Yet, he felt, some absolute values—"courage" and "righteousness" are two —ought to be taught along with critical-mindedness. Somehow a balance must be struck.

Whether the dilemma implied by *shichō-san* is being resolved by the Utsumi-shi program remains debatable. Let us consider for a moment two representative documents prepared by local schools—one a "Report on the Teaching of Moral Education" for elementary children; the other, "Annual Plan of Moral Education in Utsumi Junior High School."

The former document contains case studies for each grade. Grade One, for example, includes such topics as taking care of one's personal effects, the evils of fighting and quarreling, and making friends. Simple, graphic examples such as how to avoid losing one's books and pencils are described. Grade Two considers affectionate relations to one's mother, a healthy body, and other matters appropriate to eight-year-olds. Grades Five and Six deal with topics such as tidiness, family life, and the meaning of a "large mind."

The junior high school guide emphasizes the importance of flexibility in studying values within Monbushō's framework. Each of the three years is broken down into different themes for each month. Here are a few selected at random: freedom for the individual in relation to the group; the meaning of responsibility; loyalty to the Japanese nation and to international society; egotism; the religious spirit; and pride in work. One receives the impression that considerable pains have been taken to avoid controversial issues (sexual or political, for example); to adjust the themes of discussion to levels of maturation; and to stress the desirability (if not the workability) of teaching about values more as problem-solving than as answer-giving.

The extent to which Utsumi-shi teachers responsible for *dōtoku kyōiku* instruction can, in the extremely brief time allotted each week, succeed in relating the abstractly formulated themes of the junior high school level to everyday life is doubtful. Certainly in neither report can one discover the slightest attention paid to problems that arise because one's father is, for example, a fisherman or one's mother a full-time worker in a *kamaboko* factory. Nevertheless, that children, and parents too, do at least have the opportunity to verbalize about some of the values germane to their life in school, home, and community is a fair conclusion to draw from our evidence.

VIII

This concludes our Ebibara involvement. Throughout this Part, we have been concerned with three principal dimensions: (1) the order of the fishing community as seen both through its surrounding municipality, Utsumi-shi, and in its own structure of relationships; (2) the dynamic but at times also frustrating processes of conflict and cooperation; and (3) the goals of everyday people that thread intricately across both individual and institutional values.

How then, amidst all of these multitudinous experiences and impressions, may we epitomize the central character of this little community? Our briefest answer is this: Ebibara exerts prodigious efforts to accommodate itself in new ways of learning and earning, meanwhile striving also to preserve and nourish its own cultural identity.

Such an endeavor remains unfinished, nor can it ever be depicted as totally unique among many more or less similar communities. But Ebibara does demonstrate that over a period of scarcely more than one decade its proud and independent family owners of trawling boats have been able to subordinate, if not to supersede, timeworn practices of inefficient and illegal competitiveness, even perhaps to soften their deeply entrenched attitudes of jealousy. In reducing such conflictive behavior, the fishing co-operative (not forgetting the unofficial protective association, *kogi kumiai*) has played a formidable role, abetted by the federal, prefectural, and city Department of Fisheries, which thus often serves as an informal educational and experimental agency of doubtless stronger impact than any program of formal education. Particularly when both the expanding seaweed project and the several small marine processing plants are compounded as sources of fresh economic energy, Ebibara may be interpreted as a community of genuine distinction—a community of long-revered customs and practices that yet become interwoven with both exhilarating ventures and modest hopes for a more rewarding life.

Whether our nearby second community, Kawabara, deserves any comparable generalizations, including those that bear eventually upon education itself, becomes our next preoccupation.

Part II

A Community of Segregated People

4

PROFILE
OF KAWABARA

I

It is a cold February evening and we are talking with Kataoka-san and his wife in their simple one-story house fronting upon the main street of Kawabara. Quite unlike the bustling main street of Ebibara it is very quiet and dark outside. Kataoka-san's wife sits with us on the *tatami* (straw mat) and joins in our conversation while keeping our cups filled with steaming tea, offering us sweets, or occasionally dropping a few pieces of charcoal into the *hibachi* (brazier) which provides our only warmth.

Kataoka-san is an assistant to a truck driver and earns $70 per month, but he is looking for a better job. Every day he must travel by bus 10 miles each way to the transportation company that employs him. Aged about 55, he is taller than the average Japanese. His face is noble in structure. But when we mention that many individuals with whom we are becoming acquainted in Kawabara strike us as handsome, his wife, who is herself a fine-looking woman, replies in an unexpected way. Outsiders, she says, often mention that the people of Kawabara are unusually handsome, but whenever they do "we feel a little strange." Such compliments, however kindly intended, only serve to emphasize once more that "we" are different from other Japanese. The fact is that "we" would rather, much rather, not be different at all.

The reason is, of course, that Kataoka-san and his wife belong to the *burakumin* (literally, people of the community), the largest minority group in Japan, as do all but a few others who live in Kawabara. They, again like

81

most others, were born and grew up here, and both graduated from the nearby elementary school which all Kawabara *burakumin* children still attend. Their parents were also born here, as were both of their grandfathers, although the wife's grandmother came from another *burakumin* community. They have kinship relations with 20 households: Kataoka-san has three brothers and a sister living in Kawabara; his wife has four sisters. Altogether they are related by blood to some 75 other residents. They themselves are first cousins and products of *ren-ai*, a love marriage.

The couple has four children, but only the eldest son (aged 34) and his wife continue to live here, in another wing of the house which incidentally Kataoka-san himself built. The son and his wife have two small children, so six persons are here now. The little room in which we are talking approximates a living room, but it contains no furniture except an upright chest and small desk. It had been used as a study while Kataoka-san's younger children were still in school; before that it was a small shoe store. This enterprise collapsed, we are told, because too many neighbors failed to pay their bills. This is why Kataoka-san has been forced into his job as an assistant truck driver.

His son is a door-to-door peddler of stationery and travels throughout Yoneshima-ken. He is away from home sometimes only for a few days, at other times for as much as a month at a stretch. Kataoka-san's wife used to be a peddler too, and specialized in neckties and *okyū,* an ancient Chinese-derived folk remedy made of herbs that are burned in a little cube or cone on the bare skin. It makes one "feel good," she said, and is alleged not only to relieve pain but to cure small boys of bad behavior. It also leaves a scar, and many Japanese have several. Although *okyū* is still administered, especially in rural areas, it is becoming much less popular than it was even 20 years ago. Kataoka-san's wife, at any rate, has changed from peddling to glove-making in the one factory within Kawabara, where a few women like herself are employed.

None of the other three children (all in their early twenties) is staying at home. They live in Tokyo, to which Kataoka-san says he sent them so that they could more easily conceal their cultural origin in the anonymous environment of the largest city in the world. In the terminology of American minority relations, they are trying to "pass," much as thousands of very light-skinned persons with Negro blood attempt to hide their racial ancestry and so to become full-fledged members of the "white" community.

One of the two daughters is a bookkeeper in a Tokyo gas station; she had started senior high school but dropped out. The other daughter, a graduate of a senior high school of business, is about to be married to a factory worker. For a long time during their engagement, so her parents tell us, she could not bring herself to reveal her background to the man she planned to marry, but a mutual friend who knew her well decided to tell him. Fortunately he did not then reject her, but both are still greatly worried, as is her family, that his mother will discover her identity and seek to block the marriage. As a safeguard, their daughter has managed somehow to transfer her own citizenship record to the family register of her fiancé. Meanwhile, another hopeful element, her parents believe, is that her fiancé is a factory worker and not a *sarariiman,* for whom status is often all-important.

The second son of Kataoka-san is about to graduate from a Tokyo college, a very rare occurrence among *burakumin* anywhere in Japan. To make this possible, his parents and elder brother have managed to send him small amounts of money over a period of nearly four years, in addition to what he has earned at "any kind of job." According to both parents, their son has suffered "great agony" because he belongs to the *burakumin.* Not only must he constantly be on guard to avoid discovery, but even in high school in Yamada-shi he was a victim of prejudice. He had fallen deeply in love with a fellow student and they wanted to marry. The girl's mother, however, "tortured" her so much that the relationship was shattered. It was this affair that precipitated the young man's decision to leave home for good and to "pass," if he could, into the majority culture of Tokyo. In this decision, his parents encouraged him wholeheartedly, as they did both of their daughters, even though this meant not only a complete separation from their birthplace but severance of most kinship ties.

Although otherwise far more typical than not of Kawabara people, Kataoka-san and his wife are unusual in two respects. One is the higher-than-average level of education attained by three of their children, though not by themselves or their older son. The other respect is their wholly dedicated aim to provide a better life for their children than they themselves have been able to obtain. To do so they have exercised utmost caution to escape from the segregations, discriminations, taboos, and hostilities from which they insist many communities more or less similar to Kawabara suffer. For example, although Kataoka-san's private political views might at times be radical, and although he might like to see his transportation company unionized, he would never announce his views publicly. To do so, he said, would only jeopardize his chances, and even more his children's chances, of being approved by those of the majority culture with power to accept or reject them.

II

And yet, legally speaking, Kawabara, no less than Ebibara, is not separate at all. It is one section of the incorporated city which we have called

Yamada-shi; its inhabitants are entitled to every right and privilege that other citizens are legally entitled to; it is represented on the city council and on other civic bodies such as *jichikai* (self-governing association); and its children go to the same schools as do the rest of Yamada-shi children.

In numerous other ways, nevertheless, Kawabara is decidedly unlike Ebibara. Geographically, to begin with, it is not contiguous with the rest of the city. Whereas Ebibara is simply one very crowded area of Utsumi-shi and demarcated from the next by an invisible boundary line, Kawabara is separated from Yamada-shi proper by a riverbed (usually dry, to be sure) and can be reached only by crossing a concrete bridge, turning a sharp left, and driving for about 1500 feet along a narrow, bumpy, dusty road parallel to the river on one side and to rice fields on the other. Only then do we reach the first cluster of houses, one of them being Kataoka-san's.

From this point on, most of the small houses are crowded as closely together as they are in Ebibara. We see the tiny factory on the right. On the left, we pass the best and newest-looking building in Kawabara, the public bath. We drive between two enormous but neatly arranged piles of junk on both sides of the road which are being stored there for later sale. Suddenly we come to an open space in the dirt road, the center of the village, which is distinguished by a fire-bell tower, a dilapidated shed under which has been placed a still more dilapidated *mikoshi* (portable shrine), and finally a rubbish heap. At the farther end of the open space is another pile of salvageable junk, and opposite the *mikoshi* is a picayune grocery store and ice cream stand. The road continues, but alleyways run in various directions off from this open area in order to permit pedestrians to reach their houses. The only thoroughfare large enough to accommodate a three- or four-wheeled vehicle is the one on which we entered.

Altogether, over 600 people live in Kawabara, a total of some 150 households. There is no focal point of economic life, such as the Ebibara fishing co-operative, although Kawabara does have a community center of sorts—a neglected building containing a few low tables, holes in the floor, a few shelves of children's books, and a wobbly ping-pong table. The first impression one receives is of a stagnant, impoverished community largely isolated from the outside world, even from the rest of Yamada-shi.

First impressions are not always accurate, of course, and especially in the case of Kawabara we shall find that second, third, and fourth impressions are sometimes radically altered from our initial ones. In preparation, however, let us try to sketch the cultural order of Kawabara as it relates to Yamada-shi. For, despite severe barriers that prevail, this small city plays a continuous and crucial role in the life of *burakumin* themselves.

We select here only those characteristics of Yamada-shi most pertinent to our present interest. To begin with, Yamada-shi is somewhat smaller than Utsumi-shi: its total population is just below 34,000. There has been a decline of nearly 2000 in ten years, as more and more young people seek their fortunes in the great cities of Japan. (The decline has now leveled off, however.)

The original town is ancient indeed, having been founded in the eighth century. Its main temple, of the Shingon sect, has a history of over a thousand years, although it has been destroyed by fire more than once. Even today this temple with its spacious grounds, smaller satellite temples, and aged monuments is by far the most impressive sight in Yamada-shi. Its graceful five-level pagoda towers above the surrounding countryside. The temple is a mecca for Buddhist pilgrims, who often stop there singly or in groups even of 50 or more for a night's lodging, in order to attend 5 A.M. services conducted by its retinue of over a dozen priests, or to venerate its relics some of which are considered too sacred to be seen except by a few honored visitors.

Altogether there are 30 temples within the city limits presided over by full-time priests, and some 15 others without priests. These temples represent such famous sects as Nichirenshū, Tendaishū, and Jōdoshinshū; the last claims about twice as many members as the next largest congregation, Shingonshū. As for Shintoism, one may visit 13 shrines of various sizes and ages, one of the most impressive of which, Inari, honors the fox *kami* ("god") and is reached by climbing a high hill overlooking the great temple and city. As one climbs, one passes under perhaps a hundred small red arches, each painted conspicuously with the name of the donor, usually a businessman. Finally, the Sōkagakkai and other sects of the "new religions" have their coteries of followers, as do two small Christian churches, one Roman Catholic and one Protestant.

The city proper sprawls across several square miles of flat plain. As is typical of most recently incorporated municipalities (Yamada-shi became a city only in 1954), there is a central congested area of closely packed houses, inns, and shops, and fanning outward from it are several clusters of homes, shops, and other buildings interspersed with patchworks of farm land.

Farming is the chief occupation. Although more than 50 percent of all farmers have side jobs, 60 percent of productive work is agricultural. One of the most important institutions in the city is the agricultural co-operative, which has a small consumer store along with its large producers' department. Rice is the chief crop, but wheat follows closely after. The city is surrounded by small mountains, and orange and peach groves flourish on the steep hillsides. There are some 300 cows, 2000 pigs, and 40,000 chickens on farms within the city limits. The local experimental agricultural station, headed by an agronomist with a doctorate, is evidently having some effect in its encouragement of diversified farming. The average size of farms is a trifle larger than in Utsumi-shi but still only about half the national average.

Except for farming, Yamada-shi is economically weaker than Utsumi-shi. Since it lies inland, marine occupations are limited to a few retail fish shops. Manufacturing, too, is comparatively meager; there are over a hundred so-called factories, but very few of them consist of more than a handful of workers. Production of foods accounts for over two-thirds of manufacturing, furniture for less than a fourth, and clothing for even less. An example is the comparatively large branch factory of an Osaka company across the street from our Yamada-shi home. Here, next door to a farm, women's and children's precut clothing is sewed by a force of 25 girls in their teens and early twenties, all of whom stopped school after the compulsory nine years. Half of the girls live in a dormitory above the sewing room for the 28 eight-hour days per month that they must work; the rest travel to the factory by bicycle or bus. Almost none (even the most experienced) earns in this nonunionized factory more than a little over $40 per month.

Indeed, so far as we could discover, few employees of any commercial establishments are unionized. Although there is a central labor council with its own tidy building, its membership consists chiefly of municipal workers (especially those of the heavily staffed city hall with its claim of one employee for every 110 citizens) and local postal workers. Both of these occupations are strongly organized throughout Japan. The only other union of any significance is Jirō, which consists of people on public-works projects who would otherwise be unemployed. (Many Jirō workers are *burakumin*.) In sum, although Yamada-shi is about three-fourths the size of Utsumi-shi, it has less than half as many industrial workers, and about one-half as much manufacturing income. The rice harvest, on the other hand, is almost as large as that of Utsumi-shi.

One important source of income in Yamada-shi is not to be found in the neighboring city. Despite the new Japanese Constitution, a so-called "defense force" consisting of some 2500 soldiers is stationed here, housed in old training barracks of the prewar imperialist army. Some of the soldiers have families, while single men are eager patrons of a corps of pseudo-*geisha* estimated at about a hundred. All of the girls are booked by a "broker," who thrives on exorbitant commissions and who also happens to be a city councilman.

Besides three *pachinko* (pinball) parlors, two movies, and several cozy bars, little else in the way of commercial recreation is available. Like the few Utsumi-shi citizens who can afford it, their even fewer counterparts in Yamada-shi must travel at least as far as the prefectural capital of Hiroi-shi or to the great shrine not far from Utsumi-shi if they wish to indulge in *storippu* shows, *toruko* baths, cabarets, first-class inns, or simulated hot springs. The per capita monthly income of most occupations in Yamada-shi is a few dollars lower than in Yoneshima-ken as a whole.

Despite its sluggish industrial growth the city is comparatively flexible in political structure. At the time of our study a former Socialist, who later turned Independent, was mayor. Out of 26 members on the city council, there were 5 Socialists, 1 Communist, 1 Kōmeitō, 5 Independents, and 14 Liberal Democrats. Since the majority party is often able to form coalitions with Independent councilmen and sometimes with the Kōmeitō, Liberal Democratic councilmen oftener than not have been in political control.

Moreover, *jichikai*, the city-wide organization of common people which earlier interested us, is at least equally involved in community affairs here as it is in Utsumi-shi. Its chairman is president of the local chamber of commerce, and its executive secretary is a semiretired businessman who has devoted nearly all his time without compensation to organizational affairs since *jichikai* was founded in 1954. The structure in Yamada-shi is again pyramidal, and rests upon *kumi*—that is, neighborhood household groups. Each *kumi* has its own chairman, 250 in all, and each receives an expense account of 14 cents per year for every household in his *kumi*. The largest of these contains 150 households, the smallest five. The annual budget of *jichikai* approaches about $2500, most of which is paid by the city treasury.

Politicians evidently regard *jichikai* so useful in building support for their policies that they have even helped to finance an all-day outing by bus to a nearby prefecture for all 250 *kumi* chairmen. The climax of this outing, to which we were invited, was a lunch, replete with *sake*, at which speeches were delivered by the mayor, ex-mayor, and sundry other officials. Several *jichikai* chairmen from Kawabara, with whom we soon became acquainted, joined us on this trip. But our conversion en route was shared principally with three other chairmen who happened to ride on our bus: one a Buddhist priest dressed in secular garb, another an organizer of the local postal union, the third a bookkeeper in a local butcher shop. At intervals, several riders sang folksongs, one alcoholic gentleman with an extensive repertoire being aided only too volubly by the bus microphone.

Kamada-san, the executive secretary and one of our panel of leader informants, maintained that the purpose of *jichikai* in Yamada-shi is chiefly that of developing an enlightened citizenry by keeping people informed on local political issues and encouraging them in turn to influence the city hall. Still, no direct political actions are taken; rather, members are urged to discuss issues and to exert pressure by virtue of their opinions and recommendations. A small monthly paper of which Secretary Kamada is editor has often published critical pieces by members, which although "not too violent" sometimes "trouble" the mayor and other politicians; it serves, Kamada-san held, as a "safety valve."

Kumi themselves meet irregularly, depending on need or initiative taken by their chairmen (whose own interest may range from none at all to a great deal), and sometimes, when they do meet, the agenda may not be political at all. A *kumi* chaired by the butcher shop bookkeeper, for example, has been concerned on more than one occasion with adjudicating domestic quarrels in one or another of its member households. *Kumi* chairmen are delegated to collect national health insurance premiums and land taxes, and their commissions are used for neighborhood recreational activities such as ceremonial occasions.

Jichikai is also one indication of the vertical order of class and status levels. According to Secretary Kamada, three groups in the city consider themselves "too exclusive" to participate actively in the grassroots affairs of *jichikai;* these are the personnel of the agricultural station, the staff of an institute for training police, and the faculty of Yamada College. Although members of these groups belong nominally to one *kumi* or another, it is difficult to involve most of them in *jichikai* affairs. They suffer, he said, from "superiority complexes." In one instance he arranged a meeting to encourage socializing between housewives of the three "exclusive" groups and housewives from more typical households. He recalls that the former talked at length about how much they enjoyed *tai* (an expensive fish), whereas the latter preferred to discuss various low-priced fish. The meeting was a failure.

That others in Yamada-shi besides these three groups would be considered upper level is suggested by another leader informant, Tabata-san, former chairman of Yoneshima-ken associated women's organizations, who is often influential in Yamada-shi educational and political affairs. Although her parents-in-law were prewar landlords and her husband inherited their attractive home and remaining land, she considers herself middle rather than upper status. Political leaders, she contended, have the most status in Yamada-shi, and doctors and a few well-to-do farmers are only one level below them. She would doubtless place most, although not all, *burakumin* on or near the lowest class level, along with many of the 200 or more households (mostly Japanese evacuees from Korea and China) that occupy diminutive crumbling apartments reconverted from old army barracks in the center of town. Unlike most Yamada-shi citizens, Tabata-san sometimes visits Kawabara in order to advise the women's organization there on its own problems and plans.

Another informant, Ueno-san, a specialist in social or adult education, pictured the class-status structure in still another way. Along with politicians, he places bankers and a few businessmen in the top bracket; their monthly incomes are above $200. Municipal bureaucrats, leading school officials, experienced teachers, and prosperous farmers are middle level, with monthly incomes from $100 to $200. Lower-middle people, according to Ueno-san, include young teachers, clerks, and most farmers; their monthly incomes average $100 or less. Those with whom we are most concerned have incomes below this sum and fall into lower-class brackets.

Mention a moment ago of Yamada College leads us to discussion of education. This liberal-arts institution of some 400 students is the one exceptional feature of Yamada-shi's total program. Coeducational and residential, it has only recently become accredited. Like a number of other Christian colleges in Japan, a substantial proportion of its financial support derives from affiliated churches in the United States. Every member of the faculty of 30 members, not only the Japanese teachers but the several Americans, must be a Christian and must swear to prescribed theological tenets. However, although all are compelled to attend religious exercises and courses, only a small minority of students are Christians. Many hope to become teachers.

Schools in Yamada-shi consist of eight kindergartens (one private), two nursery schools (both private), eight elementary schools, three junior highs (one private), and two senior highs (one private). The large private senior high school attracts many students from nearby communities, so that enrollment on this level—nearly 3000 in total—is slightly above that on the junior high level. The social education department, which has sometimes been active in Kawabara affairs, is headed by Ueno-san, a part-time priest of the Shingon sect. He continues to live with his family adjacent to a temple but only on occasion performs religious rites. Altogether there are about 10,000 full- or part-time students. As in Utsumi-shi, this is nearly one-third of the entire population. The annual school budget of a little more than $250,000 is only about 17 percent of the total budget of the city, but this is still 2 percent higher than in Utsumi-shi.

III

Unlike our description of the *gyomin* community, Kawabara cannot be described so easily in terms of the network of connections with other groups or other sections. Whereas fishermen and nonfishermen are, we recall, frequently next-door neighbors, this is rarely true in our *burakumin* community. To be sure, a number of non-*burakumin* do live in Kawabara, but we shall find their circumstances to be exceptional. Likewise a few *burakumin* live in other sections of Yamada-shi. Nevertheless, to a very high degree, Kawabara is a homogeneous ingroup community. We shall consider first some economic and political features.

How do residents make their living? The mountainous piles of junk that we drove between as we traveled along the main street testify to the principal enterprise. Two entrepreneurs, both on our Kawabara panel of informants, are in this business. The first, Taura-san, who came to this community 20 years ago from Kobe, specializes in collecting bottles, of which he owned thousands at the time of our study. However, he buys anything that can be resold—worn-out bicycles, for example. The second, Hayashi-san, whose home and junk yard are adjacent to the open space on the main thoroughfare deals largely in metal—car parts, motorcycles, anything that can be melted down—but he, too, buys old tires, waste paper, bottles, and other discarded objects.

Neither junk dealer engages directly in the job of collecting. Hayashi-san, whose other interests now occupy most of his time, has turned over the bulk of the business to his eldest son. Collecting itself is done by self-styled *burōkā* (brokers). These are mostly young men, but also a few women, who live in Kawabara and work on commission. They comb the countryside, sometimes on bicycles with side cars or motorbikes with attached carriers, at other times with small trucks, and haul back their collections to the Kawabara yards. The number in this occupation varies considerably, since it is exceptional for anyone—including those with families to support, as most do—to work every day. Perhaps the main exceptions are Taura-san and his wife who are extremely industrious. Even the son of Hayashi-san divides his time between the junk business and farming, and is aided by his mother and wife. Taura-san estimated that his own staff of *burōkā* averages at most 20 days of work per month. Nevertheless, the livelihood of a dozen to 15 families depends mostly upon the junk business.

With the one additional exception of another dozen or so women employed as piece-workers in the glove factory (established by the city especially to reduce unemployment in Kawabara), other types of work are widely diversified. No household devotes full-time to the land, although a few individuals list agriculture as their chief occupation. These people own a plot of rice paddies, the largest of which belongs to Hayashi-san, but only 19 percent of all households possess any land other than building plots, as compared with nearly two-thirds in Yamada-shi. Leather work, including shoe-making, employs eight men and women workers (a slipper factory owned by a *burakumin* leader, Mitsuda-san, at the edge of Kawabara employs six full-time workers and occasional piece-workers); three citizens run food shops in the village; at least four are peddlers of shoes, clothing, stationery, and cosmetics (especially hair oil that they mix themselves), although at one time there were many more; about an equal number are clerks or factory workers. But by far the largest number, some 60 persons, classify themselves as *shittai* (men and women workers on public construction projects for the unemployed), or unskilled men and women day laborers, or a combination of the two. Exactly one person has a permanent public-service position earned by examination; he is a senior high school graduate and holds a responsible position in the Yamada-shi agricultural co-operative. Since he is also an important informant, let us call him Nozu-san.

Still, the total number of workers is hardly indicative of the economic situation in Kawabara. In terms of households rather than of individual workers, we discover that over a hundred of the 150 or so receive "economic aid" from the social welfare department of the city government. Some of these households, to be sure, receive more aid than others, and about one-third are *shittai* who earn part of their stipends (although they are not compelled to do so) under the public-works program for the unemployed. The precise total of recipients varies somewhat, depending upon the source of information and the means of recording it—an understandable ambiguity because of reluctance to offer precise data about income, and because a few families of *burakumin* live in areas of Yamada-shi outside of Kawabara proper. We can only say with assurance that nearly one-third of all households in Yamada-shi receiving economic aid are *burakumin*. Whereas the percentage of non-*burakumin* receiving aid is only about 6 percent of the city's population, it is about 75 percent of the *burakumin* population.

The amount of economic aid, moreover, is growing annually. In the last year for which figures were available, the increase was over 18 percent, somewhat above the average family increase of budget in the nation. Even so, the highest monthly stipend for a Kawabara household of five was reported as $62, intended to cover food, housing, education, and all expenses except medical care, for which another $5 or $6 may be authorized in national health insurance. Incidentally, medical expenses are relatively heavy among Kawabara people because of the higher-than-average incidence of illness, so over one-third of a family's income is often expended for drugs and physicians' services. Still, if it is learned that a family has any income other than economic aid, the $62 is reduced accordingly.[1]

Monthly incomes of many Kawabara families are, to be sure, better than this; nevertheless, comparison with average housing conditions in Yamada-shi as a whole is a striking index of wide disparity. Thus about 50 per-

---

[1] It should also be noted, of course, that most figures cited here or elsewhere have continued to expand annually since. But because inflation has also risen we may assume relatively little more improvement in purchasing power by *burakumin* than by other citizens.

cent of all Kawabara houses are limited to two rooms—an average somewhere near half of the city as a whole. Moreover, 60 percent of these rooms are occupied by four to six persons, although the average size of rooms as measured by the number of *tatami* (straw mats) is also smaller than that of the city average.

Since political patterns in Kawabara are central to the following chapter, only essential facts may be noted here. Hayashi-san, one of our two junk dealers, represents the community on the city council, a position to which he has been elected uninterruptedly since the city was incorporated. He is now a Liberal Democrat, but for many years he was active in the Socialist party of Yamada-shi, and even served as city chairman for some time.

Councilman Hayashi has his strong supporters, but many other Kawabara citizens are Socialists or Communists. Our informant Nozu-san has estimated a ratio of about one-third as many Liberal Democrats as Socialists and Communists together. At any rate, it is probably safe to assert that the Socialist party embraces the largest single group of political followers in the village. No members of the minor Democratic Socialist or Kōmeitō parties were discovered.

Even so, we must note that the Communist impact is a good deal stronger than its membership of perhaps 15 households might lead one to suppose. One of several sources of Communist influence is Jirō, the national union of unemployed workers. Although he lives in a neighboring community, the Jirō leader and organizer we came to know best, Shōda-san, is both a zealous Communist and *burakumin*. His organization, we were told, tends to discourage its members from seeking regular employment in factories or other private enterprises because it directs its energies chiefly toward winning larger and larger appropriations of economic aid from both city and prefectural governments.

Two other national organizations are important to the political dimension. Although neither is officially political, both are dedicated to the emancipation and assimilation of *burakumin* through political action as well as other means. The first, Buraku Kaihōdōmei, may be translated as Alliance for Burakumin Emancipation; the second, Dōwakai, as Society for Integration.

Tomita-san, the prefectural leader of Kaihōdōmei and another member of our leader panel, was born and brought up in Kawabara, but has recently moved to Hiroi-shi, where he devotes his time to the Kaihōdōmei program for the whole of Yoneshima-ken while keeping communication channels open with national headquarters in Tokyo. Leader Tomita is an ardent left-wing Socialist as a majority of fellow leaders undoubtedly are, although a minority such as the Jirō organizer, Shoda-san, are Communists, and although one may even detect some Liberal Democrats as well as politically unaffiliated members. This disparity is true in Kawabara itself.

The leader of Dōwakai in Yoneshima-ken is already an acquaintance of ours: the junk dealer, land owner, and councilman, Hayashi-san. Unlike Kaihōdōmei, no full-time office functions in Hiroi-shi. Actually, Hayashi-san himself appears to be the principal organizer and official. He divides most of his time between this responsibility and his office as councilman, with what little may be left over going to his commercial interests. Dōwakai, like Councilman Hayashi himself, is closer to the Liberal Democratic party than to others, although one may find occasional members here too who are Socialists or perhaps Independents.

As to the actual membership of either organization in Kawabara, our informants could never agree on the figures, and no official lists seem to have been compiled. A few households are affiliated with neither, but Kaihōdōmei members invariably claimed a substantially larger enrollment than Dōwakai, whereas some members of the latter, although still less specific, held that its own membership is larger. What is not disputable, as will shortly become apparent, is that conflict between the two organizations is acute.

Jichikai, in accordance with its nonpartisan policy, is represented by seven Kawabara *kumi*, their seven leaders by prior agreement being almost equally split along ideological lines. Four are Dōwakai members and three Kaihōdōmei; but because the chairman, a worker on the unemployment program and a Jirō unionist, is a Kaihōdōmei member, *jichikai* in Kawabara seems able to maintain a more or less precarious balance in its internal power relations. These seven leaders also participate in Yamada-shi programs of *jichikai*, although none presently holds office on the sectional or city levels. They are governed by an open agreement not to engage in ideological disputes but to confine themselves entirely to nonpolitical community interests.

A few words about the class and status ladder. Although, in the perspective of Yamada-shi, Kawabara appears to rest upon the lowest rungs, one may quickly discover sharp internal stratifications here as well. Consider, for example, the view of our woman leader, Tabata-san, who though an outsider lives adjacent to Kawabara and appears to know it unusually well. The household of Councilman Hayashi, she held, is more prestigious and more powerful than any other by virtue not only of his political position and economic status but also of his lineage, which extends back into Kawabara's past at least several generations.

Just below Hayashi-san in the vertical order of Kawabara is the household of Mitsuda-san, the manufacturer of slippers. Mitsuda-san (another informant, incidentally) holds no political office and his income is doubtless below that of Hayashi-san. Yet he is probably somewhat better educated, having graduated under the prewar high school system when *burakumin* students were almost unheard of on that level, and his family is also a very old one. We shall find him to be one of the most influential men in the whole community. The second junk dealer, Taura-san, is high in economic class but somewhat lower in status than either Hayashi-san or Mitsuda-san. His rating is probably attributable to the fact that, although he married into another old family, he himself is a comparative newcomer.

The household of Nozu-san, the agricultural co-op employee, could be ranked close to Taura-san's in the respect that both are perhaps "lower-upper" by Kawabara standards. But status may be more influential than economic position in the case of Nozu-san, since his father adds to the wide respect with which the family is regarded by virtue of his title of "social worker." It is his father's responsibility, along with two others assigned by the social welfare department, to supervise economic aid and other vital services provided for the large number of citizens whom we have found to be partly or wholly dependent upon them. Most of these people are on the lowest levels, and somewhere between them and the Hayashi, Mitsuda, Taura, and Nozu families are a few middle-level households—Kataoka is one—that more or less support themselves by such occupations as shoe-making, peddling, glove-making, or in combination with junk collecting, farming, and miscellaneous income-producing tasks.

One other upper-status *burakumin* family deserves mention. Most members of this family no longer live in Kawabara itself, but "everyone" in the city, so we were told, is aware of its *burakumin* background. It has become comparatively prosperous around Yamada-shi by owning and operating several butcher shops. And the household master is reputedly so well off as to maintain a *nigō* and *sangō*, familiar in the argot of Japanese gossip as second and third "wives."

IV

Class and status in the cultural order of Kawabara are, as we have just seen, inextricable from family relations. To complete our profile we propose therefore to comment further on the institution of the family, including kinship and marriage. Then, paralleling our Ebibara model, we must turn briefly to the three institutions of religion, recreation, and education.

As in our *gyomin* community, intramarriage among *burakumin* also prevails to such an extent that the same family names are heard repeatedly.

Hayashi, for example, is the surname of households which belong to both Dōwakai and Kaihōdōmei, and which accordingly sometimes bitterly oppose each other.

This strongly endogamous structure was highlighted when we brought a map marked with every household to Hayashi-san's home and asked him to trace the number of related families. Although we were told that common surnames do not always prove kin relationships (they may at times have been adopted by a community for convenience), it still appears true that virtually every household has at least several such relationships. A remarkable number, such as that of our truck driver, Kataoka-san, have 20 or more, and one family has nearly 30. Hayashi-san himself, one estimate suggests, has kinship ties of some sort with one-third or more of all Kawabara households.

Again, as in Kataoka-san's case, first-cousin marriages are undoubtedly more frequent than in most Japanese communities—around ten at present —although the number is said to be lower than it was a generation ago, as people have become better educated and realize that such marriages sometimes allegedly produce subnormal offspring. Cousins or not, two closely related families quite often live together in a single residence. For this reason it seems impossible, if one tries to count the exact number of households in Kawabara, to reach the same total twice.

The tradition of primogeniture also continues, although to a lesser degree than in Ebibara. We have already encountered three households among our informants—those of Hayashi, Nozu, and Kataoka—in which the eldest son and his family occupy the parental household. Councilman Hayashi is the eldest son in a family of 12 children, of whom six are still living in Kawabara itself. He received half of his father's property; the other half was divided among other sons. Indeed, a *honke-bunke* (main-branch family) pattern seems more appropriate to his family than to many others.

Because income-producing property is rarely provided with living quarters, Kawabara families often find it impossible to assure continuity or solidarity in the way that farmers or fishermen can. At the same time, according to another community informant whom we have not previously mentioned, Tanaka-san (an itinerant *burōkā* specializing in cloth remnants), one may detect almost as many instances of friction between a mother-in-law and daughter-in-law living under the same roof in Kawabara as one may discover anywhere in Japan—and abundant evidence testifies to innumerable instances.

Nevertheless, two extraordinary features of family order emerge in Kawabara. The first, which is probably more pronounced here than in most *burakumin* communities, is the presence of approximately 40 women of non-*burakumin* origin who are wives of *burakumin*. These "mixed marriages," most of them fairly recent, are invariably the result of love affairs (*ren-ai*) and not of arrangement (*mi-ai*). Like their husbands, the women are rarely if ever educated beyond junior high school, and many apparently met their *burakumin* mates in entertainment sections of Yamada-shi or other cities where they themselves were sometimes employed. Also like their husbands, they are as a group unusually attractive—so strikingly at times that it is not difficult to imagine how the erotic mutuality aroused by acquaintance with young *burakumin* must have subordinated the sacrifices which these women are often compelled to make.

We say "sacrifices" because, in the vast majority of cases, non-*burakumin* wives break every close tie with their own families. The reason is much the same as in the all-too-familiar story of Kataoka-san's younger son: there is a traditionally deep and frequently unyielding opposition by most Japanese to intermarriage with *burakumin*. It is interesting to note, moreover, that women and not men are almost always the outgroup members who have come to live in this community. Indeed, although two or three informants insisted that they knew of a few instances of a male non-*burakumin* who had entered the community as the mate of a Kawabara woman, we ourselves failed to locate a single instance.

The second conspicuous characteristic of family order is that a large but unmeasured proportion of all families in Kawabara are the result of consensual or common-law marriage. (Fifty percent was the guess of one informant, but this figure is probably too low.) One consequence is that elaborate, costly weddings very rarely if ever occur here. Occasionally, to be sure, a simple wedding party may be held in a Yamada-shi hotel or in the parents' home. In any case, the wedding party may occur, if at all, a fairly long time after a couple have decided to live together. Thus, in the case of Burōkā Tanaka's son, who had brought a non-*burakumin* woman to live with him in the family home, we heard some discussion by his mother of the possibility of a party to be held about one year afterward. The interim period, she felt, would enable the young couple to determine whether they wished to continue together.

Although other reasons for the informality of marriage and sexual patterns will be considered later, one reason is related directly to the previous characteristics of family structure. Since a non-*burakumin* woman is often disowned by her immediate relatives, any marriage ceremony that follows Japanese customs is quite impossible: the presence of parents and other close kin is essential to its performance. Thus a safer, easier, and certainly cheaper procedure is for the couple to avoid all formal Shintō or Buddhist ceremonials and, at most, to go through the routine of signing their names in the city hall register.

V

That Shintō or Buddhist wedding ceremonials do not seem important to most families in Kawabara is not to suggest that religion itself is unimportant to them. On the contrary, a majority of homes maintain a *kamidana* (Shintō shelf), the miniature shrine honoring their favorite *kami* with fresh offerings at frequent intervals. Several of the homes we visited also contained a *butsudan*, the Buddhist family altar; indeed, nearly 80 percent of all households reported possession, in some cases antique ones, passed down through several generations. (Hayashi-san's was purchased in Kyoto by his grandfather.) One *butsudan*, however, was quite new and ornate; it was given to the lady of the house, an aging widow, by her daughter who is a member of one of the famous troupes of all-girl performers on a Tokyo stage. This beautiful young woman, of whom her mother is extremely proud, has thus far apparently managed to conceal her ancestry.

Like *burakumin* everywhere in Japan, those in Kawabara belong almost exclusively to one Buddhist sect, Jōdoshinshū. Yet, rather curiously, Kawabara people rarely attend Jōdoshinshū temples in Yamada-shi itself. Rather, they are members of two temples in Hiroi-shi presided over by priests who are themselves *burakumin*. These priests often travel to Kawabara to officiate at funerals and *hōji* (commemorative ceremonials). In such cases, expenses are often considerable, since bus or railroad fare must be provided in addition to fees and accommodations. Thus, during our study, Burōkā Tanaka conducted a *hōji* in memory of his lost child. The prayer rituals lasted for three hours in the evening and three hours more the next morning. The cost to Tanaka-san was $7, which included overnight hospitality extended to the priest.

Kawabara people also travel to Hiroi-shi (a distance of nearly 30 miles) for ceremonial occasions, especially the spring and autumn festivals sponsored by their temples. Less frequently they send small delegations to the great head temples of Jōdoshinshū in Kyoto: Higashi-honganji and Nishi-honganji. Here they honor the founder, Shinran Shōnin, who in the thirteenth century declared as the chief tenet of his doctrine that any human being may be saved by the grace of Buddha. In Yoneshima-ken as a whole, one may count some 20 Jōdoshinshū priests who are *burakumin* also. But one discovers neither temple nor shrine of any sort within Kawabara itself, although a cemetery for *burakumin* lies within the village and two or three others may be seen nearby.

We do not mean to suggest that Kawabara people are excluded from other religious institutions in Yamada-shi. Over 80 percent, on the contrary, list themselves as members of a nearby shrine with which non-*burakumin* in that section of the city are affiliated also. Many *burakumin*, moreover, sometimes pray at the great Shingonshū temple in Yamada-shi, and about 30 percent, according to the co-op worker Nozu-san, occasionally utilize local folk priests (gyōja) to perform fortune-telling and other occult services. Folk beliefs steeped in Shintō lore, such as yakudoshi (bad-luck years), also continue to be respected by many Kawabarians, just as they are by Ebibarians.

VI

Turning more specifically to recreation itself, one of the most dramatic illustrations of how burakumin often participate today in public events beyond their own communities and religious institutions is the ancient festival of Shingonshū in Yamada-shi that occurs each year on February 20th. This is exactly one month after New Year's Day as reckoned by the lunar calendar. The festival heralds the coming of spring. Many farmers receive tokens of rice seed which have been blessed by priests and which are later mixed with their own rice seed to assure a bountiful harvest. But the feature of the festival most relevant for us involves a sacred ritual ostensibly brought from China a millennium ago, in which about 20 wooden blocks called hōgi become the focus of attention. Following a long evening parade—torches aflame, drums beating, flutes playing—through the principal thoroughfares of Yamada-shi, the hōgi are carried high in the pagoda by the head priest, Azuma-san (whom we shall meet again as a member of our leader panel), followed by a retinue of lesser priests, nuns, and lay officialdom.

According to Shingon theological tenets, the possessor of a hōgi is not only able to ward off seven kinds of unhappiness but to achieve seven kinds of happiness as well. In recent years the value of hōgi has been enhanced considerably by cash prizes, the Yamada-shi Chamber of Commerce redeeming them for varying amounts reaching as high as $28. The blocks are finally tossed, one at a time, to a crowd of more than a hundred young men at the base of the pagoda. These young men, although the weather may be decidedly chilly on a February night, are naked except for white loin cloths —their nakedness symbolizing purity (in olden times they were supposed to have bathed before the ceremony in a nearby stream) and hence eligibility to catch a sacred talisman.

The point to note is that among the eager crowd of shivering contestants, burakumin are conspicuous indeed. We recognize half-a-dozen young junk burōkā, a shoemaker, a peddler, several shittai—altogether probably one-fourth or so of the almost nude assemblage. Still, neither the crowd of a thousand or more spectators watching from the sidelines, nor the ring of policemen holding them back, seem in the least aware of this interesting fact; they are concentrating solely upon the wild scramble that accompanies the tossing of each *hōgi*.

Are any *burakumin* the fortunate retrievers? One cannot speak about other years, but the day after the festival that we attended we were strolling through the main street of Yamada-shi; there we chanced upon one of our friends from Kawabara whom we had observed from the pagoda with his arms stretched upward in tense readiness. He was now fully clothed, of course, but with a grin that registered because of his missing teeth he allowed us to catch a glimpse of three of the *hōgi*, which he was hugging to himself. Whether he had caught all three, or whether he had made a private deal with other *burakumin* victors, we were never able to learn.

What we did learn was that some sort of deal would have been entirely in character. Indeed, games of chance and sharp bargainings of one sort or another appear to be a special aptitude among Kawabarians—just as junk collecting and peddling, both of which likewise require skill in bargaining, are familiar occupations.

This characteristic may be noted, too, in the popularity of *pachinko* parlors in Yamada-shi. Some Kawabara citizens apparently spend substantial proportions of their daylight hours at this not very lucrative form of authorized gambling. According to Tomita-san, experts can detect slight differences between *pachinko* machines and are thus able, by skillful manipulation, to win as much as $5 or $6 in one full day. This they accomplish by illegally reselling cigarettes and other small prizes back to the parlors at a small margin of profit.

Such partially clandestine activities have been controlled at various times by two gangs in Yamada-shi, both of them reported to be headed by *burakumin,* with half of each of their memberships of about 15 likewise *burakumin.* Illegal gambling, both with dice and cards, has been one of their activities, along with collecting from indebted gamblers or bar patrons. A still more lucrative enterprise, so we were informed, has been the "protection money" that they manage to extract from bars, rooms-by-the-hour hotels, and *pachinko* parlors. Bar girls and the abnormally large number of pseudo-*geisha* entertainers have also been involved in both of these gangs, sometimes as mistresses and prostitutes, although what proportion of them are *burakumin* no one was able or willing to say.

During the time of our study, the two gangs were reported by several informants to be fairly quiescent because of police vigilance. Nevertheless, one informant was also sure that they have only been forced to operate more surreptitiously than heretofore and that the gangs' activities are actually gaining not only in Yamada-shi but in other nearby cities such as Hiroi-shi and Utsumi-shi. At any rate, whether gangs or not, it was apparent from our own observations that some Kawabarians find in the entertainment spots of Yamada-shi an unusually congenial environment—so much so that two or three young *burakumin* are even able to earn some sort of livelihood as wandering guitar-playing minstrels in search of tips from more or less inebriated celebrants.

We have been speaking of recreational activities as they relate to Kawabara adults, but little has been said about Kawabara children. A large majority of all households possess—even if they are still paying for them— television sets; unquestionably television exceeds all other forms of entertainment for both adults and children. The community itself, however, has provided almost nothing in the way of play facilities until recently. We have noted that the neglected community center has a small collection of children's books. Another community center not far from the village has conducted free programs for elementary-age Kawabara children which include singing games, card games, and abacus lessons. Children also share a nearby swimming pool on a regular schedule during the hot summer vacation period.

But within the village itself no outdoor recreational facility of any sort had ever been available until the time of our study. At that time a new slide appeared on the grounds of the public bath for the smaller tots to enjoy. Fortunately, a few months later a well-equipped playground that had been planned for several years was also constructed by the city within Kawabara, with financial aid derived principally from prefectural as well as federal funds. Less fortunately, we shall find that the playground has been another source of community dissension.

VII

Meanwhile, what of the educational program itself? That recreational facilities just mentioned overlap with this program is illustrated by the fact that community center activities have been financed by the department of social education. The swimming pool, moreover, is located on the grounds of the nearest elementary school, and Kawabara students who attend the nearest junior high school swim in the latter's pool. In both schools (let us call them, respectively, Nanyō Shōgakkō and Kitano Chūgakkō) students are also free to participate in all sports and other extracurricular activities. If they do not do so as vigorously as other children, this is largely because, so a teacher informant, Obara-san, believed, they are not on the average as strong.

Neither school, of course, is limited to *burakumin*, although these are the two nearest to Kawabara. Nanyō Shōgakkō is less than a ten-minute walk from Kawabara, and Kitano Chūgakkō is barely 20 minutes distant.

In the former school, consisting of the first six grades, about 80 children, or 35 percent of the total student body of nearly 300, are *burakumin*. In the latter school, consisting of the next three grades, there are about 55 *burakumin* children, making up 5 percent of a student body, which totals over a thousand. Six more children from Kawabara are enrolled in the two senior high schools, and we heard of two attending college—one, we already know, is the son of our truck driver, Kataoka-san; the other is a son of Councilman Hayashi. Thus it will be seen that most Kawabara children leave school as soon as the law allows—at the average age of 15. More graphically, about 10 percent of all *burakumin* children in recent ninth-grade classes continue on to senior high school, as compared with 85 percent of the entire class of Yamada-shi children who do so.

Before graduating from Kitano Chūgakkō, *burakumin* children are often given economic help to pay for study materials, class excursions, and other school expenses. Thus, among the third-year group of about 20 from Kawabara whom we became acquainted with, over half were receiving such help out of special city and federal funds provided for this purpose. Moreover, although the public employment office in Yamada-shi tries to place all ninth-grade graduates, only about one-third of the *burakumin*, so we were told by Principal Matsuo of Kitano Chūgakkō, are able to meet standards established by companies seeking new employees. The other two-thirds are dependent upon relatives to get them started in jobs—a precarious dependence indeed, since only a minority of relatives hold full-time or stable jobs themselves.

Burakumin children are also affected by at least three features of the course of study that are not equally applicable to other children. The first is a special class for slow learners; each of the two schools has one such class. About half of the children in these classes, according to the superintendent of schools, Kondō-san, are *burakumin*—a condition he attributed chiefly to the high rate of endogamy. (Another 15 teen-agers from Kawabara, in the judgment of Obara-san who teaches in Kitano Chūgakkō, are emotionally disturbed.)

A second feature is the division of third-year students during the final semester into two groups, those who are going on to senior high school and those who are not. The latter, since they are prevocational students, include almost all of the *burakumin*. In the opinion of Teacher Obara, this group loses much of its interest in education as soon as the division occurs, caring little thereafter about academic requirements or routine rules of the school.

The third feature is a venturesome program which we must consider further called *dōwa kyōiku*. This may be translated as "education for integration" or, as interpreted by Social Director Ueno, "education for the peaceful solidarity of people." *Dōwa kyōiku*, although developed on a national scale to cope primarily with problems generated by the position of *burakumin* in Japanese culture, is by no means limited to them. In Yamada-shi, for example, it is given at least cursory attention throughout the curriculum, whether children of *burakumin* are involved or not, although one elementary school—Nanyō Shōgakkō, appropriately—has developed *dōwa kyōiku* more systematically than has any other school in Yamada-shi.

Nor is *dōwa kyōiku* limited merely to teachers and children. Adults, too, are involved. In fact, several leaders in Kawabara attend annual all-Japan conferences, with travel costs again provided out of public funds. Similarly, they attend national conferences in Kyoto sponsored by Buraku Mondai Kenkyūsho (Research Institute on Buraku Problems). This organization is often in sharp opposition to *dōwa kyōiku*.

The zeal with which a few *burakumin* leaders participate in Yamada-shi education is indicated still further by their role in PTA activities. One vice-president out of three in the junior high school Kitano Chūgakkō PTA is presently from Kawabara, although at other times *burakumin* not only have occupied the majority of important offices but have dominated much of the program as well. In Nanyō Shōgakkō, the elementary school, seven out of 22 PTA officers are from Kawabara, including one vice-president. Moreover, one of the officers, Hirose-san, an informant who apparently depends almost entirely upon economic aid, devotes most of his time to this school. On several of our visits to the school he was invariably sitting with the principal discussing school activities of interest to the PTA, such as *jidōkai* and *kodomokai*—children's organizations recalled from our study of Ebibara.

One other adult organization related to education may be found within Kawabara. This is *fujin-gakkyū*, a women's study group. Weekly meetings receive modest financial support once more from the social education department. Its principal activities are *ikebana* (flower arrangement), *sadō* (tea ceremony) lessons, and incidental lessons in cooking. As we turn to the next chapter we shall find that *fujin-gakkyū*, too, is beset by tensions and conflicts that seem chronic to Kawabara's struggle for emancipation.

5

THE STRUGGLE
FOR EMANCIPATION
IN KAWABARA

I

The busiest time of day in Kawabara, judging by the number of men, women, and children who are walking about, is around sunset. Dozens are seen headed in the same direction or returning. Many are carrying towels, and if the weather is warm the men and boys are usually garbed only in white shorts. Often they stop to chat and banter. Clearly this is a time to relax and to socialize.

The magnet of attraction is of course the public bath. Unless one counts seasonal swimming pools available to children attending the two nearby schools, the public bath is the only facility for bathing available to virtually all of the approximately 150 households. Like thousands of other similar facilities in Japanese towns and cities, it is divided by an inside wall—one section for men and boys, the other for women and girls. Water is heated by a furnace on the premises, and each patron is charged a few cents for the service. The public bath is a great boon to life in Kawabara.

Yet, a former Yamada-shi mayor, who sponsored the project, epitomized the events leading to its establishment as "the bathhouse revolution." Certainly no event in the history of Kawabara illustrates more graphically how disturbed the community is or how potentially explosive its collective feelings are. Everyone in the village including the *kumi* leaders of *jichikai* seemed to agree, to be sure, that the bath was desperately needed. The nearest one available beyond Kawabara was at least a 15-minute walk along sometimes muddy and even snowy roads. Whether or not some Yamada-shi citizens may also have preferred that *burakumin* bathe separately from them, and whether this in turn could have spurred the city government to support the project, it was finally carried through at a cost of nearly $10,000, two-thirds being assumed by the federal treasury, the remainder being divided equally between prefecture and city. A running water system was installed about two years later.

Why, then, all the trouble? Why, for example, should the newspapers of Yoneshima-ken have assigned reporters to a routine dedication of a public bath, and then published instead a series of flamboyant stories about what at first glance appeared to be so beneficial and peaceful an achiever---t? Such questions are simple to ask but by no means simple to answer. Several informants brought the subject up themselves; none offered an explanation quite like any other. The only point on which agreement seemed unanimous was that this event, although it occurred several years ago, brought about a cleavage in the community which still remains both wide and deep.

As far as we are able to tell, the facility took much longer to build than would have been the case if controversy over its location had not early developed. Here, as in every recent issue arising in Kawabara, our councilman informant, Hayashi-san, played a central part. He and his followers in Dōwakai, the *burakumin* organization of which we learned in the last chapter and of which he is leader, preferred one site for the building while the opposing organization, Kaihōdōmei, preferred another. Apparently Kaihōdōmei won—indeed, since it had first petitioned the city to build the bathhouse, it decided to take major credit for the whole accomplishment. On the day scheduled for a banquet and celebration to dedicate the building, Kaihōdōmei placed its official flag, crimson in color, on the bathhouse roof and surrounded the building with members and sympathizers carrying many other flags.

By the time the mayor, vice-mayor, and other officials arrived in Kawabara the village was in turmoil. Dōwakai members protested loudly at Kaihōdōmei's belligerent tactics. The plan to have a Shintō priest purify the bath with proper rituals was canceled and the mayor substituted for him. The vice-mayor was shoved about, his necktie pulled, and there were other incidents on the edge of violence. The banquet was never held. Instead, Councilman Hayashi arranged to have the building closed, contending that it belonged to the city and not to Kaihōdōmei. Some members of the latter, meanwhile, contended that Hayashi-san's countertactics were motivated solely by his desire to regain the initiative from Kaihōdōmei and to take major credit for the bathhouse himself. At any rate, before it was opened for regular use, each organization was blaming the other for the whole fiasco. They continue to blame each other to this day.

II

That "the bathhouse revolution" was symptomatic of a vastly more complex situation would not be denied by any thoughtful observer, *burakumin* or not. Like Ebibara with its struggles to cope with changes extending both in cause and effect far beyond its own borders as a fishing community, so Kawabara is ensnared by a network of problems that not only reach deep into history but color the whole fabric of contemporary Japanese culture. If anything, Kawabara is in some ways the symbol of a conflict situation still more challenging to comprehend, much less to resolve, than is Ebibara. Particularly is this the case in one crucial respect: although we found that *gyomin* suffer from discriminatory treatment, they have not been its victims to anything like the extent that *burakumin* have. They have never been regarded outright as pariahs.

It becomes necessary, accordingly, to obtain greater perspective upon the struggles of Kawabara, and thus to review briefly the historical conditions leading to the present pattern of ghettolike segregation. This pattern still largely prevails in some 6000 communities of *burakumin*, with a population variously estimated at between one and three million Japanese citizens.[1]

Lafcadio Hearn once wrote, "Nobody can now tell the history of these outcast folk: the cause of their social excommunication has long been forgotten."[2] Happily, a great deal of historical research has since been conducted, chiefly of course by Japanese scholars but also by Americans and others. Not so happily, much of this research still leaves a good deal to be desired. Not only is its quality sometimes mediocre (most prestigious Japanese scholars studiously ignore the subject), but it is often treated from points of view reflecting some of the same differences of perception and interpretation that we have begun to observe even in so humble a community as Kawabara itself. The sketch that we now provide reflects some of these same deficiencies; nevertheless, we have tried as far as possible to present a composite of influential treatments.[3]

---

[1] Sharp variations in figures are sometimes revealed in a single source. Thus in Takashi Tōjō (ed.), *Ningen Mina Kyōdai (All Human Beings are Brothers)* (Kyoto: Chōbunsha, 1965), the figures of 6000 *burakumin* communities and three million population are indicated in some pages while lower figures are indicated in others. This disparity is due largely to the fact that no official census of *burakumin* is available. The actual number is probably somewhere between the low and the high.

[2] Lafcadio Hearn, *Japan—An Attempt at Interpretation* (New York: The Macmillan Company, 1904), p. 273.

[3] For sources, consult Appendix IV, Bibliographical Notes.

Several theories have been advanced to explain the emergence of *burakumin*. It has been said, for example, that they were originally Korean and Chinese immigrants, even Filipinos or descendants of a Hebrew tribe. Such racial theories were popular toward the end of the nineteenth century and again during the period of fascist nationalism in the 1930s; they still have a few advocates. Consensus now prevails, however, that *burakumin* are as purely Japanese as anyone else. Their emergence must therefore be explained on other than ethnic grounds.

The most influential alternative contends in general that *burakumin* are the product of a class and caste order that underwent various transformations over the course of approximately two thousand years of Japanese history. Slavery, for example, was an accepted institution in the first century A.D., and doubtless many slaves were captives of war from the Asian mainland. Status levels, moreover, were clearly defined by the third and fourth centuries. Although *burakumin* as we now know them did not appear as a distinct group until much later, their precursors were numerous.

Particularly conspicuous were *senmin* (lowly people) who had emerged by the seventh and eighth centuries. Although near the base of the social pyramid, *senmin* were nevertheless a cut or two above the earlier slave classes from which at least a portion surely descended. This was because some *senmin* developed considerable skill as painters, sculptors, musicians, gardeners, and actors who contributed much to the classical arts. Indeed, they are said to have played a predominant part in shaping Japan's two most original dramatic forms: *nō* and *kabuki*. Other *senmin* were artisans in jewelry, bamboo, rice, straw, and leather. But still others, probably the great majority, were unskilled laborers. These people were assigned to such menial jobs as digging wells and ditches, removing sewage, and obtaining food for dogs and hawks belonging to aristocratic sportsmen, especially those who lived in the national capital, Kyoto, and who were devoted to the popular sport of falconry.

Food catchers are especially important to our story because of the name for their occupation, *etori*. Its shortened form, *eto*, eventually became corrupted, according to various historians, into the term *eta*. The Chinese characters for this term are sometimes translated as "defilement abundant," which in less elegant language is often taken to mean simply "very dirty." The term *eta* is still the most common label used for *burakumin* by non-*burakumin* and sometimes even by *burakumin* themselves, and it is considered just as insulting to most *burakumin* as "nigger" is to most Negroes (except when they use it among themselves, often in a bantering way)—so much so that for a time after *burakumin* had been formally granted equal rights the term was prohibited by law. Under such circumstances, we cannot avoid wondering about the insensitivity of several American scholars who in their own writings persist in the use of *eta* without apology.[4] It is as though Japanese scholars were to publish accounts in their learned journals of "Niggers in America." For decades the preferred term has been *burakumin*, meaning simply people who are residents of hamlets, although even now the term may be qualified as *tokushu burakumin* (residents of special hamlets; that is, segregated people).

But why was the work of *etori* in earlier times considered so defiling? Here the influence of both orthodox Shintoism and Buddhism was doubtless important—Shintoism, because of its high regard for spiritual and physical purity, including abhorrence of blood (recall the taboos mentioned in Ebi-bara); Buddhism, because of its key principle of the sanctity of all life. True, long before Buddhism swept Japan, meat was common enough as a food and eventually became so again. But, as Buddhism grew in influence, sanctions against meat-eating also came to be loudly proclaimed; these sanctions at the same time conveniently reinforced economic pressures to preserve horses and other stock threatened by periods of drought.

What thus began as a fairly restricted and simple occupation slowly developed into a whole group of major ones, all involving the handling of animals—butchering, skinning, bone and leather processing, burying. These occupations are perpetuated to this day by the several Kawabara residents who make slippers, sell shoes door to door, and own or work in meat markets. Added to this circumstance was the fact that meats, including entrails, must have been eaten by these people simply because, unlike the grains available to farming people, little other food was accessible.

Yet it would be in error historically to suggest that *senmin* who originally became involved in such "defiling" occupations were inevitably or exclusively the direct ancestors of present-day *burakumin*. Between the dawn of Japanese Buddhism in the sixth century and the mature feudalism that emerged a millennium later, social upheavals were frequent. Farmers and artisans were struggling intermittently for greater freedom, warriors and regional rulers were fighting for more and more power, some *senmin* succeeded in becoming land owners, and on occasion even the lowliest joined with others above them in revolts against the extreme poverty and oppressions of the long era.

In any case, motley groups of lowly artisans and unskilled workers were often relegated to fringe areas of the larger towns under the name, *eta*. Here they were gradually joined by increasing numbers of beggars, gravediggers, cremators, vagabonds, outlaws, debtors, and other disfranchised souls known as *hinin*. The two groups thus tended to be linked together and *eta-hinin* became a familiar term, as did *kawaramono*. This term referred to people

---

[4] Cf. Appendix IV, Bibliographical Notes.

who lived at the edge of rivers where land may be useless or floods often threaten, but where the flowing streams could also be utilized for such trades as leather and butchering.

The foundations thus were tortuously laid for the full-fledged appearance of *burakumin*, the ancestors of Kawabarians. This event did not occur until the feudal Tokugawa (Edo) era, an era that extended over the largest part of three centuries, from the early seventeenth to the final third of the nineteenth. The emergence of feudalism was accompanied by tremendous upheavals in which even occasional *eta-hinin* or *kawaramono* succeeded in becoming warriors and landlords. Yet, uncounted numbers of the lowest classes were cast more ruthlessly than ever into segregated areas, where they were compelled to work at specified trades. Leather work became especially important because of its usefulness during long civil wars, most notably in the production of saddles, drums, and protective armor against swords and arrows. Slumlike communities of *burakumin* can still be seen today situated in the shadow of the great castles of *daimyō* (feudal lords) that survive in Nagoya, Matsuyama, Kochi, and other cities.

The single most important influence leading to the appearance of *burakumin* as a pariah class was, however, the formation of a rigid status structure by the great feudal ruler, Ieyasu Tokugawa, who brought peace to Japan at the cost of virtually absolute power for himself and his heirs. Status, occupation, and residence were all predetermined and proclaimed as eternally unchangeable, a system that successfully prevented any unification of forces that might have led to revolt. There were three large categories— aristocrats, citizens, and *eta-hinin*—all three in turn being subdivided into fixed levels. Thus farmers and merchants belonged to the middle category, whereas feudal lords, warriors, and priests belonged to the upper category. *Eta-hinin*, too, had their internal hierarchies; one family was regarded as chief of them all and passed down its position of status through many generations. Yet to all classes above them *eta-hinin* were considered so extremely low (even their usefulness as artisans of war implements was no longer in demand) that such groups as farmers and merchants who themselves were treated as inferior beings by the aristocratic class found comfort in the assurance that others were still more inferior.

This assurance was reinforced by sumptuary laws. Although strict etiquette was prescribed among various classes, *eta-hinin* were required by the early eighteenth century to wear certain kinds of clothing and slippers, to avoid conventional hair styles, to stay out of other households, to remain in their own hovels at night, and to prostrate themselves before citizens upon meeting them. Even their family records were segregated in the official archives. Lafcadio Hearn epitomizes their condition in a poignant sentence: "Between the lowest of the commercial classes and the Eta, the barrier was impassable as any created by caste-tradition in India; and never was a Ghetto more separated from the rest of a European city by walls and gates, than an Eta settlement from the rest of a Japanese town by social prejudice. No Japanese would dream of entering an Eta settlement unless obliged to do so in some official capacity."[5]

Nevertheless, with the deterioration of feudalism in the late eighteenth and early nineteenth centuries, *burakumin* began, at first timidly, to protest their lot. Some joined with farmers in revolts against ruthless landlordism, although others were enlisted to fight against such rebellious groups. At any rate, the Meiji Restoration of 1868 finally repudiated the Tokugawa era and ushered in the era known as modern Japan. Three years later, in 1871, the Emancipation Act was passed. It proclaimed full economic and political rights for all those now called *shin-heimin* (new citizens). But the act was perfunctory. Although a few non-*burakumin* leaders sought genuine reform, the new democratically inclined government of the Meiji era did as little to implement its own proclamation as the United States government did after the Civil War.

The parallel is striking in other ways. Farmers and other groups resented vociferously and at times violently any attempts at equalization for *burakumin;* no doubt such a change would threaten their own lowly status. (But upper-class intellectuals were not always supporters of emancipation either; thus it is reported that a teacher of Crown Prince Hirohito once proposed that *burakumin* be sent en masse to the South Sea Islands.) Meanwhile, the Meiji regime discouraged exclusive enterprises for particular groups, so that the virtual monopoly in leather and butchering trades that *burakumin* had hitherto reserved for themselves was often taken over by other groups with larger capital. The consequence, of course, was still further shrinkage of income.

The first groping toward emancipation on the part of *burakumin* themselves did not develop for nearly 30 years after the Act of 1871. Only at the turn of the century did groups of young men begin to organize for their cause, but their efforts were too sporadic to be effective. Moreover, they were opposed by some conservative *burakumin*, especially those who had somehow managed to rise a rung or two up the class and status ladder. To be sure, a few strikes by leather workers occurred, some *burakumin* publications began to appear, and a famous novel *Hakai (Transgression)* aroused

[5] Hearn, *op. cit.*, p. 273.

many readers for the first time to the plight of *burakumin*. Yet, by and large, other more pressing problems, particularly wars, preoccupied the Japanese people.

It was not until 1921 and 1922 that a momentous step forward occurred. Suiheisha (Organization of Levellers, a term borrowed directly from English history) was organized in Kyoto with some 2000 delegates present. Here is a quotation from its declaration of principles:

> People of the special communities . . . throughout the Country, unite! To our long-suffering brethren.
>
> The fact that the reformative undertakings attempted in our behalf by many men and by recourse to various methods during the past half-century have not brought any appreciable results should be taken as due punishment for the violation of the sanctity of humanity by us and others. And when we realize that these sympathetic movements, on the contrary, have degraded many of our brethren, it is inevitable that we should organize a collective movement at this time by which we may emancipate ourselves by our own effort by means of self-respect. . . .
>
> Our ancestors worshipped freedom and equality, and practised these principles; they were the victims of despicable class rule; they were manly martyrs of industry; they were skinned alive in recompense for their work in skinning animals; their warm hearts were ripped out as the price for stabbing the hearts of animals; and they were spat at with the spittles of ridicule. Yet, all through these cursed nights of evil dreams, the glorious human blood has kept on flowing. And we, who have been born of this blood, have come to live in an age when men may turn into gods. The time has come when the oppressed shall throw off the brand-mark of martyrdom, and the martyr with the crown of thorns shall receive blessing.[6]

In another dramatic manifesto, issued about a year later, Suiheisha also declared, in part:

> Comrades: Proletarians of the whole world, oppressed and exploited by the capitalists of Europe, of America, and of Japan, all the oppressed nationalities under the yoke of capitalistic imperialism, we appeal to you!
>
> We, the *eta* people in the Far Eastern corner of the earth, who have been oppressed and insulted for a thousand years past, appeal to you, who are fighting valiantly the final class war with blood-thirsty capitalism!
>
> We, the *eta*, are the Jews of Japan, and if there is any difference in social position between the real Jew and us, ours is in all probability

---

[6] Quoted in Shigeaki Ninomiya, "An Inquiry Concerning the Origin, Development, and Present Situation of the *Eta* in Relation to the History of Social Classes in Japan," *The Transactions of The Asiatic Society of Japan*, Second Series, vol. X (1933), pp. 128f.

worse. We are the remnants of the ancient slave system in Japan. We have been totally deprived of the liberty to choose occupations, but are forced to slaughter animals, to tan skins, to mend clogs, and no more. We have had no human rights. What we have received from society in general is but mockery. Thus our forefathers lived in dark resignation with unquenchable curses. No wonder, then, that when many attempts to save us failed, these age-long curses and desperation crystallized into our vehement revolutionary movement of to-day. The rise of the *Suihei-sha*, through which we intend to liberate ourselves by our own efforts, is the outcome.[7]

Thus Suiheisha, obviously enough, was influenced almost from the outset by Marxian ideas and particularly by the appearance of the Japan Communist party which was formed at the same time. That Suiheisha was quickly infiltrated by political radicals, and that the goal of emancipation came to be interpreted in the context of the class struggle and the classless society, is an indisputable and paramount fact in its history. In 1925, the man who was to become the single most famous leader of *burakumin*, Jiichirō Matsumoto, was elected chairman of the annual Suiheisha convention, and from then until his death in 1967 his influence as a left-wing Socialist and national Senator was prodigious. At one time, in fact, he was expelled from the Diet for refusing to placate himself before the Emperor, although he was later reinstated. He spent various periods of his life in prison and died in office.

But Suiheisha soon became badly split internally over ideological disputes of whether or not to regard the history and struggles of *burakumin* primarily in terms of the Marxian interpretation of history or more pluralistically and moderately. The term "conciliationism" *(yūwa-shugi)* entered the dispute often and the question was whether and, if so, how *burakumin* should attempt to conciliate or compromise with other sections of the population, including the government. Thus, although Suiheisha claimed a membership of some 200,000, it was rarely unified. Frequently a virtual stalemate prevailed; at other times it veered from its original policy of extreme aggressiveness toward the liberal and democratic mood that captured the enthusiasm of many Japanese in the 1920s.

Concentration upon economic problems and the necessity for *burakumin* farmers as well as workers to affiliate with the growing labor movement were often urged, but so too was vocal expression reinforced by direct action. Chapters of Suiheisha became involved in numerous struggles in behalf of their rights, which sometimes led to boycotts of schools, refusals

[7] Quoted in Ninomiya, *op. cit.*, p. 144. It should be noted that *eta* is used here by *burakumin* themselves, but within a decade or so later it was almost entirely rejected.

to pay taxes, withdrawal from civic organizations, and numerous arrests. Finally, as Japan moved into the nationalist-fascist period leading to World War II, Suiheisha (although it managed for a time to hold together more or less illegally) suffered from such bitter persecution and suppression that in 1940 it disbanded.

Not until the war had ended and a new democratic Constitution which prohibited discrimination against any citizens had been adopted, did Senator Matsumoto and his associates decide to organize a new and militant group. The Buraku Emancipation National Committee, formed in 1946, grew quickly and became so politically effective that it was soon able to send three *burakumin* to the Diet as Senators in the House of Councilors and six to the House of Representatives. Matsumoto-san's own popular vote was so extraordinary that he even served for a time as vice-chairman of the House of Councilors. Nine years later, in 1955, the National Committee changed its name to Buraku Kaihōdōmei, the organization with which we were earlier becoming acquainted and which remains today the most aggressive national spokesman.

Once more, however, not without dissent. Just as Suiheisha had often been riddled with internal disputes of policy and tactics, so too has its heir. To be sure, Kaihōdōmei has remained under the strong influence of leftist coalitions, but latter-day *burakumin* "conciliationists" have objected to them. Almost as soon, indeed, as the new organization was launched, splinter groups in various localities began to appear so that, by 1960, the gap was too wide to bridge and a new national organization, Dōwakai, was formed. Its leaders were Liberal Democratic politicians; for example, one of its recent national chairmen, Masao Yanai, has been a *burakumin* member of the House of Representatives. Like Kaihōdōmei, its headquarters are in Tokyo, but also like the latter its strength lies chiefly in local chapters to one of which, in Kawabara, we have already been introduced.

The general orientation of Dōwakai may be epitomized by this statement of national policy:

> It is in the spirit of democracy to solve Burakumin problems through cooperation with the political party which the majority of people support, since Burakumin problems are those of the entire nation. Because they must be considered as realistic problems, Dōwakai does not advocate an immature utopia or a revolutionary view based on radical thought . . . [It] opposes resolutely distorted education for the realization of the class struggle.[8]

[8] Zen Nippon Dōwakai, *Dai Gokai Zenkoku Taikai Shiryō* (Materials for the Fifth National Meeting) (Tokyo, 1964), pp. 4, 34.

III

Kawabara was established during the Tokugawa era, probably about two centuries ago. The original community specialized in leather artisanship such as drum-making. In the midnineteenth century, only about ten households were gathered here on the riverside, and even several decades later it consisted of a hamlet of less than 50 families, roughly one-third of the present number. The big influx occurred in the 1930s during the period when the city was an important military center. Today, although a few *burakumin* continually move out, others constantly move in, particularly people who have found it too difficult to make a living elsewhere and who find in Kawabara a harbor of security.

In these respects as well as in several others, Kawabara is more similar to than different from other segregated communities in Yoneshima-ken—such at least is the judgment of the prefectural government specialist on *burakumin* problems, Yamasaki-san. The majority of the ten or more thousands who live in these communities are more dependent on economic aid and on jobs for unemployed workers than on any other resource. The chief exception, apparently, is a *burakumin* village of hard-working farmers not far from Yamada-shi, many of whom are also part-time peddlers.

This is not to suggest that Kawabara is merely a prototype. Each community of *burakumin*, no less than other kinds, has its own unique features. Thus Yamasaki-san regards Kawabara as considerably below the average of the total of nearly 50 in Yoneshima-ken, but in an interesting way: the village environment, he thinks, may be somewhat above average, the economic level somewhat below, but the "emotional situation" is very near the lowest of all *burakumin* communities under his jurisdiction.

Here we return to the internal conflicts which we saw coming to a head at the close of our overview of *burakumin* history, and which were already approaching an explosive stage in "the bathhouse revolution." Indeed, if we adopt Yamasaki-san's own characterization and for the moment consider Kawabara's situation most crucially as an "emotional" one, terms like "schizophrenic" are suggestive. When we regard a schizophrenic patient as one in whom two parts of his personality tend to be divided from one another, then Kawabara tempts just such an analogy. But, also like other analogies, this one is far from perfect. We have already observed how the group of *jichikai* leaders, although members of opposing organizations, are still on occasion able to act in concert. It was they who originally supported the public bath; it was they, or at any rate six of them, who offered to cooperate with our own study;[9] and it was they who unanimously endorsed the recent proposal to build a playground for Kawabara children.

[9] Cf. Appendix I, Research Methodologies: Ebibara and Kawabara.

Even so, obstacles encountered in any attempt to achieve communal unity in behalf of the common cause of emancipation are exemplified again by this latter proposal. As in the case of the public bath, charges and countercharges were far more profuse than cooperative actions. Likewise, as in the earlier case, much of the dissension was over the question of location. Strips of public land near the riverbank had seemed the most feasible spot; hence a petition in its favor, circulated by the *jichikai* officers themselves, was endorsed by Kawabara households overwhelmingly. Was the playground project finally to move from blueprint to reality?

Not yet. Many months after the petition reached city hall, weeds continued to grow on the selected location and another stifling summer came and went while Kawabara children played on the single dusty street or in refuse-littered lots. Moreover, if we are to believe an upper-echelon *jichikai* leader who lives perhaps a mile from Kawabara, one impressive explanation for the delay brings us back again to the tactics of our *burakumin* councilman, Hayashi-san. Sometime in the past, according to this explanation, riverside strips of land had been rented from the city for trivial sums by Kawabara residents, ostensibly for gardens but recently for little except rubbish piles. In any case, among those who rented these strips, and who in turn arranged to subrent from a number of strip-holders for even more trivial sums (a few cents for each strip), was Councilman Hayashi himself.

In the playground petition not a single Kawabara citizen requested reimbursement of these rentals. Nevertheless, we were told that Hayashi-san expected the city to compensate all renters, of whom he was the largest—a total close to $6000. This amount exceeded the entire budget for playground construction. Finally, although not without vituperative exchanges between him and the mayor of Yamada-shi, a compromise settlement was reached and a small fraction of the demanded payment made. Only then, although plans for the playground had begun nearly four years earlier and funds had been appropriated some months before, did construction actually start. At the same time, it became feasible to release adjacent strips of land on which half-a-dozen small dwellings have now been erected and are rented by the city; these are occupied by a few of the more desperate Kawabara families included in a prefectural study of substandard housing among *burakumin*.

Shall we accept the *jichikai* leader's explanation? Probably not altogether. Councilman Hayashi himself insisted that after all it was he, Kawabara's sole elected representative, who had acted to seek public funds for the playground and new dwellings in the first place. Moreover it was he, he said, who had persuaded *jichikai* to accept a slight increase in the public bath fee (up to about four cents, the lowest in the city) that the city council had requested, in return for which he would persuade his political colleagues to support the playground venture. Besides, how could anyone wish to benefit financially from a facility designed solely for the children's welfare?

Behind the pros and cons of this incident, nevertheless, are three major factors. The first two we have begun to consider: on the one hand, the mutual hostility of Kaihōdōmei and Dōwakai; on the other hand, the community power structure. The third factor centers in the relations of Kawabara to the outside world, not only to Yamada-shi and Yoneshima-ken but, as our quotations from Suiheisha foretell, to Japan and the world as a whole. In the remainder of this chapter, we propose to examine further all three of these factors as they affect the dynamics of Kawabara culture. In the next chapter we return to some of them again.

IV

The fact that *jichikai* leaders had succeeded in forming something of a united front on the question of the playground should not lead us to suppose that Dōwakai and Kaihōdōmei had at last resolved their dispute. Councilman Hayashi himself was explicit on this point, and accused Kaihōdōmei "behind the scenes" of blocking his efforts. Its leaders were fearful, he contended, that Dōwakai would receive too much credit if the playground were actually built. Our co-op worker, Nozu-san, himself a loyal Kaihōdōmei member, agreed that Dōwakai and especially Chairman Hayashi would gain in community status, and felt that this would be unfortunate. Actually neither Dōwakai nor Kaihōdōmei, Nozu-san felt, were sufficiently concerned with the playground to take much initiative. From our own perspective, whether the alleged low level of enthusiasm was due more to community lassitude than to the fact that a project for children does not, after all, offer a suitable forum in which to vent personal and ideological hostilities, it would be difficult to say.

It is not difficult, however, to adduce further evidence that these hostilities are rife. In the words of Tomita-san, Kaihōdōmei prefectural leader, the two locals effectively "paralyze each other." Let us illustrate further.

A number of informants both in and out of the community recalled how Hayashi-san, who had originally been a president of Kawabara's Kaihōdōmei chapter, was openly accused of absconding with public funds. These funds had been provided from city and prefectural treasuries to finance a new regional publication for *burakumin*. The accusation was made by another informant, Hatano-san (he divides his time between peddling, farming, and *shittai* or public project labor), who went so far as to distribute throughout Yamada-shi several thousand copies of a circular inserted in the morning newspaper which detailed his charges. In return, Hayashi-san, pointing out that one issue of the newspaper had been published, sued Hatano-san for libel. The dispute was finally shelved when the councilman withdrew from Kaihōdōmei and organized Dōwakai. Hatano-san then became president of the Kaihōdōmei chapter. But soon Mitsuda-san, our slipper-maker informant, issued his own printed circular and challenged Hayashi-san to defend before the public not only his grounds for the suit but several other incidents, such as his role in the bathhouse conflict, his allegedly "violent" language in the city council, and his withdrawal both from Kaihōdōmei and the Socialist party.

Yet, quite surprisingly, none of the three Kaihōdōmei leaders just mentioned—Tomita-san, Hatano-san, or Mitsuda-san—should be regarded as Councilman Hayashi's most powerful opponent. Rather, this most powerful opponent is Okubo-san, a non-*burakumin* resident of Yamada-shi, a busy physician, a member of the city council, and the foremost spokesman for the Communist party in Yamada-shi. His influence upon the people of Kawabara is especially felt through two important functions—first, through the group of *burakumin* households who are affiliated with the Communist party and who, though small in number, are aggressive and vocal; second, through his profession, since many more *burakumin* are patients of his than of any other physician in the city.

These two functions are not as disparate as they might first seem. As a physician, Dr. Okubo has ample opportunity to know Kawabara families, and they in turn have often come to respect him for his sympathetic concern with their troubles. Still more pragmatically, it is he who signs the majority of health certificates that not only qualify local *burakumin* for free medical services but that specify frequent physiological disabilities. Many of the Kawabara citizens on economic aid are able to document that they are incapable of regular employment.

Thus Dr. Okubo, finding *burakumin* to be promising recruits for the Communist party, often visits Kawabara not merely as a physician but as a politician. He regards Dōwakai, of course, as merely a pawn of the controlling class; since its leaders are members of the Liberal Democratic party, they prove to be political servants of Japanese capitalism and international imperialism. To promote his cause still further and thus to persuade *burakumin* that they are the victims of exploitation, a separate group has been formed in Kawabara which attempts to influence the membership of Kaihōdōmei, Jirō workers, and other citizens. Called the Association for Protection of Life and Health, it is a national Communist-affiliated organization for people on economic aid. Not all who attend its meetings are party members, but Dr. Okubo and his comrades make sure that party policy governs its program.

This program focuses, understandably, upon the theory and practice of class struggle. Indeed, the struggle for emancipation is held to be futile otherwise, a position more or less shared by a majority of national Kaihō-dōmei leaders as well as by rank-and-file members, including Kawabarians. Even though most of these, furthermore, are certainly not Communists, many have come to prefer Dr. Okubo to Councilman Hayashi—a preference indicated in a recent election when the latter received fewer Kawabara votes than his opponent (but both were elected), and despite the fact that the latter is a *burakumin* while Dr. Okubo is not. As the shoemaker, Akie-san, another informant and one of the very few male non-*burakumin* living in the village, put it, that particular election was one of such "indescribable conflict" and bitterness that in more than one case brother turned against brother.

Although one would be exaggerating to assert that most *burakumin* admirers of Dr. Okubo are sophisticated in their grasp of the theory of class struggle (on the contrary, we shall later produce evidence to reveal remarkable degrees of moderation and even conservatism in Kawabara[10]), one would not be exaggerating to point out that at least a minority are familiar with this kind of practice. The point is dramatized whenever workers in the unemployment program who are members of Jirō (All-Japan Free Labor Union) demonstrate or picket. We ourselves observed a noisy demonstration outside the Yamada-shi city hall where red Kaihōdōmei and Jirō flags were prominent indeed. On another occasion Jirō demonstrators surrounded the homes of the mayor and director of social welfare and, if our informant Ueno-san is correct, kept both officials "captive" for the better part of a day. On the principle, moreover, that such issues as higher economic aid are never exclusively *burakumin* issues, Jirō extends invitations to other unions to participate in such demonstrations. These are sometimes accepted.

Within our entire panel of Kawabara informants almost none denied, whatever their organizational allegiance, that class conflict is an important phenomenon of Japanese political-economic life. Only one, Taura-san, the junk entrepreneur, mentioned the rising middle class as possibly tending to placate the conflict, although he and his wife favor the Communist party. Nozu-san, a Socialist by preference, held that, notwithstanding a rising per capita income, the cleavage is actually widening: under the surface of prosperity, capitalist power becomes more and more consolidated while wages increase disproportionally to the cost of living.

Yet only two or three informants had ever read Marxian sources. One of them, Tanaka-san, the itinerant *burōkā*, at one period subscribed to a Communist newspaper, but changed his allegiance from Socialist to Liberal

10 Cf. for example, pp. 185–188.

Democrat because, he maintained, the Socialist party seems too concerned with workers who belong to the huge Sōhyō unions and too little concerned with the weak and unorganized. As we remember, Hayashi-san (a brother-in-law, incidentally, of Tanaka-san) also changed his allegiance, his own professed reason being the "prejudice" he felt among members who resented a *burakumin* as their city chairman. But even while still a Socialist, not only did he experience a "nervous feeling" about class struggle; at no time did he regard himself as a follower of Marxism. True, although he said he had opposed Japanese militarism and nationalism, and although as an "independent" he occasionally goes so far today as to support the Communist party on a specific piece of legislation, nevertheless he believes that social change must come mainly through "parliamentary processes" and not through the pressure groups and class conflicts that he finds rampant in present-day Japan.

Councilman Hayashi's statements lead us to distinguish still more sharply between the tactics of Kaihōdōmei and Dōwakai. While remembering the contention of Yamasaki-san, prefectural expert, that Kawabara's problems are largely "emotional," we must also remember that both local chapters belong to national movements with programs of action established at national and prefectural conferences. What, then, are these programs?

A Dōwakai meeting of all Yoneshima-ken chapters that we attended appeared to be a rally in behalf of the Liberal Democratic party. To be sure, the national Dōwakai chairman gave a speech, as did Hayashi-san, but so also did the prefectural secretary of this party as well as politicians running for office. The two or three hundred *burakumin* present were urged to support these candidates as the best assurance of their own welfare. After all, they were told, is not the federal government controlled by the Liberal Democratic majority? And is it not true that this majority, sympathetic as it is with Dōwakai's program, has already begun to provide grants for the construction of *burakumin* housing, for *burakumin* education, and for other benefits?

On the national level, Dōwakai platforms of action have emphasized such steps as the following: developing women's auxiliaries, expanding *dōwa kyōiku* (the educational program for emancipation), supporting the expansion of industry, and repudiating the notion sometimes expressed that the safest policy is to avoid any kind of disturbance. But all such advances must be achieved first of all by "enlightenment" (*keimō*), which in turn means understanding and awareness eventuating in "common consent." Here is the guiding procedure.

Compare this procedure with those emphasized in reports of recent prefectural and national Kaihōdōmei conferences. The term *keimō*, for example, is not to be found in any of these reports, but the terms *tōsō* (struggle) and *tatakai* (fighting) are used frequently. Dōwakai must be "crushed," for "conciliationism" is depicted as a "poisoned hand," offering *burakumin* feeble concessions at the price of complacency and compromise. A great deal of stress is placed upon Japan's subservience to American "monopoly capitalism," and the Ministry of Education is accused of retreating from early postwar democratic education to reactionary policies. Stress is also placed upon the need for unity not only within the *burakumin* minority itself but in solidarity with other people of the working class, including farmers and fishermen. The common tasks of all these people are largely similar to those advanced in the platforms of the Socialist and Communist parties.

Still, it would distort the picture to imply that Kaihōdōmei's strategies are always strictly in line with either or both of these parties. Occasionally Liberal Democrats even hold national leadership positions. About 10 percent of the Kawabara chapter itself, so we were told by its chairman, Hatano-san, consists of Liberal Democratic sympathizers, and, according to Hirose-san, the *burakumin* PTA enthusiast, some local Dōwakai members belong to Jirō. This situation hardly guarantees anything like the solidarity that both Kaihōdōmei and Dōwakai advocate—each, of course, on its own terms. Even so, just as the latter organization maintains a reform program that might be called one of liberal moderation, the former has moved well beyond the confused gropings of Suiheisha, with its furious reactions to centuries of minority isolation. Rather, Kaiōdōmei supports a radical orientation in which *burakumin* differences from other working people are subordinated to their common interests.

Returning to Kawabara, the fact noted above that some overlappings of political and other organizational affiliations do after all occur suggests that, with all its "schizophrenic" symptoms, the community is by no means totally polarized. Certainly both Kaihōdōmei and Dōwakai reject any policy of mere acquiescence or subservience. Nor would ideological disputes be likely to prevent many of its citizens from uniting in the face of what they considered to be an insult to their sense of dignity. Undoubtedly, too, the conflicts that we have described are regarded especially by more thoughtful residents, such as the well-trained co-op employee, Nozu-san, as debilitating in the extreme.

One modest beginning toward rapprochement has been made by the 50 or more Kawabara women nominally affiliated with the city, prefectural, and national women's federation. For example, the wife of our junk dealer, Taura-san, though fervently leftist herself, has recently joined with the hope that possibly Dōwakai and Kaihōdōmei women could reach working agreement at least on higher levels of the federation. This hope has been shared by our woman leader informant, Tabata-san, who though not a *burakumin*

is concerned about Kawabara and is convinced that some progress is being
made through the women's study group, *fujin-gakkyū.*

Yet, even such a noncontroversial topic as how to arrange flowers more
beautifully can cause disputes. No wonder that the wife of Burōkā Tanaka,
a strong Dōwakai supporter, has become pessimistic. Although both organizations are represented on the board of directors, Kaihōdōmei women, she
said, frequently boycott meetings—even a New Year's Party which they
themselves had helped to plan. Whether they do so mainly because they
consider such topics as flower arrangement too innocuous and bourgeois, or
because, unlike Dōwakai women, they want the department of social welfare to defray most of the lesson costs, or simply because of indifference, we
could not clearly determine. Still, it is hardly astonishing that this same
lady, who happens also to be a sister of Councilman Hayashi, confessed to
us that she has no close friend among Kaihōdōmei housewives, although one
neighbor might be considered as a "kind of friend."

V

If the first primary factor in trying to understand the involutions of Kawabara life is interorganizational strife, the second, certainly, is the dynamics
of local power.

Ever since the Tokugawa era (and doubtless vastly earlier in less or-
dered ways), *burakumin* communities have maintained their own internal
hierarchies of status, class, and influence. This is really only to say that these
communities like most others in Japan have retained strong vestiges of their
feudal past. Kawabara is no exception, and in this respect, at least, it is far
more typical than not.

What appears to be less typical is the extent to which hierarchical
control, centering first of all in Hayashi-san, is being constantly challenged.
In this respect the primary factor examined above intermeshes with the
second factor. Although it is true that Dōwakai itself serves as a brake upon
Kaihōdōmei's favorite tactics of aggressive action, it is equally true that,
without Kaihōdōmei, Hayashi-san would less frequently be placed on the
defensive or compelled to make various concessions. With Kaihōdōmei,
however, we have found that Dōwakai's influence is strictly limited—indeed, that the two local chapters, to recall Tomita-san's terse phrase, often
seem to "paralyze each other."

But what, meanwhile, constitutes the source of Hayashi-san's considerable strength? No one, so far as we were able to discover, denies that he is a
shrewd politician and clever businessman. Everyone, moreover, whether
burakumin or not, apparently agrees that he is immensely preoccupied

with his own interests ("selfishness" was the attribute preferred by less charitable critics). Perhaps still more significantly, he has the advantage of a long family history in Kawabara. Both his grandfather and father were full-time land-owning farmers, a remarkable feat for any *burakumin*. Hayashi-san himself goes considerably further in expressing family pride: not only did his father precede him as village representative in wider community affairs; but one of his Kawabara ancestors must have been a Shinto priest, for he recalls that as a boy he inspected family heirlooms once belonging to this man. The implication is, and historians provide considerable support, that some *burakumin*, although not themselves considered well-born, at least were able to climb higher in the social order than feudal patterns ordained.

Yet, none of these contributing conditions seems sufficient to answer our question. Probably most important of all, certainly so in the view of our woman leader, Tabata-san, is the influence of a widespread practice in Japan commonly known as *oyabun-kobun*. Let us quote Beardsley again on the meaning of this practice:

> The *oyabun* is a ritual father who protects or stands as a patron to *kobun* or ritual sons in return for their loyalty or service. He is also their boss and is often referred to by this term, *bosu*, in Japan today; his gang or team of subordinates work under his orders on the job and also must clear with him any significant actions off the job or between jobs. . . . Be it noted that everyone gets some sort of reward for submitting to an *oyabun*; consequently followers remain faithful to their leader when times are hard, as they never would for a man who has used sheer power to subordinate others.

Beardsley adds, however, that *oyabun* and *bosu* are both loosely used in present-day Japan. Actual "rituals" may no longer be performed; rather *oyabun-kobun* relations "are merely tacit hierarchical systems of patronage from above and loyalty from below. . . ."[11]

At any rate, the characterization applies very well to Hayashi-san. Not only is he often called *bosu* both by his friends and foes, but his behavior is consistent with this title. Thus, at a gay pre-New Year's Party in his home where he was surrounded with Dōwakai followers, the convivial host at all times dominated the proceedings and commanded guests intermittently to be quiet when he wished to sing a folk song or make a little speech. Through the years, moreover, he has been able to strengthen his authority by hiring *burōkā* for his junk business, by personal loans to *kobun* in exchange for

[11] John W. Hall and Richard K. Beardsley, *Twelve Doors to Japan* (New York: McGraw-Hill, Inc., 1965), pp. 83f. Cf. Edward Norbeck, *Changing Japan* (New York: Holt, Rinehart and Winston, 1965), p. 5.

their loyalty, by political maneuverings, but most of all, no doubt, by kinship connections.

As noted previously Kawabara is a complex web of such connections, and the Hayashi extended family may be largest of all. Within Dōwakai itself one discovers many close and distant relatives—the number being estimated by different informants as anywhere from 30 to 70 percent of the entire membership. In addition, Hayashi-san has extended his influence through kinship ties well beyond the village: thus in the *burakumin* community of Utsumi-shi one of his daughters is married to the first son of its own *bosu*. This arrangement, according to one admittedly hostile informant, netted Hayashi-san a very substantial fund with which to conduct successfully his first campaign for city councilman.

It is impossible to measure the precise extent to which the powerful values of *giri* and *on*, which we found to be so significant to the Ebibara subculture, are involved in such family and intergroup affairs.[12] Since Kawabara is after all a Japanese community, it does seem plausible to suppose that *oyabun-kobun* must prove to be considerably more than merely a boss-underling device; it must also be strengthened both by the network of kinship relations and by the cluster of traditional values that more or less invariably permeate that network. Let us restate the most influential: *on*, the beneficence extended by a person of superior position to one below him; *ongaeshi*, the obligation created toward the benefactor as a result of *on*; and finally *giri*, the inclusive value of mutual obligation, whether status relations are involved or not.

One must not of course presume that, to the extent a value such as *on* applies also to Kawabara, this fact refers exclusively to Hayashi-san's power constellation. In varying degrees other family networks have their own constellations. The wife of Taura-san, for one, belongs to another of the largest in Kawabara; most of its members are probably more zealously oriented toward Kaihōdōmei than are most members of Hayashi-san's extended family oriented toward Dōwakai. One of her brothers, for example, is the militant leader of the local Communist group; four other brothers, all living within the village, are devoted to Kaihōdōmei; and her husband is surely able, given his staff of *burōkā*, to develop his own *oyabun-kobun* as something of a counterbalance to the councilman's. Nor should we overlook Mitsuda-san, the second most prestigious Kawabara citizen and a long-time rival of Hayashi-san, who frankly conceded his own community influence to be heavily dependent upon kinship ties. Even *yoboshigo* (the waning custom of ritual adoption noted in Ebibara) is still, he said, occasionally practiced.

[12] Cf. pp. 56–57.

We conclude anew, then, that the flow of power within Kawabara is by no means constricted to a single stream. Conceding from our evidence that Hayashi-san remains *bosu* "number one," nevertheless he is unable to control completely even his own extended family. A few of his relatives openly support his strongest political opponent, Dr. Okubo. Others continue to manifest obligations toward him in personal relations—after all, *on* is hardly a tradition that one can shrug away—but in public matters reject his support of the Liberal Democratic party.

Thus, to return to the two competing locals, Kaihōdōmei and Dōwakai, what must have appeared to be a situation of badly confused allegiances may now at least seem understandable. It is hardly surprising that the village president of Dōwakai is a cousin of the prefectural director of Kaihōdōmei, and that both are named Tomita. Some citizens, moreover, presumably belong to Dōwakai because of the power of *giri* or *oyabun-kobun*, or both, yet may vote consistently Socialist. Conversely, a few Kaihōdōmei members may for reasons of family loyalty feel that they must support Councilman Hayashi at election time, yet resist his *oyabun-kobun* in favor of, say, Jirō strategies.

And yet, granting all such countervailing forces, it is neither *oyabun-kobun* nor the extended family with its cluster of customary values that totally accounts, if Mitsuda-san is right, for Kawabara's reservoir of potential power. Rather, it is drastic "economic needs" combined with severe "feelings" that centuries of discrimination have instilled in his people. The time has now arrived, he insists, when these needs and these feelings must finally be galvanized into sufficient strength to achieve full emancipation.

VI

Mitsuda-san's statement provides a bridge from Kawabara, which we have been viewing mainly from inside the community, to its relations with the outside world—the third primary factor of which we spoke earlier.

Perhaps the most graphic evidence of how our *burakumin* friends feel about this outside world is the readiness and frequency with which they relate incidents of discriminative treatment by non-*burakumin*. Many of these incidents have become famous; others are simply personal and local.

One of the most famous, related to us by Kaihōdōmei Leader Tomita, is the story of how, a few years before the Emancipation Act, a young *burakumin* in Edo (later renamed Tokyo) was beaten to death in a quarrel with a young non-*burakumin*. When a leader of the segregated people demanded that the murderer be punished, the chief magistrate of Edo replied that, since the life of a *burakumin* is worth one-seventh of the life of another person, it would be necessary to execute six additional *burakumin* along with the murderer himself.

Tomita-san also displayed the photograph of a half-century-old stone post located only a few miles from Yamada-shi at the entrance to a shrine. Although some incriminating symbols have become blurred, the post still reads, "Dirty persons not allowed to enter." *Burakumin* worshiped in a segregated section of this shrine.

We accompanied Leader Tomita and the Jirō activist, Shōda-san, to another shrine, also near Yamada-shi, where a festival was in progress. Here, too, *burakumin* of a local ghetto seemed to have congregated in one area of the grounds where they performed a traditional dragon dance. Incidentally, we were told that only a few weeks previously one of their own young women had won a beauty contest and had promptly received several proposals of marriage, all of which were withdrawn with equal promptness after her place of residence became known.

Most of our informants related unpleasant personal experiences. Tomita-san himself became involved in a bloody fight with a fellow high school boy who had called him "the square root of 16"—one implication of which is a four-footed animal and hence a being who is regarded as sub-human. (Both boys were expelled and later reinstated, but Tomita-san refused to return.) Four, indeed, has long been the supremely insulting number to *burakumin*. Even the term "B29" is suspect in conversation; it refers to a four-engine plane! Worst of all, if any one holds four fingers up before *burakumin* there is almost sure to be trouble.

Two common incidents involving Kawabara children may be mentioned. In one case, when the teen-age daughter of Entrepreneur Taura became ill and had to stay home from school, a girl friend who wished to visit his daughter in Kawabara was refused permission by the girl's mother. The other incident concerns the same performer in the all-girl theater whom we previously mentioned: when as a high school student she once held a party for school friends in her Kawabara home, one of her guests confessed that she had been instructed by her parents not to eat any "very dirty" (*eta*) food. This incident, according to her mother, precipitated her daughter's decision to withdraw from school; too often, she felt, she had been "treated with contempt."

As might be expected, the most virulent instances of discrimination reported to us occurred in two other areas: job opportunities and relations of the sexes. Repeatedly we were told how men and women have returned to Kawabara to live because they could not obtain steady work. As Taura-san and his wife explained, when two persons of equal competence apply for a job, the non-*burakumin* is almost surely chosen although never of course with any hint of the underlying reason. Even Nozu-san, whom we recall is the only Kawabarian holding a permanent public-service position in Yamada-shi, spoke of sensing in his early associations an undercurrent of hostility on the part of fellow employees, a hostility which largely disappeared as they came to know him. However, he is still sure that no girl among these employees would ever consent to marriage, regardless of how strong the mutual attraction might be.

Such conflicts involving love and marriage were conveyed to us most poignantly by a young *burōkā* on Taura-san's staff. After falling in love with a non-*burakumin* girl in a nearby town, he brought her to Kawabara as his common-law wife. Her father immediately sent police to bring her back home (she was not quite 20 and hence below the legal age for marriage without parental consent) where she was locked inside. A brother-in-law of Taura-san visited her parents to try to persuade them to change their minds, but he was "surrounded by relatives" who remained adamant. Indeed he could only report that the father's face appeared "like a mask of death." Soon after, the young man smuggled a note to her which said, "Whatever happens, I will be waiting for you." The very next day the young bride reappeared in Kawabara. She had escaped from her home and in her bare feet had run to the nearest railroad station where she caught a train to Yamada-shi. Then, knowing that her parents would command her to return, she was spirited to the home of the young man's aunt in a nearby prefecture. She went into hiding, there, and the cooperative aunt managed to have the girl's letters forwarded to her parents from Osaka, where she pretended to hold a job. Two months later, when she reached legal age, she returned to Kawabara. They have since registered their marriage in the city hall.

"My story could become a novel," our young informant said, and perhaps he is right. For, although he contended that several of his Kawabara friends could relate equally eventful tales, his own has reached a climax happier than most. Where no one else could succeed, their lovely baby daughter has reconciled his parents-in-law and him and his wife. Both families have begun to visit each other. "I hope," he concluded, "that my daughter will never have to endure a similar experience, though quite possibly she will." Unfortunately, he reminded us, it is even harder for a young woman than a young man of *burakumin* background to search beyond one's community for a mate.

No wonder the outside world is viewed by many Kawabarians as much more hostile than friendly. No wonder either that, as *burakumin* have learned to unite and to press for what they consider their just rights, their belligerence in turn has encouraged images of themselves to develop among many other Japanese that are even more hostile—images strengthened, of course, by the stubborn persistence of ancient cultural taboos, by centuries of isolation, and by xenophobic fears.

Nor have all *burakumin* outgrown the extremist tactics promoted in earlier decades by their first influential movement, Suiheisha. Although both Dōwakai and Kaihōdōmei now regard its policies as narrowly conceived and clumsily exploited, nonetheless these tactics sometimes continue to manifest themselves not only in the hypersensitivity of individual *burakumin* to allegedly prejudicial attitudes, but likewise in the vociferous and pugnacious demonstrations which Jirō particularly (oftener than not abetted by Kaihōdōmei) constantly promotes.

But whatever one may think of the effectiveness of militant strategies of change, one fact is clear. Within scarcely a generation, *burakumin* in general and Kawabarians in particular have more completely accomplished the feat of calling national attention to their plight and their demands than all the uncounted legions of their ancestors were ever able to accomplish. Though perhaps ironically, it is no small achievement when, for example, the mayor of Yamada-shi confesses (as he frankly did to us) that his single greatest official worry is how to cope successfully with issues the Kawabara people constantly raise. Moreover, *burakumin* are a source of concern, as we shall discover in Chapter 8, to every informant on our leader panel.

Nor is such concern mere verbalizing. Largely because of pressures from Kawabara itself, the city has built a public bath, a playground, and several city-owned houses, installed running water, and constructed a dike along the village riverbank to prevent damage from flash floods. Even more, various levels of the government provide increasing sums for economic aid as well as health and other public services for a large proportion of *burakumin;* help to underwrite programs of both Dōwakai and Kaihōdōmei; and appropriate funds for educational activities such as *fujin-gakkyū* and *dōwa kyōiku.* We must now consider, finally, how other educational activities are mirrored in Kawabara's relations to the public schools of its surrounding city.

VII

Just as the mayor of Yamada-shi considers the community of *burakumin* his single most worrisome problem, so also does the superintendent of schools. In both of the institutions where Kawabara children are enrolled, it became clear to us that their principals, Matsuo-san of the junior high school, Kitano Chūgakkō, and Takagi-san of the elementary school, Nanyō Shōgakkō, are more troubled by the minority of Kawabara students than by all other problems combined.

This concern embraces the other students as well. For, just as conflict situations are found to be chronic within Kawabara itself, fears are constantly expressed that conflicts also will flare up between *burakumin* and other enrollees. That such fears are not wholly without substance may be exemplified by four events reported to us.

In the first event five *burakumin* girls in Kitano Chūgakkō invited several non-*burakumin* of the same second-year class to hold a rendezvous with them after school hours in the yard of another school. There the five girls proposed that the whole group form a "friendship club." All but one of the non-*burakumin* agreed and so, as a ritual popularized in movies, the hosts proposed that all of them cut their fingers slightly with a small knife and mingle drops of blood to symbolize their unity. But the knife only frightened their guests. One girl who had refused the invitation was slapped and told to undress. When her crying deterred them, the "friendship club" collapsed precipitously, and the five Kawabara girls took all the change, about fifty cents, that their guests carried in their purses.

An incident of this kind can disturb many more persons than the few involved directly. The moment that the uncooperative girl revealed it to her parents, they and other parents called upon their city councilman. He in turn informed both the mayor and Superintendent Kondō. Then, since the students were all enrolled in Kitano Chūgakkō, Principal Matsuo became involved and brought together such *burakumin* leaders as Mitsuda-san and Hatano-san, together with the parents of the five Kawabara girls. All of these parents, he said, were apologetic and made no attempt to react with the hostility that he had half expected.

The second event occurred in Nanyō Shōgakkō some time before we arrived. A teacher was accused by *burakumin* parents of applying corporal punishment to three of their sons because the boys had been negligent in attaching their name tags to uniforms according with school rules. The teacher denied the charge, and insisted that he had merely patted their heads gently. A public meeting, with both Superintendent Kondō and Principal Takagi in attendance, was called by Kawabara parents. According to our informant, considerable quantities of *sake* had been consumed prior to the meeting presumably, he said, to fortify some of the fathers who wished to speak up. At any rate, before the issue could be clarified, accusations and counter-accusations became so thunderous that the accused teacher was urged to go home, and soon thereafter the meeting was adjourned by Mitsuda-san, the chairman.

The third event illustrates how Dōwakai-Kaihōdōmei conflicts spill over into the schools. Members of Dōwakai had borrowed a tape recorder from Nanyō Shōgakkō without explaining their purpose. It turned out that the recorder was being used by Dōwakai in a demonstration of its own at City Hall, a demonstration which Kaihōdōmei disavowed. It also insisted that public school property cannot be used for political purposes. The head teacher of Nanyō Shōgakkō forthwith rushed to the demonstration and withdrew the recorder.

The fourth event occurred some years ago, but has left a deep scar. On a field trip of Kitano Chūgakkō students to Osaka and Kyoto, a *burakumin* girl developed pneumonia and subsequently died. The accompanying teachers and principal were accused by *burakumin* parents of negligence, and the case was brought before the city council by the Communist councilman, Dr. Okubo. The principal was finally forced to resign, an event that may well have influenced the ultracautious policies of his successor. So cautious is Principal Matsuo, indeed, that according to our student informant, Anasaki-san, he did nothing when a *burakumin* boy once struck him. Also, whereas he is strict enough about enforcing rules such as "no smoking" on the school grounds so far as non-*burakumin* are concerned, he is said to overlook infractions by *burakumin* students.

Typically Kaihōdōmei remains, of course, the more aggressive of the two organizations in its relations to the schools. Its Communist segment, especially, has opposed parental donations to the cost of school swimming pools on the ground not only that *burakumin* are too poor to contribute but also, no doubt, because such facilities should be entirely provided as a matter of policy out of public funds. (This position is frequently maintained also by Sōhyō unions.) On one occasion it succeeded in reversing a PTA decision to purchase a number of school desks. It has also demanded that more attention be given in the curriculum to *burakumin* problems. Finally, in order to exert greater influence upon school affairs it has maneuvered, as we noted earlier, to have its own leaders elected as local PTA officials. To weaken such previously almost total control, however, Principal Matsuo, so we were informed, has been urging non-*burakumin* to run for office and to send fathers to PTA meetings who can stand up to the vocal Kawabara fathers.

But by far the most striking reaction of the Yamada-shi majority has been for as many as 50 parents to withdraw their children from one or both of the two schools in a single year, and to send them to other public and private schools where *burakumin* children are not enrolled. Some of the more affluent or influential parents send them more than 10 miles away to schools in a neighboring town. This practice, to be sure, is not unique to Yamada-shi nor is it motivated merely by the presence of *burakumin* but also, as the *jichikai* leader Kamada-san pointed out, by ambitions of upward mobility. Nevertheless, the practice of transferring students, especially from Kitano Chūgakkō, is such a serious one (two parents involved in the incident of the "friendship club" withdrew their daughters immediately) that both the mayor and school superintendent have pleaded with Yamada-shi parents to reduce the practice. They have also pointed to a rule that prohibits transfers to other public schools outside a child's residential district, a rule frequently circumvented either by registering a child at the household of a relative or simply by disregard.

These conflicting reactions do not entitle us to draw an entirely negative picture of Kawabara's relations to public education. Nor would we be correct to imply that all non-*burakumin* parents hold identical attitudes toward *burakumin*. One female vice-president of the PTA at Kitano Chūgakkō told us, for example, that her son remained in that school precisely because of the official plea to reduce transfers. Moreover, at least a minority of *burakumin* parents are as ready to criticize the misbehavior of their children and even their own habits as are non-*burakumin*. We shall also note later that, whereas it is undoubtedly true that many teachers and administrators have tried to shy away, a few others, notably at Nanyō Shōgakkō, have manifested genuine interest in the difficulties of adjustment faced by Kawabara children. Very rarely indeed are teachers in Yamada-shi accused these days of prejudice; more commonly they are praised by *burakumin* parents themselves for concern and fair-mindedness. The wife of Taura-san, an especially critical Kawabarian, is one of these parents. (And yet her teen-age daughter, although she could recall no prejudiced teacher, admitted that she felt "unhappy" when one of her high school instructors stressed the importance of investigating family backgrounds when a marriage is being arranged.)

How, actually, do children of *burakumin* and non-*burakumin* feel about each other when they have the opportunity to mingle? In Nanyō Shōgakkō, some teachers contended that non-*burakumin* children very early become fearful of *burakumin* because the latter are "always fighting." But sociometric tests that we examined gave rather different impressions: in five elementary classes out of nine the *burakumin* children are liked as well as others; in two classes several *burakumin* are liked by both groups more than average; and only in two others did the children of *burakumin* like children of their own group more than they did others. This is surely an indication of a high degree of acceptability.

Although no similar objective data were obtained from Kitano Chūgakkō, our impressions are less positive. Student Anasaki spoke of many "fights" that take place in this school between *burakumin* and other students; one of the most recent, according to rumor, required hospitalization for a non-*burakumin* boy who had been attacked by two Kawabara boys in a corner of the school yard. Anasaki-san had also been warned by friends even before he entered the school to avoid all contact with Kawabara students because they are "violent and fearful." It does seem clear from our evidence that dislike and exclusion intensify as Yamada-shi children reach their teens and become increasingly aware of the pariah group among them.

Yet, just how reliable is this awareness? What, basically, is the character of the people of Kawabara, not as perceived at a distance by fellow students, but by people both within the community itself and others outside who claim familiarity with that character? What, above all, do *burakumin* hope to achieve from a nation that has regarded them historically as hardly deserving of hope? In short, what are their patterns of value? Questions such as these are our next concern.

6

VALUE PATTERNS
IN KAWABARA

I

What is the average *burakumin* "really" like? Only a meager few Japanese
are able to answer this question with any more accuracy than average
Americans are able to answer it about, say, Navajo Indians or Mexican-
Americans. The reason is similar: opportunities to become familiar by informal face-to-face associations, or even by formal but competent study of
ethnic or minority groups, is very much the exception rather than the rule.

Let us try to penetrate this wall of separation and distortion by utilizing, as we did in our *gyomin* community, the still hardly refined concept of
"modal personality." Again we stress the *valuational* aspects of personality as perceived this time both by Kawabarians themselves and by Yamada-
shi informants who have claimed some experience with these fellow citizens.

With little doubt, the most reiterated characteristic proved to be "aggressiveness." This term or some rough equivalent was mentioned less often,
to be sure, by *burakumin* than by non-*burakumin*. Yet the former did not
deny aggressiveness; on the contrary, it was treated as a kind of virtue. Observe, for example, the frankness with which *burakumin* PTA officers speak
at meetings, the vehemence with which Kawabarians argue among themselves, and above all the militant unity that they are able to muster when
they decide to express animus against an alleged instance of discrimination
or to demonstrate publicly for some improvement of their lot.

Next to aggressiveness the quality most often stressed was "hypersensitivity." Thus the non-*burakumin* leader of *jichikai*, Kamada-san, spoke of
the importance of accepting refreshments like tea or *sake* when he is offered

them in a Kawabara home; not to do so is sure to be misinterpreted as an abhorrent reaction. Such phrases were heard as "feelings of persecution," "fantasies of oppression," and "inferiority complex," although the most common term was simply "suspiciousness." This was interpreted by one or two informants to mean extreme sensitivity to prejudice manifested by out-group people—that is, a constant anxiety and half-conscious trepidation on the part of *burakumin* that non-*burakumin* secretly harbor hostile or even loathsome feelings. Here is one important reason, according to Taura-san, the junk entrepreneur, why many young men and women return to the community after having tried to hold jobs elsewhere; they simply do not wish to "endure such hardships" any longer. In all fairness, however, this reason is not always separable from the easy, undisciplined ways of living to which so many Kawabarians seem to be addicted.

It is hardly surprising that the third most accentuated trait appears to be "instability," a trait related particularly to work habits. Reluctance to hold a steady job, irregular schedules of, say, junk *burōkā*, and the lack of household budget planning too often result in overspending, overborrowing, overindulgence, and such other manifestations of "reckless" and "erratic" behavior as a propensity to gamble at *pachinko* or dice. As Director Ueno of Yamada-shi social education expressed it, *burakumin* tend to be "present-oriented" in that they rarely plan for the future and try rather to subsist from day to day.

Almost as frequently stressed is "irresponsibility." Thus, according to various informants, numerous *burakumin* try to obtain all they can in the form of welfare grants without commensurate concern to provide information requested of them by the city for purposes of accurate economic, health, or educational records. Nor do many even file tax forms if they can possibly avoid it. They rarely reveal, moreover, any appreciation for whatever services may be rendered them. The commoner feeling seems rather to be that such services of financial benefit or community improvement (the bathhouse and playground are apt examples) are only their just due. After all, retribution for centuries of discrimination and suffering is not quickly fulfilled. Besides (here the Marxian ideology is apparent) *burakumin* have only been the more extreme victims of a pernicious system of exploitation that extends to virtually the whole Japanese working class. They do not feel that the people owe special obligations for the meager portions that the government provides; rather the government has neglected to provide anywhere near enough in either family aid or public services.

Not all *burakumin* agree with this rationale. Probably the most critical Kawabara informant is our slipper maker, Mitsuda-san; though deeply concerned over his own people, he is surely not defensive. For example, presently none of his own skilled workers are *burakumin* simply because, he admitted, their stability is little if any better now than it has been in centuries past. In one sense, many *burakumin* today are even less stable workers than they once were when they were regarded as leather artisans. As this semi-monopoly has dwindled (shoe-making, especially, has turned more and more into a mechanized and mass production industry) it is scarcely surprising that so many *burakumin* workers have become careless. At the same time they justify increasing dependence upon economic aid with the frank encouragement of such influential allies as the Communist councilman, Dr. Okubo.

Nor is it very surprising that Mitsuda-san, concurring with several others, chose "parasitism" as still another term of character delineation. We have noted that about 75 percent of all households, a total of more than 400 persons, are primarily dependent upon economic aid. (About 80 percent of the cost, incidentally, is provided by the Federal treasury.) Recall further that, although able-bodied men and women are encouraged to find jobs through the city placement office, only about one-third of these households have participated in the program for unemployed workers *(shittai)*, since there is no legal requirement that they enroll. Of those who are enrolled, moreover, not a single Kawabara household includes more than one *shittai* worker, although two are eligible.

Voluntary social workers, who receive preliminary training and frequent briefings, are primarily responsible for supervising the welfare program in Yamada-shi. Kawabara has three such workers whose primary tasks are to determine the needs of families and to recommend monthly stipends. But subterfuge is rife. Some common-law wives live with their husbands secretly in order to list separate addresses and thus to qualify for double stipends. Others supplement stipends by various kinds of part-time jobs, *pachinko* gambling, or other devious activities which they fail to report, knowing that their checks would be reduced if they did. One official in the Department of Social Welfare estimated for us that applications of Kawabara residents may be considered, at best, as 50 percent accurate. Thus the maximum stipend of $62 for a family of five (provided only if no member presumably is earning an income) is often only part of the total income, although doubtless the largest part.

That parasitism is too harsh a label, certainly in some instances, is revealed by a random sample of Kawabara welfare cases which we were permitted to examine without identifying names. In one case, a divorced man with a young son is responsible for his aged mother who suffers from tuberculosis and other diseases. He is a *shittai* worker. The second case reports that the household master is syphilitic and neuralgic, with a wife and two small children to support. In the third case, the man was recently imprisoned for theft, his wife is alleged to be tubercular, and there are again two small children. (In the social worker's file on this case, it is noteworthy that questions were raised as to the authenticity of the medical report, which was held to be affected by political interest in the applicant on the part of the physician in charge.) The fourth case is complicated by a pregnant common-law wife and two children in elementary school, although the man is without regular work. In our fifth sample, a young man with a wife and baby is regarded as "too neurotic" to hold a job, he suffers also from physiological ailments according to medical records filed by the same doctor, and his only occupation seems to be "twanging a guitar" in the bars of Yamada-shi. Our final sample describes a greatly troubled household where there is continuous conflict not only between the wife and her husband but also between the wife and her mother-in-law. The husband is away from home much of the time, although no one is sure where he goes; one of her small sons died from diptheria; another suffers from an eye disease; and she herself was hospitalized so that her work in the Kawabara glove factory has been curtailed. The family grows vegetables estimated to be worth $1.30 per month, this sum being deducted from economic aid totaling about $48, plus medical services. Only the constant intervention of social workers has prevented the wife from leaving this household permanently.

Yet granting, as all informants did, that tragic cases are common, the consensus still prevailed that parasitic behavior remains pronounced. Thus our single non-*burakumin* informant living in Kawabara, Shoemaker Akie, insisted that most *burakumin* do not really need to depend upon economic aid, that their repeated failure to hold steady jobs is due much more to their unfortunate habit of "impatience" with work than to prejudice against them. He is especially resentful of the fact that many Kawabarians who receive monthly stipends can afford higher standards of living than he and his wife, both of whom work full time, she in the local glove factory and he as a shoemaker for ten hours of six and often seven days a week.

Resentment is also detected among hard-working farmers in Yamada-shi who observe what appears to them, comparatively speaking, to amount to a life of leisure. The common knowledge that Kawabarian applicants for economic aid often resort to what Entrepreneur Taura appropriately termed *kamofuraaju* (camouflage) concerning their status with the hope of gaining larger stipends hardly lessens such skeptical reactions. As Director Ueno expressed it, this is "discrimination in reverse," discrimination in favor of *burakumin* as against other underprivileged citizens whom the government continues to neglect perhaps because they have not learned to act with sufficient militancy.

Are we then compelled to regard the integral values of the Kawabara personality type in chiefly negative terms, that is, as *dis*values? Any unqualified answer would, we think, once more oversimplify. Although ag-

gressiveness, hypersensitivity, instability, and parasitism are certainly rec-
ognizable attributes, they are tempered by other more positive ones. Thus
we have already noted how aggressiveness may be perceived in more than
one perspective. True, it often antagonizes and even frightens non-*burakumin*. But true, too, it serves as a channel through which *burakumin* not
only express their "righteous indignation" at the shabby treatment long
accorded them, but demand and sometimes win a more equitable share of
the resources of life that have been promised them (on paper at least) for
nearly a full century.

Aggressiveness, moreover, suggests another positive value: "mutuality."
We have seen how both Kaihōdōmei and Dōwakai—not to forget Jirō—
utilize techniques of direct collective action. Though we did not observe
any local situation that called for a solid front of all Kawabara groups, they
are certainly capable of forming one if sufficiently disturbed by an offensive
incident. At the same time, although ingroup cooperation thus emerges as
another important concomitant value, Kawabarians who picket the mayor's
home or set up a blockade around the public bath generate such severe
counter-hostilities among the majority group that one may understand why
they are sometimes accused of "violent" behavior and even collective "sad-
ism." This kind of accusation is no doubt colored by still vivid memories
among middle-aged Japanese of Suiheisha's rashly belligerent tactics in the
1920s and 1930s. A vicious circle is thereby generated as hostility begets
hostility.

To say, however, that *burakumin* unite firmly and aggressively in joint
expressions of common grievances is not to say that they always behave in
similar ways as individuals. In face-to-face associations even with the most
bellicose leaders such as the Communist organizer of Jirō, Shōda-san, or
with rank-and-file Communist residents in Kawabara, we found them to be
consistently polite and respectful, even at times cordial. True, such personal
"amicability" is not always the case. Some *burakumin* do behave with extreme pugnacity, even as individuals. The most vigorous Communist in
Kawabara, for example, was described by another left-wing leader as one
who "annoys" many people because of his inveterate hostility, one whose
troubles are so deeply psychological that no real change in his personality
is likely.

Or consider the case of two brothers, nephews of Councilman Hayashi.
Both have attacked their father, a shoemaker, with knives. One, a gang
member and twice divorced by the age of 21, also attacked his wife and
father-in-law and was confined to the psychiatric ward of the national hospital in Yamada-shi for several months. The other brother, age 18, was
recently arrested for stealing a watch but has not been jailed because he is
still a "minor." Yet their father, though deeply troubled over his sons' be-

havior, has not only defended them on occasion; possibly they have acquired some of their volatile behavior directly from him. He once traveled to Hiroishi to protest to the prefectural superintendent of schools about a teacher who, he claimed, had treated one of his sons in a prejudicial manner, a complaint which he withdrew after official investigation.

But such cases as these are hardly representative. At most they highlight the fact that emotional illness, no less than other kinds, is of higher incidence among *burakumin* than among the general population. More representative of positive factors in the Kawabara personality type is the impression that *jichikai* leaders apparently make upon representative assemblies in Yamada-shi. According to Jichikai Secretary Kamada, these leaders are cooperative and amenable participants, a judgment supported in another setting by our leader informant, Azuma-san, head priest of the great Shingonshū temple. When, he said, *burakumin* participate in the lively February festival described earlier, or borrow one of his halls for a conference, their conduct is impeccable and their manner congenial.

Positive values are even better exemplified by the same young Kawabarian whose tale about his marriage woes was reported in Chapter 5. Once, while sharing a hospital room over several weeks with a non-*burakumin* patient, the latter confessed that he had wholly changed his mind about the *burakumin* character. Never having met such a person previously, he had always supposed that *burakumin* were invariably mean, rude, and hostile. But now, through close daily association, he had discovered otherwise. Had these young friends heard of a concept familiar to social psychologists they might have agreed that the fiction shattered in that hospital room was a *burakumin* "stereotype."

In recapitulation, what may we then infer as a fusion of the Kawabara personality? Perhaps the term, "double character," emphasized by another teacher informant, Inoki-san, is fair enough. The personal amicability that we have noted is often manifested, he said, in the attitudes of such *burakumin* as Hirose-san, the PTA enthusiast who spends much of his time at Teacher Inoki's elementary school. Yet one can never be quite sure of Hirose-san's motives; he changes his mind and mood from day to day. Indeed, the often professed interest of parents in good education for their children seems all too frequently to be offset by their still stronger interest in gaining as much as possible in the way of benefits for themselves. For example, a large majority of all Kawabara families have managed to obtain television sets, although only a minority of teachers, if Inoki-san is correct, have been able to afford them. Again, although kindness and compassion, especially to the downtrodden, and a reciprocal desire to be liked were mentioned as noticeable traits, so too were cunning, selfishness, and jealousy of another's larger stipends which even lead at times to informing on each other. As Nozu-san put it, one reason why Kawabara seems bogged down by its own conflicts is that "every leader wants to be a general." Yet it is also apparent that collective action even on the part of *jichikai* leaders representing opposing organizations has sometimes been productive.

The "double character" of *burakumin* may be highlighted further by another concept familiar to social psychologists known as "the frustration-aggression complex." Although its significance has been modified since it was first made famous by John Dollard and others, the essential proposition for our purpose remains apropos: "the occurrence of aggressive behavior always presupposes the existence of frustration and, contrariwise, . . . the existence of frustration always leads to some form of aggression." [1]

Clearly the picture of Kawabarians that we have drawn in the preceding two chapters, and particularly in this one, suggests this complex. Aggressiveness, for example, is commonly accompanied by suspiciousness and insecurity; both of these characteristics imply in turn how frustrated a Kawabarian must often feel in the face of unspoken prejudice, ostracism, and blockages that deny either steady jobs or free choice of marriage partners.

Several informants would still wish to qualify this sort of characterization, however. The ever-critical Mitsuda-san is convinced that the aggressive behavior of his people oftener than not is misdirected toward false targets; that is, fellow *burakumin* become furious over minor matters such as an alleged insult—the epithet *eta*, particularly—but rarely do they act to effect really important change. Most *burakumin*, he insisted, ought to take the initiative to leave Kawabara for a healthier environment. Nothing legally prevents them from doing so. But too many find it easier to remain as residents and to nurse their frustrations in the comforting circle of their fellows.

Nor were Mitsuda-san's harsh opinions necessarily resisted by other informants. Nozu-san, for example, implied agreement when he conceded that suspiciousness among Kawabarians, even though grounds surely do exist for such an attitude, is at times exaggerated grossly. Similarly, our non-*burakumin* women's leader, Tabata-san, confessed that she has usually "failed" to motivate most of her Kawabara friends to seek a better life for themselves outside, a failure she attributes to related factors: rejection by outgroups, delinquency, long-established routines of segregated living, and below-average intelligence. This last factor was implied by still others in several ways: a seeming lack of self-awareness concerning the negative impressions the *burakumin* sometimes make upon outsiders; a strong tendency

[1] John Dollard and others, *Frustration and Aggression* (New Haven: Yale University Press, 1939), p. 1.

to conceal difficulties from themselves and others; ignorance of such ideologies as communism which nevertheless are loudly proclaimed; and lastly "immaturity."

Two final observations must complete our profile. One is an analogy offered by Hatano-san, local Kaihōdōmei chairman, between Jews and Burakumin. Both are "branded," he said, as minority groups and both have been forced to wear insignia at various times in history that identify them in the same way that a ranch identifies its cattle; yet neither Jews nor Burakumin, any more than cattle, are physically distinguishable except by such insignia. The analogy extends still further: the ratio of Jews in the United States happens to be fairly close to the ratio of Burakumin in Japan; both groups adhere to their religious faiths somewhat more tenaciously than does the public at large; both often tend to cling to their own ingroups for comfort and security (a phenomenon sometimes known as "clannishness"); and both are noted for the exceptional numbers that have engaged in peddling and junk collecting—the latter business possibly traceable to the historic travails that compelled these minorities at various times to scavenge in order to remain alive. Both, finally, are noted for their shrewd businessmen. (Hatano-san might have added that otherwise the current economic status of the two minorities is often far from comparable.)

Our second observation raises the question of whether, despite their Japanese genesis, *burakumin* are in any way "visibly" identifiable as a cultural group. Our own research team could detect no such differences. In speech habits, Kawabara and Yamada-shi citizens seem identical, although the people of the city as a whole do speak with a regional "dialect" quite apparent to visitors from other areas of Japan. Nevertheless, some Kawabarians insist that they can speak, if they wish to do so, in such a unique *burakumin* argot that strangers would find it impossible to follow their conversation. Thus Burōkā Tanaka said that often he became acquainted with *burakumin* in hotels and other meeting places by sending out "wave lengths" in the form of phrases familiar only to them. This practice is common, he said, throughout Japan among the older generation of *burakumin* but decreasingly so among younger people, few of whom any longer speak fluently in the old forms. Probably many parents even discourage their children, Tanaka-san thought, for then they cannot be detected as *burakumin* by their style of speech. But Kaihōdōmei Leader Tomita did not quite share this opinion: he found that one obstacle confronted when trying to teach Kawabara children in after-school classes to speak standard Japanese was the colloquial habits acquired from their parents, even the use of special terms for numbers.

No other differentiating features were noted. Probably Entrepreneur Taura is right in pointing out that outsiders who contend that they can detect *burakumin* by appearance are simply projecting a preconceived image —in our terms, stereotypes. Dress, to be sure, is typically very informal, but this must be attributed mainly to low income, not to ingroup eccentricities. Facial features in Kawabara may often seem comparable, too, but this may be largely the consequence of more frequent endogamous marriage than one finds elsewhere in Yamada-shi.

II

The value patterns to which we now turn focus on marriage and sexual morality in Kawabara. As anticipated in Chapter 4, the characteristic that first stands out is the extraordinary degree of informality that prevails by comparison with mores of the Japanese majority culture. Thus we have seen that many marriages, probably a large majority, are common-law or consensual, that is, without benefit of clergy, Shintō or Buddhist. Because of this, one question in an early stage of our study on the frequency of divorce in Kawabara appears in the light of subsequent knowledge to have been naive. Most informants answered that they knew of almost no divorces, the principal reason being, of course, that formal dissolution of marriages is rare. For example, non-*burakumin* wives who eventually decide (as some do now and then) that they can no longer endure the stringencies of Kawabara life have little trouble in terminating their marriages. They simply go home.

Such informality is doubtless also affected by the avoidance of traditional wedding ceremonies, an extravagance that Kawabarians can afford even less than Ebibarians. But a more pervasive reason, perhaps, is a general unwillingness to be constrained by the customs of a culture that already has constrained *burakumin* much too long and much too rigidly. The primary goal, after all, is the right to enjoy just as much freedom to marry whomever one chooses as anyone else enjoys; if this is in any way enhanced by avoiding ceremonies and legalities then let them be avoided.

In the case of Kawabara, certainly, the consequence appears to justify this attitude. Not only have we noted that the number of non-*burakumin* wives approaches one-third of the total number; we are able to report further that two of our informants, Mitsuda-san and Tomita-san, are both married to non-*burakumin,* and a third, Hatano-san, told us that two of his sisters, both of whom live elsewhere, are likewise married to non-*burakumin.*

Thus it is quite consistent for most of our grassroots panel to prefer *ren-ai kekkon* (love marriage) to *mi-ai kekkon* (arranged marriage), especially since all marriages with non-*burakumin* have, so far as we know, understandably been of the former kind. Yet Nozu-san, for one, reflected the already familiar opinion that a combination of *mi-ai* and *ren-ai* is better than either way alone—in short, that whereas a man and woman should have ample opportunity to decide whether they are attracted enough to marry each other, negotiation by means of a *nakōdo* (go-between) reduces the risks inevitable to merely romantic love. This opinion was largely shared by Tanaka-san whose own marriage (though his wife confessed to us that she had done her best to resist the *nakōdo's* overtures for three full years) is, like Taura-san's, a product of *mi-ai*. Taura-san, however, did admit that *burakumin* find much less reason as a rule to perpetuate *mi-ai* than do Yamada-shi farmers: being relatively propertyless, the necessity of assuring stable households that will preserve the family heritage of land is almost nonexistent among Kawabarians.

That *ren-ai*, as Enterpreneur Taura also contended, sometimes leads to marital instability and anguish not only for the married couple but often for other kin is borne out by some of our earlier evidence. Particularly is this true of marriages that attempt to break through powerful taboos prohibiting exogamy. Take another example: Teacher Inoki described the case of a druggist in Yamada-shi who committed suicide because his daughter had married a young Kawabarian with the start of a police record; as Inoki-san expressed it, the "shame" was just too great for the father to bear. One final example: just before we left, Burōkā Tanaka's pretty non-*burakumin* daughter-in-law, whom we had met several times and who only a few months earlier had come to live in the Tanaka household with the 19-year-old son, was suddenly taken to a psychiatric hospital. We were told by Tanaka-san's wife that both parents of the young woman had angrily resisted her decision to move to Kawabara, and she herself had been suffering from the effort to adjust to this new and, for her, strange community.

These two cases are not necessarily representative. They do suggest that the life of *burakumin* is far from conducive to simple adjustment and stability in matters of marriage and morality. Still more specifically with regard to sexual behavior, it was a recurring though not unanimous judgment that premarital and extramarital relations occur oftener in a community such as Kawabara than they do in the average Japanese community. Thus Dr. Okubo who, after all, should have grounds for his statement (we remember that he treats by far the largest number of *burakumin* patients of any doctor in Yamada-shi) is positive that a large majority of all teen-age girls in Kawabara lose their virginity before they graduate from Kitano Chūgakkō. Our truck-driver informant, Kataoka-san, seemed to concur. He said that the intimate associations habitual to a small homogenous community easily lead to sexual relations, a situation not comparable to huge cities where people are more cautious because they are mostly strangers. Shoemaker Akie supported this contention. He had heard, for example, of extramarital affairs in Kawabara among various wives, not to mention husbands, who engage in such affairs while their conjugal partners are absent sometimes for weeks on peddling expeditions. Also, he once chanced upon a secret rendezvous in the dilapidated attic of an unused house where teen-agers regularly met for sexual indulgence. (After discovering a small pornographic library, he decided to report the rendezvous to a local social worker.) On another occasion, Akie-san witnessed erotic play between a ten-year-old girl and a young adult shoemaker apprentice employed by her father.

Still, it is necessary to record that the picture sketched by other Kawabarians sharply differed from this one. Particularly, Nozu-san and Tomita-san, both of whom grew up in Kawabara as Akie-san had not, emphatically portrayed the community as quite conventional in its moral standards. Neither professed to know of any exceptional licentiousness; and neither they nor other informants would admit knowledge of a single case of incestuous relations. The most they would concede was the employment of a few girls in Yamada-shi bars. Neither could think of a prostitute or pseudo-*geisha* presently from Kawabara, and although they admitted that movie-going by boys and girls together has increased since they themselves were in their teens, they equally insisted that average Kawabara parents are no different from other parents in their disapproval of unconventional behavior especially by their teen-age daughters. Indeed, Nozu-san drew quite an opposite conclusion from Kataoka-san's point that people in close proximity tend to be more intimate; on the contrary, Nozu-san held that such proximity only dampens the zest for sexual adventure. Again, in opposition to Dr. Okubo, Tomita-san was sure that only about one in ten junior high school girls is no longer a virgin by the time she graduates, although it is also true, as another informant, a mother and grandmother, pointed out, that a single promiscuous girl can harm the reputation of the other nine. The fact is, she added with approval, that since a number of young Kawabara women are now obtaining jobs as barbers and beauticians they must scrupulously avoid indecorous conduct.

Whereas our evidence here is inconclusive if not downright contradictory, there seemed to be agreement that, whatever the truth about Kawabara women, most Kawabara men do have premarital sexual relations, although again in no greater proportions than other Japanese men. In the words of one informant, to do so is only consistent with the male "character." Another informant, about 35 years of age, estimated that before his marriage he had experienced intercourse with something like a hundred women, most of them available professionals in Yamada-shi itself and none particularly distinguishable from others in erotic artistry.

Although most informants seemed to condone this double standard, two or three did not. Thus Kaihōdōmei Leader Tomita was not only vehement in denouncing prostitution as an evil stemming from economic deprivation; he was equally so in holding that unmarried men as well as women should remain chaste. Burōkā Tanaka took a different view: it is all right, he thought, for a man and woman to have premarital intercourse provided they are deeply in love; what is wrong is for a man to enjoy sexual freedom but not for a woman to do so. Only the single standard can be justified.

Partly for this reason, perhaps, Tanaka-san favors frank sex education in high school, beginning gradually on the junior level and reaching such topics as contraception and abortion on the senior level. Also, he feels, it is important for parents to develop in their children wholesome attitudes toward masturbation: to encourage them to vent their pent-up energies in sports, but at the same time to help boys, especially, to see that masturbation is preferable to intercourse with prostitutes. Fortunately, Tanaka-san added, books and magazines on sexual behavior are now readily available so that parents have an easier time talking frankly, as he does with his own three sons, than when he himself was young. Tomita-san, in the same spirit, objected to the suggestion sometimes made that mothers alone should teach their daughters about sex and fathers their sons. This is only "half learning," he insisted, for each sex needs to understand the other. Too many women, for example, are still ignorant of the nature of genitalia, even of their own.

No informant on our Kawabara panel objected to sex education, and all with whom we discussed the matter favored birth control, including abortion if other means fail. As one spokesman pointed out, such education is imperative as a consequence of the "new morality" of the postwar decades, induced as it is by disparagement of outworn feudal codes. If an abnormal degree of moral laxity now prevails, this is not unusual to Kawabara but is rather symptomatic of the culture as a whole.

More usual may be two additional conditions among average *burakumin* communities. One is the frequent absence of parents from home during many hours of the day, at times even for a month or longer at one stretch. If young Kawabarians often feel neglected and frustrated as a consequence, if in certain cases they are said to lose respect for their own parents, one may surely appreciate why some of them turn elsewhere for affection or for gratification of too many unsatisfied desires.

A second factor, according to Shoemaker Akie, is the dearth of viable choices. Children, living in cramped quarters and early observing erotic activity on the part of other family members, take it for granted that here is something they, too, must try. Moreover, with no playground available until very recently, with few invitations to cultivate close friends beyond the limits of their own ghetto, with little at home to hold their interest (although television has become one significant exception), it is scarcely surprising that, notwithstanding the perhaps defensive statements of Tomita-san and Nozu-san, moral laxity might more frequently be the case in such a community as this than in more generous environments. Neither should one be surprised that, on the average, according to Dr. Okubo, women in Kawabara suffer more acutely during menopause than do women outside, a trouble he attributed directly to the strain of living in a milieu of severe insecurity and tension.

III

Unlike what a Western observer might expect, the values central to marriage and sexual conduct were not explicitly related by our local panel to religious values. The only exception was a non-*burakumin* leader, the Shingonshū priest, Azuma-san. We shall consider his views later.

And yet, as anticipated by Chapter 4, religious values appear to be more important to Kawabarians than to many Japanese citizens. Several resource persons stressed the historical contention that Jōdoshinshū (the Buddhist sect, we recall, to which most *burakumin* belong) first befriended this pariah group during an age when it was almost entirely excluded from other sects. Priest Azuma himself, though of a rival sect, was emphatic in his admiration of Jōdoshinshū for having challenged the "hierarchical structure" of feudal times in favor of a more egalitarian gospel. For taking such initiative, he said, other sects should be grateful just as many *burakumin* apparently feel grateful to this day.

Not all do, however. Among our *burakumin* informants, Leader Tomita of Kaihōdōmei particularly criticized Jōdoshinshū priests in Hiroishi because they "don't lift a finger" to share in the struggles of *burakumin* for a better life on earth. Rather, they limit their roles, even though they too are *burakumin*, to performing *hōji* (ancestral commemorations), funeral services, and similar rites for which fees provide their livelihood. In the spirit, moreover, of the Marxian philosophy which has influenced many leaders of Kaihōdōmei besides himself, Tomita-san readily endorsed the famous adage that religion is the opiate of the people. But even he confessed to keeping an inherited *butsudan* in his own home and to performing abbreviated *hōji* on appointed anniversaries of his family ancestors.

Thus although Tomita-san considers himself an "atheist," he reflects a continuing ambivalence among many *burakumin* with regard to religious values. Recall Suiheisha, the "levelers' movement" that we found to be so influential three and four decades ago: one of its earliest policy decisions was to recommend a 20-year boycott against the head temples of Jōdo-shinshū in Kyoto on the ground that even their own priests, although gladly accepting financial contributions from *burakumin*, also made invidious comparisons between the latter and other Japanese. Still other objections to the sect were raised—for example, priestly hierarchies have at various times in history been the allies of political autocrats in forcing *burakumin* to join Jōdoshinshū temples for the purpose of further subjugation. Again, the familiar complaint was heard several times that religion only diverts human energies away from present-day problems in favor of escape into a realm of other-worldly salvation. One group of Suiheisha members tried to counter this criticism by proposing that *burakumin*, rather than completly repudiating their Buddhist faith, should seek to redirect it toward this-worldly tasks. That the Jōdoshinshū priesthood could not have been wholly oblivious to this kind of redirection may appear from the fact that the original declaration of emancipation, issued in 1922,[2] was written by a priest named Saikō. According to one account, Saikō-san labored over this historic document while hiding from Kyoto police on the roof of a prostitute's house.

But let us return to our quest for explanations of the appeal of religion in general and of Jōdoshinshū in particular. Ueno-san, who, it should be remembered, doubles as Director of Social Education in Yamada-shi and as an inactive priest of Shingonshū, contended that Jōdoshinshū, unlike his own sect or one or two others such as Zenshū, is a "soft" religion. That is, one may attain Buddhahood with almost no personal sacrifice, no arduous rituals, and no prolonged training or study in depth of its theology. Director Ueno questioned the historic claim, therefore, that Jōdoshinshū has been the dominant sect among *burakumin* because it succored them when others did not. (One or two informants mentioned, incidentally, that Nichiren was another saint who did.) The primary reason, he contended, was that Jōdoshinshū attracts not only *burakumin* but others among the untutored masses mainly because it is easy and simple to accept. To believe that Buddha assures one of heavenly bliss demands little more effort than utterance of sacred chants at proper intervals.

Among Kawabarians, Burōkā Tanaka seemed most distinctly to reinforce Ueno-san's interpretation. More conscientiously than some of his neighbors, he prays before the *butsudan* every evening, never forgetting his deceased parents and children in his prayers, and beseeching Buddha to guide his spirit after death to Paradise. His family briefly joins him. When asked why he remains faithful to this ritual, his frank reply was that although life on earth is important it is, after all, a steppingstone to life after death.

[2] Cf. p. 110.

Moreover, he said, *burakumin* have suffered so much that they are understandably attracted by this expectation, although it is also true that the sheer persistence of religious custom may be a stronger reason. Meanwhile, although nothing more is required of him than to beseech Buddha's benevolence, Tanaka-san also regularly prays to his Shintō *kami* and occasionally visits the popular shrine of the fishermen's *kami* in a nearby town.

Shoemaker Akie is somewhat more pragmatic. While he was suffering acutely (he was once in jail and has experienced abject poverty), he felt a "desperate need" to obtain help from a "supernatural power." Now that he is somewhat better off he admits to diminished religious fervor, but he also wonders whether such fluctuations of devotion do not reveal his own "selfishness."

Akie-san's wife is the only Sōkagakkai member in the community, and although she and her friends have done their best to persuade her husband to join the movement he has refused. His greatest faith, he feels, is in himself: "If I live straightforwardly I can build my own life"—his implication being, of course, that he need not depend upon the blessings of Saint Nichiren. Besides, Akie-san dislikes the requirement that family *ihai* (ancestor plaques) be burned by its members.

Others shared his dislike. Although several hundred Sōkagakkai members are said to live in Yamada-shi, they have had no success within Kawabara itself. Such unresponsiveness, to be sure, is not always the case among *burakumin;* thus in the Utsumi-shi ghetto, a number of households not only have recently joined, but we were told that they have become more energetic than either Kaihōdōmei or Dōwakai groups. The judgment of our own informants, nevertheless, remained vehemently negative. Even our rival junk entrepreneurs, Hayashi-san and Taura-san, fully agreed for once: the Sōkagakkai movement plays upon the "weaknesses" of people, by offering them soporifics and exploiting anxieties of the insecure and goalless. As for Kōmeito, the political front of the movement, it is merely a scheme to promote the ambitions of insincere people. Its international line is equally a sham. Interestingly, Burōkā Tanaka, who agreed that Jōdoshinshū is a "soft" religion, criticized the Sōkagakkai because it invites religious "laziness" by persuading followers that illness can be cured by prayer when in fact it can only be cured by medicine. One should never expect Buddha to respond to supplications, he said, whether for health or for money; hence no good Jōdoshinshū member ever prays for divine help.

Entrepreneur Taura, incidentally, is the only person we met in Kawabara who had ever shown the slightest interest in Christianity: as a boy, he attended a Christian Sunday school for about one year. True, missionaries representing various Christian sects in Hiroshima, Osaka, and particularly Kyoto, have at times shown impassioned concern over the plight of *bura-*

kumin, and history records that at least one segregated village was converted to Christianity. So far as we know, however, none of the several missionary teachers in Yamada College a mile or so away has ever crossed Kawabara's boundary lines.

IV

Social, economic, and political values are frequently and explicitly traced by Kawabarians to the Constitution of Japan. Adopted in 1947, this noble document is so thoroughly democratic in its guiding principles that one can readily understand why *burakumin* everywhere appeal to it when they press political leaders for belated recognition of their rights.

Consider such Articles as the following:

> *Article 11.* The people shall not be prevented from enjoying any of the fundamental human rights. These fundamental human rights, guaranteed to the people by the present Constitution, shall be conferred upon the people of this and future generations as eternal and inviolable.

> *Article 13.* All of the people shall be respected as individuals. Their right to life, liberty, and the pursuit of happiness shall, to the extent that it does not interfere with the public welfare, be the supreme consideration in legislation and in other governmental affairs.

> *Article 14.* All of the people are equal under the law, and there shall be no recrimination in political, economic or social relations because of race, creed, sex, social status or family origin.

> *Article 18.* No person shall be held in bondage of any kind. Involuntary servitude, except as punishment for crime, is prohibited.

> *Article 24.* Marriage shall be based only upon the mutual consent of both sexes, and it shall be maintained through mutual co-operation, with the equal rights of husband and wife as a basis.

> *Article 25.* All people shall have the right to maintain minimum standards of wholesome and cultured living.

> *Article 26.* All people shall have the right to receive an equal education corresponding with their ability, as provided for by law. [3]

Our Jirō official and Communist party member, Shōda-san, was one of those fond of citing such Articles in behalf of the struggle of his people. He felt, as did several other *burakumin* whom we interviewed, that there is no significant difference between the goals of democracy and those of either

[3] Quoted from Esler Dening, *Japan* (New York: Frederick A. Praeger, Inc., 1961), pp. 245–257.

communism or socialism. Differences that do emerge are not chiefly on the point of ends but rather of means, that is, technically speaking, of "instrumental" values. Hence a number of loyal Kaihōdōmei members, while repudiating the exploitative means of capitalism, also criticize Communist party tactics as "too radical" and as socially alienating: *burakumin* who become Communists simply sharpen the stereotype of a "difficult" and "hostile" group. But the Socialist party was criticized too: to quote one informant, this party scatters its energies "as a hen scatters grain." To quote another: it suffers from "immaturity."

These were not unanimous judgments. Communist Shōda was emphatic in pointing out that organizations like Kaihōdōmei have been able to progress only because they have been militant enough to compel federal, prefectural, and city politicians to yield to their demands for better housing, scholarships, and jobs, and even for financing organizational activities. Also, the familiar contention was reiterated that the struggle of *burakumin* embraces oppressed people everywhere in the world. Exploitation, the common denominator of every sort of oppression, whether educational or economic, includes equally the Untouchables of India and the Negroes of America. Shōda-san reminded us that a cable had once been dispatched expressing the solidarity of *burakumin* with Harlem Negroes in their common troubles and common hopes. Yet even Shōda-san freely admitted that too often his people are overaggressive. This is chiefly due, he held, to inadequate education: when people are ill-informed it is difficult for them to think of alternatives; hence their frustrations produce explosive feelings.

Only one of our *burakumin* panel, Councilman Hayashi, disagreed with the strong consensus of support for socialist-communist goals. To be sure, we may recall that he, in accordance with Dōwakai policies, endorses the goal of emancipation. What he does not endorse is, again, the instrumental value of radical tactics advocated both by the Communist and Socialist parties of Japan as well as by Jirō and Kaihōdōmei. He favors rather a "welfare state" or, in language familiar to Western economics, a "mixed economy" partly socialist and partly capitalist as found in countries like England. Such a moderate or eclectic orientation toward politics is best symbolized by the Democratic Socialist party, the closest Japanese equivalent of the right-wing socialist movements of Europe. Too often, however, this third-rank party, according to Hayashi-san, vacillates or falls under the influence of the more aggressive Socialist party. Here, indeed, is a key to the trouble with all political goals in Japan; not only the Democratic Socialist party but others, too, including the Liberal Democratic party, are vague and equivocal, he held, as to any long-run political objectives.

Thus, although the councilman was himself once local chairman of the Socialist party, and whereas he privately favors the Democratic Socialist party (he was once asked to form a branch in Yamada-shi where none as yet exists), he is now a Liberal Democrat although a critical one. This incumbent party is riddled, he maintained, with factionalism and corruption extending all the way up to chiefs of state; but, because so many people are dependent upon political favors for jobs, it seems impossible to eradicate this evil. Still, the Socialist and Democratic Socialist parties are not immune to corruption either; after all, they do accept donations from businessmen. And should the Socialist party ever become strong enough to win control of the government, the power of the great trade unions would then become just as one-sided as is the present domination of government by big industry.

In perspective, then, Kawabarians tend to reflect in their wider social values many of the same disparities that were noted earlier in their everyday experience. The slipper maker, Mitsuda-san, is perhaps more typical than not: he has supported Dr. Okubo for election on the Communist party ticket, yet during our own study he also endorsed at least one Liberal Democrat who ran for the national Senate. Again, although Nozu-san is a devoted Socialist and an employee of the Yamada-shi producers' co-operative, he revealed almost no interest either in consumer co-operatives or in promoting any program of co-operative education for school children. Rather, he apparently accepted the co-operative almost exclusively as a device by which farmers obtain better prices for their harvest within the capitalist economy. The director of his own co-operative, incidentally, is an influential Liberal Democratic councilman.

Such instances of vacillation in economic-political values are hardly astonishing. Recall from the two preceding chapters how within each major organization, Kaihōdōmei and Dōwakai, one may discover members of both conservative and radical parties. Recall, too, the continuous influence of the historic virtues, *on* and *giri,* which on many occasions conflict with ideological allegiances; or the still influential custom of *oyabun-kobun,* which binds a considerable number of Kawabarians regardless of political sympathies to the structure of ingroup control centering in the local *bosu;* or what often encompasses both of these traditions, extended families with their tenacious web of kinship connections.

Nor should one forget the conflicts engendered, though seldom stated explicitly, between a deeply engrained religious faith with its hope of otherworldly redemption, on the one hand, and the combative this-worldly values of Marxian-influenced doctrine, on the other hand. Finally, but by no means of least importance, are the value conflicts that we have discerned between the "outer" and "inner" worlds of Kawabarians: their desire, above all, to be accepted as full-fledged citizens, along with the need for security and mutuality that many seek to satisfy in the relative seclusion of ghetto existence.

Here we return to the poignant dilemma that opened our study of Kawabara. This is the dilemma of Katoka-san, the truck driver, who had to decide whether or not to help his children "pass" into the wider society. Kataoka-san and his wife finally decided to sacrifice the values of a closely knit family in favor of the future happiness of their two daughters and younger son. Therefore three of their four children are seeking a new life in Tokyo by trying to conceal their origin and identity as *burakumin*—at the price of severing all Kawabara ties.

Do others approve? The impression that we receive is, again, one of ambivalence. Taura-san, for example, confessed that at times he has been torn between loyalty to this community and the welfare of his family; his decision, however, is to remain in Kawabara, to work hard at his growing junk business, but to send his children away to college where he hopes they will marry non-*burakumin*. His same young *burōkā*, whose harrowing tale of marriage we reported earlier, held that it is quite all right for people to try to pass if they can, except that then they are no longer able to help others who remain behind. He himself does not wish to conceal his identity; rather his policy is simply to shun anyone suspected of prejudiced attitudes. The view of our local Kaihōdōmei chairman, Hatano-san, is even more straight-forward; he could pass, he said, if he really desired to do so since he has had some college education and is an experienced typesetter. But then he would only consider himself a traitor to his cause.

Perhaps the most tragic response to this dilemma, however, was Tomita-san's. A considerable number of *burakumin* have, he said, already moved out of Kawabara into other sections of Yamada-shi. Yet, since everyone in the city knows who they are, they rarely become "close" to non-*burakumin;* on the contrary, one always detects unspoken feelings of reserve. Here is one explanation of why passing does not often succeed; even or perhaps especially where they manage to conceal their backgrounds, the yearning of *burakumin* for the comradery of their fellows is frequently more impelling than the demand for extreme caution. Thus they are torn again by ambivalence—on one side is the need for personal identity, on the other side the wish to be respected as equals. Only too frequently, according to Leader Tomita, it is the former of these two magnetic values that ultimately triumphs.

In answer then to the further question of whether *burakumin* are "progressing" in the sense of improvement of their overall condition, we could hardly anticipate unanimity. Nozu-san, although he saw little improvement in the life of his own community, discerned considerable improvement in one respect: the federal government has finally appropriated funds for new housing and other urgent needs. At the same time, undercurrents of prejudice may actually have deepened due to continuing indignation if not outright fears on the part of the majority society ever since the days when it was first aroused by the tactics of Suiheisha. The mere fact that hostility toward *burakumin* is seldom exposed in public any longer is hardly proof, Nozu-san felt, that prejudice is not at least as virulent as ever.

Others wavered, too, between optimism and pessimism. Hatano-san held that the single greatest token of progress in Kawabara has been the remarkable influx of non-*burakumin* wives. But offsetting this fact, as Taura-san reminded us, is the depressing economic situation; for example, although the standard of living has risen slightly in Kawabara, this is due chiefly to more substantial economic aid—a dubious value at best since it also encourages disvalues (parasitism most conspicuously).

In discussing this same question, the prefectural official assigned to *burakumin* affairs, Yamasaki-san, contended that the only significant achievement since formal emancipation was proclaimed nearly a century ago (federal grants, he insisted, are little more than tokens) is outlawry of segregation in the public schools. How, he asked, can one speak of other kinds of progress, as long as economic problems among *burakumin* and prejudice among non-*burakumin* both remain acute?

Yamasaki-san's evaluation tended to be supported by two informants who live outside the community but closely follow its affairs. Women's Leader Tabata has observed little recent improvement in the deviant behavior of most Kawabara children, although there are exceptions. Likewise, Jichikai Secretary Kamada has failed to discern any genuine improvement in the condition of Kawabara. Although confessing a feeling of "hopelessness" about the situation, he did admit that a few Kawabarians are not to be characterized so gloomily; among them he included both Kaihōdōmei Leader Tomita and Dōwakai Leader Hayashi.

This discussion of political-economic values concludes with much the same group of controversial questions that were asked unevenly of our Ebibara panelists. Most who responded, both within and without Kawabara proper, opposed any change in the Constitution that would permit rearmament. Most wished to see Red China admitted to the United Nations. Most wanted America to withdraw from Vietnam. On only two issues did the majority of the panel reveal beliefs perhaps not wholly consistent with others: they saw no serious objection to American atomic submarines visiting Japan, and they were skeptical of the workability of a democratic world order. At the same time, all but one unanimously endorsed world order as an ideal. This informant was skeptical because "it sounds too much like the Sōkagakkai."

V

Turning next to educational values it is well not to forget that, although many of the values attributed to the schools of our previously studied sub-culture, Ebibara, apply equally to Kawabara, we confine ourselves again to characteristics revealing certain distinctiveness. Even so, we can hardly avoid one characteristic of value shared equally by both the *gyomin* and *burakumin* communities: since Kawabara children, like Ebibara children, attend public schools entirely outside of their own neighborhoods, they are inevitably affected by the ways education in each city as a whole includes the valuational dimensions.

Consider, to begin with, a question addressed to various informants as to whether education in Yamada-shi is or should be concerned primarily and deliberately with rebuilding cultural institutions toward desirable goals, or whether its principal role is or should be that of transmitting and reinforcing those institutions with supportive values already well established and commonly accepted. So far as Kawabarians are concerned, the answer is straightforward: even though education does not as yet do so at all effectively, it should nevertheless direct its attention first of all to changing those habits and attitudes of Japanese life that encourage prejudice and that perpetuate discrimination. But when we turn to Yamada-shi educators the answer becomes less clearcut.

Superintendent Kondō, for one, held that while the primary function of the school is to "stabilize" culture, he has no objection to programs of social education for adults (especially if these take place in factories or community centers) that deal directly with matters of economic and other kinds of change. Still, he sees no clear way by which schools can cope directly in solving problems of *burakumin*, except to help ghetto students to become more industrious so that when they do seek jobs they will be better qualified. Indeed, experimental projects of any kind that deviate from the prescribed curriculum are wholly impractical; even now the schools can barely accomplish all that they are expected to. Nor, said Kondō-san, do citizens of Yamada-shi normally make suggestions for curriculum innovation; with the exception of a few Kawabarians, they seem quite content to accept courses of study as they are.

At first Principal Matsuo of Kitano Chūgakkō appeared to be more resilient in his answer to this same question. He does not, he maintained, regard Japanese education as chiefly a conservative force; after all, especially since World War II, students have been exposed constantly to such democratic values as freedom and participation. Parents, too, are encouraged through their PTAs to share these values with their children.

Yet, on closer scrutiny, Principal Matsuo proved to be even more equivocal than Superintendent Kondō. Although he criticized school requirements for repressing creativity and spontaneity in learners, he saw little opportunity to resist them. Still more revealing, he opposed any direct discussion whatsoever of *burakumin* problems in the curriculum. The only practical policy, he insisted, is *fure-nai:* "don't touch." The clear choice is between two and only two alternatives, explosive conflict or strict avoidance of the problem, and to his mind the latter alone is feasible. Democratic discussion of *burakumin* problems might be all right in theory, but not in practice; the extremism of a few *burakumin* just won't let it work. Matsuo-san's general attitude, moreover, extends quite consistently far beyond this specific issue: the obligation of the school, at least until the senior level, is to remain "neutral" toward controversial questions of every variety, and thus to confine its obligations at most to helping students develop ability to cope with any such questions when they become adults.

Social Education Director Ueno agreed with Principal Matsuo. The primary function of the school, he said, is to teach knowledge and skills objectively, not to "take sides." Recently, for example, when a group of senior high school students wished to form a "radical" political group, he opposed it zealously because he held that they are not mature enough to understand such matters. As for problems of discrimination, it is unnecessary to deal with them in the curriculum at all. The old adage, *Neta ko o okosuna* ("sleeping children should not be awakened"), continues to be appropriate: most children know little or nothing of *burakumin;* why arouse them? Nor does evidence show that Ueno-san, as an adult educator, considers his responsibilities to include any attempt to bring school and community into closer partnership.

Teachers among our informants agreed more than they disagreed with the general orientation of their administrative leaders. Even Teacher Inoki, our progressive-minded informant at Nanyō Shōgakkō, thought that it would be dangerous to expose children to problems such as class differences and conflicts; to do so might lead them to become "pessimistic" about Japanese society. Certainly in the elementary school, students must not be confronted with ideological issues because such an effort would only distort meanings. And yet, as seems true of most other professional informants, one detects considerable eclecticism in Inoki-san's educational beliefs; perhaps they reflect his history as a former member of the Japan Teachers' Union who had been "exiled" to teach on an isolated island, but who came to Yamada-shi after assuring administrators that he had resigned from the union. He is now a vice-president of the local chapter of Kyōshikai, the proadministration organization of teachers. Yet he remains in attitude an educational liberal. For example, he favors the "problem-solving method" of "scientific inquiry" concerning questions of value, and he regrets that this method of teaching and learning is no longer encouraged. As long as this remains the case, he says, the school cannot hope to function as an instrument of change.

The single widest critical consensus within our panel of school people appeared here. In other words, Teacher Inoki's attitude toward what he more or less privately regarded as the constricting if not debilitating power of Monbushō (Ministry of Education) is shared in varying degrees not only by other teacher informants in Yamada-shi but by local PTA officers, by students, and even by some administrative officers. We must be careful to note, indeed, that the largely conservative mood prevailing among teachers and administrators is not necessarily defended as a desirable mood; rather, the commoner attitude seems to be that education presently can do very little to become a reconstructive force as long as rigid controls from the top down continue to hold.

On this point Principal Matsuo proved to be quite spirited. Because of academic demands placed upon his school both by Monbushō and by prefectural authorities, such modern techniques as the discussion method, social problem-solving, and field trips have had to be curtailed to a minimum. In place of them, what he called the "installment principle" has become virtually the only method of learning. The primary goals of education in Yamada-shi have become the taking of examinations, winning high enough scores to assure advancement, and competitive striving to do well in Kagawa testing programs so that the prefecture can continue to place at or near the top of the National Achievement Tests (NAT). Simultaneously, a high-level value of Japanese education after the war, to enable the child to develop as a "whole person," has been more and more subordinated.

Here the value judgments of our student-informant, Anasaki-san, are apropos. This fifteen-year-old regarded his present education chiefly as preparation for further education, not at all as intrinsically worthwhile in the sense of enabling him to understand or to cope with problems of his own life and time. Far from holding that Kitano Chūgakkō performs any discernible role in effecting social change, he insisted that the opposite is true: since rote-learning and subservience are the primary habits acquired by junior high school students, one could hardly expect them to speak up, much less to question or participate of their own volition. It is not only the problems of the 50 or so *burakumin* students in his school that are neglected, so too are all other problems of the Yamada-shi community.

Student Anasaki, incidentally, is an officer of *seitokai*, the student organization of Kitano Chūgakkō. It has, he said, achieved considerable autonomy including budget-making because the administration quickly yields to almost any kind of pressure, even from students. Nevertheless, *seitokai* cannot become an effective organization, since neither teachers nor administrators wish it to cause any kind of trouble.

Our teacher-informant from the same junior high school, Obara-san, was not as vehement as Student Anasaki. Yet he too appeared to be negative more often than positive. True, he regarded the NAT as serving the useful purpose of measuring levels of ability; yet he agreed with several other informants that it places primary value upon scores, an opinion shared by Director Ueno, who could see no alternative as long as teachers are untrained to motivate children to learn except by the incentive of examinations.

Although our impression is that most teachers in Yamada-shi dislike the NAT, they are resigned (if Teacher Inoki is right) to this kind of imposition as long as "competition" remains a primary value of Japanese culture. According to Student Anasaki's calculations, this also means that students like himself who wish to compete for admission to senior high school must take some "27 big examinations in a single year." In preparation for these, about half of the student body of Kitano Chūgakkō are enrolled in tutoring classes in addition to their regular programs. Special tutoring now occurs even in Nanyō Shōgakkō for about half of the fifth and sixth grade children who are hopeful of continuing not only into senior high school but possibly to still higher levels.

To restate our original question differently, let us ask one other informant, Kikuchi-san, a PTA officer at Kitano Chūgakkō, her opinion of education as a means of change toward more or less enunciated cultural goals. From the standpoint of a parent, her answer supported an opinion expressed by others on our panel. The schools, she felt, "conceal" the most urgent problems of our age from the eyes and thoughts of students. And yet neither Monbushō at the national level nor teachers and school officials at the rank-and-file level can really be blamed too much: on the one hand, parents themselves constantly urge their children to pass examinations as the be-all and end-all of learning; on the other hand, parents do little or nothing to question or criticize the system of education as it now exists. Therefore the ineptitude that one detects in school personnel as they continue to circumvent such problems as the *burakumin* is, Kikuchi-san declared, one consequence of habits of indifference and passivity among parents and other citizens themselves.

If any major exceptions may be offered to the scarcely glowing picture thus far sketched by our informants of the valuational dimension of Yamada-shi and therefore Kawabara education, these may be considered within two remaining spheres. The first is the program called *dōwa kyōiku*, earlier translated as "education for integration." The second is a series of community recommendations for improving the local school program. *Dōwa kyōiku* is not a Yamada-shi innovation; rather it is nationwide. More accurately the program is a double endeavor: one part is supported by a movement known as Zendōkyō, an abbreviation for the National Assimilation Study Conference; the other part by Monbushō. The conference itself has met annually since 1953, with as many as two or three thousand delegates representing teachers, administrators, parents, and other groups. It has been leftist in orientation, with Kaihōdōmei influencing planning and programs. Problems of discrimination are central to conference deliberations, but repeatedly its official proclamations have emphasized that the guiding purpose is to promote democratic education as a whole, without which prejudice and related evils cannot be eradicated. The Marxian ideology has also been influential in the insistence of leaders that capitalism is at the root of these evils for the reason that the profit system requires exploitation. In more recent conferences the emphasis has shifted, however. Thus the one attended by a member of our research staff did not conspicuously play up the anticapitalist theme; rather its many symposiums dealt with such topics as guidance, children's organizations, and in-service training for teachers of *dōwa kyōiku*.

Monbushō's program began in 1958, its own organization being called the Japan Association for Assimilation Education. Its guiding principles have been much more temperate than Zendōkyō's; indeed, it has apparently been promoted as something of a counterfoil. Critical, direct analysis of the social order and of such evils as discriminatory employment is minimized in favor of teaching broadly democratic human relations to all children. Therefore, whereas the Monbushō enterprise likewise formally approves of assimilation and equality for *burakumin,* it views this goal as achievable by gradually improving the present economic and political order. Understandably, Dōwakai, the *burakumin* organization that we have come to know as an ally of the dominant Liberal Democratic party, endorses the Monbushō program much more enthusiastically than it does Zendōkyō's. According to Councilman Hayashi, Dōwakai also has its own education and research center, financed by Monbushō, at the head temple of Jōdoshinshū in Kyoto (Honganji); on our visit to this temple, however, we failed to discover either regular staff or organized activities.

Finances for Zendōkyō derive chiefly from its own publications (including a monthly magazine), Kaihōdōmei support, and miscellaneous contributions. Also, it has been associated with the influential Kyoto-based Research Institute on Buraku Problems, which publishes numerous books and brochures on the history of *burakumin* and other pertinent themes.

The Monbushō *dōwa kyōiku* program, by contrast, is financed directly from the federal budget. In a meeting with the *dōwa kyōiku* director of Monbushō in Tokyo, we were informed that a special committee with Kaihōdōmei as well as Dōwakai representation was about to recommend to the Prime Minister a budget of $70,000 earmarked for scholarships for *burakumin* students who want to attend senior high school. Another national project, already under way, is an annual three-day session for in-service training of teachers specializing in *dōwa kyōiku*. Yet, like Yamada-shi educators, the national director is dubious of any "direct" approach to the study of *burakumin* problems in the curriculum, even under carefully trained teachers. Possibly this could be done through "special clubs" in the schools; possibly, too, a "direct" approach could be attempted "a few years from now" if parents could be reached at the same time through effective social education.

In Yoneshima-ken, the Monbushō program has been carried out chiefly through an independent prefectural organization in which *dōwa kyōiku* tries to emphasize democratic goals, not just for *burakumin* but for all children. Considerable talk, nevertheless, was noted in this organization about the need to affiliate with Zendōkyō. We attended an all-day program sponsored by an elementary school not far from Nanyō Shōgakkō, which featured demonstrations of how *dōwa kyōiku* can be carried out in everyday learning (one class we visited was having a lesson on *Uncle Tom's Cabin*). It was also attended by several Kaihōdōmei members. Here is one indication, apparently, that the two wings of the *dōwa kyōiku* movement do sometimes join hands, just as Kaihōdōmei and Dōwakai occasionally manage if only precariously to do so in Kawabara.

Meanwhile, the Monbushō program has provided grants to selected schools where special *dōwa kyōiku* projects could be attempted. In Yoneshima-ken, to which $500 was originally allocated, one of these schools was Nanyō Shōgakkō. Its own project began in 1958 and evolved from year to year. Psychological needs of Kawabara children were emphasized in an early program, academic ability in another, group guidance in still another. One of the most imaginative ventures was to seek better communication between *burakumin* and non-*burakumin* parents, with teachers serving as intermediaries through actual visits to many homes in the district. A questionnaire was also prepared to determine how the two groups felt about each other, although according to Tabata-san many responses were too evasive to be useful. Local Kaihōdōmei spokesmen, reflecting Zendō-kyō's orientation, also remained critical of the Nanyō program, insisting that direct attack upon such problems as prejudice were being soft-pedaled.

Certainly it seems evident when one examines most of the materials prepared for the Nanyō project that the Monbushō "indirect" approach continues to overshadow Zendōkyō's preference for a "direct" approach. True, one of these documents, prepared as a classroom guide, not only refers briefly to discrimination but points to such handicaps as absenteeism, below-average IQs, unbalanced diets, and poor environments from which Kawabara children particularly suffer. Even so, the document is couched in general language such as "respect for human beings" and "building character," and its specific activities (for example, dental examinations and games) apply equally well to all Nanyō children.

Only two features strike us as unusual. One, teachers and parents have engaged in writing "liaison notes" to each other about their children, so that both sides can be better informed. And two, a twice-yearly magazine has been published by the school in which children, teachers, and parents together try to share some of their deeper feelings and interests. This magazine has the touching name "Whispers—little desires." Here is just a sample, written by a second-grade child: "You come back so late at night, Daddy. Do you know that I wait for you to come home? Daddy, please come home earlier."

Here please recall that *dōtoku kyōiku* (moral education) is practically mandatory in all public schools of Japan. Hence we may suppose that *dōwa kyōiku* would on occasion overlap with *dōtoku kyōiku*. In the case of Nanyō Shōgakkō, such overlapping has been deliberate: in utilizing the practical guide books provided to all public schools by Monbushō for teaching moral education, the staff seeks to relate at least verbally such precepts as "respect for personality" to the task of educating against any kind of prejudice. Again, the precept of "inquiry" is compared with the concern for socioeconomic factors that cause segregation; and the value of "respect for labor" is associated with the problem of discrimination in employment.

In short, faced by persistent prodding from education-minded *burakumin,* the school closest to Kawabara has tried, we think valiantly, to move step-by-step toward a more "direct" approach. To be sure, its most interested teachers are far from satisfied for several reasons. Some parents of non-*burakumin* children oppose *dōwa kyōiku* because, they say, it devotes time and money to a program intended to benefit only a minority of children. Also, Teacher Inoki among others finds that a wide gap still prevails between theoretical precepts as embodied in written materials and daily classrooom practice. Again, the time allotted to moral education, one hour per week, is altogether too limited (and even this often seems to be curtailed in favor of practice for tests).

The legitimate psychological question, moreover, of when children are ready to come to grips with problems of discrimination is far from clear. And even were it clearer, age-graded resources prepared by Zendōkyō affiliates in, say, the history of *burakumin* are only now becoming available. Then, too, the contention that Monbushō is attempting to indoctrinate its own values continues to trouble some teachers, especially those who may have been influenced by Nikkyōso (Japan Teachers' Union). Finally the ever-irksome task of dealing honestly with issues of prejudice, without at the same time offending hypersensitive parents, remains hazardous; thus it is hardly difficult to understand why so many Yamada-shi teachers prefer to steer away from the controversy altogether rather than to run the risk of embroilment.

At any rate, and notwithstanding that *burakumin* problems often become acute on the teen-age level, no effort remotely comparable to Nanyō Shōgakkō's could be discovered in Kitano Chūgakkō. Moral education is also required in the junior high school, but this consists of formal lessons prescribed by Monbushō. Principal Matsuo, supported by Superintendent Kondō, therefore avoids any kind of *dōwa kyōiku* that treats of discrimination; as suggested earlier, to do so would, they were sure, simply inflame the situation. Since, after all, the trouble is said to lie chiefly with *burakumin* themselves, and since few non-*burakumin* students are in any case aware of prejudice or indeed of *burakumin* problems at all, *dōwa kyōiku* must be confined strictly to developing more positive democratic values in all Kitano students. To this end, meetings are held regularly in the school auditorium for the third-year class, during which teachers lecture on moral principles; no discussion is provided. The pressure of academic requirements, moreover, makes it impossible, according to Principal Matsuo, to develop special materials even in *dōtoku kyōiku*. The only exception, it seems, occurs in the PTA where once each year a lecture on *dōwa kyōiku* has been offered chiefly at the instigation of *burakumin* officers.

A number of positive proposals, a few already under way, conclude our overview of education's place in the value patterns of Kawabara. They reveal, we believe, the genuine concern of some citizens that their public schools exercise more of a creative and aggressive role in improving the life of Yamada-shi. In no particular order, let us list the eight most interesting proposals.

1. *Establishment of the Yamada-shi study group on burakumin problems.* This study group was launched during our period of involvement, several meetings being held at Yamada College. The 15 or so participants consisted predominantly of public school teachers and administrators although the chairman was an official of the college faculty. Only one *burakumin*, Mitsuda-san, was a member. He seemed to agree that others

should be judiciously selected to prevent Kaihōdōmei-Dōwakai bickering from destroying the group's effectiveness.

Several proposals emerged at these sessions. One was a plan for inter-visitations between schools enrolling many *burakumin* children and schools consisting entirely of non-*burakumin*. The assumption behind the idea was, of course, that direct, friendly association between children of various cultural backgrounds is one fruitful means of alleviating stereotypes and encouraging mutual respect.

Another proposal weighed by the study group was that the newly constructed playground in Kawabara be utilized both as a further opportunity for intervisitations of children, and for a well-supervised program of recreation to be instituted during summer vacations. This playground program would aim to develop more constructive social behavior among *burakumin* children, most of whom reflect a good deal of the same difficult personality patterns that we have noted in their parents.

2. *Strengthening of Seitokai.* Gaps between student officers and other members of the junior high school organization, as well as gaps between students and faculty, could be narrowed if a program were developed involving many more young people in school activities and responsibilities. These could well include *burakumin* students.

3. *Revitalization of moral education.* At least an average of two hours per week (that is, double the present time) should be devoted to moral education, based on the once influential "whole man" concept of learning and teaching *(zenjin kyōiku).* Discussion of problems geared to the interests of children of various ages; intensive in-service training for teachers of *dōtoku kyōiku;* more sharing and searching by teachers and students together in dealing with moral questions; more analysis of tensions engendered between Western and Eastern values (for example, the postwar emphasis on individualism versus traditional respect for *oya kōkō,* filial piety); frank consideration of problems of sexual morality; re-establishment of the core corriculum so that moral questions may be considered in relation to areas such as social studies; examination of conflicts between value orientations of the older and younger generations, including serious attention both by adults and children to shifting patterns of family order—all of these reforms were suggested by various informants.

4. *Less stress on rote-learning, more stress on the arts.* The two hours out of 37 per week presently devoted to the arts in the junior high school curriculum, and the two hours out of 31 in the elementary school, were called grossly insufficient. To provide greater balance, less time and energy should be devoted to competitive examinations, NATs, and drills in mathematics and other skills; more time should be devoted to music, painting, and other creative arts. (Resistance to NATs, homogeneous group-

ing, and competitive examinations also meshes, we remember, with Nik-kyōso attitudes, although teachers' union members have virtually disap-peared from Yamada-shi. Such resistance is in accord with Zendōkyō and Kaihōdōmei; both consider these practices discriminatory against lower-class children, especially *burakumin.*)

  5. *More educational involvement in the culture of Yamada-shi.* Only a few hours at most are now devoted to local history in the entire junior high school; otherwise such aspects as the social, political, and religious are almost wholly bypassed. This neglect is even more severe in Kawabara. The need, we were told, is for more leeway in the curriculum, more freedom to innovate, and more participation in community life.

  6. *Establishment of a Center for the Growth of Children.* This center was actually inaugurated during our stay in Yamada-shi, and has been financed by both federal and prefectural social welfare funds. Since its principal aim is to reduce juvenile delinquency, it has special relevance for Kawabarians. Superintendent Kondō is director, and the staff of five includes both policewomen and teachers. One of their chief duties is to patrol the streets in the late afternoon and evening. Thus in a single month over 80 instances of delinquent behavior were recorded by the Center, and various kinds of remedial treatment including psychotherapy were recommended.

  7. *Establishment of a Society for the Improvement of Chil-dren—a new parent-teacher group in the elementary school, Nanyō Shōgakkō.* Contrary to the previous practice of teacher-parent conferences on an individual basis, the aim of this society will be to encourage uninhibited monthly group discussions of daily problems, especially among *buraku-min* children, with as many parents and teachers as possible. Since parental devotion often transcends ideological differences, this suggestion (which emanated, incidentally, from Kawabara parents) could become, according to Teacher Inoki, another common link between Kaihōdōmei and Dōwakai.

  8. *Establishment of a new elementary school venture, gakkyū-kai* (a term suggesting "classroom meeting"). This venture plans to utilize homeroom hours in Nanyō Shōgakkō for discussion of the children's problems in their own rather than their teachers' terms. Thus it becomes another step in the evolution of *dōwa kyōiku* and *dōtoku kyōiku* considered as reciprocal endeavors. With minimal supervisory control, Kawabara as well as non-*burakumin* children will be encouraged to conduct their own meetings and to express their own feelings frankly. Guidance will be strengthened, hopefully with the aid of at least one full-time specialist well informed in both *dōtoku kyōiku* and *dōwa kyōiku. Gakkyū-kai* will also attempt to enlist the cooperation and interest of the two elementary

student organizations already active, *kodomokai* and *jidōkai*. All of the nine classroom teachers at Nanyō Shōgakkō will be involved by keeping diaries of *gakkyū-kai* sessions and by seeking to improve their guidance roles. In-service preparation for the venture was already under way when our own research in Kawabara and Yamada-shi drew to a close.

VI

How, in concluding this Part, shall we pinpoint the character of Kawabara? Our many-faceted delineation of its patterns of value may have left the reader with too artificial and tepid an image. Such has not been our intention: despite their forlorn record, Kawabarians, if they are at all fairly typified by their children, are often overflowing with the sheer zest of everyday living. The eagerness, for example, with which crowds of boys and girls vied to take turns holding our hands as we walked along the earthen pathways beside their rows of simple houses, or the gleeful chatter that filled our car when on occasion we volunteered to escort them on frequent joyrides through the countryside, remain indelible memories.

And yet, looking back at the three-stage interpretation that has likewise governed Ebibara, one impression again looms above all others. This is of a community at once beset by almost chronic internal disturbances, but nonetheless able to demonstrate remarkable and even militant vigor at moments of crisis in behalf of its paramount commitment to the goal of full emancipation. As we have also found to be true of Ebibara, no one could properly maintain that Kawabara is thereby radically different in many respects from hundreds of comparable communities or, for that matter, from Japanese villages in general. Still, the more patiently one seeks to probe beneath the surface of Kawabara life the more one begins to detect its own idiosyncracies. These, we have found, gain sharpest focus through the extraordinarily bitter conflict of several years' duration between local members of two *burakumin* organizations—Dōwakai and Kaihōdōmei—the former endorsing a policy of "conciliationism" toward the municipal, prefectural, and national power structure; the latter supporting emancipation by means of aggressive and sweeping strategies directed against that structure.

Inevitably again, to be sure, the community situation as a whole is far less simple than any compressed statement such as this can suggest. When confronted by specific issues, Kawabarians at times reveal inconsistent, erratic behavior both in their personalities and in their professed organizational as well as family allegiances; at other times they are able to unite sufficiently to carry concrete tasks through to completion. The collaborative plan to construct a desperately needed playground is one instance of the latter that we observed; the cooperative and friendly spirit (despite a recalcitrant minority) displayed by the majority toward our own involvement in Kawabara is another. The fact, too, that local *burakumin* leaders have undertaken persistent roles in educational affairs, notably through PTAs and *dōwa kyōiku* ("education for integration"), is an indication that, despite the reluctance of Yamada-shi school administrators and most though not all teachers, Kawabara does take very seriously indeed the mandate of universal, democratic human rights enshrined by the Constitution of Japan.

But further inquiries now emerge. In the final Part before us, we propose to consider both Kawabara and Ebibara not only comparatively but evaluatively. This endeavor once more embraces three successive steps, although quite different from those familiar to Parts I and II. The first step will view our two communities in common perspectives. The second will perceive them through the eyes and judgments of a group of leaders whose experiences and postures are likely to prove both similar to and dissimilar from those of Ebibarians and Kawabarians. The third and final step will try to channel both descriptions and prescriptions of our total investigation through one central institution—Japanese education.

Part III

Perspectives

7

FROM
THE BOTTOM UP:
A COMMUNITY
PERSPECTIVE

I

Twenty miles, less than an hour by bus or car, separate Ebibara from Kawabara. No matter how often you drive from one to the other over a fine concrete road you are charmed by the vistas on all sides— the fertile rice fields in geometrical precision, the phalanxes of orchards, the gentle hills of lovely hues of green.

One would suppose that this countryside must indeed provide its residents with a fair share of the modest, life-sustaining satisfactions that they expect in exchange for their toil and the honor they pay to their families and their gods.

It is true that increasing numbers of citizens in Yoneshima-ken, perhaps as in any rural section of Japan, do receive satisfactions such as these. Rarely, to be sure, do they receive them quickly or easily: to earn enough from land or factory, from office or sea, demands vast patience and endless exertion. Considered as a whole, Yoneshima-ken is the home of hard-working, modest, and persevering people.

And yet, generalizations about cultures, even very small ones, often prove hazardous indeed. Even such simple generalizations as we have just ventured would require substantial refinement before one could claim to have pictured this region with any real precision.

Ebibara and Kawabara are cases in point. Officially, both our *gyomin* and *burakumin* friends are full-fledged citizens. The great majority of both, moreover, have lived in their respective communities for generations—

165

further back in time than can usually be determined from family records preserved in their local temples. The consequence is that they have absorbed into their personalities and their ways of life a myriad of qualities that reflect not only the national character of Japan but still more, no doubt, the regional character. Even so, the more we focus upon each of these communities the more sharply we discern two further somewhat paradoxical features. On the one hand, both reveal a variety of characteristics in common that are much less conspicious among many other Japanese communities; on the other hand, they are different in various striking respects even from each other.

This chapter compares the most pronounced of both these similar and dissimilar characteristics, drawing not only from the resources of preceding pages but from a brief investigation, not hitherto reported, of the value orientations prevailing in both subcultures. We conclude with a frankly interpretative evaluation of our own.

II

The people of Ebibara and Kawabara are regarded by the majority of their neighboring citizens with invidious feelings that range from acute prejudice to mild contempt or condescension. One must immediately qualify, of course; such feelings, we have found, are typically stronger toward Kawabara than they are toward Ebibara residents. Nevertheless, they remain endemic toward both. It was scarcely a generation ago, after all, that marriage between an Ebibarian and a young person from a nearby community would have seemed to the latter little short of a disgrace. Today, although the pattern of exclusion has weakened, many outgroup people still prefer to avoid marital ties with ingroup Ebibara families, just as they shun any such ties with Kawabara families.

Invidious feelings result, of course, from multiple causes. In the cases of the *gyomin* and *burakumin* whom we have come to know, some of those causes, actual or alleged, may be summarized:

The lower-lower and upper-lower class status of most citizens in Ebibara and Kawabara;

Their consequent "culture of poverty," [1] with such attendant features as higher than average rates of illness, crowded slum housing, lack

---

[1] This term as used by Oscar Lewis is not always strictly applicable to our two communities. Nevertheless, similarities of meaning are abundant. Cf. Oscar Lewis, *La Vida* (New York: Random House, Inc., 1966), pp. xlii ff.

of household and personal cleanliness, low educational level, and lax sexual mores;

A propensity to gamble away earnings at *pachinko*, cards, dice, coin tossing, and other games;

A concomitant tendency to live from day to day, with minimal economic planning and maximal insecurity;

A high ratio of menial workers, both men and women, including door-to-door peddlers;

An abnormal incidence of juvenile delinquency, which in turn is partly attributed to frequent absence of both parents from their households;

Considerable disregard for legality by adults as well as children;

A reputation for erratic temperaments, especially in the form of volatile if not on occasion violent behavior, coupled with feelings of inferiority;

Endogamous kinship networks, with marriages often—much too often, in the view of various observers—occurring between close relatives, including first cousins.

This summary could be extended. Our concern has been simply to indicate some conspicuous influences generating adverse attitudes. This is not to suggest that other attitudes of a more favorable nature are not discernible as well. Consider, for example, that Ebibara and Kawabara both are known to manifest a greater than average degree of religious devotion, a devotion usually not expressed in allegiance to the same sects, yet equally confined to orthodox forms of Buddhism and Shintoism (there are no Christians). It is symbolized, too, by the frequent display of a costly *butsudan* (Buddhist household altar) and a *kamidana* (Shintō shelf), by the practice of such ceremonials as *hōji* (ancestral commemoration), and by severe hostility to such heterodox sects as the Sōkagakkai.

Again, certain character traits common to both communities are mentioned in terms of commendation. These include a willingness to cooperate in *jichikai* programs of the respective cities; a readiness to join hands, sometimes by only a few families but sometimes by large numbers, when confronted by serious trouble; a respectful, often congenial manner in face-to-face relations; and, above all, the zeal with which both communities have tried recently to attack what they consider to be the most serious problems confronting them.

These quite affirmative traits are reinforced by the fact that, in addition to comparably distinctive features, Ebibara and Kawabara also reveal features more or less common to their immediate cultural environment. Because of this, the people of Utsumi-shi or Yamada-shi can scarcely regard their Ebibara or Kawabara neighbors in too deprecating a fashion without deprecating themselves as well. Again in abbreviated fashion we select more or less random examples of such common features:

The tradition of *honke-bunke* (main-branch family) with its cluster of loyalties and obligations;

At the same time, slowly increasing democratization of family order and of boy-girl relations;

The widespread practice of birth control;

Participation in political affairs by both sexes, at least to the point of exercising voting rights;

Levels of social class, with power and prestige centering in a few relatively upper-level families;

Perpetuation, though with declining enthusiasm, of various folk rituals such as *yakudoshi* (protection against bad-luck years);

Nine years of compulsory education (about one-third of the population of each city is in school) with standardized curricula prescribed at the national level;

Availability of, although far from universal enrollment in, senior high school and social (adult) education programs;

Active student and parent organizations;

Widespread out-of-school tutoring, chiefly in preparation for the multitudinous examinations;

Predominantly rural environments relatively distant from great urban centers, but modified at accelerating rates by the smallness of farms (about one-half the national average in both municipalities), by the speed of transportation, by widespread utilization of the great media of communication (periodicals least, movies and radio somewhat, television most), and by increasing industralization.

III

However impressive one may regard such common cultural denominators, still more so, we think, are the features that place Ebibara and Kawabara in contrast.

Take, to begin with, marriage and family practices. The tradition of *mi-ai kekkon* (arranged marriage) and the more modern practice of *ren-ai kekkon* (love marriage) seem to be moving in almost opposite directions. Not exclusively so, of course: none of the contrasts we consider are without overlapping elements. With this precaution in mind, it is still evident that *ren-ai* is primary in Kawabara, more and more so as non-*burakumin* women (some 40 at present) come to live with their *burakumin* mates whom they met outside. In Ebibara, on the other hand, *mi-ai* is increasingly preferred. This preference is attributable partly to the lessening of sexual permissiveness but probably to a much greater extent to the economic need of young fisherwomen, even more than of young fishermen, to locate partners from outside their own community. It is above all this need for security that therefore often requires the services of a go-between (*nakōdo*), occasionally a professional one. To state the point in a different way, both communities incline toward more frequent exogamous marriage, but in Kawabara this is enhanced more and more by the popularity of *ren-ai* (a trend prevalent throughout Japan), whereas in Ebibara it is enhanced best by reverting to *mi-ai*.

Marriage rites reveal no less striking differences. In our fishing community, we learned that these rites are typically elaborate and very costly, so much so that they place an almost unbearable financial burden on parents, especially of the bride. Thereby they also assure one important sanction of stable marriage. But compare our *burakumin* community: the majority of marriages, being common-law, more often than not consist of signing a register at the city hall and sometimes apparently not even this.

Interwoven in complex ways with differing marriage rites in both communities are differing reactions to such wellworn practices as primogeniture, the adoption of sons, the main-branch kinship pattern, and the values of *on* and *giri*. All of these practices and values, we recall, are affected by customary patterns of relationship between those who bestow beneficence and those who acquire obligations as a result of such bestowal.

But again we perceive striking variations. Primogeniture, for example, is the rule in Ebibara; in Kawabara it is the exception for the reason that, unlike its neighboring community where particularly fishing boats are valuable property, the eldest son of a *burakumin* is rarely able to make a living from his parents' holdings. *Muko-yōshi* (male adoption) therefore is also less frequent, and marriage ties in turn appear less secure because they are less essential to family perpetuity. *Oya kōkō* (filial piety) likewise is weakened in so far as respect for parents may be associated with respect for economic status together with the power that this status manifests.

Such variations must not easily lead us to suppose that patterns of reciprocal obligation influenced by *on* and *giri* do not remain influential in Kawabara too, nor that the *honke-bunke* structure of the extended family which reinforces these values is merely trivial. What does appear to be frequently the case is that, since primogeniture and inheritable property are meager, obligations are most effectively exacted through *oyabun-kobun* ("ritual father—ritual son") relationships rather than through the more dominant

Ebibara pattern. Through these relationships, a *bosu* such as Hayashi-san is able to maintain impressive influence not only over numerous members of his extended family but over other associates who become socially, economically, or politically indebted to him. In Ebibara, by comparison, we can assume that the *oyabun-kobun* pattern has weakened inversely to the strengthening of other patterns—most importantly, perhaps, the fishermen's producer co-operative which substitutes membership rights for hierarchical obligations. No such institution exists within the *burakumin* community.

A further factor is that in contrast to Ebibara *gyomin*, who often reside next door to farmers or other citizens of Utsumi-shi long imbued with customs of family mutuality, Kawabara people live in almost total isolation from fellow citizens of Yamada-shi. Hence they have less cause to perpetuate the customs of these citizens or to be concerned for fear others think ill of them for failing to do so.

Even so, such isolation does not in the least deter Kawabarians from involvement in the city's political activities. Here is another sharp distinction from Ebibarians. Most of the latter, even though they may exercise their voting franchise and share in *jichikai* responsibilities, are usually lukewarm if not indifferent about political affairs. On the contrary, Kawabarians seem to be much better informed and more concerned not only about Yamada-shi politics but about prefectural, national, and even international affairs.

Even more dramatically, we have found that explicitly Kawabara political values are, taken as a whole, well to the left of those in Ebibara. Whereas nearly all *gyomin* are Liberal Democrats (indeed, they seem abjectly loyal to Kasuga-san, the Utsumi-shi representative in the lower house of the Diet, whom they regard as one of their own), the majority of Kawabarians support the Socialist party. In addition, the Communist party although small in membership is extremely active among *burakumin* (we discovered no Communists among our *gyomin* friends). Even local members of the Liberal Democratic party, including Councilman Hayashi, seem more amenable to a moderately leftward posture in Kawabara than would be true of Liberal Democrats in general.

But the same phenomenon of greater political awareness and concern also leaves an impression of much greater political disharmony in Kawabara than in Ebibara. Not only are ideologies acutely at odds; the conflicts of family loyalties with *oyabun-kobun* connections, and the prevalence of opportunistic motivations added to chronic intergroup hostility, all contribute to an overall impression that our *burakumin* are far less unified in the sphere of political interest than our more conservative fishermen.

It is not surprising, consequently, to find a greater degree of solidarity prevailing likewise in the economic life of Ebibara than of Kawabara. This is neither to forget that *gyomin* are not without their own severe conflicts, nor that *burakumin* are capable of elements of unity. What we do discover is that Ebibara is bound together not only by an age-old occupation fraught both with danger and courage but by the vitally important fishermen's cooperative. Nor are such unifying forces merely economic: recall both the young fishermen's "sleeping clubs" (sometimes called *neyado*) that have continued for many generations, and the vigorous "matriarchy" of the co-op auxiliary. And although it is true that numerous Ebibara citizens are not actually fishermen, it is equally true that the great majority, including wives, daughters, sons, and other relatives, are engaged in one form or another of wage-earning directly related to the sea.

If Kawabara, by comparison, could be said to possess any single predominant economic feature it is dependence upon public-welfare grants. We remember that, including *shittai* (workers on unemployment programs), over one hundred—some two-thirds of all households—are partly or wholly dependent upon these grants as compared with but two or three Ebibara households. The only other noteworthy economic features are the junk business of Hayashi-san and Taura-san, who together hire some 20 or 25 *burōkā* or collectors though rarely full-time, and the glove factory that employs about a dozen women. Thus, with the exception of the latter and a few sundry workers such as peddlers and shoemakers, Kawabarians can hardly be compared with Ebibarians on the score of industriousness. Fishermen have managed to maintain and even to increase their incomes primarily by stretching the length of their working days, often to well beyond 12 hours. Among *burakumin* it is probably safe to estimate that a rough average of the working day for the total work force is less than half this total.

Turn now to one of our main concerns—the process of cultural change. Granting that poverty, with all the evils it connotes, is the root of the problems of both these communities, what has each done to cope with it?

Here again contrasts are more pronounced than similarities. The *gyomin* program is a concerted effort to upgrade the local economy through several innovations: seaweed farming most notably, including plans to push back the sea by a long breakwater so that acreage may be substantially increased; the construction of "fish apartments" for stationary fishing; other co-op projects that include a new warehouse for dried sardine; the beginnings of a consumer co-op sparked by the women's auxiliary; and the several thriving marine-processing factories that employ many Ebibarians.

The single venture in the *burakumin* program resulting in any noticeable employment improvement is the tiny glove factory. Other changes are of three sorts: limited upgrading in living conditions (the public bath, running water, a few small city-built apartments, the playground); annual increases in welfare stipends; and the educational program for integration or emancipation known as *dōwa kyōiku* which centers in the elementary school, Nanyō Shōgakkō.

The tactics by which the two communities have sought to cope with their respective situations also differ markedly. Whereas the most powerful force within Ebibara undoubtedly is the producers' co-op, Kawabarian dynamics centers chiefly in political agitation through Kaihōdōmei and Jirō, to a lesser extent through Dōwakai, and finally through political affiliations that are strongly though not exclusively leftist.

The response of prefectural and federal governments to problems and needs of the two communities also varies. Granting that the difference is not always clearcut, efforts to improve Ebibara life seem to be instigated more often "from above" whereas, in the case of Kawabara, changes that have recently occurred are more the consequence of almost constant pressures "from below." Remember that the innovation in seaweed growing, particularly, was fomented by the prefectural Department of Fisheries, not without resistance and even intracommunity conflict. Remember, too, that Yoneshima-ken has launched a five-year plan geared to a national plan to reduce overpopulation of fishing households, and at the same time has strengthened the marine economy by various kinds of subsidization.

We do not mean that the changes effected in Kawabara are exclusively the consequence of local struggle, and that those in Ebibara are not. Both communities, for one thing, are interconnected with hundreds of others in Japan that confront similar problems. The fishing co-op is part of a national network with long experience and substantial economic resources (the affiliated credit union of Yoneshima-ken is one impressive example). Similarly, Kaihōdōmei, Jirō, and Dōwakai are national organizations which, with a history of militant activity extending back half a century or more, are largely responsible for growing public concern with the plight of *burakumin* communities. National political parties enter the picture also: not only have the Socialist, Democratic Socialist, and Communist parties all expressed such concern; so too, reluctantly or not, has the ruling Liberal Democratic party. Due partly to pressures of minority parties, partly to the persistence and aggressiveness of *burakumin* organizations, and partly to the fact that many Liberal Democrats are themselves more disposed toward welfare state policies than one would expect from a more monolithic conservative coalition, the total effect has been one of annually increasing appropriations earmarked for *burakumin* programs extending all the way from *dōwa kyōiku* to publicly financed housing projects.

Nevertheless, it still remains clear that Kawabara has more frequently taken grassroots initiative in seeking various changes than has Ebibara. The absence of a fishermen's union or other affiliation with the powerful forces of organized labor; the lack of local political organization; an almost total disregard both by the co-op and the public schools for any kind of educational program geared to the special needs and interests of *gyomin;* the heavy hand of traditional obligations and customs—all account substantially for even fewer public improvements in Ebibara, such as a much needed playground, than in Kawabara.

The one partial exception is, again, the Ebibara co-op. Certainly devoted leaders such as Director Oka do on occasion take initiative with admirable energy, just as they seem ready to listen to proposals for change by prefectural officials. At the same time, such activities are almost exclusively concentrated upon improving the fishing economy, almost never upon improving the community in any other way. True, the women's auxiliary may concern itself with broader problems such as family life. Yet, being a voluntary appendage of the male-dominated co-op and without any real authority, auxiliary leaders are often stymied in their good intentions. Nor must we forget *kogi kumiai,* that ingenious "defense force" of the Ebibara fleet, whose purpose is to come to the support of members caught fishing illegally. The difficulty is that *kogi kumiai* rarely if ever functions as an agency of planned community improvement; rather it is a device that aims to perpetuate such practices as poaching or overfishing. In this sense it serves more to retard than to advance progressive economic change.

Returning to education, this phase of our perspective concludes by noting several additional differences in the two communities—differences despite the fact that the school systems of both cities are compelled to maintain virtually identical structures and programs. One difference is the continuing if limited vigor of the teachers' union (Nikkyōso) in Utsumi-shi, as contrasted with Yamada-shi where the teachers' union is virtually moribund. (We did learn, to our surprise, of two teachers in Kitano Chūgakkō who continue to hold membership.) A certain irony may be detected in this situation. Left-wing *burakumin* leaders are understandably sympathetic to Nikkyōso, and Nikkyōso to them; consequently Kaihōdōmei, for example, frequently opposes policies of the Ministry of Education (Monbushō). Thus, if aggressive Kawabarians are seldom able to muster support among Yamada-shi teachers in behalf of their own struggles (Inoki-san and one or two others are exceptional), this may be partially because the only other teachers' organization, Kyōshikai, acquiesces in Monbushō's often conservative policies much more than Nikkyōso does. Yet it remains questionable whether, even if the teachers' union were still active in Yamada-shi, it would make any difference to *gyomin.* Certainly in Utsumi-shi we could detect minimum concern on Nikkyōso's part with local community problems.

Another provocative distinction follows from a tendency on the part of Ebibara teen-agers to form strong cliques in the schools, a tendency re-peatedly mentioned by teacher informants in Utsumi-shi but never once by their counterparts in Yamada-shi. Not that Kawabara children, at least on the junior high school level, fail to cluster together; it is inevitable for them to do so for no other reason than that invidious feelings between *burakumin* and non-*burakumin* become severe by the time of adolescence on the part of both groups.

Even so, it seems plausible to suppose that clique-forming among Ebi-bara students should be more visible than in Kawabara. In the first place, Ebibara is sufficiently stable that children have the opportunity to develop close ties with one another in a way that Kawabara, with its constant inflow and outflow of population, does not so easily permit. Again, the acute or-ganizational rivalries in Kawabara that we have observed are likely to be reflected in the children of families who belong to opposite ideological camps. (This division does not occur at all in Ebibara where rivalries are much more manifest in the form of personal jealously or vindictive gossip.) Still further, the fading but by no means forgotten custom of ritual adoption known as *yoboshigo*, added to the *honke-bunke* pattern of family ties and obligations that exert such dominating influence in Ebibara, is bound to influence children's relationships more directly than in Kawabara where such traditions are decidedly less firm.

Most interesting of all, one detects subtle differences in communal spirit. In Kawabara this seems to be induced largely by the defensive iso-lation into which *burakumin* are forced; in Ebibara it appears more strongly in the form of a vaguely articulated fraternalism rooted in the mores of a venerable occupation. Such fraternalism is observed in the sleeping clubs, the local summer Shintō festival, and the informal talk-fests of acquaint-ances referred to as *hiyori-moshi* and *mōshi-awase*. Clique-forming among *gyomin* children is, in short, a natural consequence of compound cultural factors.

One final point of difference is again rather ironic. Although both com-munities send much less than the average number of students to senior high school, although the older generation of *gyomin* has had meager regard for schooling, and although *burakumin* leaders have been far more active in PTA activities and special educational projects than have *gyomin* leaders, considerably fewer Kawabara students go beyond the ninth grade than do Ebibara students. This discrepancy is, we think, due less to profound psy-chological changes than to a material but crucial fact of life: whereas Ebi-bara and Kawabara both remain relatively impoverished communities, the former has managed to attack and sometimes to solve its most critical eco-nomic problems; the latter, due to causes by no means exclusively its own, has thus far largely failed to do so.

IV

We now turn to an investigation of similarities and differences between Ebibara and Kawabara revealed by their value orientations. The reader who does not wish to follow the technical details of this section may skip to the next section (pp. 184–188) where we weigh their significance for the comparative theme of the present chapter.

The instrument constructed for and the findings of this investigation, as well as the methodology by which it was applied, are described in Appendix II.[2] A few important points, however, should be kept in mind. In Ebibara, 98 households cooperated fully in this phase of our study; three refused to do so. In addition to this "saturation survey," we administered exactly the same instrument to a random sample of 119 Utsumi-shi households so that we might discover useful comparisons between our chosen subculture and the surrounding municipality. Utilizing the same instrument, we obtained results from 102 households in Kawabara, with 16 others refusing to cooperate, and in Yamada-shi we obtained a random sample of 100 households.

The principal model of value choice that we utilized in both communities, as well as for our leader panel, shall be called the *Innovative-Moderative-Transmissive Continuum* (I-M-T). We were chiefly interested in the degree to which our subcultures reinforce and perpetuate traditional value orientations, as symbolized by the *right* end of the continuum; to what extent they tend to support novel, unprecedented value orientations, as symbolized by the *left* end; or to what extent they tend less toward either the "conservative" or "radical" choice than toward a "liberal" choice somewhere along the *middle* of the continuum. The I-M-T model is, we think, appropos to our inquiry: we are especially concerned with the dynamic character of Japanese culture and education, and therefore with attitudes and beliefs about values that are indigenous to this dynamic character.[3]

One further point by way of methodology: the I-M-T continuum weaves across all of the institutional areas of cultural order symbolized by the model of concentric circles utilized in earlier chapters. Values infiltrate

---

[2] Cf. Appendix II, The Value Study: Model and Findings.

[3] I-M-T is not, of course, the only possible model of value orientation that could be developed for this study. It symbolizes, rather, the author's particular interest in an anthropological philosophy of education regarded as a complex agent of cultural reinforcement and cultural reconstruction. As indicated in the Introduction, it therefore exemplifies our concern at times to venture beyond strictly descriptive values toward an interest in prescriptive and normative values. At the same time, granting the selective character of this value study, safeguards of research methodologies have been kept as objective as possible. (See footnote 4.)

every aspect of human life, whether we are concerned with family, religion, education, politics, or any other institution. A subsidiary question that arises from this all-embracing conception is the extent to which the value orientations of Ebibara and Kawabara are consistent or inconsistent when the several institutions are compared. Centrally, however, the same two questions continue to preoccupy this chapter, but now in the light of our I-M-T model: In what respects are the two communities alike? In what respects are they unlike?[4]

We begin this time with the family, and therefore with the kind of interpersonal values related to love and marriage. As the schedule shows, eight items bear most directly upon this core institution, although others touch upon it. Consider, then, the implications in item 1 (see p. 280) which dramatizes the familiar but often poignant question of whether a young Japanese woman should follow the traditional way of obeying her father's wishes with regard to the choice of a marriage partner, or whether she should follow her own wishes. Immediately we find a difference in preference, although not a strong one. Kawabara respondents choose the latter Innovative alternative as first choice, whereas Ebibara respondents prefer the Moderative alternative of discussing the problem fully with the family. Both communities largely reject the Transmissive alternative of abiding by the father's wishes. Specifically, less than 10 percent of both communities support patriarchal authority, and vary by a margin of roughly 4 percent between the Innovative and Moderative choices, a difference hardly impressive enough to be significant. Nevertheless, the first preference, strictly speaking, is M in Ebibara and I in Kawabara, and the second preference is the converse. The T orientation is a very weak third in both communities.

Before leaving item 1, it is interesting to compare the value orientation of our two subcultures with that of the small cities surrounding them. Utsumi-shi, like Ebibara, prefers M, although Utsumi-shi prefers M still more emphatically. But Yamada-shi differs from Kawabara: it strongly prefers M whereas Kawabara mildly prefers M only as second choice. Thus Kawabara is the single one of the four cultural groupings to choose I as the first preference. But all four emphatically reject the T choice which symbolizes most distinctly the traditional ethics of the family, and all four place considerable weight upon the M choice, which indicates a quite non-Confucianist emphasis upon family participation in decision-making.

[4] The influence of the pioneer study of Florence Kluckhohn and Fred L. Strodbeck will be apparent in some of the terminology and other aspects of this investigation. It is important to emphasize, however, that their work is far more comprehensive in scope and refined in methodology than ours. We have not attempted to follow theirs except loosely. Cf. Florence Kluckhohn and Fred L. Strodtbeck, *Variations in Value Orientations* (Evanston: Row, Peterson & Company, 1961).

A second family item (13) expresses three alternatives open to a women who, already having three children, finds herself again pregnant. We find in both Ebibara and Kawabara that M receives by far the strongest preference: "She should have the child, but from then on strictly practice birth control or be sterilized." The next strongest preference is T: "She should have as many children as Divine Nature intends her to have." The weakest preference, I, is for "abortion in a city hospital." Thus we find that, whereas the order of value preference in the two communities differs slightly with regard to item 1, here the order is $M > T > I$[5] for both. But note a shift in the T choice: whereas in the first item it was relegated to a weak third, here it becomes the second choice, that is, accepting the ordinances of Divine Nature is preferable to abortion. The same $M > T > I$ order also prevails for Yamada-shi, though not, of course, to the same quantitative degree.

To analyze each of the remaining 30 items with equal precision would demand much more attention than could be justified. What we do wish to sketch more fully is the picture of Ebibara's and Kawabara's agreements and disagreements in value orientations, together with how they compare with their respective cities.[6]

Let us take the areas of agreement first. On each of a total of 19 items, both subcultures completely agree in their sequence of the three alternative choices. Of all the items, moreover, the strength of the first preference is weightiest in item 24, where respondents are asked to accept (T), reject (I), or modify (M), the traditional ethics of *on* (obligation) and *oya kōkō* (filial piety). More vehemently than in item 1, their preference is M, whereas I and T are both repudiated by substantial majorities.

The next heaviest weight of agreement as to preference is indicated in item 14, which considers attitudes of approval or disapproval toward the Sōkagakkai. Both communities vigorously oppose the I choice (joining the organization) and strongly prefer M (admiration for the zeal of the Sōkagak-kai while still remaining loyal to the Buddhist sects to which respondents already belong).

Third in strength of preference is item 9 and again M is preferred to I or T. If a fishing boat is lost in a storm, the family of owners should neither be left to its own devices (I) nor become dependent upon the main-branch family (T), but should seek help from the co-op credit union (M).

Fourth in strength is shared equally by two items, 19 and 28. In the

---

[5] The symbol $>$ means "preferred to."

[6] For details of computation utilized in the remaining summary of this section, cf. pp. 294–298.

former, when respondents are asked to choose among national patriotism, its repudiation, or a "new ideal of patriotism in which the Japanese nation is united with mankind as a whole," a large majority selects the last of these alternatives (M). In item 28, dealing with motivations to study, the I choice (to become independent) is much preferred over either merely liking to study (M) or deference to parents (T).

Turning to those items toward which strength of preferential agreement between Ebibara and Kawabara is feeblest, item 2, dealing with education, is feeblest of all in the sense that preferences are distributed widely between all three choices. Only a small majority in both subcultures supports the I choice to the effect that study of "the present tasks of Japan" in the school curriculum is more important than the "traditional arts" (T). The next weakest preferential agreement is revealed in item 21, which by implication favors democratic over autocratic leadership (I), although T (by implication favoring the latter) is almost equally strong. The third weakest is item 7 which reveals the M preference of supporting, though reluctantly, National Achievement Tests (NAT). The fourth weakest item is 23 which again favors M, in this case a rather opportunistic interest in "fair wages and good working conditions," whether unionized or not.

What now of disagreements in the comparable value orientations of Ebibara and Kawabara? Only 13 items reveal such disagreement as compared with the 19 that reveal agreement in sequential ranking of preferences. The strongest ratio of disagreement appears in item 15. Here the question is whether and how faithfully fishermen are expected to pray to their great Shintō *kami*, Ryūōjin, before they go out to sea. A majority of Ebibarians prefer M (to pray "maybe once a month") to T (to pray "almost everyday"), whereas Kawabarians strongly prefer the latter. The reason for this disparity may well be due, however, to stereotype notions among outsiders of how fishermen behave religiously rather than how (as implied by their M preference) they actually behave.

The second strongest item of disagreement is item 3, concerning what should be done about couples who have retired. Ebibara emphatically favors the tradition of living with eldest sons (T), but Kawabara favors M ("they should live separately"). Both communities think very little of community centers for retired people (I).

Two items, 25 and 31, are tied for third in rank on the disagreement side. The former raises the question of whether a young *burakumin* should remain in his own community or seek a livelihood outside. In this case both Kawabara and Ebibara strongly endorse I; he should seek a job in Osaka but continue to struggle for emancipation. But they sharply disagree as to the second choice—that is, more Ebibarians than Kawabarians think the young man should stay in the community where he feels secure (T). This choice may reflect misunderstanding by *gyomin* of *burakumin* attitudes, just as the question of praying to Ryūōjin may reflect a converse misunderstanding. But both communities rank lowest the third choice of "passing" (M).

The other tied item of fairly strong disagreement, item 31, raises the question of how wives like to spend their spare time. Ebibara respondents seem to prefer to spend it with their families watching television (M), but Kawabarians prefer to attend meetings of the community women's association (I). Both rank T lowest: attending an *ikebana* (flower arrangement) school.

Disagreements in value orientation range, like agreements, from strong to weak. The two items of weakest disagreement are 1, (the rights of a young woman thinking of marriage), and 22 (how much time the schools should devote to drilling in the skills of language and arithmetic). We have found that, with regard to item 1, the two communities waver between M and I. In item 22, however, although neither community considers that too much time is spent in drilling (I), Kawabara and Ebibara both waver between T and M, for each community is almost equally divided on whether the amount of time is too little (T) or about right (M). Kawabara tends here toward more conservativism than does Ebibara.

How do our two subcultures compare in their value orientations with the wider municipalities of which they are part? Ebibara and Utsumi-shi agree in ranking all but 6 of the 32 items. Kawabara and Yamada-shi agree in all but 11 of the 32. Striking an average, the two subcultures together agree with the two cities embracing them approximately three-fourths of the time.

For purposes of illustration, let us note some instances of agreement and disagreement between the smaller and larger communities. Ebibara and Utsumi-shi share strongest agreement of preference on item 24; so also do Kawabara and Yamada-shi. This is the item dealing with *on* and *oya kōkō*, which we have already found also indicates the strongest agreement between Ebibara and Kawabara. Thus we may observe that on this issue, M is the strongest preference for all four cultural groupings: "Japanese people should not ignore *on* and *oya kōkō*, but should combine them with the democratic idea that all family members should discuss and reach decisions together."

Item 29 is second in strength of preferential agreement between Ebibara and Utsumi-shi. It raises the question of what one does in the event that a net is lost on the beach: Should one expect his relatives to help (M), go to a *gyōja* (fortune teller) (T), or "stop searching and buy a new net" (I)? By far the heaviest support goes to the third alternative (I). Kawabara and Yamada-shi also prefer I but differ slightly on the second preference, which is M for Kawabara and T for Yamada-shi.

Nearly as strong preferential agreement between the smaller and larger communities is manifested in item 14, which we have also noted previously. Here all four groupings agree on the dominance of M: respect for the enthusiasm of the Sōkagakkai, but still more respect for traditional Buddhist sects. The second preference is T, which implies repudiation of the Sōkagakkai movement.

A few disagreements between our smaller and larger communities are also sufficiently revealing to deserve comment. Taking Ebibara and Utsumi-shi first, the strongest disparity in value orientation appears in item 15. This item, we remember, raises the question of whether or not to pray to Ryūōjin before one goes out to sea. Here again outsiders, in this case even citizens of the same municipality, may well suppose that fishermen pray much oftener than they actually do. In other words, while Utsumi-shi citizens select the T alternative as their first preference, *gyomin* themselves select M as their first preference.

The second strongest item of disagreement in preference is item 3, which deals with retired elder citizens. Just as we have found that Ebibara and Kawabara disagree on this item, so too do Ebibara and Utsumi-shi: the fishing people are strongly T-directed, whereas Utsumi-shi is more M-directed.

The third strongest disagreement is in item 8. Here respondents are asked to choose between teaching children to respect religious traditions (T), to do nothing about them (I), or to think seriously about the possibility of modifying these traditions (M). Ebibara and Utsumi-shi choose M as dominant, but T is second preference for the city and I for the village.

The weakest degree of disagreement is found in item 30, dealing with sex education. A majority in both Ebibara and Utsumi-shi favor such education for high school students (I), but again there is mild disagreement on the second preference: more Ebibara citizens prefer that sex education be left to parents (T) than do Utsumi-shi citizens.

What of disagreements in preference between Kawabara and Yamada-shi? Of the items revealing disagreement, item 18 shows the widest disparity. Raising the question of centralized versus decentralized control of education, over twice as many Yamada-shi as Kawabara citizens believe the American system would be impractical in Japan (T). The larger community seems to favor most strongly, (at least by implication), the Japanese to the American system, whereas the small one leans by implication toward the latter (M).

The next widest disagreement between Kawabara and Yamada-shi is found in item 1) and the third in rank is another familiar one, item 25. An additional word on the latter is called for, since it is the only one of the 32 dealing explicitly with *burakumin*. Yamada-shi, like Kawabara, prefers the I alternative—to seek a job outside the ghetto but to "struggle proudly with other *burakumin* for full emancipation." Nevertheless, this preference among Kawabarians is much stronger than among people of Yamada-shi, who are also attracted rather markedly by T—to remain in the ghetto.

At the weak extreme of the continuum of items showing preferential disagreement between Kawabara and Yamada-shi, the weakest of all has been noted above in item 29, concerned with the "god" of fishermen. Two other items not previously mentioned, however, also waver on the borderline between agreement and disagreement, 6 and 10, both dealing with political values. The former raises the issue of whether Japan should join a "world federation of nations." Both Kawabara and Yamada-shi almost equally agree in their first preference that "it is all right in theory but impossible in practice" (M), but they differ otherwise: almost twice as large a percentage of the *burakumin* community favors such a federation (I) as does the city at large, whereas almost twice as large a percentage of city residents opposes it (T). Item 10 is concerned with public versus private ownership of industry. Both communities reject all-out private enterprise (T), but Kawabara favors public ownership (I) more strongly than does Yamada-shi, which is more attracted to a "mixture of both kinds of ownership" (M).

Consider next the several concentric institutions represented in our value inventory. How do the four communities compare in their value orientation toward the family, religion, economics, politics, recreation, and education? Starting with the cluster of eight items on the family, love, and marriage, Ebibara's first choice is M (four times); I and T are the first choice only twice each. Thus one may symbolize the preferred value orientation of Ebibara here as $M \begin{matrix} > \mathrm{I} \\ > \mathrm{T} \end{matrix} \left(4 \begin{matrix} > 2 \\ > 2 \end{matrix} \right)$. Kawabara may be symbolized as $M > I > T$, since first choices are $4 > 3 > 1$. (We shall hereafter refer to such ranking of the frequency only of first choices as the "dominant value orientation.")

Following the same procedure, let us compare again the two sub-cultures with the surrounding cities in their attitudes toward family values. In Utsumi-shi, the "dominant value orientation" is $M > I > T$ as compared with Ebibara's $M \begin{matrix} > \mathrm{I} \\ > \mathrm{T} \end{matrix}$. In Yamada-shi, it is $M > I > T$, which thus agrees with Kawabara. Ebibara and Utsumi-shi also agree in six out of eight items when compared in sequence of first choices, and Kawabara and Yamada-shi agree in seven out of eight. Taking all four groupings together, $M > I > T$ is obviously the "dominant value orientation" in terms of first choices.

Without comparable detail, we now consider the value orientations related to other institutions. The five religious items indicate that here the "dominant value orientation" for Ebibara is $M > I > O$ (T is not chosen at all) and for Kawabara it is $\frac{M}{T} > I$. The two communities agree on the sequence of choices for two items but disagree on the rest. Placing each community in relation to its city, Ebibara and Utsumi-shi slightly disagree on their "dominant value orientation," as do Kawabara and Yamada-shi. If we pool first choices of the total of all four groupings, the "dominant value orientation" is $M \genfrac{}{}{0pt}{}{> I}{> T} \left(12 \genfrac{}{}{0pt}{}{> 4}{> 4} \right)$.

In the economics cluster of four items, Ebibara's preference is $M > I > O$, whereas Kawabara's is $\frac{M}{I} > O$. When we compare the smaller with the larger communities, Ebibara and Utsumi-shi accept the same "dominant value orientation," but Kawabara and Yamada-shi do not quite agree. The four groupings together reveal a "dominant value orientation" of $M > I > O$.

In political values, Ebibara and Kawabara accept the same "dominant value orientation": $M > I > O$. Ebibara and Utsumi-shi almost agree, as do Kawabara and Yamada-shi. On the sequence of choices in the five political items, Ebibara and Kawabara agree on three pairs, Kawabara and Yamada-shi on two, and Ebibara and Utsumi-shi agree four times on the same sequence of $M > T > I$ and once on $I > T > M$. The "dominant value orientation" of the four communities combined is $M > I > T$.

Since only three items are classified under recreation, and at least one of these, item 2, belongs just as properly under education, let us say about these three items only that Ebibara and Kawabara differ in their "dominant value orientations," whereas Ebibara and Utsumi-shi agree completely. But Kawabara disagrees here with Yamada-shi: $I > T > O$ as compared with $T > I > O$. The "dominant value orientation" on recreational values for all four groupings is $\frac{I}{T} > M$.

Education, represented by six items, reveals a "dominant value orientation" of $M > I > T$ in Ebibara and also in Kawabara. But Utsumi-shi somewhat disagrees with Ebibara, and Yamada-shi agrees with Kawabara. The "dominant value orientation," when spread across all four communities, is $M > I > T$.

Our justification for subjecting the reader to such a bloodless dissection will become apparent, we hope, in the concluding section of this chapter. Meanwhile, let us go one step further. How do our communities compare when viewed as a whole?

To begin with, Ebibara's overall "dominant value orientation" is $M > I > T$ and Kawabara's is also $M > I > T$, as determined by the total frequency of first choices for all 32 items. With regard to how Ebibara and Kawabara react to the several cultural areas, only in one case does the I preference prevail, namely, in Kawabara's "dominant value orientation" toward recreation. M again is distinctly dominant: in both communities it takes first preference in the family, politics, and education; in Ebibara it is also first in religion and economics.

The two connecting cities are still weaker in their reaction to the I alternative: neither community selects it even in one area as first preference. T is preferred once—in Yamada-shi's recreational value orientation. M is dominant for both of the larger communities in the case of the family, religion, economics, and politics. Yamada-shi also prefers M for education.

Full agreement in the "dominant value orientation" is discovered between the fishing community and its municipality in recreation and in economics. No full agreement is discovered between the *burakumin* community and its municipality.

Finally, taking the four communities together, we find that in the sequence of first choices for each item, full agreement exists in 13 of the 32, with heaviest agreement in family values and weakest agreement in recreational and educational values. The $M > I > T$ value orientation is dominant in the family cluster of items, as well as in economics, politics, and education. Religion is fairly close. The sharpest departure is in recreational values.

We may conclude by asserting that the strongest preference is clearly M, the next is I, and the least strong is T. Translating these preferences into rough percentages (again based on the total of first choices only), M is a little stronger than I and T together (approximately 54%–29%–17%). Or, looking at this distribution still differently, about 25 percent more of our respondents choose M in preference to the next strongest choice I, whereas about 12 percent more of them prefer I to T.

Returning to our chief foci of interest, Ebibara and Kawabara, it thus becomes evident that their combined value orientations tend to reinforce those of the larger municipalities, and vice versa. To be sure, taking Utsumi-shi and Yamada-shi together in terms of the frequency of first choices, they prove to be about 12 percent more weighted in favor of the T preference by comparison with Ebibara and Kawabara, whereas the latter together are about 12 percent more weighted in favor of the I preference by comparison with Utsumi-shi and Yamada-shi. Nevertheless, M is the heaviest weighted preference for all four communities. Although Ebibara and Kawabara together are therefore somewhat more inclined to the Innovative than to the Transmissive value orientation, both of them join with their municipalities in most strongly favoring the Moderative value orientation.

V

At the outset of this chapter it was re-emphasized that generalizations are often difficult to justify in the study of cultures. Surely the perspectives thus far obtained support this familiar if not trite observation. Even so, and with appreciation of the risks involved, several we think are amply warranted.

Perhaps the most apparent generalization is that Ebibara and Kawabara, when viewed in the perspective of our "impressionistic" as well as "objective" evidence, are both decidedly alike and decidedly different, both consistent and inconsistent, both unified and disunified. Then, when we view them further in the perspective of their larger municipalities, we reach the same conclusions still more emphatically.

A number of additional generalizations are less apparent but more intriguing. In the first place, the central contention that value orientations vary both within and between cultural groupings is clearly supported by our study. Equally pronounced are the wide ranges in value preferences both within and between cultural clusterings; in no instance do we discover total rejection or acceptance by the combined tested groups of any one of the three alternative responses provided for each item. Dominant preferences, to be sure, are much stronger in some cases than in others; yet in still other cases one observes such a wide distribution of preferences that variant choices practically counterbalance the dominant ones. The familiar anthropological insistence on relativity and plurality of value orientations is thus doubly reconfirmed.

Other interesting comparisons appear between our study and one conducted in Japan sometime earlier by William Caudill and Harry A. Scarr. First, the latter supports the thesis of other prior studies not only as to variations in value orientations between groups but also in the range of preferences within groups. Second, a considerable degree of rough correlation may be noted between their categories and our own overall $M > I > T$ value orientation. In family relations, for example, the category most closely resembling our Moderative choice is much preferred to the choices we have termed the Transmissive and Innovative. The greatest noticeable distinction appears to be a heavier emphasis upon the I type of preference in the Caudill-Scarr study, an emphasis quite possibly due to the fact that its sample populations were located in or near the great city of Tokyo and that a much larger proportion of senior high school students was included among respondents than in our populations. These conditions, urbanism and educated youth, might well encourage value orientations toward the left end of the continuum to a greater extent than would be expected from rural and older age groups of less education. Both studies, nevertheless, resist what we call the T preference much less frequently than they do either of the others: M or I.[7]

More broadly and less technically, what may we infer as to the "philosophy of life" of our grassroots communities when these are viewed by comparison not only with the other research studies mentioned above but with the picture that we have tried to draw from our field involvement? Surely one of the pronounced features that must strike observers is a remarkable quality of resilience—that is, a willingness to support practices and values that accommodate themselves to dynamic cultural patterns provided that change is neither too swift nor too sweeping. Rather, it is likely to be welcomed enthusiastically only if it is both gradual and piecemeal.

Thus the prevailing mood of these communities may be described as a pragmatic one, pragmatic in the cultural-philosophical sense of aversion, on the one hand, to too firmly or permanently established principles or practices of whatever sort, and affinity, on the other hand, for policies and activities that try by multiple, flexible, modifiable, and testable means to perform tasks and meet needs generated out of the present period of economic, political, or other expressions of rapid transition. Granting that variant attitudes are plainly observable also—some in the direction of ancient ways, others toward fresh and even radical ways—nevertheless these attitudes less frequently are as sharp or influential as are attitudes of concession, temperateness, and conciliation.

Such a pragmatic mood is, of course, more congenial to the Moderative than to either the strongly Innovative or the strongly Transmissive value preference. This mood is so apparent from our inclusive data that one sometimes detects, for example, considerable discrepancy between the radical social and political ideologies, particularly of many Kawabarians, and what may be the more deeply rooted values and attitudes that lie beneath these ideologies. Item 5 is a fair case in point. One might suppose, to listen to

---

[7] Cf. William Caudill and Harry A. Scarr, "Japanese Value Orientations and Culture Change," *Ethnology*, vol. 1 (1962), pp. 53–91.

zealous Kaihōdōmei members, that advocacy of militant labor strategies would be almost overwhelming; yet only one-fifth of our respondents in the value study favor this sort of strategy. True, even so small a proportion is greater than in Ebibara, or for that matter in either of our large adjoining communities. Nevertheless, a majority of Kawabarians agree with all three of these communities in preferring most strongly the M alternative of, say, organizing a committee and talking with the boss in a friendly way.

Item 23 reveals the same kind of M preference. On the question of whether the common practice of paternalism in employer-employee relations is desirable, Kawabara again joins with Ebibara and both municipalities in rejecting the strictly union position (that paternalism is undesirable) in favor of a grossly opportunistic form of pragmatism: any system is all right "as long as it provides fair wages and good working conditions."

In another related item dealing with socialist and capitalist alternatives (item 10), Kawabara appears in a more consistent light. It is the only one of the four clusterings to prefer I (public ownership of the means of production). But it is worth noting that M, indicating a "mixed economy," is also quite heavily supported, and that Ebibara despite its lack of any explicitly radical ideology favors the radical choice almost as much as it does the liberal one—more so indeed than does Utsumi-shi. This item, incidentally, is perhaps as typical as any in exemplifying how both Ebibara and Kawabara tend to the Innovative preference more than do their encompassing municipalities despite pockets of Transmissive resistance, despite also the still stronger attraction of the overall Moderative choice.

This latter choice is likewise popular in the way that Kawabara reacts to the reputation of Nikkyōso (the teachers' union) as a radical movement (Cf. item 11). Reflecting the ideology of some leaders, Kawabara endorses Nikkyōso's tactics a little more sympathetically than does Ebibara or either of the two small cities. Nevertheless, like them, its own first preference is clearly toward a policy of moderation. Quite possibly, this prevalent attitude suggests that, in any degree that our evidence might apply to Yoneshima-ken as a whole, the decline of the teachers' union in this prefecture is due much less to disapproval of the principle of unionism than to Nikkyōso's frequently radical policies.

But just as Kawabara often appears to be more moderately liberal than radical, so Ebibara often appears to be more moderately liberal than conservative. To clarify the point, if it is true that more Kawabarians vote the Socialist or Communist ticket than they do any other, and that Ebibarians vote the Liberal Democratic ticket with still greater solidarity, it does not follow that Ebibara any more than Kawabara is always consistent in attitudes with its formal political allegiances. An instance of such incongruity is in the fishing community's orientation toward socialized medicine (item

20): although not as emphatically as Kawabara or even Utsumi-shi, it still favors "completely free medical care to all citizens" by an impressive margin.

In family relations, too, Ebibara seems to be much more liberal than one might be led to suppose from some of our other impressions. It will be remembered that the strongest single item of preferential agreement between all four groupings is item 24, which rejects the purely traditional ethics of *oya kōkō* in favor of a middle ground in which democratic family relations are encouraged. True, Ebibara remains steadfast toward primogeniture, and disagrees here not only with Kawabara but with both Utsumi-shi and Yamada-shi. Yet in other family items, such as those involving the rights of a young woman in her relations to young men (Cf. items 1, 17, or 26), or in other family relations (Cf. item 9), Ebibara is again more moderate than otherwise. Even in religion, an alleged stronghold of tradition, we find this same temperate attitude predominant: toward a combined use of science and religion in matters of illness (item 4), toward religious education (item 8), and toward praying to the Shintō *kami* Ryūōjin, (item 15). Although it is true that Ebibarians, like other respondents, have little patience with the orthodox Buddhist sect backed by the Sōkagakkai (item 14), they have even less patience with the value of magical rites (item 29).

Are our communities equally pragmatic about education? Less agreement is discernible concerning this institution than any other, indicating quite possibly that the program of the schools either is not well understood by rank-and-file citizens or is itself so confused in much of its theory and practice that such understanding is hardly to be expected. At any rate, although M is again the strongest preference, there does appear to be abnormal disparity in the sequence of choices in the way that our four groupings respond to the cluster of educational items.

The perception that crystallizes from our several perspectives is, then, of subcultures that are at once rooted deeply in a revered traditional order, are amenable to and on occasion even prepared to adopt audaciously new processes, but yet are drawn again and again toward conglomerate policies and programs that appear short-range and sometimes disjointed in a highly tractable period of Japan's evolution. This predominant Moderative preference, we must reiterate, is by no means always consistently expressed: variations not only in value orientations and means of change, but in major institutional structures themselves, are frequently multiple, sometimes conflictive, and even at moments bewildering.

Such a complex situation also produces disturbingly negative effects, only one of which is recalled here. This is the ubiquity of illegal practices manifested in considerable gangsterism, political bribery, and underground gambling. But it is perhaps most obtuse both in the widespread violation by

Ebibarians of fishing regulations and in the equally widespread falsifications of records perpetrated by Kawabarians who seek as much welfare aid as possible. Our impression is that such local illegalities, however frowned upon and threatened by authority, are frequently condoned and even ignored. Yet one may doubt whether comparable illegalities (political corruption, most notoriously) are much less chronic elsewhere in Japan.

Let us recapitulate. From the variety of evidence available to us, the dominant mood of our communities tends to be strong in qualities of accommodation and conciliation, but weak oftener than not either in devotion to and celebration of the values of a profoundly rich cultural heritage or in any conspicuous sense of direction toward well-articulated cultural goals.

These impressions may be crystallized in one further way by reactions to issues involving Japan's international relations. Although our panels of informants usually oppose rearmament and support a United Nations strengthened by admission of Red China, the tenor of their responses when reinforced by our value study is one of ambivalence. For example, when asked about a world federation of nations in which Japanese sovereignity would be subordinated, two-thirds of our total respondents indicate that the notion "is all right in theory but impossible in practice" (item 6). Yet on item 19, over three-fourths of all respondents prefer "a new ideal of patriotism in which the Japanese nation is united with mankind as a whole."

But we do not wish to underestimate the positive characteristics symbolized qualitatively as well as quantitatively throughout this work by the "dominant value orientation," $M > I > T$. Granting the frequency of variations, inconsistencies, and conflicts, it should not be forgotten that these characteristics also protect our two communities from dangers of rigidity and authoritarianism—dangers that continue to lurk uncomfortably close to the surface of Japanese history. Finally, that our two communities frequently prove ready to respond to and participate in cultural change—change oftener than not in the direction of values harmonious with a democratic ethic of widening participation and increasing human fulfillment—augurs for a future that would be welcome to both *gyomin* and *burakumin*. To this and related evaluative judgments we shall return in the pages ahead.

8

FROM THE TOP DOWN: A LEADERSHIP PERSPECTIVE

I

Ebibara and Kawabara, we have learned, are accompanied by waves of cultural life that inevitably, constantly ebb and flow. Particularly intricate are the patterns of relation between these little communities and the municipalities with which they are connected: Utsumi-shi and Yamada-shi. Only on occasion thus far, however, have we referred to the surrounding prefecture of Yoneshima or its capital, Hiroi-shi, and even more rarely to the region with which this prefecture is integral or to the country of Japan as a whole. The present chapter strengthens our understanding of Ebibara and Kawabara by placing them more clearly in the perspective of these wider environments.

Appendix III[1] relates how our explorations on the prefectural level were organized and conducted. The only point to underscore is that we concentrated upon a panel of 16 upper-level leaders representing something of a cross section of occupations and professions. A few of these citizens have already assisted us at specific points during our involvement in the subcultures: the Liberal Democratic mayor of Utsumi-shi whom we have called Miyakawa-san; the head priest of the largest and most venerated Shingon-shū temple in the prefecture, Azuma-san; the executive director of the Yoneshima-ken fishing co-op credit union, Adachi-san; the prefectural chairmen of the two rival *burakumin* organizations, Hayashi-san (for Dōwakai)

---

[1] For details, cf. Appendix III, Research Methodologies: The Leader Panel.

189

and Tomita-san (for Kaihōdōmei); the Communist leader of Jirō (union of unemployed workers), Shōda-san; the pioneering ex-president of Yoneshima-ken's women's organizations, Tabata-san; and the Yamada-shi executive secretary of *jichikai*, Kamada-san.

In addition to these individuals, from whom we must learn more, let us now introduce the remaining members of our panel:

Nagashi-san, a prestigious artist and founder of the Hiroi-shi art museum;

Doi-san, organizer and officer of the Yoneshima-ken division of the Japan textile workers' union;

Natsui-san, chairman of the prefectural board of education;

Ishioka-san, vice-president of a large bank in Hiroi-shi;

Okumura-san, executive director of the agricultural co-operatives of Yoneshima-ken;

Kamijō-san, lawyer and ex-president of the Hiroi-shi Rotary Club;

Enomoto-san, organizer and officer of the Yoneshima-ken division of the municipal workers' union of Japan;

Sumida-san, director of the department of social welfare in the prefectural government.

II

Since value orientations were the concluding interest of our preceding chapter, we continue with them here. Limiting ourselves for the moment to our "objective" study of value orientations, we find that the leader panel agrees with rank-and-file people in preferring more strongly the Moderative (M) to either the Transmissive (T) or Innovative (I) choice. In fact, the proportion of first choices of M is a little higher (about 59 percent as compared to an average of 53 percent in the four communities). At the community level, however, we find that the I or second choice is somewhat more attractive than at the leader level (a difference of about 9 percent), and that the T or third choice is a little less attractive (about 3 percent).[2]

Several other points emerge. For example, close parallels are discerned between the higher and lower levels in the sequence of choices for a total of 22 of the 32 items (but note that in some items our leaders completely reject one or another of the alternative choices). This proportion compares fairly closely with Ebibara and Kawabara, which together agree in 19 of the

[2] For details, cf. Appendix II, The Value Study: Model and Findings, and Appendix III, Research Methodologies: The Leader Panel.

32 items, as well as with Utsumi-shi and Yamada-shi, which agree with the two subcultures on an average of 23 out of the 32 items. The implication is that considerably more harmony than disharmony seems to prevail in the value orientations of citizens living in this prefecture though not always, of course, on precisely the same items.

Strongest agreement of preference between leaders and community people is found in four items. Item 16 raises the issue of whether people should regard neighborhood organizations as more important than their families, or vice versa. Leaders completely reject the former alternative whereas grassroots people reject it by about 79 percent. Item 29 deals with the question noted earlier of whether, when a fisherman loses a net, he should simply buy a new one rather than resort either to family assistance or to a fortune-teller. Here leaders are unanimous in preferring the first alternative, whereas the rank-and-file agree by 87 percent. Item 24 is the familiar one involving traditional family ethics; both levels vigorously support the M alternative of a balance between older obligations (such as *on*) and new democratic relationships. Our final example of strong agreement refers to leadership itself (item 32): here our high-level panel is again unanimous in believing that "The people have to trust their national political leaders to do what is best, but they should watch them carefully and change them often." Our four communities agree with this preference by about 77 percent, although it is perhaps significant that over 15 percent still hold that "It is best to trust important decisions of policy to national political leaders because most people don't understand enough to make good decisions themselves." This reaction probably reflects the persistence of feudal attitudes among an impressive minority.

As for strong disagreements, item 21 ranks first. Here the question once more concerns leadership: Do co-op and other local community groups require autocratic direction or should they be condemned for this kind of direction? Our leader panel is almost evenly divided between I (outright condemnation) and M (democratic leadership can only develop slowly). But it totally repudiates the T alternative ("This is the way organizations have to be run if they are to be efficient and active"), whereas about 40 percent of our community people prefer this alternative to either of the others, another indication that feudal values among the latter remain attractive. At times, too, leaders seem more strongly to prefer the I-oriented choice; thus in item 22, only about half think that "We spend too much time drilling children in reading, writing, arithmetic," whereas less than one-fifth of the lower-level groups think so.

On certain other items of strong disagreement, the tendency found earlier of these lower-level groups to be more I-directed than their municipalities is reconfirmed by comparison with the leader level. Thus in item 10, although the strongest preference of both levels is for M (a "mixed economy"), one finds striking disparity in the second preference, I: only about 8 percent of our leaders favor a completely socialist economy whereas over 36 percent of our community people do so. Or compare item 20: both levels vehemently reject a return to purely private medical services, but over two-thirds of the lower-level endorse "completely free medical care to all citizens," whereas over half the upper-level sample is satisfied with the present system (again a "mixture" of private and public services), "because most people can afford to pay more than they used to." It would seem that a large majority of *gyomin* and *burakumin,* or for that matter other small-city people, may not be ready to agree that "most people" include *them.*

Without further concern for exact strength of preferential agreement or disagreement, a few other comparisons deserve note. The leader level is much more T-oriented than the community level in favoring substantially increased time in the schools to learn such traditional arts as the tea ceremony (item 2). The same T-orientation appears in item 23 where a larger proportion of leaders endorses the paternalistic pattern of employer-employee relations, and in item 11 where more leaders than others completely reject the teachers' union as "too radical."

Yet our upper-level group tends to be distinctly more I-oriented than the grassroots in believing to a greater extent that older parents should live apart (item 3). The same observation may be made of supporting the right to strike (item 5), in endorsing the American system of decentralized education (item 18), and in believing that "only medical science," not a combination of science and prayer, can save a sick child (item 4). In several instances, however, it should be noted that only a minority of leaders favors the I alternative.

Eight of our 16 leaders attended or graduated from college, six attended or graduated from senior high school, and two probably did not go much beyond elementary school. If then the question is raised whether their markedly higher than average level of education is also reflected in their value orientations, we can only conjecture that probably it is. For example, leaders are more critical than grassroots people of National Achievement Tests because NAT stresses "memory ability and not other kinds of learning, such as critical thinking" (item 7), and their much stronger opposition to drilling children in the three R's has already been noted (item 22). Also, they have greater regard for liking to study (item 7), and they endorse sex education even more emphatically (item 30).

Higher levels of education likewise may influence their value judgments concerning religion. We have found previously that leaders are more inclined than grassroots people toward scientific attitudes in the case of illness. We have not called attention thus far to even greater hostility on the part of leaders to the Sōkagakkai (item 14). Yet, on the question of whether parents should be concerned about the declining religious faith of their children, both upper and lower groups of respondents are almost equally uncertain as to what, if anything, should be done about it (item 8).

The greatest degree of congruence between our two major levels appears in the cluster of items dealing with marriage and the family. In all eight items, the sequence of preferences is paralleled in the two groupings and the weight of difference is fairly small, although the value orientations themselves differ from item to item. One cannot say with certainty whether formal education at either level has played a significant role in producing this situation. One can, however, infer that since family practices and values are studied in Japanese schools much less thoroughly than, say, natural science, these patterns and values must have been acquired chiefly by way of personal and community experience and, regardless of formal teaching or learning, have permeated all levels of the population.

If this judgment is correct, it is understandable why leaders and community people react similarly to family and marriage questions more often than they do in other areas such as science. Yet the informality and looseness of this kind of learning may also help to explain why both levels exhibit troublesome disharmonies within the family cluster of items when we note the disparate sequences that appear in their parallel responses on the two levels: $M > T > I$ (three times), $M > I > T$ (twice), $I > T > M$ (twice), and $T > I > M$ (once). In this light, Utsumi-shi's family education project described in Chapter 3 could become, we believe, one important effort both to perceive and to reduce such extreme disharmonies. It apparently proceeds from the premise that school and community could become partners, and that fluctuations in family values should be of at least as much concern to public education as NAT competitions.

III

Reference to values of the family draws us back to our familiar model of concentric circles of institutions through which, in Parts I and II, our subcultures were viewed in terms more or less successively of the family, religion, recreation and art, politics, economics, and education, with due regard for the interwoven cultural dimensions of order, process, and goals.

Turning now to qualitative interviews with the leader panel, what are their most relevant perceptions of these same institutions? In the pages ahead we shall rarely attempt to make further explicit comparisons of similarity or dissimilarity with the community level, saving these comparisons primarily for the concluding chapter.

The age range of our panel was from 32 to 75, the median approaching 50. All 16 were married and their mates were still living, although one leader became divorced during our study. (He and his wife had endured ten years of "strain," he maintained, in order that their two daughters might not suffer from any stigma before their own recent marriages.) All 16 were also parents, the largest family consisting of seven children, the smallest of one. The median was slightly above three. Nine were grandparents.

Although our top-level spokesmen all live in a predominantly rural prefecture, we should also note that half live in its largest city, Hiroi-shi, and only one of the 16 is even a part-time farmer. Hence their combined views of the changing pattern of Japanese family life probably reflect more of an urban environment than would be true of our community panels. Certainly these leaders concede that the historic pattern has been changing toward more rights and participation for wives and children, a change that they seem inclined, at least verbally, to approve.

Yet in all but one of the leader households that we visited, it became apparent that wives continue to play predominantly traditional roles as housekeepers and mothers. Only one wife had attended school above the senior high level. This exception was our woman leader, Tabata-san, who had been a teacher for many years as indeed her husband still is, and as are her son and daughter-in-law, all of whom live in the same household along with two small grandchildren for whom she is now chief baby sitter. Even our two labor leaders seemed to prefer that their wives remain at home most of the time, although they themselves rush incessantly from one union conference to another.

As might be expected, 1945 was repeatedly cited as a major turning point in the history of Japan. Since all of our leaders were born before World War II and most were well into adulthood, it is understandable why patriarchal patterns have remained fairly firm. Thus only two leaders, one the youngest in the group, frankly admitted that their marriages had been *ren-ai* (love) rather than *mi-ai* (arranged) and even then the older of these two had made sure that a *nakōdo* (go-between) formalized the engagement. In several cases, leaders had no personal acquaintance with their spouses before marrying them. Yet, whereas no one unqualifiedly endorsed this tradition any longer, neither did they approve of the extreme alternative; most insisted, rather, that *ren-ai* combined with *mi-ai* is the safest procedure— that is, let young people have more opportunity than formerly to make friends with the opposite sex, but let them also be guided by parents or others older and wiser than themselves. Impulsive, romantic decisions to marry are at least as likely to lead to catastrophe as those between strangers.

In any case, most marriages among their own children have continued to reflect the *mi-ai* pattern, and this in turn, as Kamijō-san, the lawyer, reminded us, reflects the ancient tenet that the institution of marriage is not so much for the sake of love as for the sake of family solidarity and continuity. Even one of our most liberal spokesmen, the labor leader, Enomoto-san, regretted too great weakening of the "2000-year-old tradition" of parental veneration. Priest Azuma expressed it this way: the proper goal is a "middle way" between the modern Western notion of "horizontal" family relations and the ancient "vertical" structure of Eastern hierarchical authority.

Still further traditional attitudes were discernible. Premarital and extramarital sexual experiences, for example, which have been more or less condoned for centuries, are still, we were told repeatedly, widely practiced throughout Yoneshima-ken. Although our panel was unable to agree as to whether or not premarital intercourse, mostly with prostitutes, is on the increase, several reminded us that one of its chief causes has long been the parental restrictions placed upon informal social relations between young men and women. For example, any kinds of rendezvous such as movie dating are often still frowned upon. One leader-informant did concede, to be sure, that it is wiser to allow his teen-age daughter to go to movies with a boy friend openly than to invite surreptitious meetings, and another went so far as to sanction the practice for daytime hours only. Incidentally, this latter gentleman, who had been a senior high school principal for many years, always prohibited social or even folk dancing among his students on the ground, he maintained, that it enflames erotic urges.

Our panel again could not agree on whether extramarital relations are increasing. One leader contended that rising incomes of upper-class men enable them to support at least one mistress more easily than ever, an important dividend of which is the admiration of their friends for both their affluence and virility. (Another leader knew a fellow citizen who zestfully supported six mistresses until he died at a venerable age.) The trouble with this contention, however, is that rising incomes invite more ways to enjoy higher standards of living. As still another spokesman wryly pointed out, it must sometimes generate quite severe conflict to decide between acquiring a new mistress or a new refrigerator!

On the whole, then, the pervasive attitude was one of considerable tolerance toward sexual patterns. The increasing ease of divorce, although still below 10 percent in Yoneshima-ken, was strongly approved, as were equal rights for wives who find, for example, that they can no longer endure their mothers-in-law. One financially successful informant, although he condoned the possible decline in extramarital liaisons (the people today, he said, would not tolerate an Emperor Meiji who, once had 14 "wives"), nonetheless frankly endorsed the double standard: after all, men are entitled to "relief" without emotional involvement, whereas women (for reasons that remained ambiguous) apparently are not. Only one informant held that the titillating *toruko* baths and *storippu* shows should be prohibited, much less their lurid advertisements scattered widely on Hiroi-shi billboards.

Only one or two others condemned prostitution on the ground that it perpetuates feudal customs of female exploitation and subservience. Considerable division of opinion prevailed, indeed, as to whether federal outlawing of prostitution (since 1958) is any real solution. In an earlier chapter we found how profitably the pseudo-*geisha* system continues to thrive with the blessing of politicians in Yamada-shi. Also, there is said to be less prevention of venereal infection than in some earlier periods when prostitutes were medically supervised. To be sure, in Hiroi-shi a rehabilitation center for bar girls, hostesses, and other "entertainers" is maintained by the prefectural government, but the number of inmates decreases when times are profitable (during our study about 15 girls were housed there, three-fourths of capacity).

Even so, the views of Kamada-san, *jichikai* executive, may be more typical of the panel than not. Legalized prostitution and its allied activities not only reduce the likelihood of contagion, they also reduce the danger of violations of better-class girls who wish to retain their premarital virginity. Most important of all they provide employment for many young women who could not do as well otherwise. Certainly one must be impressed by the estimate of our labor leader, Doi-san, that about one million Japanese females are presently employed in erotically stimulating occupations. Incomes vary widely, of course, but in one of the better Hiroi-shi night clubs the more popular hostesses with whom he himself was on very friendly terms earn considerably more than a well-trained office secretary could ever hope for.

But on the question of abortion our panel proved rather conservative. Although no one favored its outright abolition, all held that today it is much too easy to obtain. True, legalized abortion has been needed to reduce the population rate, but destroying the living fetus not only violates a sacred Buddhist tenet but may jeopardize the mother's health. Our panel disagreed, moreover, as to the propriety of abortion for an unmarried woman although, because both mother and child are stigmatized by illegitimacy, a majority still favored it.

A far better solution than abortion is, of course, birth control. With one exception, to whom we shall return in a moment, our leaders were enthusiastic about the widespread use of contraception. Two recalled the great influence upon Japan of Margaret Sanger who hastened its widespread acceptance. Sterilization, the "rhythm method," the condom, and the medicinal douche are, we were told, still the commonest means; other means such as the diaphragm, pill, and uterine loop were not yet in widespread use in

Yoneshima-ken during our study, although all were becoming obtainable. Diaphragms are least popular because women are shy about having them fitted by physicians. But even at local agricultural co-operatives, where other contraceptives are dispensed at low cost, a woman prefers to ask for them by the delicate name of *suisen* (daffodil). In drugstores they are often concealed conspicuously by newspaper wrappings.

Sex education, most leaders also contended, is much weaker than it ought to be. Among adults groups, to be sure, it is frequently quite effective: not only do agricultural co-ops sponsor programs on family planning, so too do many unions such as the textile and municipal. Yet in a survey that Jichikai Secretary Kamada once conducted in Yamada-shi, he found that farmers particularly wanted to learn more. No one, moreover, could recall seeing a PTA program or movie on birth control (although movies are available), and on lower school levels sex education is almost exclusively limited to the physiology of reproduction (in some physical education and home economics classes, topics such as menstruation are included also). But here again our panel tended to be cautious. Although most informants freely admitted that sex education should include moral questions, they were not specific as to what or how except to point out that the Ministry of Education largely avoids them, and that in any case methods of birth control are too hazardous a matter to study even on the senior high level—certainly until teachers are better prepared to handle the topic. Besides, various women's magazines are filled with uninhibited discussions of the varieties of sexual experience, which millions of teen-agers avidly read at home.

Although our leader panel was rarely unanimous or wholly consistent on sex, marriage, and family questions, by far our most articulate dissenter was the Shingon priest, Azuma-san, who viewed the whole matter strictly in terms of the tenets of his own "hard" sect. Thus he condemned both premarital and extramarital relations; unlike several others, he regarded masturbation as sinful; his staff of priests never consent to pray for couples who hope for no more pregnancies; and he disapproved of birth control as well as of abortion except in cases where a mother's health is seriously threatened. (Only for like reasons, one may properly kill a mosquito.) He did frankly admit that Buddhism has not been effectual in eliminating the mistress syndrome and that some Buddhist sects, especially the newer "soft" ones, are much less stringent than his own—in fact, some extremists have encouraged sexual freedom by the practice of erotically-flavored ceremonials. Also, although his own marriage had been *mi-ai*, he refused to endorse either the *mi-ai* or *ren-ai* alternative, for the choice is artificial. The more correct conception derives from *in-nen:* a "cause-effect" pattern of total relations between husband and wife aimed at maximum harmony. How marriage is brought about is thus of trivial significance.

Priest Azuma here approached what he considered to be the master key to Buddhism itself—its opposition to all dualisms (including those of Christian theology) and its central regard for the harmony of nature and the universe. A primary concept thus is *arayashiki,* which he defined as the "foundation of life," the primordial force that unites and propels all beings. Precisely for this reason, sexual expression is considered a natural and vital dimension of *arayashiki,* and although it demands regulation it must not be treated as of subordinate or merely instrumental worth. On the contrary, it is a richly intrinsic value, a value which the artist, Nagashi-san, compared to that of a beautiful plant.

Our priest's patient efforts to clarify his own theological interpretation of sexual and family ethics became considerably more elaborate than we are able to convey here. Nevertheless, one may infer that despite its strictures the core of his position is still shared by a majority of the leader panel in their own affirmative attitudes toward sexual and marital experience, with due regard for modesty, social restraint, and respect for parents. Indeed, as Azuma-san also pointed out, such respect is deeply rooted in religious tenets: the proper relation to Buddha is not one of obeisance before a stern, forbidding God but rather one of loyal devotion to a wholly natural Father who is prepared to return that devotion in full.

IV

We find ourselves, then, well within the second sphere toward which our panel expressed concern, that of religion. Art, too, entered our discussions here, particularly with Nagashi-san.

Religious attitudes varied all the way from the deep sense of dedication revealed in Priest Azuma whom we came to appreciate at one extreme, to the bitter hostility toward religion's alleged soporific influence manifested by Tomita-san, Kaihōdōmei leader and professed atheist, at the other extreme. All leader respondents, nevertheless, had been affiliated at least in childhood either with Jōdoshinshū (to which the majority still belong) or with Shingonshū, and everyone apparently continues at least the practice of ancestral commemoration (*hōji*). Virtually all own a *butsudan* (Buddhist altar) in which they regularly place offerings, but only a minority still maintain a *kamidana* (Shintō shelf). Within recent years, the married daughter and son-in-law of one of our respondents and the married son of another have been converted to Christianity. All three are college graduates.

The majority seemed troubled over what they regarded as a widespread decline in religious faith. Several spoke of the total indifference of their children, with whom they contrasted their own devout youth. Lawyer Kamijō, for example, recalled praying often at a shrine when he was preparing for college examinations, whereas his son and daughter only occasionally visit a shrine and then apparently for its recreational more than its religious attractions. Yet, next to Priest Azuma, only one informant, Okumura-san, the agricultural co-operative director, revealed any powerful religious motivation. A lay leader of Jōdoshinshū, he has for some years personally sponsored two meetings per month in his own home, one featuring lectures on Buddhist theology, usually by a priest, the other bringing together a group of teachers and other friends who discuss practical moral questions and their religious foundations. In addition, he sponsors a public lecture in a nearby temple once every year.

Director Okumura professed that his own role, a highly influential one in prefectural economic life, should be regarded as a "gift from God." He has, he said, a historical mission to perform without any thought of "reward." Yet he can hardly be characterized as sectarian-minded: any particular sect, including those of other great religions, can only provide alternative routes toward the meaning of God—the "ultimate power" of the universe. Moreover, whereas it is true that millions of people have deified Buddha, this is because of lack of sophistication: Buddha is a magnificent teacher of God's ways, certainly, but never should he be regarded as God Himself.

Less fervently, a number of other spokesmen such as Nagashi-san, the artist, and Natsui-san, the Yoneshima-ken school board chairman, likewise recognized the existence of some supreme universal power. Thus, while calling himself a "naturalist," Artist Nagashi, with remarkably Aristotelian overtones, spoke of God's universal "forms" which are expressed distinctively through the media of his own lacquer work and painting.

The banker Ishioka-san, always conscious of his high socioeconomic status, insisted that few of similar status to his own would any longer think of displaying a *kamidana*—indeed, that today the strength of religious faith is usually inverse to one's class level. He himself emphatically rejected personal immortality (friends of comparable status would consider him *baka*, a fool, were he to profess any such belief). Actually the only sense in which he could justify "immortality" at all is through the birth and survival of his direct descendants. Yet he admitted that his father, a large-scale prewar landlord who lived in the Ishioka home until his death, had been a deeply religious man; and even today our informant's family scrupulously practices both *hōji* and *bon* to honor ancestors.

Still others, among them Lawyer Kamijō and Jichikai Secretary Kamada, noted how people often return to the Buddhist faith as they grow old. Kamijō-san quoted a common saying, *Kurushii toki no kami-danomi*, which freely translated means: "When people suffer they turn to supernatural powers." Here a fundamental difference, he contended, between Buddhism and Shintoism centers in the focal concern of the former with the after-world and of the latter with this world. Hence the frequency of Shintō shrines dedicated to *kami* ("gods") of business, education, soldiering, fishing, marriage and almost every other aspect of the life cycle except death. The distinction is not absolute: Buddhism, too, has its this-worldly aspects. (What better proof than the first saint of Shingonshū, Kōbō Daishi himself, who over a millennium ago built irrigation systems that still function near where he was born?)

Nevertheless, even Jichikai Secretary Kamada, who belongs to no sect at all and does his best to tackle personal problems through his own efforts, also confessed that he sometimes "fears God" as he approaches old age. As to what "God" means he was not clear; nor did he pretend to know whether to expect personal immortality. Yet he could not help wondering whether an astronaut must not experience a feeling of awe at the vast mystery of the universe as he whirls through space. In Lawyer Kamijō's quite different terms, the truly religious person is one who experiences "reverence, piety, and benevolence," virtues which he regretted too few Japanese any longer manifest.

Priest Azuma would doubtless agree, but he would also insist as a loyal disciple of Kōbō Daishi that Buddhism, as exemplified in attitudes toward sex, is by no means so exclusively other-worldly as some panelists seemed to imply. One should not forget, he held, that vices and virtues are of three main varieties—of the mind, of words, and of acts—and that no one variety is paramount over the other two. Nor, he said, should one forget the tripartite reality of substance, form, and usage, a reality which encompasses all dimensions of nature, even so simple an object as the common drinking cup.

Although our priest no less than other leaders was more than a little interested in the Sōkagakkai, the militant Buddhist social organization to which we have referred, he was more cautious than most in his judgments. Professing as he did so often that his knowledge was derived from limited sources, yet in this case he aimed directly at the heart of the movement—the Buddhist doctrine of Nichirenshōshū and its most sacred of all relics, the *ita-mandara*. This is a black lacquered plaque on which Saint Nichiren, the "true Buddha," is said to have written the most sacred words of all time. (On our own visit to Taisekiji, the head temple of the sect at the foot of Mount Fuji, we were not permitted close to the *ita-mandara*. Other Nichiren sects, however, dispute the relic's authenticity.) A "true believer" is one who accepts abjectly this source of divine power. Worship of it, best expressed through lengthy rituals, is the one absolute assurance of health, happiness and the solution of every sort of human problem.[3]

Priest Azuma does not, of course, subscribe to the tenets of Nichiren-shōshū, nor for that matter does any one of our other 15 leaders. The technique of conversion known as *shakubuku*, which is said to have been invented by Nichiren himself as a way of persuading people, was just as severely criticized by upper-level panelists as by our lower-level panel. (Artist Nagashi, laughingly recalled how, when an acquaintance once tried *shakubuku* on him he answered that he already belongs to the "Bokkei sect"—Bokkei being his given name.) Fears are frequently played upon (a favorite routine is to visit hospital patients) and, if Labor Leader Doi's information is correct, members who wish to withdraw may even be threatened with "violence." The pseudo-militaristic, "totalitarian" structure of the organization all the way from top echelons in Tokyo to the simple neighborhood units of Yamada-shi and Utsumi-shi; the "opportunistic" and "insincere" motivations of most college-educated, salaried officials; the demagogic character of its political programs; the "childish" quality of much of its propaganda; and the below average socioeconomic status of the majority of members—these were among the more frequently reiterated criticisms.

Why, then, has the Sōkagakkai grown so phenomenally, with estimates of membership ranging from 2 or 3 million by Kamada-san to 15 million by its own officials? However disputable, the answer was an emphatic consensus among our panel: the Sōkagakkai is even more successful than well over a hundred other "new" religions with often more or less common tenets and rituals (Tenrikyō is one of the best known), because it fills a "spiritual vacuum" among vast numbers of people who have lost their bearings in the decades since the end of World War II. They are people, we were told, for whom traditional ways of religion fail to satisfy; for whom Japan can no longer be regarded as an invincible nation governed eternally by its Emperor-God; for whom the increasingly Westernized technology creates a serious lag in economic skills; or finally for whom rational, scientific ways of attacking everyday human problems are still beyond their comprehension or ability.

For perhaps several of these reasons, two of our panelists compared the Sōkagakkai to the Communist movement, except for one important

---

[3] Cf. the official English interpretation, *The Sōkagakkai* (Tokyo: The Seikyo Press, 1960). Cf. also pp. 65–67, 145, for a community perspective.

difference: the former grounds its program in an ancient theology, the latter refuses to do so. Another panelist echoed our Ebibara informant, Masumi-san: the Sōkagakkai, both insisted, is too uncomfortably reminiscent of Nazism and Fascism. Yet on one other question of whether the movement would nevertheless continue to grow or instead had already reached its crest of membership and power, there appeared to be, once more, sharp differences of opinion.

We punctuate our present discussion of religion by returning to Nagashi-san's keen interest in its relations to art. He discerns, he said, a close affinity particularly between the finest traditional arts of Japan and the Zen sect of Buddhism. Beauty of form as familiarly expressed in *sadō* (tea ceremony) and in certain types of *ikebana* (flower arrangement) is typical of Zen. Likewise his own *shitsugei* (lacquer art) exemplifies, despite its practical uses, much the same sort of esthetic qualities. In fact, although *shitsugei* is not a Zen creation, nonetheless it often contributes to the precise rituals of *sadō* itself. Here *wabi*, a Zen concept connoting perfect simplicity and quietness, is a revealing principle.

Nagashi-san did not intend to attribute to Zenshū all that is most indigenous to Japanese art. Confucianism and Taoism, for example, were also mentioned, especially their preoccupation with right order, a preoccupation reflected not only in the arts but in the correctness of human relationships including, of course, the master imperatives of obligation: *giri* and *on*.

Nor would Artist Nagashi wish to leave the impression that he is merely a traditionalist. Though disliking Picasso's erotic unconventionality, which he regarded as decidedly non-Oriental, nevertheless he gladly conceded not only that such behavior has often seemed indispensable to Occidental artists but that Picasso himself is today supreme in the totally free expression of his creative genius. Nagashi-san himself, moreover, is hardly constrained by any single esthetic mode. Western abstract art, for example, has profoundly affected some of his own work, as in a lovely painting of cliffs and sea that he presented to us.

Even so, historic religious influences continue to weigh upon him. The quest for distinctive ways of expression is again, he maintained, a Zen-like quest for continuous rediscovery of esthetic form. Yet, since it must always fall short of final satisfaction and is therefore bound to fail, there remains in all of us, artists or not, an existential fear of death. After all, is it not alone in the attainment of unqualified perfection, a perfection to which Artist Nagashi constantly aspires in his works and through which lies his single hope for immortality, that this fear could ever be assuaged? But Zenshū teaches us, too, that such perfection ever eludes our mortal grasp, and so the shadow of fear accompanies us always.

V

Politics and economics, no less than the family and religion, were institutions of great interest to our upper-level panel. Of the 16 participants,
seven are members of the ruling Liberal Democratic party, two are active in
the Socialist party, one in the Democratic Socialist party, and one in the
Communist party. Of the remaining five who declared themselves to be
"independent," at least three fairly regularly support the Liberal Democrats.
Roughly, the panel thus tended to reflect the distribution of political allegiances in the nation as a whole.

A similar distribution could be observed in answers to the specific
political questions that were also asked of the community panels. Thus,
as to whether Article 9 of the Japanese Constitution should be amended to
permit an armed force, a minority answered "no" and a majority "yes,"
with vigorous support for nuclear weapons by at least three. One leader
proposed, however, that Article 9 should become part of an international
federal constitution; no one opposed membership in the United Nations;
and most favored the inclusion of Red China. Likewise, while a majority
approved the visits of United States atomic submarines to Japanese ports,
the panel was somewhat more divided on the Vietnam issue—at least five
favored withdrawal but one went so far as to defend the position of America
both because it must "keep face" and because armaments boost its economy.
On the question of whether the Communist party should be outlawed,
more respondents than not held that it is safer to permit freedom of
organization than to force it underground. Nonetheless, two leaders
responsible for large staffs of workers sharply disagreed on whether to
employ party members: one would simply refuse; the other, who already
employs several, held that they have as equal legal right as any qualified
employee, so long as they do not disrupt normal operations.

Perhaps the most liberal propensities of our panel centered around
the question of public enterprise. None opposed NHK, the nationally
owned radio and television system, although neither was enthusiasm
revealed in favor of public operation of the several private networks.
Similarly, whereas no one wanted to see the Japanese National Railways
turned over to private enterprise, most also seemed content with the
numerous private lines. The self-styled "conservative," Banker Ishioka,
held that only one natural resource, water, should be publicly owned and
controlled, a view somewhat counterbalanced by that of another Liberal
Democrat, Mayor Miyakawa, who went so far as to concede with no sign
of disapproval that public ownership of at least the largest industries is
only a matter of time.

The dominant impression that emerges here is, then, the eclectic one of a "mixed economy," with Liberal Democratic members somewhat more inclined toward a public-service image of the state than would probably be true of a comparable sample of United States Republicans. The director of public welfare, Sumida-san, appeared to represent several Liberal Democrats besides himself: service to the people should always be the chief criterion, not private *or* public enterprise. Thus he especially favored greatly strengthened benefits in medical care, in geriatrics, and in education. At the same time, unlike Shōda-san, Communist, or Tomita-san and Enomoto-san, Socialists, Sumida-san would not welcome a socialist political economy.

Yet it could hardly be said that Director Sumida arrived at his critical opinions on the basis of familiarity with Marxian ideas. True, although a number of leaders (not only those of leftist orientation) had at some time more or less carefully studied Marx's works, few were emphatic to admit that they had been influenced. More unusual was the co-op leader, Okumura-san, who proudly mentioned the influence of the Utopian Socialist, Robert Owen. Nevertheless, although he recalled how, in the prewar period, he had fought with the Farmer's Union to break the grip of feudal landlordism and was sometimes called a Communist, he views himself first of all as an "enthusiastic Buddhist."

Here Priest Azuma, although of a different sect, would doubtless applaud Leader Okumura. For, despite our priest's frank admiration of socialist ideals, Marxism for him is much too materialistic. More than this, it tends to glorify the worker as such rather than the whole individual. The Liberal Democratic party, because its concern is with the latter and not merely with the former, is accordingly closer to Buddhist principles than are Marxian-influenced parties. After all, Buddhism too is "democratic" in its key political principles: How could it be otherwise when we perceive that "identity, uniqueness, and relatedness" are readily transposable to "equality, freedom, and fraternity"?

For very different reasons, Doi-san, our textile union director, likewise rejected the doctrines of Marx. Because it substitutes clichés and outmoded formulae for psychological and other kinds of scientific approaches to workers' problems, it becomes increasingly obsolete. More than this, Marx himself, a cloistered intellectual, was not only ill-informed of day-to-day economic struggles; he failed to anticipate the rise of the middle class, largely a twentieth-century phenomenon that has caused much of the theory of class struggle to become outmoded.

Thus Doi-san's own Democratic Socialist party, backed by the Japan Federation of Labor Unions (Dōmei), is not to be considered revolutionary. Whereas it joins with the much larger Socialist party on specific issues, a more urgent need is to find ways for workers and owners to cooperate. He himself is one of several representatives of organized labor who serve on prefectural boards of mediation, together with employers and "neutral" representatives of the public at large. After all, workers are not necessarily good managers; both are essential to economic progress. The goal is a middle-class democracy made possible by gradual upgrading of the standard of living of all citizens. For this reason, although it still remained his not very spirited hope that a coalition of Socialists and Democratic Socialists might eventually defeat the Liberal Democrats, Doi-san has on one occasion, at least, supported a Liberal Democratic candidate for the national Senate.

Yet he consistently supported the right to strike not only for industrial unions—his own already has that right—but equally for those that have not, notably the municipal and postal workers, railroad workers, and teachers. (This position, as might be expected, Banker Ishioka opposed, although it is only fair to note that he also opposed management-controlled "company unions" that still flourish among small establishments.) Doi-san blamed extremist movements after the war for bringing about a severe curtailment: both the Socialist and Communist parties, he insisted, have been rigidly controlled by left-wing ideologies that even now continue to waver between pro-Peking and pro-Moscow policies—policies that have led to dictatorship and the muzzling of freedom.

Enomoto-san, the municipal union leader, although a staunch Socialist, would not completely disagree with Doi-san. True, the huge General Council of Trade Unions of Japan (Sōhyō) with which his union is affiliated is the backbone of the Socialist party. (Doi-san was frank to admit, incidentally, that 90 percent of Sōhyō members vote Socialist as compared to only some 65 percent of Dōmei members who vote Democratic Socialist.) Nevertheless, granting that a socialist order is the ultimate goal, the immediate task, according to Enomoto-san, is to strengthen collective bargaining. Then, as employers become more conciliatory, so simultaneously does Sōhyō become more pragmatic and hence less doctrinaire. Meanwhile, the fact remains not only that rural conservatism is a powerful brake on radical social change, but that a "mood of security" is developing among workers themselves as they seek such objectives as the standardized minimum wage and increasingly upward mobility. Certainly his own municipal employees develop "ambivalent feelings" of class status; after all, nearly all of them wear "white collars." Thus even for Labor Leader Enomoto, the concept of class struggle appeared less relevant than it once was—a view from which, of course, both of our left-oriented burakumin leaders, Tomita-san and Shōda-san, would vehemently dissent.

Other spokesmen held still different views on the relevance of class struggle to Japanese society. Educator Natsui refused, for example, to assert whether it is currently weakening or strengthening, though he did regard it as "serious." Our women's leader, Tabata-san, said that whereas doubtless it is real enough she herself could not take sides in such a struggle. Several of quite varied political persuasion agreed that the vast majority of workers are not, in any case, class conscious in the Marxian sense; they are simply not informed. The more common situation, they held, is for workers and indeed for citizens at large to vote for candidates toward whom they have developed some sort of personal attraction, rather than from any clear political convictions.

On only one point did there seem to be unanimity. Virtually every panelist, whether Liberal Democrat or not, reinforced what Councilman Hayashi had stated earlier,[4] namely, that corruption is rife in the dominant party. "Bribery" (up to the highest officials of the national government), "bossism," "factionalism," and "selfishness" were among the pejoratives mentioned. In Yoneshima-ken, too, large sums have been spent to elect Liberal Democratic candidates, much in the form of "gifts" that range all the way from trips to hot spring resorts for local leaders to aprons and packages of sugar for voter-housewives.

Leaders did not, to be sure, agree as to whether or how far corruption also infects the opposition parties. One or two held that these parties are almost equally suspect, a view emphatically denied by Labor Leader Enomoto. After all, he said, the Socialist party has access to nothing like the funds of the Liberal Democratic party. Thus, in a prefectural campaign for national senator that took place during our residence (won, incidentally, by a Socialist), Enomoto-san calculated that the cost to his own candidate had been less than $9000, as compared to well over $50,000 to the Liberal Democrat. The latter sum, incidentally, was less than two-thirds of the expenditure in comparable campaigns. Corruption was also said to have been far below average. Even so, we can appreciate the caustic remark of Lawyer Kamijō that it will take another full century before a single clean election is likely to occur.

Here one is reminded of the young Clean Government Party, Kōmeitō, the political arm of the Sōkagakkai. More readily than in the case of any other party, our panelists were prepared to concede that it has not been contaminated by corrupt maneuverings. Labor Leader Doi, for example, confessed that although he dislikes its opportunistic platforms (it borrows when convenient from the Democratic Socialist party), and although its "fanaticism"could conceivably become more dangerous than that of the Communist party, nevertheless Kōmeitō may continue to grow if only because of disillusionment with the Liberal Democrats. Whereas others disagreed on the question of further growth, Co-op Leader Okumura went

[4] Cf. pp. 147–148 and pp. 67–68 for a fisherman's view.

further: just possibly, unless other parties reform, the Kōmeitō party may eventually come to power.

Mention of Okumura-san draws us back to the movement which he heads, the Yoneshima-ken agricultural co-operatives. Like the fishing co-operatives, which we discussed in Part I, they are primarily an economic rather than a political movement. Even so, their impact which extends back some decades has probably been as far-reaching upon this prefecture as anywhere in Japan. Although they consist chiefly of producer co-ops with nearly 200 branches (including Yamada-shi and Utsumi-shi), they also maintain nearly 100 consumer co-ops, proportionately far more than among the fishing population, and this despite the same kind of opposition from privately-owned stores. Fertilizer is the main commodity, but some co-ops are presently expanding to include many products all the way from groceries to motorcycles. One, in Hiroi-shi, is even called a "supermarket," while a co-op housing project for farmers was also being considered at the time of our research.

The co-op movement, Leader Okumura pointed out, is not to be identified with any party ideology. Though the Communist party has termed it an "agent of American imperialism," the fact rather is, he said, that the movement favors the "coexistence" of capitalism and socialism. Moreover, although most members, being farmers, are Liberal Democrats, no attempt is made to influence anyone's vote. As in the case of fishing co-ops, members formally determine all policies. Seventy percent of the members attend annual meetings where programs are considered and adopted by majority vote.

Rural co-ops are, in short, an important index to the economic life of Yoneshima-ken as a whole. Although here as elsewhere the farm population is steadily declining, it still remains larger than the urban population. Meanwhile, chiefly through the effectiveness of co-ops, farmers now control the prices of their crops more equitably than at any time in their history; thus many in turn have been able not only to retain their holdings of land but to perpetuate much of the historic family patterns that depend upon them.

Co-op Leader Okumura agreed, to be sure, that farms are much too small. Hence, although he firmly opposed both absentee ownership and Soviet-type collectivization, he did endorse a radical change of policy that would permit one household to own as much as 100 acres, up to the maximum that it could manage by itself with highly mechanized efficiency. In this way, the likelihood of too severe an imbalance between industry and agriculture in Yoneshima-ken could in part be redressed, and the decentralized, democratic practices to which agricultural co-operatives have contributed so much could continue to evolve.

That others on the panel were capable of audacious proposals was illus-trated by our prefectural executive of the fishing co-op credit unions: Ada-chi-san. The problem of over-centralized political and economic control could best be attacked, he argued, by consolidating the 46 present prefec-tures into seven or eight much larger ones. Each of these would then have considerable autonomy in directing its own affairs; at the same time its re-lations to the federal government could function more effectively. We were told that both the ruling party and at least one minority party, the Socialist, already include some advocates of this idea. Director Adachi himself be-lieves that its adoption would go far toward providing a more equitable balance between centralized and decentralized operation of all sorts of en-terprises, mainly private but perhaps public as well.

VI

How thoroughly and effectively, in the judgment of our panel, does public education in Yoneshima-ken deal with the sort of controversial questions that we have been trying to epitomize? Only one leader, the chairman of the prefectural school board, Natsui-san, held that development of the class-room discussion method after World War II has made it possible for students and teachers to engage in active and critical rather than merely passive learning. Yet, on second thought, even Educator Natsui qualified his judg-ment: the discussion method has been developed primarily in the elemen-tary schools; in the junior and senior high schools it is much more limited, especially in the latter where preparation for examinations is of primary importance. Arai-san, the prefectural superintendent of schools (Natsui-san and his fellow board members appointed him during our residence) did profess some interest in developing new ventures on the junior and senior levels, but whether or not these might concern controversial issues such as politics was left ambiguous. In any case, most teachers, Superintendent Arai implied, are at present no more qualified to handle such issues than they are course units in sexual morality.

It hardly comes as a surprise that when we asked our respective leaders in co-ops, religion, labor, and politics whether they could provide specific evidence of critical or comprehensive educational attention to any of these areas, their replies were almost wholly negative. Thus neither Doi-san nor Enomoto-san, labor leaders, could recall instances of their teen-age children relating at home any classroom discussions of political or economic ques-tions. (Enomoto-san's daughter did tell us that her social studies teacher once reported the results of an election; otherwise he faithfully followed textbook assignments. Still, she asked, why shouldn't he do so as long as her fellow students seem to be indifferent?)

But panelists were themselves divided on whether the curriculum should devote more attention to the crucial problems of our age. One in particular, Banker Ishioka, held that Oriental young people are generally too immature, too volatile, even at times fanatical (witness, he said, student demonstrations in Korea, or for that matter in Japan itself). Hence, whereas it is perfectly legitimate to teach the "principles of politics"—after all, "order" and "peace" are Japan's two most important goals—it is definitely not safe to study such issues as Vietnam or the pros and cons of atomic weapons. Students, he maintained, should remain aloof of politics and concentrate on "the most basic things." Yet to outlaw demonstrations is not the answer either; one cannot legislate radical attitudes out of existence.

Two other leaders, both usually of moderate views, would disagree with Banker Ishioka. Labor Leader Doi, a Democratic Socialist, and Lawyer Kamijō, a Liberal Democrat, equally insisted that the great purpose of public education should be to develop critical-mindedness in young citizens which is attainable only through scrupulous examination of every sort of human concern. Kamijō-san cautioned, nevertheless, that the task is hazardous: to become deeply involved in the study of, say, democracy almost inevitably leads in turn to consideration of communism. Perhaps this is one reason why most teachers, he maintained, are reluctant to become involved in controversial studies at all.

We detect still other reasons for such reluctance, one of which is the highly competitive examination pressures already alluded to. If, as Doi-san put it, school children have little time to be children (his own, he said, can hardly "breathe"), then teachers certainly must be compelled to expend a large proportion of their own classroom energies on testing requirements. Although the contention might be disputed, we were even told that as a result of these requirements teachers are subjected to a higher rate of "overtime" work than those of any other prefecture. In any case, Yoneshima-ken's exceptionally high ranking in the National Achievement Tests (NAT)[5] and the heavy load of regular course requirements, can well explain why concern with other educational matters tends, in Lawyer Kamijō's apposite term, to become "peripheral"; why, moreover, the stress on learning science as a subject has not, he said, necessarily transferred to scientific ways of thinking about personal and social problems; or possibly even why, according to other information provided to us (although again perhaps disputable),

[5] For community views on the NAT and other educational questions, cf. pp. 151–154.

Yoneshima-ken school children have a higher ratio of eye strain than those in any other section of the country.

This is not to say that most leaders repudiate the examination program. More than one seemed proud of the remarkable success of Hiroi-shi Senior High School in the number of its graduates who succeed yearly in winning admittance to the supremely prestigious University of Tokyo. True, Women's Leader Tabata, an experienced teacher, objected to the program on the ground that it deflects education from the more vital task of free personality development. Priest Azuma echoed a similar view: entrance examinations encourage uniformity at the price of individuality. But others maintained that for many Yoneshima-ken citizens, especially those with rural backgrounds who are ambitious for better economic opportunities, only a strict subject-centered curriculum governed by rigorous standards could effectuate such opportunities. For example, Doi-san, who deals daily with industrial workers, explicitly praised the prefecture's ranking in NAT scores. Less sanguine leaders, however, preferred to characterize the testing and examination system by a well-known phrase: *Shikata ga nai*, "it cannot be helped." In Educator Natsui's view, even if one grants that the system could be improved, it remains on the whole both unavoidable and fair. Teachers, meanwhile, may also incline toward the attitude of *Shikata ga nai*, since their competence is said to be evaluated largely by the test scores of their students.[6]

Another reason for their pervasive attitude was attributed to the teachers' union, Nikkyōso, always a lively controversial topic wherever education is discussed. Previously we reported that Nikkyōso has shrunk in the prefecture to a fraction of its original size, and that this reduction has accompanied a proportional strengthening of the contents and methods of education as endorsed, on the one hand, by Monbushō (Ministry of Education) and as condemned, on the other, by Nikkyōso. One consequence is that whether Yoneshima-ken teachers approve or not of NATs or other features of the educational program (and we have found that many apparently do not), they seem incapable organizationally of resisting them.

But here disagreements within our leader panel again became severe, this time on the question of Nikkyōso itself. Only one-fourth of our leaders appeared to be emphatically in favor of Nikkyōso: the two Socialists, the Communist, and one Liberal Democrat (the retired teacher and women's

---

[6] A personal communication from a Yoneshima-ken school administrator assures us, however, that some modifications in the curriculum and entrance requirements in the junior and senior high schools have been effected since our research was conducted. He also noted more emphasis on development of the "whole child," with Yoneshima University leading in this liberalizing trend. The children now look more "cheerful," he said. But other communications have sounded much less optimistic.

leader, Tabata-san). Although we were told that it is not extraordinary for Liberal Democrats to belong to Nikkyōso, Tabata-san said she has earned the hostility of many political associates. It happens that she also chairs the local women's section of her party.

The single bitterest opponent of Nikkyōso was Educator Natsui. Well before he became chairman of the prefectural board of education, he found it impossible as a high school principal to cooperate with the then strong union locals in Yoneshima-ken. Nikkyōso, he said, is responsible for false propaganda that Japanese education has been regressing from the progressivist philosophy that influenced it so heavily in the late 1940s and early 1950s. The trouble is that Nikkyōso is controlled by "communists," probably the most dangerous of them being professors at the University of Tokyo and the Tokyo University of Education who, he contended, were once equally extreme "nationalists." (In both institutions, incidentally, we were told during personal visits that a substantial proportion of their faculties still belong to Nikkyōso, which is not true of most Japanese institutions of higher learning, including both Yoneshima University and Yamada College.)

At any rate, with most of Educator Natsui's opinions, Banker Ishioka heartily concurred. Nikkyōso leaders, he maintained, are mostly "radical agitators" who want Japan to become a "red nation." It should be disbanded. But Ishioka-san did concede that the impoverished economic status of teachers over a great many generations could well account for counter-extremisms in the postwar profession. Moreover, consistent with his opposition to company unions, he opposed Kyōshikai as long as it remains an administrator-dominated organization in the educational profession. This is one point at least on which he appeared to be more liberal than Natsui-san, who endorsed Kyōshikai. Prefectural Superintendent Arai also seemed to differ with his board chairman on this point: Kyōshikai, he said, is merely a "study group," but he would not object if it were to become a genuine teachers' union so long as it found its model in certain European unions rather than in Nikkyōso.

Our initial question—whether public schools should give close attention to such major issues as we have been reporting in this chapter—was also related to the Nikkyōso dispute. Several informants insisted that for some years after World War II many zealous union teachers had sought to convince their students of the evils of the capitalist system and the virtues of a communist or socialist society. This radical exuberance produced a conservative reaction spearheaded by Monbushō but with the backing, of course, of the Liberal Democratic party.

To understand the present extremely cautious stance of many teachers concerning economic and other fevered questions, one must therefore appreciate the political context of the Nikkyōso-Monbushō feud. Our impression was that most leaders would agree with the Dōwakai chairman, Councilman Hayashi: the attempt of Nikkyōso teachers to "color" the curriculum with its own ideology (one consequence of which, he maintained rather ambiguously, was to stimulate juvenile delinquency) has only produced much tighter centralized controls. Whether these controls (as the Kaihōdōmei spokesman, Tomita-san, would doubtless contend) have already resulted in other kinds of "coloration" congenial to Monbushō as representative of the prevailing power structure, Hayashi-san, although himself a former Socialist, did not venture to judge. What he did willingly admit (so, too, did Labor Leader Enomoto) was that Nikkyōso, after its long period of far-left policies, seems now to be veering toward a more conciliatory and "realistic" strategy which could even conceivably approach his own ideal of teaching as a neutral and objective function.

The extent to which the national and prefectural goals of Nikkyōso would now meet with approval by some of our informants depends, we suppose, on how these goals are to be interpreted. At any rate, as summarized for us by Tamura-san, the veteran Nikkyōso teacher and leader in Yoneshima-ken whom we met in Chapter 3, they include the following: higher salaries, shorter hours, strengthened social security such as pensions, smaller classes, the rights of labor, democratic education, the achievement of peace, and the growth of political democracy.

Different leaders were interested, of course, in quite different educational questions from those we have been reviewing thus far. Education in the arts, to take one instance, was understandably championed by Nagashi-san more than by any other spokesman. Having been a teacher of art at Yoneshima University, he expressed mild indignation at what he regards as the relative neglect of all the fine arts including music by the school curriculum. Compared with science or technology, he estimated a ratio of something like one to ten. One finds, to be sure, a "high school of art and crafts" in Hiroi-shi (the only one in the prefecture) with an art faculty of about 15. But even this school provides training in limited fields: sculpture, for example, is missing, although painting, mostly in its traditional forms, is emphasized. Moreover, since numerous students pursue technological subjects, even this school is not quite accurately named.

Elementary schools, except the "laboratory school" of Yoneshima University, employ no special art teachers, but upper-level schools ordinarily have at least one on the staff. The University includes several professors of both the graphic and musical arts, their main responsibility being that of training teachers. Thousands of public school students also visit the Hiroi-shi art museum. All in all, despite certain strictures, Nagashi-san is optimistic: not only is more art available in education than before the great war, but students are now permitted, as they rarely if ever were in earlier times, to develop original styles. His hope is that the curriculum will eventually achieve a balance between the sciences and arts.

Another area that invited comment is moral education (*dōtoku kyōiku*), an area to which we recall some community informants also reacted strongly. Quite unlike sex education, however, *dōtoku kyōiku* won from our leaders but feeble applause. Only Educator Natsui chose to endorse it both as a necessary substitute for religious instruction and as a way to develop respect for traditional values by means of discussion techniques. In contrast, Banker Ishioka perceived no need for moral education at all: right principles are imperative, certainly, but these can never be successfully instilled by formal prescription; they must derive from the moral fiber of the culture itself. To attempt to impose such principles on youth is, indeed, only bound to invite rebellion.

Co-op Director Okumura, although not as negative as Banker Ishioka, was likewise skeptical. Consistent with his religious propensities, the trouble with *dōtoku kyōiku*, he argued, is that it concentrates upon prudential morality—that is relativist rules of practical conduct, not upon basic standards. This is not to deny that such rules have a place in culture, but they hold a subsidiary place. The great task is to seek the "truth" about the supreme goods of life, not as Monbushō tries, at least obliquely, to accomplish through moral education, but by continuous dialogue between students and teachers with teachers serving as guides rather that as peremptory authorities.

Okumura-san's position was shared once more by Priest Azuma. But the latter was still more critical of *dōtoku kyōiku*: it becomes, he said, too exclusively a process of passive mentation (or, in Welfare Director Sumida's term, it is much too "formalistic")—a superficial device of Monbushō to help preserve the established social order. In any case, to attempt to dichotomize moral and spiritual values is mischievous.

Priest Azuma was among several who favored, as one corrective, the introduction of courses in comparative religion especially for the secondary level. Himself an ex-director of a Buddhist high school and college, he related how such courses are already offered on both the senior and college levels of some accredited Buddhist institutions. One course with which he is familiar devotes a full semester to Buddhism, a second to Christianity, and a third to other world religions. The strict Constitutional separation of church and state need not, moreover, deter similar comparative religion projects in public institutions so long as no one sect or creed is treated as the only true one. Meanwhile, although religion, he held, remains a tragic "blind spot" in public educational programs (indeed, one major reason alleged for the rising rate of crime), it is a weakness that unfortunately cannot be removed until the indifference and incompetence of teachers so far as religion is concerned are ameliorated through workshops and other sorts of special preparation in comparative education.

Such a proposal is not even now entirely impractical. Already in Yoneshima-ken a day-long annual conference is held on problems of religious education in which groups such as PTAs and representatives of various religions, including Priest Azuma, participate. It would doubtless encourage him to know that Prefectural Superintendent Arai, Lawyer Kamijō, and Welfare Director Sumida were other leaders favoring some form of comparative religion projects. Sumida-san went so far as to propose that they be attempted even in the elementary school.

But it was our lawyer who pointed to a related problem: the education of Buddhist priests themselves. Speaking as a lay consultant to the head temple of his own Jōdoshinshū, Kamijō-san maintained that priests are too rarely dedicated any longer to their calling, partly because they are too preoccupied with making a meager living, but partly also because they have become too separated from their congregations and too indifferent to everyday human concerns. One consequence is that people do not always "trust" their own priests, even though the lack of rapprochement should be blamed on both sides: congregations are all to frequently indifferent to their faith. Lawyer Kamijō's indictment of theological education was inadvertently reinforced, moreover, by Priest Azuma himself: since the training of priests has been chiefly confined to "metaphysical subjects," those who teach in Buddhist colleges are usually not qualified to teach secular courses such as natural science—courses which might, in any case, distract them from their prime obligations.

A few further reactions are apropos concerning the two ends of the learning continuum—early childhood and adult education. Only one leader, Welfare Director Sumida, chose to discuss the first of these. With the rapid increase of working mothers (a trend which, incidentally, he seemed to welcome much less than did our Women's Leader Tabata), the demand for nursery schools and kindergartens chiefly as child care centers is increasing far more rapidly than the supply. (One exclusive kindergarten in Hiroi-shi, however, is best-known for another purpose: any parent fortunate enough to have his children admitted is virtually assured that they will end up in a top-ranking university!) Many of these establishments are privately owned and nursery school teachers called *hobo* (loosely, "teaching mothers") are trained in a special two-year course after senior high school. Tuition is still charged for both nursery schools and kindergartens, public as well as private, although the federal government pays part of the cost. Sumida-san himself endorsed compulsory education for at least part of the day from the age of three, a rather heretical proposal, especially for a Liberal Democrat. He also seemed to favor a federal plan whereby nursery schools and kindergartens would both become a tuition-free division of the regular school system.

Our panel presented both discouraging and encouraging views of adult education. On the negative side, social education (the formally supported adjunct of Monbushō concerned with adult programs) was seldom spoken of enthusiastically. The only outstanding exceptions reported to us are in the area of family and old-age projects. Some 500 recreational and educational clubs for retired citizens are, according to Welfare Director Sumida, already functioning in this one prefecture. As for family education, a good example of one impressive program has already been described in our study of Ebibara. According to Women's Leader Tabata, however, it is increasingly difficult to motivate young mothers who, being better educated than the preceding generation, feel less need for such programs.

On the positive side, what impressed us most are the adult programs sponsored both by the agricultural (though rarely the fishing) co-operatives and by some of the large trade unions. Because, according to our spokesmen for these movements, the public school curriculum largely avoids both co-op and labor problems, it becomes essential to find a way to fill the vacuum. Thus applicants for co-op positions are often, according to Okumura-san, ill-informed of the movement, a weakness which the national co-operative college in Tokyo is helping to reduce.

Members who join either of the great unions represented on our panel are also given orientation. Doi-san's textile union provides a two-month program that includes one intensive and strictly sober week at a "labor college" with professors and trade-union leaders as lecturers, with a full-time union staff in charge, and with the cost being shared both by locals and by national headquarters. The employers' only contribution is the free time from work allowed each participant. (But here it should be noted that, in Doi-san's view, orientation programs are needed not only to correct anti-labor biases but also ideological distortions often inculcated by Nikkyōso teachers.)

The municipal workers' union could claim a still more elaborate program. In the Yoneshima-ken office alone, six staff members are assigned to educational work, one a specialist in Marxian theory, workers' rights, and other ideological themes. Young people's programs are likewise active, such as a Socialist party discussion group. About 60 professors from various universities are said to be utilized as resource experts by the national union, many of whom visit Hiroi-shi and other locals.

Still further, annual regional and national conferences on a wide range of themes are sponsored by this union, both with the aid of public funds and with representation by community people such as farmers' and women's groups. Thus during our period of residence, a national conference in a nearby city was attended by some 6000 persons who spent four days pooling the findings of preceding local and prefectural conferences (four or five of them in Yoneshima-ken alone). Symposia topics ranged all the way from agriculture and pollution to taxation and *burakumin.* Conclusions and recommendations were "fed back" to the local level, but it is noteworthy that these conferences apparently avoid explosive controversial issues. The chief reason, according to Labor Leader Enomoto, is that although the sponsoring union is affiliated with Sōhyō and hence the Socialist party the conferees themselves include citizens of widely varying viewpoint. The major aim seems to be that of generating cross-sectional community involvement.

Workers' education of this kind appears to us more clearly as a viable democratic force than as the instrument of a doctrinaire position. To the degree that our impression is sound, it supports the point made above by Hayashi-san and one or two others that the left-oriented movement may now be developing more pragmatic and viable approaches to the problems of Japanese culture than was formerly the case. In this endeavor, public education may prove to be less of a major reconstructive influence than the kinds of adult education that we have been describing.

Indeed, from Enomoto-san's viewpoint, it would be foolhardy for him or other labor leaders even to approach educational authorities with any proposal that problems of, say, unions be reintroduced into the curriculum. He remembered that, some years ago, teachers who did try to include the history of the labor movement in their courses were expelled for their efforts; and today, too, he himself would simply suffer "exile." Thus the best alternative is to circumvent Monbushō and the public schools by way of adult programs such as those of his own union.

VII

At this stage, if we retrospectively glance at the several institutions to which our panel has been reacting, beginning with the family and concluding with education, it becomes possible to catch glimmers of one additional perspective. This appears as a concept already utilized in both of our subcultures— modal personality. In this case it emerges from and throws light back upon the character of Yoneshima-ken as a whole.

As if most leaders had pondered on some such concept many times before, nearly all seemed eager to tackle it again. A remarkably high ratio of consensus emerged, furthermore, to confirm our preceding evidence: the value preference of citizens living in the area is, in our terms, predominantly Moderative rather than either Innovative or Transmissive. This characterization was supported by an extraordinary variety of terms: people in Yone-shima-ken, so we were told, tend to be mild-mannered, calm, acquiescent, harmonious, cooperative, compromising, tactful, cautious, frugal, compla-cent, approval-seeking, provincial, docile, polite, proficient, unadventurous, and imitative.

One consequence of such a cluster of qualities was said to be the paucity of national leaders who rose originally from Yoneshima-ken. True, it is possible to name a handful who have won ministerial or other high political posts, and one president of the University of Tokyo was born here; yet no one has ever reached the position of prime minister. Similarly in the field of the arts, our leaders largely agreed that almost no painters, writers, or musicians from Yoneshima-ken have as yet gained national stature. More-over, although many citizens migrate to the vast nearby cities, very few engage in large risk-taking enterprises; rather, more and more people seem content to settle for the kind of bland security congenial to the typical sara-riiman.

This soft-hued portrait was marred in one glaring respect. If Jichikai Secretary Kamada is right, the Yoneshima-ken personality type also tends to be crafty, petty, envious of success in others, and somewhat untrustworthy. It should be pointed out, however, that Kamada-san is not a native of the area, and that only one native-born leader, Artist Nagashi, singled out similar features for comment. To be sure, still another, Educator Natsui, went so far as to admit that some citizens possess these characteristics, and Labor Leader Enomoto agreed that such characterizations are commonplace.

At any rate, according to Lawyer Kamijō, one causal factor may be traceable to Japanese history. During the Tokugawa era of feudal rule, Yone-shima-ken was exploited by the ruling lords as a "watch dog" over nearby prefectures where the insurgent spirit was far more aggressive. Meanwhile, peaceloving sects (Jōdoshinshū most, Shingonshū somewhat) were rewarded with political and economic protection in return for their loyalty to the regime—one probable result being that, by comparison, militant sects like Nichirenshū still remain of minor influence in Yoneshima-ken. This historical contention may also help to explain why, although a few violent uprisings such as farmers' strikes of the prewar period have occurred in this prefec-ture, they have been less frequent than in various other areas of Japan, even in adjacent ones.

It is not possible to determine the degree to which such emollient influences may have delayed the eventual overthrow of Tokugawa power. There were certainly other factors too, at least one of which, according to Co-op Director Okumura, was the feudal practice of more or less deliber-ately alienating various sections of the country from one another. This was accomplished largely, he contended, by the ingenious device of constructing and imposing a different dialect upon each area so that no area could effectively communicate with any other. The remnants of this device are said to be apparent in the variety of dialects that one still detects in areas of close proximity.

But the problem before us requires a second causal factor; we may call it the "ecological interpretation of modal personality."[7] A number of informants quickly turned to this factor; they were convinced that one cannot hope to understand the human archetype of his region until one understands the distinctive geographical, meteorological, and geological features of the natural environment. Thus, over and over, they contrasted the environment of Yoneshima-ken with that of the regions closest to them— above all, with one that we shall rename Ōyama-ken.

Certainly contrasts between the ecology of these two prefectures are dramatic. Whereas Yoneshima-ken also includes hills and small mountains, the observer is struck by the relatively wide areas of terrain that are level enough to permit rice and other crops twice a year in generous abundance. Ōyama-ken, on the other hand, may at times seem still more beautiful but also rather awesome. Not only is it divided from its sister prefecture by a rugged mountain range that extends well into its interior, but it borders the Pacific Ocean. Because of these two facts and its unprotected location Ōyama-ken suffers from frequent floods, typhoons, and other catastrophes.

The conclusion drawn by our panel amounts to something like this: just as the terrain and climate of Ōyama-ken are comparatively harsh and severe, so the people have long been considered rebellious, passionate, and stubborn; contrarily, just as the ecology of Yoneshima-ken is relatively gentle and compliant, so its inhabitants are themselves conciliatory and mild in their general manner. One is reminded here of the cultural polarity made famous by Ruth Benedict: the Dionysian and the Apollonian.[8] One is reminded, too, of a remark by one of our informants to the effect that he has found from intimate personal experience that the women of Ōyama-ken are vibrant and responsive by comparison with those of Yoneshima-ken who tend, he said, to be placid.

More than one leader referred in addition to the lovely, graceful scenery of so much of Yoneshima-ken, and not only drew analogies with

---

[7] Cf. Julian Steward, *Theory of Culture Change* (Urbana: University of Illinois Press, 1955), for a point of view that could be considered congenial. Nevertheless, anthropological authorities on Japan such as Edward Norbeck (whose critique of this work in a preliminary draft has been immensely helpful) are skeptical of our informants' "ecological interpretation" as oversimplified and outmoded. Even more so, perhaps, would they question Okumura-san's historical account above of superimposed dialects.

[8] Cf. Ruth Benedict, *Patterns of Culture* (Boston: Houghton Mifflin Company, 1934).

certain elusive qualities of "femininity" which they detect in its personality type, but also compared these with the more "masculine" qualities of people in areas not far distant. Such "femininity," Nagashi-san contended, is in turn directly reflected in the extraordinary delicacy of his lacquer work manifested in fineness of line and softness of design that enables any connoisseur to identify instantly the bowls, trays, and other productions of this art that abounds in Hiroi-shi. And after all, he asked, how could it be otherwise? Just as one discovers various species of plants in Yoneshima-ken that are not to be found in Ōyama-ken, so one detects different inimitable personality styles in each prefecture.

To return for a moment to Ebibara and Kawabara, can the prefectural modal personality as the leader panel has patterned it be juxtaposed with that of our two subcultures? Obviously our answer is no more than conjectural; certainly one can never expect the two to fit together perfectly. Thus a propensity toward the Innovative value preference that was found to prevail in greater degree among *gyomin* and *burakumin* than either in their surrounding municipalities or in the leader panel is one distinction not to be ignored. What it implies, at the least, is that neither of the two subgroupings is typified by a personality quite as amenable or quite as "other-directed" as the prefectural type depicted by our leaders. In the case of Kawabarians, introverted behavior perhaps abetted by the frustration-aggression complex appears from our evidence to be a significant deviation; whereas in the case of Ebibarians, extroverted behavior appears also somewhat more conspicuous than among, say, "typical" farming people.

VIII

Though the question of "fit" between subcultural and prefectural personality types invites much further exploration, a related question enables us to come full circle to our point of departure—our two communities. How, in short, does our leader panel characterize people such as those with whom we have become acquainted in Ebibara and Kawabara?

This question may be answered at the outset by turning briefly again to our value study. Recall item 15, in which fishermen are discussing their foremost *kami*, Ryūōjin. Previously we learned that Ebibara people, at least in terms of this item, are less devout about religious faith than any of the other three communities think they are. The same conclusion could be drawn when we include leaders: they may suppose that more fishermen pray to Ryūōjin every day than is actually the case. At the same time, if leaders are simply responding in terms of how they themselves would act rather than how they imagine fishermen act, then they are more skeptical of the value of prayer than are any of the four community groups. About one-fourth of the upper level reject prayer altogether, as compared to about one-tenth of the lower level.

The one item on *burakumin* (item 25) is equally provocative. Although a majority of leaders agree with the community majority that a young *burakumin* should find a job in Osaka but struggle valiantly for "full emancipation," closer scrutiny once more reveals deviancy. Nearly a third of our leaders as compared with less than a tenth of our community participants including Kawabarians, believe that the young man should try to "pass" into the larger community.

Turning to more substantial and qualitative impressions concerning modal personality, it is necessary to appreciate that disparities among leader informants are even more acute than usual. Since three of the panel are themselves *burakumin*, one is an ex-fisherman, and all 16 reveal pronounced personalities of their own, the most we can expect are both dominant and deviant reactions.

A composite of views on the fishing people is considered first. Although not all leaders presented their notions of the *gyomin* modal personality, enough did so to help us determine the extent to which our characterizations as developed from "the bottom up" (especially in Chapter 3) are reconfirmed here "from the top down." Some leaders knew no fishermen personally, yet they were seldom reluctant to express emphatic opinions. Three independently of one another, for example, reminded us of a famous Japanese saying, the gist of which is: "beneath the bottom of one's boat lies the terror of the depth." This existential condition, several maintained, is also the key to the fisherman's character. Although few ever venture into the open Pacific, nevertheless their occupation is still much more fearsome and precarious than most and thus tends to develop such qualities as courage, forthrightness, virility, and pride. But this very condition likewise invites attitudes sometimes described as "fatalistic," and hence less concern with either the yesterdays or tomorrows than with what each day may bring. Gambling, which we remember to be almost addictive, is concomitant with such an attitude: After all, is not life itself a gamble?

In other respects, *gyomin* were regarded less sympathetically. Excessive drinking, below-average intelligence, "loose" sexual behavior, chronic indebtedness, in-group clannishness (including too frequent marriage among relatives), crudeness of speech, slovenly and frequently unhygienic home conditions were among the more negative characteristics discussed. Two leaders, particularly, stressed that certain diseases of the eye and skin have until recently been common among *gyomin*—a condition due, they said, to carelessness in handling infectious kinds of fish.

Our leader panel also suggested that *gyomin* are temperamental—that is, quickly given to explosive feelings, yet just as quickly given to meekness. Children of fishermen are notorious for comparable qualities: their erratic behavior not only reflects the manners of their parents but also the insecurities engendered by the absence both of fathers at sea and of mothers who peddle fish or work in factories.

The perspectives provided by leaders further sensitize us to one or two significant differences between Ebibarians and other fishing communities in Yoneshima-ken. Earlier we referred to Kazaki-shima, the offshore home of *gyomin* who remain within the jurisdiction of Utsumi-shi. This island community, due perhaps to its relative isolation, appears to be still more traditionally oriented than is Ebibara. One conspicuous reason is the continuance of the feudally-influenced system of ownership and control of a fleet of fishing boats by a single individual. Under this system, it would seem probable to us that somewhat similar ties of obligation prevail here between employer and employee as were observed in Kawabara's *oyabun-kobun* pattern of "boss-worker" relationships. In Ebibara, however, such a feudal influence no longer exists; hence, although we have found that the whole network of ancient values inherent in *on* and *giri* remains influential, the fact remains that individual family ownership of trawlers appears to encourage a spirit of greater competitiveness and independence than would be true of such fishing communities as Kazaki-shima.

Another distinctive feature of Ebibara, also observed by various leaders, is that it has succeeded to a greater extent than most of the approximately 65 Yoneshima-ken communities of fishermen in strengthening its economy. Selecting Kazaki-shima once more for comparison, most of its families (as in several other not far distant communities) combine farming with fishing; unfortunately, this is still rarely sufficient to provide liveable incomes. The result is a decline of population as families migrate to the cities. This uprooting likewise helps to account, in the eyes of Doi-san, for the foothold that the Sōkagakkai has managed to obtain among the insecure who still remain on the island. Meanwhile, Ebibarians, although fishing and farming are never combined in the same family, do usually manage successfully to supplement their income through such innovations as the seaweed project and marine processing factories. Thus its fishing population continues to be comparatively stable and has repelled every effort of the Sōkagakkai to convert its citizens.

But we should be in error to imply that Ebibara is regarded as more atypical than not of fishing communities in the region. For example, Adachi-san, our most knowledgeable leader in the fishing culture, would doubtless insist that the social immaturity of *gyomin* in Ebibara is little different from that of *gyomin* elsewhere. This is manifested perhaps most disturbingly, he said, in their inability to distinguish clearly between customary patterns of human relationship, again well exemplified by *giri*, and the newer more democratic patterns of "contractual obligation." Unlike the former, the latter do not properly depend at all upon family ties, the prestige of seniority, *oyabun-kobun*, or other forms of traditional paternalism; rather they depend entirely upon mutual and open agreements on what the contracting parties ascertain to be of common benefit.

In fact, however, even fishing co-operatives, according to Director Adachi, are still a confusing and often debilitating mixture of both the older and newer forms of obligation. This is a consequence, in part, of relatively low education among *gyomin*, although Adachi-san was careful to emphasize that biologically and psychologically they are capable of being fully equal to other Japanese. It is also partly due to the seasonal nature of their occupation which forces fishermen to undertake short-range, poorly planned tasks; to lack of sophistication in organizing themselves effectively (although some deep-sea fishermen have organized unions elsewhere); to stubborn retention of habitual practices; and finally to ineffective leadership.

Next to the co-op, perhaps the single most graphic example of how fishermen do nevertheless learn how to strengthen themselves through collective action is *kogi kumiai,* the extralegal "mutual protective association" that comes to the aid of Ebibarians caught illegally fishing. The trouble with this organization, Adachi-san implied, is its faulty assumption that "the sea is free to everybody." Therefore it would appear to function not so much to promote constructive unity as to delay solutions to those severe problems that Ebibara *gyomin,* no less than their fellows throughout Yoneshima-ken, have thus far failed to resolve.

Attitudes of the leader panel toward our *burakumin* community, ranged from severe prejudice at one extreme to fierce dignity by our three *burakumin* panelists at the other.

The most obtuse instance of prejudice was the admission of Ishioka-san, a graduate of Tokyo University, that he could no more imagine his attractive teen-age daughter marrying a young man from this minority group than he could imagine her marrying a leper. True, he has never visited a ghetto nor become acquainted with any *burakumin*. People of his class, he said, do not wish to live near them, although farmers and other lower-class people may not care.

His own business establishment, moreover, would never consider hiring a *burakumin,* even if one were to apply. This is most unlikely not only because above-average intelligence, he maintained, is required of employees, but because the family background of every applicant is carefully investigated. Should this somehow occur, any *burakumin* employee would eventually be recognized by patrons or fellow workers (much in the same way, he contended, that Jews often are in America) and this would surely generate such protest that the wisest policy is exclusion in advance. Nevertheless, this informant firmly avowed that he is devoid of bias! Rather his only concern was with what others would think—members of his own extended family in the case of marriage, his associates and customers in the case of business.

Several others were also resistant to the suggestion of intermarriage. This did not, of course, include our *burakumin* leaders, two of whom are already married to non-*burakumin*, although one reported that his wife and he had been totally rejected by her family until after their two children were born. No other panelists with whom we discussed the question were unequivocal in favoring the right of their own children to marry whom they choose. Even Labor Leader Doi once opposed an intermarriage with a *burakumin* in his own union, and confessed that he would feel most "uncomfortable" at the prospect for one of his children.

Another spokesman, Artist Nagashi, did admit that erotic drives are often so powerful that such a marriage is always possible and must be accepted if it occurs. But, as he also pointed out, much depends again on the power of family sanctions: for anyone to whom these sanctions are paramount, the consequences of this kind of intermarriage are far more painful than for one like himself to whom they are not. For similar reasons, marriage between two races may also prove undesirable, though we should note that the same spokesman who compared *burakumin* with lepers would not object to his daughter marrying a Caucasian provided that the latter's class position were equal to her own.

The one notable exception to the clear tone of non-*burakumin* distaste for marriage with *burakumin* was expressed by our Buddhist priest, Azuma-san. Whether he would feel the same if his own children were involved was not clear, but on religious grounds he definitely opposed any kind of discrimination, marital or otherwise. Since World War II his own Shingonshū has, he said, sought to advance emancipation through the efforts of Dōkō Undō, a movement roughly meaning "going together" that encourages intermarriage as one of its goals.

The common practice of investigating a person's background is undoubtedly a major stumbling block to both marital freedom and economic progress. According to Welfare Director Sumida, the *koseki* (family record) can be obtained from city hall files by anyone, either a company or an individual, by paying a fee of 14 cents. Since this practice appears to be prevalent throughout most if not all of Japan, it is widely taken for granted even though actually it should not be permitted, so Sumida-san agreed, without authorization by the person being investigated. The *koseki* does not, to be sure, identify anyone as a *burakumin;* nevertheless it does indicate both family connections and place of birth. Hence the investigator rarely has trouble in discovering whether an applicant was born in a ghetto like Kawabara.

No employer, of course, publicly rejects applicants simply because they are *burakumin.* He knows that discrimination is unconstitutional. But he also knows, as exemplified by the ease with which he obtains *koseki,* that little is done legally (with the important exception of integrated education) to enforce the guarantees stipulated in Articles 11, 13, 14, and 24 of the postwar Constitution. To be sure, as various informants both on the lower and upper levels emphasized, it is only fair to recall that on a strictly impartial basis *burakumin* less often qualify in terms of ability or skills than do rank-and-file applicants. Even so, it remains indisputable that the kind of employment policy disclosed above by Banker Ishioka is much more typical than not.

Moreover, so far as we were able to determine, no concerted campaign has been undertaken by employers anywhere in Yoneshima-ken (or anywhere in Japan) to provide job opportunities for *burakumin* in ways comparable to recent efforts of some American firms to employ minority group workers. More than this, when the question was raised as to why such a program should not be attempted, the answer even by leaders tending toward an Innovative value preference was that such an effort would be "impractical." Welfare Director Sumida's view is typical: what is most needed is gradual enlightenment among employers, not legal pressures against discriminatory practices. Even our Kaihōdōmei and Dōwakai leaders, who usually disagree on policy and practice, oppose antidiscriminatory employment laws of the kinds now widespread in the United States; the proper procedure, they contend, is on the one hand to educate the public at large on the evils of prejudice and discrimination, and on the other hand to provide much more effective skill training for *burakumin* so that they can qualify for jobs on their own merits.

Only Labor Leader Enomoto of the several panelists with whom we discussed this problem took a somewhat different posture. True, even his left-oriented union provides no special machinery through which to persuade employers of the need to employ *burakumin.* Nevertheless, it does officially oppose discrimination, frequently cooperates with the national *burakumin* organization, Kaihōdōmei, and pays special attention to problems of *burakumin* in its educational programs. It is also concerned with such practical objectives as raising minimum wages which, in turn, are bound to raise the economic level of *burakumin*, since the latter are often among the first victims of exploitative working conditions.

Job-training, which appears to be inextricable from the objective of fuller and fairer employment practices, has made modest progress—apparently because of *burakumin* pressures more than any other single influence. Thus in Yoneshima-ken, Sumida-san estimated that over $8000 has been appropriated out of prefectural and municipal funds in a single year so that 150 young *burakumin* could undergo driver training, and thus qualify for possible positions as bus and truck drivers or chauffeurs. In addition, loans at less than 2 percent interest are provided the trainee's family to tide it over during his training period, and scholarships of a few dollars each are provided to junior high school graduates who go on to senior high school.

Further education, obviously, does not in itself guarantee economic or social upgrading. Although some 70 percent of the driver trainees qualify and even receive jobs, about a quarter of these soon quit. Less than half-a-dozen *burakumin*, so we were told, hold positions anywhere in the prefectural government, since they must pass the same qualifying examinations as anyone else. Moreover, if Leader Tomita of Kaihōdōmei is right, only two *burakumin* teachers may be found in all Yoneshima-ken, although in the area's textile union a few *burakumin* members, according to Labor Leader Doi, have been elected to local offices.

It is also true that more and more funds, although still comparatively meager, are being appropriated each year on several governmental levels to alleviate *burakumin* conditions. These funds are earmarked for a wide range of activities such as *dōwa kyōiku* (integration education), scholarships, and housing. Perhaps most surprising to foreigners is the fact that the two rival *burakumin* organizations, Kaihōdōmei and Dōwakai, both receive appropriations for virtually all the activities amply exemplified in Kawabara itself. It is as if, in America, the National Association for the Advancement of Colored People or Core were to be blessed by public appropriations. The situation in Japan does not surprise Tomita-san in the least, however: after all, since the Constitution explicitly guarantees equality to all citizens the government has no choice but to support organized efforts to advance that right. Or, as Councilman Hayashi put it, government aid amounts simply to "a confession of guilt."

All members of our leader panel would probably agree with Tomita-san and Hayashi-san that, as Lawyer Kamijō reminded us, it is not too difficult to approve of equality in principle so long as one is not required to deviate from traditional habits in everyday practice. Or, as Artist Nagashi frankly confessed about himself, one may consciously believe that he is completely democratic toward one's fellowmen, yet remain unconsciously prejudiced.

Both informants were among several who confessed that they had almost no personal acquaintance with *burakumin*. Yet the image that emerges among our leaders of this minority's modal personality proves to be far more in accord with than different from the community image drawn in Chapter 3. Kamijō-san, for example, spoke of the unstable behavior of *burakumin* as well as of their "violent" and "thoughtless" temperaments. (More precisely than most, however, he emphasized that they are not inherently inferior at all, but rather are the victims of a tragic history that could be alleviated by a better environment and better opportunities. He spoke approvingly of Chicago as an example of a great city that has been trying to effect such improvements for the Negro population.) Other leaders reiterated such qualities as resignation and alienation, suspiciousness, ambivalence, over-sensitivity, and lower than average intelligence partly due to the high ratio of endogamous marriage.

Thus the *burakumin* character is pictured here in even more grossly negative terms than the *gyomin* character. Although some leaders were anxious to qualify their generalizations—Doi-san, for example, was sure that any kindness extended to *burakumin* will be met by kindness—nevertheless the characterization that unfolds could hardly be termed a happy or optimistic one.

Two top-level panelists, Tabata-san, our women's leader, and Kamada-san, *jichikai* executive secretary, who know *burakumin* better than do most non-*burakumin* on our panel only confirmed this impression. Although Tabata-san did insist that prejudice has markedly diminished since she was a school girl, Kamada-san considers even the American Negro problem to be more correctible than the *burakumin* problem which, he felt, would continue to resist full amelioration for at least another 50 years. Nor was he willing to lay all the blame upon majority group behavior. Granting that most non-*burakumin* are too preoccupied with their own problems to care one way or another, *burakumin* themselves, he felt, are also sorely at fault if only because of their deeply entrenched parasitic habits of dependence upon welfare support. They are habits which, until overcome by others based firmly upon self-reliance, serve to perpetuate not only patterns of discrimination but all the related evils that keep the vicious circle in erratic rotation.

But let our three *burakumin* leaders have the last word here. None would deny the seriousness of the situation as depicted by Kamada-san, yet all three would doubtless place much more weight of responsibility upon non-*burakumin*. Councilman Hayashi reminded us, for example, of the severe difficulty of finding teachers sufficiently informed about or concerned with the plight of *burakumin* children. Most teachers do not even wish to work in schools near ghetto neighborhoods. Hayashi-san might also have pointed out that one reason for their reluctance is the fear of conflict with *burakumin* parents. Nor can teachers hardly be blamed, when the penalty for any such conflict is likely to be compulsory transfer to some distant school district by officials acquiescing in the "don't touch" policy of *fure-nai* endorsed by principals like Matsuo-san. As Shōda-san, the Jirō leader, would insist, much of the trouble here stems from the fact that "educational leaders are weak."

As for Kaihōdōmei Leader Tomita, he could well remind us that some communities have succeeded in breaking parasitic habits by providing stable economic opportunities. Recall the *burakumin* community of farmers as one example. We ourselves accompanied Tomita-san to another small community some miles from Yamada-shi where a glove factory supports 30 *burakumin* families. Here only two other families depend upon welfare aid. Skilled workers, mostly women, were receiving about $45 per month which has doubtless increased modestly since. It must be remembered, after all, that Kawabara has been described as well below the economic average of the 50 or so ghettos in Yoneshima-ken.

IX

To pursue further here the proliferation of differences and similarities that has emerged in the course of our search for perspectives, first from "below" and then from "above," would seem redundant. We confine ourselves, accordingly, to but four summary statements concerning our leaders.

1. Our panel demonstrates once more the substantially supported thesis that value orientations are various indeed. These have been observed in the many variations that appear not only between the community and leader levels but within the latter itself. Unanimity among our 16 leaders, whether we weigh the evidence of either our quantitative value study or our more probing qualitative interviews, is decidedly less frequent than varying degrees of disparity.

2. When these two kinds of evidence are compared, still further disharmonies as well as harmonies of viewpoints appear (just as they do at the community level) on the part of leaders. Recall only two examples. Our qualitative findings indicate, on the one hand, more respect for religious institutions and traditions than appear from the decidedly limited revelations of our quantitative study. Yet, on the other hand, the fairly critical if not always consistent attitude of leaders toward current practices in education seems on the whole mutually reinforced by both pools of evidence.

3. The manner in which our leaders respond to various controversial issues (Marxism is one instance) testifies to their considerable sophistication and expertise by comparison with typical responses at the

community level. Nevertheless, one of the most significant observations is the frequency with which informants on the lower levels reveal perceptions and values strikingly akin to those at the upper level.

4. The generalization immediately above pertains especially to the "dominant value orientation," $M > I > T$, which we recall embraces not only all four grassroots samples but the leader sample as well. In this respect, our attempt toward the close of the preceding chapter to epitomize the character of our communities as "a highly pragmatic one" of temperate accommodation—that is, as directed more toward moderate and functional goals than toward either deeply traditional or audaciously novel goals—is substantially reconfirmed (once again granting exceptions) by our leader panel. Indeed a few of our more "extreme" informants, such as Banker Ishioka toward the right end of the continuum or Labor Leader Enomoto toward the left end, have seemed at various moments attracted more to the liberal posture than to either a conservative or radical one. Equally so, even were we to concede the complete legitimacy of the characterization presented above by our leader panel of Ebibarians and Kawabarians, and further were we to recall that the Innovative value preference proves somewhat more attractive to either Ebibarians or Kawabarians than it does to their surrounding municipalities or to the leaders themselves, nevertheless we must not overlook the fact that Ebibarians and Kawabarians are, like our leaders, decidedly more Moderative in their overall dominant value preference than they are Innovative or Transmissive.

More impressively in terms of this Moderative quality than of any other, our higher and lower perspectives tend, we think, to synchronize. It provides, moreover, a link to our next and final chapter where we hope by means of one major institution—education—to compare more succinctly and graphically the principal evidence derived from our "lower" and "higher" perspectives.

9

EDUCATION
AS AN AGENCY
OF CULTURE

I

"Perhaps no other educational system in the world is so continuously and so earnestly fought over."[1] Thus writes R. P. Dore, a foremost Western interpreter of the culture of Japan.

Why is this the case? A partial answer, at least, may be found in preceding chapters. Most comprehensively this answer is that the struggles, confusions, and variations in both values and practices that pervade education are themselves inextricable from both cause and effect of other major dimensions of the culture.

It has been, in short, our crucial presupposition that all kinds of learning and teaching, informal as well as formal, must be viewed in the contexture of institutional patterns. We have tried to convey the image of a highly intricate grid: the vast structure of the Japanese educational system, the complex dynamism with which it functions, and the immediate as well as overarching purposes that shape and direct its course—these can be understood and appraised only in close proximity to all other cultural structures, cultural dynamisms, and cultural purposes.

Since the same presupposition should likewise undergird any useful study of the family, politics, economics, recreation, art, or religion, it would be possible at this stage, other things being equal, to discover significant

[1] "Education," in Robert E. Ward and Dankwart A. Rustow (eds.), *Political Modernization in Japan and Turkey* (Princeton: Princeton University Press, 1964), p. 196.

implications for any of these institutions just as well as for the one we have selected. But, as was earlier remarked in an entirely different connection about the fishing culture of Ebibara, "other things are *not* equal": our own principal interest and experience lie in the philosophy and practice of education, and it is accordingly here that we wish to draw together and to interpret our chief findings. Still we must not suddenly dismiss the myriad institutional relationships that interlace with our focus of attention. Though not at every moment in the foreground, these relationships are always close at hand.

Of the many steps by which it is possible to approach this concluding task, we select three: one step is backward into a glimpse of educational history; two steps are forward to certain considerations of the present situation and of future opportunities. All three steps, but primarily the last, are to be regarded as deliberately evaluative and sometimes prescriptive; at the same time they rest upon the body of descriptive evidence hitherto presented.

II

Why, then, to reiterate Dore's statement, may one speak of the never-ceasing struggles of Japanese education? The record surely bears him out; indeed, every student of its history must be struck by the constancy of the "withdrawals and returns," the movements and countermovements, the strains and stresses, that especially characterize the modern period. Of course it follows from our configurational approach that the same judgment applies equally well to other major periods of Japanese history.

Or, to state it differently, education like the encompassing culture echoes a kind of Hegelian philosophy of history—in familiar terms, a dialectic of theses and antitheses superseded by periods of temporary synthesis. Something of this evolutionary-revolutionary process has already been observed in our sketch of *burakumin* history:[2] the long, tragic struggle for emancipation of this pariah group has been a jagged one of regressions, stalemates, and progressions that continue to this day with no sign whatever of abeyance.

The Tokugawa era (often dated as extending from 1603 to 1867), which exerted such a crushing and baleful influence upon the career of *burakumin*, is regarded by authorities as creating the foundations of modern public education in Japan. It is not our purpose to recapitulate a fascinating story

2 Cf. pp. 105–112.

that has been told often and well.[3] What we do wish to emphasize is that, in addition to such considerable achievements as a rate of literacy at its conclusion above that of any other Eastern country and even above many in the West, the Tokugawa era also left a deposit of traditions that continue to permeate educational movements a full century after the Meiji era opened in 1868. Thousands of schools flourished, both private and governmental (the latter chiefly for the elite *samurai*). Curricula varied, depending on clientele, but all taught at least reading and writing interlarded with a stern Confucianist morality. *Oya kōkō* (filial piety) was, of course, primary; so too was the virtue of loyalty both to the family and community. Students thereby learned that a good society is one of strict hierarchical levels with everyone finding his proper place. Future leaders were also trained in political and military know-how and in the concept of public well-being as feudally conceived. Yet, both preceding and following the Tokugawa policy of national isolation, the people exhibited a remarkable capacity for cultural osmosis as well. This is illustrated not only by fascination with Western ideas and practices but, centuries before that, by the diffusion of Chinese artifacts, language, religion, and philosophy.

The point of main concern is that the pioneers of the Meiji Restoration had thus inherited a deep respect for the importance of education. Based upon the five ancient virtues of benevolence, justice, courtesy, integrity of character, and learning itself, the dominant method of teaching and learning which for centuries had stressed repetition and memorization continued to be taken for granted as virtually the only practicable method. To be sure, the spread of literacy and marketable skills, as well as respect for rationalism, offered a ladder to personal improvement and upward mobility for more and more citizens, even for those of lower status. Any suspicion, however, that education might eventually provoke severe misgivings toward the paternalistic order apparently worried the benevolent elite very little. After all, why should they be worried? Not only was the principal purpose of education to develop respectful and loyal citizens, not only were virtues such as *oya kōkō* woven through the moral fabric of all education, but formal learning itself was predominantly a process of passive inculcation rather than of critical inquiry.

Nevertheless, from 1868 until 1890 an extraordinary fermentation took place that was surely symptomatic of the amazing energies and great expectations released by the post-Tokugawa regime. In education alone, at least four major educational influences, all from the West—the French, Swiss,

---

[3] For sources on Tokugawa education as well as other sources that have influenced this historical sketch, consult Appendix IV, Bibliographical Notes.

American, and German—became enmeshed with Japanese philosophy and life. France's system of centralized control was borrowed as a model for the public schools, though not for the universities. The Swiss philosopher of education, Johann Pestalozzi, with his child-centered approach to learning, became something of a vogue. Two practical-minded American educators, William S. Clark and David Murray, exerted unusual influence as visiting authorities.

But the democratizing mood created by men such as these was increasingly resisted by powerful factions to whom it was thoroughly distasteful. The appeal of German thought and ideology, especially Johann Herbart's philosophy of education, became influential in turn. Herbart's stress upon the primacy of moral instruction combined with the Prussian concept of schooling as a servant of the state seemed to these factions far more harmonious with their own heritage. A subsequent and intensive absorption of various expressions of German philosophy and scholarship thus became so fashionable that its effects are conspicuous in higher learning down to our present day.

No less than our comments upon the Tokugawa era, these encapsulated comments on the first Meiji decades merely underline our thesis: education, far from being the unified and stable institution that its leaders doubtless wanted it to be, was already racked with disunity and instability. On the one hand, education even near the beginning of the Meiji era was interpreted in an official document as a process by which each individual might rise according to his own ability and ambition. The influence of American patterns was undoubtedly substantial, even to the adoption of schoolrooms modeled after those in Boston schools of the 1870s. Yet, on the other hand, by 1890 the trepidations of the Emperor and his closest advisors that policies and programs were moving too fast and too far from their moorings in the feudal past was brought to a climax by the issuance of the Imperial Rescript, the single most famous and influential statement ever produced in Japanese education. Barely 200 words in length, it is Confucian in morality, affirms the divine origin of the Emperor, and considers the state as the end to which individuals are the means. Throughout 55 years thereafter it was read on countless ceremonial occasions, memorized by millions of children, and remained the keystone of the educational arch everywhere in the land.

But the Imperial Rescript by no means meant that education had at last achieved equilibrium. Certainly it was expansive. As early as 1906, 95 percent of all children were said to be in school, and by 1908 six years had become compulsory for both sexes. Institutions including colleges mushroomed. Even more impressively, Western ideas as well as technologies continued through the early decades of the new century to infiltrate the culture at a rapid rate—some of them conservative but many others liberal and radical. John Dewey, particularly, made a vast impression upon educational thought: not only were some private schools (Tamagawa Gakuen is perhaps the most famous) influenced by his ideas but in piecemeal fashion public schools, too, were affected by progressivist practices. Through the years some 42 translations of Dewey's works and 58 books about him have appeared in Japanese, surely a record for any educational philosopher.[4] The John Dewey Society of Japan remains active today.

Meanwhile, opposition to cautious if not reactionary practices in politics and economics spread contagiously both among university faculties and student organizations. Marxism, as a philosophy of protest and a guide to militant social action, became more influential than any other imported doctrine critical of the Establishment. Yet as its influence and related movements grew, so too did their antithesis of militaristic and autocratic nationalism more and more firmly and grimly occupy the seats of governmental power. Already in the 1920s, arrests and purges of educators and students were numerous. By the 1930s and early 1940s a nazified and militarized regime had converted the schools into centers of indoctrination in the supremacy and infallibility of the Emperor and nation. How far the pendulum had swung is epitomized by recommendations of Monbushō (Ministry of Education) in 1936:

> Japanese institutions should be interpreted in accordance with national aims, which should be contrasted with the individualism and materialism of the West. . . . All things not in conformity with national policy should be excluded from Japanese thinking. . . . University professors should be chosen not only for scholarship but also for loyalty to Japanese tradition. . . . In the elementary schools, especially, the Japanese spirit and ancestor worship should be stressed. . . . Courses, such as morals and civics, should be taught in such a way as to strengthen filial piety, loyalty, obedience to law. . . . [5]

Following surrender, recommendations such as these were of course discarded. Certainly one of the most sweeping and abrupt reconstructions in the history of any nation's schools was sparked by the United States Educational Missions of 1946 and 1950, notably by the first. Nine years of continuous, free, compulsory education through the junior high school, an optional three-year senior high school, adult education, a nation-wide system of public universities, and coeducation were among the reforms that were

---

[4] Cf. Victor N. Kobayashi, *John Dewey in Japanese Educational Thought* (Ann Arbor: School of Education, University of Michigan, 1964).

[5] Quoted in Ronald S. Anderson, *Japan: Three Epochs of Education* (Washington, D.C.: U.S. Department of Health, Education, and Welfare, 1962), p. 15.

not only quickly adopted on a national scale but, as we have found exemplified in our own two communities, still remain in effect.[6]

A number of other sweeping innovations, however, were either modified or dropped entirely by the mid-1950s. Decentralization of educational control through popular election of local school boards has been replaced by politically appointed and largely ineffectual boards. The curriculum structure and instructional processes have been almost entirely centralized in the Ministry of Education. Moral education (called *shūshin* before the war but now called *dōtoku kyōiku*) has been reinstituted. The core curriculum in science and mathematics, but especially in the social studies interrelating such fields as government, geography, history, and ethics, has been largely superseded by separate courses. Textbooks are carefully screened at the national level. Time spent on developing habits of critical thinking through discussion methods and direct concern with problems germane to learners (including those of neighborhoods where the children live) has diminished, most conspicuously in the upper grades, to a small fraction of the total schedule.

The following Monbushō statement of 1953 is surely candid in its succinct repudiation not only of the social studies program but, by implication, of much of the philosophy of education that pervaded the major reforms of 1946:

> (1) Social studies is not nationalistic. In order to awaken the national self-consciousness of the people it is necessary to teach straight history and geography.
>
> (2) Social studies is not methodical. Basic subjects, systematically taught in separate courses are the only way to insure real learning. . . .[7]

Even more bluntly, the Minister of Education proclaimed in 1957 that "It is necessary to hammer morality, national spirit, and to put it more clearly, patriotism, into the heads of the younger generation."[8]

But Monbushō's counterplans of the 1950s, many of them implemented, were not approved without bitter resistance that at times approached violence. Particularly, the teachers' union (Nikkyōso) was in the forefront of this resistance. Nikkyōso based much of its own educational policy on the Fundamental Law of Education (1947), a codification of original postwar reforms. The spirit of this law is conveyed by the following excerpts:

---

[6] For a sketch of one fairly typical school system (Utsumi-shi). cf. pp. 17–20.

[7] Quoted in Anderson, *op. cit.*, p. 116.

[8] *Ibid.*, p. 31.

> Education shall aim at the full development of personality, striving for the rearing of the people, . . . who shall . . . esteem individual value, respect labor and have a deep sense of responsibility, and be imbued with the independent spirit. . . . In order to achieve the aim, we shall endeavor to contribute to the creation and development of culture by mutual esteem and cooperation, respecting academic freedom, having a regard to actual life and cultivating a spontaneous spirit. [9]

Many educators and other leaders not necessarily sympathetic with Nik-kyōso's political orientation have likewise resisted Monbushō, notably those who conceive of education as a potential agent of cultural change and creative renewal as well as, or even more than, an agent of cultural stabilization and reinforcement.

Thus we conclude that the zigzag course of education continues to portray much the same sort of erratic patterns that it has been portraying for a very long time, particularly so in the century since the close of the Tokugawa era. Still, it is by no means our intention to draw a second conclusion of painful futility from our first. Quite the contrary, the story of education is more correctly to be seen as symbolic of an eager, however uneasy, quest for a deeper and wider expression of Japanese national character. This quest is discernible, not just in the higher echelons of disputation between Monbushō and Nikkyōso, certainly not just in the exhausting polemics of the Liberal Democratic and opposition parties. Its core of vitality is likewise to be found, omnipresently so, in the styles of life befitting rank-and-file citizens. In brief, it is our conviction that the meaning of education, no less than the meaning of politics, art, or any other facet of its ethos, is finally and most significantly grounded in the kinds of communities and schools that become more and more familiar to us. Let us return to them now.

III

Contemporary education, if it is to be reappraised through the aggregate of evidence provided both from "below" and from "above," may be grouped around four overlapping issues: (1) the control of the schools; (2) the teaching-learning process; (3) the curriculum; and (4) educational goals.

In recapitulating and evaluating these issues, limitations should be kept

---

[9] Quoted in Herbert Passin, *Society and Education in Japan* (New York: Bureau of Publications, Teachers College, Columbia University, 1965), p. 302.

in mind. First, the abundance of detail and multiple variations characterizing our exploration thus far cannot, of course, be duplicated here. Second, the extent to which the picture drawn principally with the aid of our informants reflects the total culture of Japan is not possible to judge. With regard to the first qualification, we must assume that the reader is familiar with what has gone before. With regard to the second, we can only warn him once again that generalizations about cultures are always hazardous. At the same time, it is only fair to observe that we are viewing an extraordinarily compact country bound together not only by geographic insularity but by such phenomena as a single language and a unilaterally directed educational system. Our assumption therefore is that some, if not many, of the highlights that we select for attention below have pertinence for much wider ranges of educational and cultural experience, conceivably even well beyond the nation as a whole.

The *control* of public education, we have just been reminded, is pyramidal and hierarchical, with the authority of Monbushō at the peak, thousands of rural and urban schools under its orders at the base, and 46 prefectural departments that serve as channels of communication connecting the two extremes. Although essentially the same structure (granting secondary modifications in time and place) was originally borrowed from France early in the Meiji era, it is by no means agreed that this is the most desirable structure.

How, for example, may our own evidence help us to focus upon the question of centralization versus decentralization of administrative control? As one point of departure, note item 18 of our value study:[10] judging by this sample of citizens at both the upper and lower levels, the question reveals uncertainty as to what they think the proper structure ought to be. To be sure, a majority, perhaps remembering the policy of decentralization imposed in the postwar period, rejected the American system; yet it is worth noting that a fairly substantial minority (a majority in Kawabara alone) favored a combination of both centralized and decentralized control.

This impression of ambivalence is strengthened in other ways. We recall that Nikkyōso, which has consistently fought for much more decentralized control than has ever been attempted, was not enthusiastically endorsed by most informants. Thus in item 11 the teachers' union was found to be "too radical" by all of our groupings, even by Kawabara. Yet a majority plainly endorsed the principle of a teachers' union, provided that it could be more temporizing than Nikkyōso has usually been.

The fact, moreover, that Yoneshima-ken teachers have been withdraw-

---

[10] Cf. Appendix II, The Value Study: Model and Findings.

ing from Nikkyōso in droves (although the phenomenon is far from typical of most parts of the country) by no means proves their wholesale rejection of teacher unionism in general or, by implication, of more completely decentralized controls in particular. Many withdrawals could hardly be called voluntary: pressures by administrative echelons from Monbushō down have been exceptionally strong in Yoneshima-ken. By the same token, the growing membership of Kyōshikai (Japan Teachers' Association) does not necessarily demonstrate enthusiastic endorsement of its administrator-dominated program. Rather it may simply mean (as Nikkyōso members remaining in Utsumi-shi insisted) that large numbers have been intimidated by such devices as the principal's rating scale for teachers, a device through which promotions, assignments, and other decisions regarding their status are said to be markedly affected.

What are we to conclude about the issue of administrative control? The Moderative value preference that has emerged as dominant from our amalgam of perspectives suggests that neither the highly centralized system restored by Monbushō in the 1950s, nor the principle of decentralization favored by Nikkyōso since its founding in 1947, may be acceptable to the majority of citizens. Each kind of control has been tried up to a point and each has been found wanting. The unresolved task is increasingly clear: to develop a workable formula that would enable the center of gravity to shift away from the present extreme of centralized authority toward a middle ground.

But the issue of control extends further than administrative power; it raises questions of the respective roles that students, parents, and teachers play within schools themselves. As for students, it is encouraging to find that their own organizations, most importantly seitokai in the lower and upper secondary schools and jidōkai in the elementary, are thriving. Yet it has also been found that although seitokai is conducted democratically (more fully, we suspect, than jidōkai) in that officers are freely elected by the entire student body, and although student responsibility is assumed for tasks such as helping to maintain discipline and keeping school property clean, nevertheless a good deal of superimposition by the professional staff is often said to prevail. Particularly our student informants, although proud of their organizations, expressed the desire for more vigorous participation in budget-making and other school affairs. However, that this desire might extend to cooperative planning of courses of study never seemed to occur to them, perhaps because the curriculum is already heavily preplanned.

As for student involvement in political activities, our most revealing evidence derives from a substantial consensus of informants that public demonstrations should not be forbidden by law but that they should have advance authorization by school and city officials (Cf. item 12). It is also our impression that the extreme postwar militancy of Zengakuren (National Federation of Students' Self-Government Associations) would not meet with their majority approval today.

Parents, too, are involved in school affairs through their organizations— PTAs, most notably. Still, from our observation, their activities (if more energetic than in many other countries) are narrowly circumscribed for reasons perhaps comparable to those on the student level. Parents, it is often said, rarely consider it their prerogative to intrude upon school officialdom. This attitude no doubt derives in part from the traditional prestige accorded the educational profession, in part too from the hierarchical structure of the system.

Recall how both of our labor leaders, though privately critical, doubted whether they ought to express openly their reservations about subject matter or teaching methodologies. While PTAs, moreover, have been extremely active in raising munificent sums for such worthy additions as gymnasiums, swimming pools, and libraries, recall also the forthrightness with which Kikuchi-san, a grassroots PTA officer, criticized herself as well as her fellow parents for their apathy and indifference toward such urgent problems as control itself.

As usual, however, qualifications are in order. Certainly in Yamada-shi it could hardly be maintained that all parents quite deserve Kikuchi-san's indictment. We are thinking especially of those *burakumin* leaders who take such an active part in PTA affairs as to cause Principal Matsuo of Kitano Chūgakkō severe discomfort. This is not to overlook the fact that local *burakumin* (Hatano-san, local Kaihōdōmei chairman, for one) hardly as yet typify attitudes of the majority of citizens. But they do betoken the equally important likelihood that, within the ranks of Japanese parents, many thousands reflect varying degrees of dissent from the status quo of education.

Nor can it be said that all members of the educational profession whom we came to know best are themselves complacent. True, one of the most conservative of all informants was our ex-teacher and ex-principal, School Board Chairman Natsui. True, too, much the same sort of acquiescent attitudes noted among parents seem frequently to characterize teachers—attitudes which, as has been mentioned, may well be connected in Yoneshima-ken with the weakening of Nikkyōso. Equally impressive, nevertheless, are those teachers among our informants who not only implied dissatisfaction with the line-staff structure of control and approved of widening student participation in school affairs, but who in one or two cases (most prominently in Nanyō Shōgakkō, the elementary school with the largest proportion of *burakumin*) were even planning to involve both parents and children in experimental projects.

Nor should we leave the impression that faculties of the four schools with which we were best acquainted have become mere order-takers. For one thing, Nikkyōso remains vigorous in Utsumi-shi Junior High School. Within all four schools, for another thing, we found teachers' study groups constantly at work and, on both the prefectural and national levels, conferences and research programs are multitudinous. That some of these high-level proceedings filter down to rank-and-file schools is surely to be hoped for—from Monbushō, especially by way of the National Institute for Educational Research; from Nikkyōso, through its People's Education Research Institute. In addition, both Monbushō and Nikkyōso hold their own national conferences that are attended by teachers and other educators from throughout the nation, and the smaller organization of Kyōshikai has defined itself as a "study group."

IV

The *teaching-learning* process may be viewed in two complementary phases, both of which have also been anticipated. One occurs because people everywhere are constantly, actively teaching and learning simply by virtue of the fact that they belong to cultures. Here is the "informal" phase of education sometimes referred to as *enculturation*,[11] the universal way of transmitting, modifying, and sometimes sharply altering man's evolutionary course. Informal enculturation has been exemplified in different but equally dramatic ways both by Ebibara and Kawabara: by the former, through such ventures as the precedent-breaking seaweed project; by the latter, through such valiant struggles against segregation as those of the two *burakumin* organizations, Dōwakai and Kaihōdōmei.

The "formal" phase of enculturation includes all the kinds of teaching and learning that take place within institutions established for this purpose. Obviously, while the "informal" and "formal" phases are never wholly separable, comparative educational history does show that they often tend to become separate. In much of Japan's history the discontinuity between them appears to be wide indeed—a discontinuity which the Fundamental Law of Education of 1947 aimed, we believe, to reduce, but which prevailing policies have tended to maintain.

Consider the examination system. All students are subjected to an almost constant barrage of examinations, increasingly so as they move upward. In Yoneshima-ken, moreover, one requirement has until recently preoccu-

---

[11] For a critical and comprehensive application of this concept, cf. Nobuo Shimahara, *A Study of the Enculturative Roles of Japanese Education* (unpublished dissertation) (Boston: Boston University Libraries, 1967).

pied citizens more than any other, the National Achievement Tests (NAT). We remember that this prefecture succeeded in winning one of the topmost NAT ratings.

What have our informants thought of this requirement? Again objectively, a majority across all groupings seemed to express the mood earlier epitomized by "it can't be helped," an aphorism which in this instance suggests that even though we may dislike the NAT we must accept it as a kind of necessary evil (Cf. item 7). Here one detects again something of the same ambiguity of attitude that was noted above with regard to the issue of control. In one perspective, students and teachers (parents seemingly less) often appear so hostile to the entire examination system, not just to the NAT, that the term *shiken jigoku* ("examination hell") is apparently quite as commonplace in our communities as it is everywhere else. Yet in another perspective the opinion of Labor Leader Doi is commonplace, too: "minds have to be trained well." Without such training, he held, most people cannot hope to improve their lot in a period of keener competition for better positions and better rewards than the country has ever been able to afford before. In this respect, since vocational education in particular becomes a powerful tool for individual advancement, it could hardly be denied that the teaching-learning process here has made and continues to make a vast contribution to cultural mobility and growth. Nevertheless, taken as a whole, our upper-level panel appeared to be more critical of stimulus-response, mechanized types of teaching-learning than did our lower level. For example, increased time for drilling children in the "three-R's" was disapproved (Cf. item 22) by a majority of the former although approved by the latter.

One may doubt, to be sure, whether either level of informants objects to ordeals such as the NAT with anything like the concern displayed in a lengthy and severe critique prepared by a commission made up of educators from Tokyo University and other institutions. We cite it here because considerable attention is devoted to Yoneshima-ken; we also wonder, incidentally, whether a subsequent reduction of prefectural involvement was in any way its consequence. In any case, although the document sympathizes with the desire of parents to improve the learning ability of their children, it firmly opposes any notion that drilling for NATs is a defensible educative means of satisfying this desire. In the anxiety, moreover, of administrators and teachers to show up well in the tabulations, supplementary drilling of children with the aid of special drill books is said to have occurred in certain schools during early mornings before regular sessions begin, in late afternoons, or even on Sundays, in addition to some regular class sessions and periods otherwise set aside for physical exercises.

The tests themselves are indicted by the commission for developing abnormal competitiveness and strain among both students and teachers. They are said to add substantially to the teacher's workload, to weaken "we-feelings" within classrooms, and to deflect attention away from more urgent needs, such as reduced class size and higher compensation for teachers. They demoralize by encouraging various subterfuges in order to raise scores (such as sometimes providing correct test answers in advance). Their methods of absorption and memorization cultivate social habits of acquiescence and conformity. As a result, and by far most seriously, they stultify "critical, thoughtful, living and creative learning . . . about nature and society."[12]

Still, we must repeat that the extent to which this bill of particulars could convince our own panels of informants is unclear. What does seem clear is that to the extent the critique is apropos to the NAT, it is equally so not only to the arduous prefectural achievement tests but to the system of entrance examinations required traditionally of all applicants for senior high school and college. It is also quite revealing that among the four top-level panelists probably most conversant with education (the retired lady teacher, Tabata-san; the ex-principal of a Buddhist high school, Azuma-san; the welfare director, Sumida-san; and the prefectural school board chairman, Natsumi-san), only the last seemed willing to condone that system.

Other informants were distressed with the learning-teaching process in still further ways. It is true that at both the elementary and secondary levels one hour per week is set aside to encourage "special class activities" and the development of "independent attitudes." Yet please remember how more than one leader doubted whether students are learning scientific and critical ways of thinking merely because they are compelled to pass courses in scientific subjects. And remember, too, that even our cautious Principal Matsuo severely criticized the "instillment principle" which, he said, has largely replaced the famous postwar ideal of *zenjin kyōiku* ("whole-man education"). As for our young informant, Student Anasaki, he could detect little in his learning requirements to stir his imagination or excite his interest. Preparing for and taking tests occupies, he said, by far the largest share of his waking time and energy.

We are compelled to conclude, accordingly, that the primary methods of formal enculturation have in recent years gravitated in some respects closer to tradition than away from it. At the same time, and notwithstanding the heavy emphasis upon mastery of pre-established subject matters, it would grossly mislead to imply that no significant recent changes in the teaching-

---

[12] *Gakute Hakusho Undō no Matome* (Summary of Report on the Movement Against National Achievement Tests) (Tokyo: Nippon Kyōshokuin Kumiai, 1964), p. 62.

learning process have occurred at all. The crucial point is that these appear to be far more conspicuous in the specifics of efficiency and technique than in altered social-psychological premises of that process.

Let us try to crystallize the import of this judgment by returning to another question asked of various informants during our Kawabara study: "How far, if at all, do you conceive the role of education as an agency of cultural change?" From Superintendent Kondō and Social Education Director Ueno all the way to various teachers, students, and parents, the dominant consensus that emerged was a fairly concerted one: although education, ideally, *should* serve much more actively as this kind of agency the fact is that on the whole it most assuredly *does not.*

The import of this consensus is double-edged. One edge sharpens, as it were, the fatalistic overtones of *Shikata ga nai* ("it can't be helped"): after all, what can we do but accept the situation? The other edge exposes something of the same currents of discontent with educational policies and practices that have been coursing so restlessly through much of modern history.

Yet, however endemic such discontent may prove to be, it must definitely not, we contend, be diagnosed as proof of cultural ill health. No one can feel the exuberance of children as they burst from their classrooms into the playgrounds; no one can listen to their laughter or share their eager friendliness; no one can observe teachers manifesting concern for the growth and well-being of their young charges; no one can sense the eagerness with which thousands of teenagers endlessly travel long distances to pay homage to the beautiful and hallowed creations of centuries long past; no one can experience firsthand something of the zest with which citizens learn to wrestle with and sometimes to conquer the rugged obstacles of their socio-economic life—no one, in brief, can gain impressions such as these without coming to appreciate that the teaching-learning process is by no means as circumscribed as one might otherwise narrowly suppose. Perhaps a charitable judgment of the Japanese educational system is that, in its most comprehensive sense, enculturation as creative growth occurs almost as much in spite of as because of the vast apparatus of that system.

V

Is a similarly charitable judgment demanded when we turn to aspects of the *curriculum?* Surely, so far as one of the remarkable innovations of the early postwar period is concerned—namely, the core curriculum—our answer must be principally negative. We recall well how, during our final conference at Monbushō, a high-ranking educationist informed us smilingly that the core curriculum is now quite extinct. Instead of problem-centered patterns of study, courses have proliferated once more into discrete and conventional subjects. The only remnant of the core curriculum that we were able to detect is in the upper secondary school where "civics-ethics" and "political science–economics" are formally linked, although even here not necessarily integrated in terms of human problems.

Let us consider these curriculum problems further by returning to important educational questions. (*a*) Should the creative arts receive greater recognition along with the sciences? (*b*) Should students have frequent opportunities to study their own communities? (*c*) Should the doors of learning be opened wide to lively controversial issues that arise in every major institution of the culture? (*d*) Lastly, how if at all should the schools treat moral education?

Beginning with the question of art education, we have noted that, according to our objective sample, leaders and grassroots people disagreed on whether to include more of the traditional arts (Cf. item 2); a majority of the former said yes and the latter no. In social education, we did discover a few classes in *ikebana* (flower arrangement) and *sadō* (tea ceremony). But as for public education, only our artist, Nagashi-san, expressed eagerness to bring the graphic and musical arts into fairer balance with the sciences.

Possibly additional informants on both levels might have agreed with Artist Nagashi had they been challenged to express their views. Considering Japan's great reputation as an esthetically-tempered culture, we were nonetheless surprised at the relative lack of spontaneous concern.

What of community involvement as a curriculum experience? Utsumishi school administrators with whom we discussed this question surely spoke for many of their colleagues: such involvement is unworkable. And how could it be otherwise when NATs, course schedules, or other routines are already overwhelming?

One discovers exceptions nonetheless. Certain periods in the social studies may be devoted to local history, and teachers' study groups have been known to develop resource materials for this specific purpose. Also, many elementary children are escorted to nearby parks, railway stations, or other convenient establishments. Nor should we overlook the personal visits that teachers annually make to the homes of their students, a time-consuming but admirable enterprise.

From our own observations the most persistent attempt to bring the curriculum into closer proximity to the community has been instigated less directly by the schools themselves than by certain parents. We refer to *dōwa kyōiku* (integration education) through which Kawabara leaders seek to

develop greater sensitivity to problems of *burakumin*. Faculty plans underway during our visits to the elementary school, Kitano Chūgakkō, that aimed
at coping with these problems suggest to us that, despite rigidities, initiative
is not impossible for dedicated principals and teachers.

The conception of the community as a learning laboratory was implied
in the School Education Law of 1947 for the elementary school: "To develop
a proper understanding of the actual conditions and traditions . . . of children's native communities. . . .[13] And even for the upper secondary level,
Monbushō issued a directive in 1950 that included "meeting the needs of
the local community" with teaching materials "selected from the local situation."[14]

Nevertheless, in our own communities, directives such as these have
in greater part either remained on the verbal plane or simply been ignored.
Thus it had apparently not occurred to Utsumi-shi educators that the fishing
co-operative, to consider only one resource, offers fertile opportunity not
only to learn about but to share vicariously in the life and work of Ebibara
people. But why should it occur to them when fishing people are hardly regarded by so many of their fellow citizens as an admirable lot? And even if
they were regarded otherwise, it was, after all Yoshida-san, junior
high school principal and Kyōshikai chairman, who considered it
improper for the schools to single out this or any other group for particular
attention.

Principal Yoshida leads us to our next question—the place of controversial issues in the school curriculum. At this stage, we must also grasp the
final opportunity to compare while summarizing some of our more relevant
findings concerning two other major institutions, the economic and political.
How are these perceived in terms of education from the comparative perspectives of our communities and leader panel?

Return for purposes of illustration to the fishing co-op. As was discovered from our contacts with another and much larger co-operative movement, the agricultural, public schools pay so little critical attention to this
movement (though they may on occasion refer to it) that many adult programs have had to be established in order to instruct co-op members in their
social-economic roles. Actually, any searching examination of the theory
and practice of co-operatives is itself bound to be controversial: not only do
producer policies modify traditional assumptions of capitalism, but consumer policies go still further by superseding the usual private profit-making
process with a co-operative one. Simultaneously, people learn through both

---

[13] Quoted in Passin, *op.cit.*, p. 294
[14] Quoted in Anderson, *op.cit.*, p. 104

sorts of policies that economic practices can operate according to democratic principles.

The point is significant to public education as well. Just as *gyomin* (as the fishing co-op executive, Adachi-san, well reminded us) may be enculturated gradually to subordinate older customs such as the *honke-bunke* network of family obligations in favor of democratic principles, so their children, too, could learn directly to compare both the older and newer practices and to consider the strengths or weaknesses of both. Even more than this, a country like Puerto Rico already attests to the practicality of student organizations conducting miniature co-operatives according to precisely the same rules that are followed every day by some of our own informants—Oka-san, farmer, or Watanabe-san, fisherman, to recall but two.

It is not possible to say whether either of these gentlemen, or for that matter any other of our resource persons, would endorse such a venture. Very few if any, we are reasonably sure, have ever considered it, apparently not even Nozu-san, *burakumin* employee of the Yamada-shi farmers' co-op. Still, that they have not done so thus far does not necessarily mean that critical study of the theory and practice of co-operatives would be repugnant to them, certainly not as long as members of our panels are prepared to agree with Labor Leader Doi and Lawyer Kamijō that study of all kinds of controversial issues are indispensable to vital education. In the light of our present interest in the curriculum, let us review several similar issues.

One of the most flamboyant, surely, centers in problems of class structures and class conflicts. Yet almost from the moment that these terms are confronted one becomes aware of the need for dispassionate enlightened guidance both as to what they actually mean and what their current practical relevance may be. Earlier it was found that informants on both levels held confusing perceptions of the class structures of their own communities; the one consensus that became apparent was that class conflicts are deepseated indeed. A very few informants (the junk dealer, Taura-san, for one; the trade union leader, Enomoto-san, for another) drew our attention to the emerging middle classes which they regarded as a buffer against such conflicts. The Marxian theory of class struggle appears to have deliberately influenced only three or four informants at most.

A closely related issue is the role that the national trade union confederations (Sōhyō and Dōmei, primarily) play in the affairs of political parties. Not forgetting that only in Kawabara was the dominant Liberal Democratic party a minority, when we compare our principal clusters of informants they seem to be far from agreed as to the import of this role even in their own communities (Cf. items 5 and 23). Nor is their agreement any less conspicuous in their political views: recall how a majority of Kawabarians alone among our groupings favored a socialist order yet how strongly a minority of all but our leader panel also favored it (Cf. item 10). These disagreements protrude quite as plainly from our impressionistic evidence: contrast the views of Banker Ishioka and Kaihōdōmei Director Tomita on the leader level, or those of Social Director Ueno and Teacher Masumi on the community level.

More specifically, the strongest but never total consensuses among both levels of informants emerged in support of several political issues. These were admission of Red China to the United Nations, the ideal (but not necessarily the practicality) of a democratic world government, the right of the Communist party to function legally, and the right of atomic submarines to visit Japanese ports. The sharpest differences prevailed over two other issues: Vietnam (only in Kawabara did a majority seem sure that the United States should withdraw), and Article 9 (Ebibara and Kawabara both opposed any amendment that would permit rearmament, but a majority of leaders did not).

We are tempted to extend this discussion to wider aspects of both the economic and political spheres; they provide abundant resources for any curriculum concerned with the realities of Japanese culture. But let us once more illustrate only from our two focal communities: the efforts of Ebibarians to attack their economic problems in the face of resistances from Utsumi-shi industrial and allied political forces; and the almost violent pressures brought to bear against Yamada-shi politicians by Kawabarians bent on bringing about such village improvements as the public bath. We must emphasize now that neither of these situations is exclusively a local one. On the contrary, one could trace the connections of each with the whole economic-political power structure not only of the municipality itself but likewise of the prefecture, indeed of the national government. Specifically in the case of Ebibara, such connections are traceable most directly through the Department of Fisheries; in the case of Kawabara through the Department of Social Welfare.

In the light of this contention, recall how the modal personalities of both *gyomin* and *burakumin* are perceived pejoratively by most of our upper-level panel.[15] The question that follows from this perception is whether the dominant political and economic authorities of Yoneshima-ken may only reluctantly and tardily respond to the needs of *gyomin* and *burakumin* because these authorities are acting partly or even primarily according to their own constricted preconceptions of *gyomin* and *burakumin*.

This question is likewise controversial, certainly. Yet one may ask whether it is not precisely just this kind that deserves scrupulous consideration in the curriculum of public education. Not that any of the questions thus

15 Cf. pp. 216–219.

far reviewed could or should receive equally frank and intensive treatment on every level of learning; we are not unmindful of the admonition of Teacher Inoki that children in the lower grades can hardly be exposed to such problems as class conflict with the sophistication that they could consider at a more mature age. Still we are not unmindful, either, that it was also Inoki-san who advocated learning as a process of critical inquiry—a process which, unless it is patiently and constantly cultivated in the early years of a child's development, is much less likely to develop at all.

We find it difficult, therefore, to applaud the posture taken by Principal Matsuo and certain other school administrators. It was he, we recall, whose frankly professed policy toward discussion of *burakumin* problems is crystallized in a single phrase—*fure-nai* ("don't touch"). The best policy, in other words, is to avoid controversial problems at all.

Whereas some of our informants would not agree with such a policy, others on both levels probably would. Thereby they help, we believe, to perpetuate much the same kinds of discontinuities already considered in the process of teaching-learning. These discontinuities guarantee in the case of the curriculum that students shall be provided with minimal opportunity either to analyze or to evaluate urgent political-economic issues— until by some strange metamorphosis they become suddenly endowed with the capacity to understand and act as responsible adults.

A last troublesome question in the area of curriculum must now be confronted: What of the requirement known as *dōtoku kyōiku* (moral education)? We propose to tackle this thorny question with the aid of two other major institutions, the family and religion. Our informants have surely demonstrated that these are also fraught with controversy.

Dōtoku kyōiku is itself controversial. Stemming from the Confucianist philosophy which placed moral axioms at the heart of Tokugawa education, this subject was required of all students for many generations until it was excluded on the recommendation of the United States Educational Mission in 1946. Within scarcely a decade, nonetheless, we have found that a modified policy of moral education was restored to the two lower levels and by the mid-1960s to the senior high school, despite the protests of Nikkyōso. The one partial exception has been *dōwa kyōiku* (integration education) which the union not only differentiates from *dōtoku kyōiku* but interprets quite differently from Monbushō's interpretation.[16]

Our present problem may be approached first by way of the family, the core of traditional morality. That the family has been changing rapidly is a commonplace observation. The weakening of primogeniture; the modi-

[16] For brief descriptions of *dōtoku kyōiku* and *dōwa kyōiku* in theory and practice, cf. pp. 75–77 and 154–159.

fying of *honke-bunke* (main-branch family structure), together with the complex pattern of interpersonal obligations symbolized especially by the ethical precepts of *on* and *giri;* the diminution of patriarchal authority; the increasing popularity of love marriages (*ren-ai kekkon*) as compared with the more customary arranged marriages (*mi-ai kekkon*) have already been discussed.

They are also topics about which, objectively as well as impressionisti-cally, variations in value orientations have proved to be widespread. Take the question in our objective study of whether retired parents should live with their oldest son (item 3). Leaders and Ebibarians sharply disagreed; the latter emphatically favored perpetuation of the custom, the former even more emphatically rejected it, and the average of all community groupings was split down the middle. Several other issues, too, revealed divisions though often less sharply. Thus, although the weight of preference was found to be invariably against strictly authoritarian rules concerning the rights of young women (Cf. items 1, 17, and 26), substantial proportions on both higher and lower levels either supported these rules or favored compro-mise between individual freedom and family obligations. Such, too, was the usual impression gained from our qualitative probings.

On the much discussed topic of *mi-ai* and *ren-ai* both levels also tended to prefer a combination of the two practices; each by itself, they held, can lead to marital catastrophe. Even so, one of the most striking distinctions between Ebibarians and Kawabarians has been the increasing popularity of *mi-ai* among the former and *ren-ai* among the latter.[17] Here leaders differed from community respondents: the former, if judged by their behavior and despite verbal approval of a balance between *mi-ai* and *ren-ai,* have con-tinued usually to prefer arranged marriage.

As for sexual morality, our two principal perspectives reveal more con-vergence. Tolerance of premarital and to a lesser extent extramarital experi-ence for males (although not necessarily for females) appears extremely common, with strains of "puritanism" running through both levels. Much of our impressionistic as well as objective evidence points, furthermore, toward approval of birth control (sterilization included), although abortion was accepted only reluctantly (Cf. item 12).

Returning now to *dōtoku kyōiku,* how might moral education be af-fected by these considerations? Remembering that one of the chief ideolog-ical reasons offered by some informants for its re-establishment has been the alleged need to develop stronger regard for ancient virtues such as *oya kōkō* (filial piety), one might suppose that required class sessions in moral educa-tion would seek to emulate Tokugawa and post-Tokugawa habits of outright

[17] Cf. pp. 58–61 and 139–140.

indoctrination. The fear, indeed, that just this practice could easily recur and eventually support another period of chauvinistic nationalism has been the dominant reasons why Nikkyōso, especially, continues to resist the entire enterprise.

In any case, whether chiefly because of Nikkyōso's stand or because of painful memories of past tragedies, it is, we think, to the credit of Monbushō that *dōtoku kyōiku* has officially rejected such indoctrination.[18] As noted in Chapter 3, syllabi material is if anything innocuous and dull, although considerable latitude is also afforded as to how teachers shall carry out the requirement. So much is this the case that demands have even increased for detailed syllabi and lesson plans. In this one case at least, in the judgment of some teachers, Monbushō has been too lenient.

The weakness of *dōtoku kyōiku* thus becomes almost the converse of those strongly prescribed course contents in science, mathematics, and language that constitute the bulk of the curriculum. Several community informants called our attention to what they regarded as the unmotivated petty content of typical *dōtoku kyōiku* classes. Leaders too, Co-op Director Okumura perhaps most forcibly, were skeptical oftener than not. And yet, judging by a program we observed conducted in a rural junior high school many miles from Yoneshima-ken, such ineptness is by no means inevitable; on the contrary, children can become very much involved and immensely stimulated.[19] Our conclusion and that of several informants is that, if dynamic and meaningful moral education is to occur in communities such as Ebibara and Kawabara, it should become just as controversial as any other kind of relevant study of political and economic problems. Why are not moral problems quite as inextricable from *dōtoku kyōiku* as principles of nuclear physics, say, are inextricable from the natural sciences?

But our discussion has been concerned especially with moral questions that arise in family and other interpersonal relations. As earlier noted in the lively family project conducted in Utsumi-shi, some of these questions have already been raised with limited numbers of parents. We gladly commend such a venture. Equally commendable is the provision, though probably much too limited, for units on family life in the social studies. What is still missing, however, is concerted attention to other problems that we have been recalling: tensions, for example, induced by patriarchal versus democratic family relations; or the counter-attractions of *mi-ai* and *ren-ai* mar-

[18] Recent developments have raised contentions among critics, however, that Monbushō has veered again toward a more traditional and conservative policy approaching closer to indoctrination of such moral precepts as patriotism. Cf. Appendix IV, Bibliographical Notes, p. 307.

[19] For a brief report of this program, cf. Theodore Brameld, *Education as Power* (New York: Holt, Rinehart and Winston, Inc., 1965), pp. 86 ff.

riage customs; or the rights and privileges of younger members of the family, including female members. Also there is almost no attempt to connect these issues to the learning-teaching process as an opportunity to become involved in the day-to-day moral experiences of real communities.

Most saliently of all, *dōtoku kyōiku* appears to circumvent any kind of forthright attention to experiences induced by changing patterns of sexual behavior. That these issues can create severe disturbances, the testimony of no less an expert than Dr. Okubo (the non-*burakumin* physician doubtless most familiar with intimate layers of Kawabara life) seems to confirm. Yet that sexuality is almost totally ignored in the curriculum (except as a biological process) seems no less disputable. While most informants, moreover, heartily favored sex education (Cf. item 30), they were uncertain as to precisely what moral problems ought to be considered, or at what stages of maturation such urgent matters as contraception might be introduced.

One of the ironies of this disregard is that sexual ethics is said to be grounded in religious imperatives to a much lesser extent than would be true of the Western world. It could be argued, indeed, that the comparative liberality with which both our lower and higher informant groups looked upon sexual experience may reflect this cultural phenomenon. And yet a contention of some Japanese scholars—namely, that precisely because their contemporary culture lacks a firm religious foundation, moral education becomes far more of a necessity than it would be otherwise—seems almost wholly bypassed so far as sexual values and patterns are concerned.

Here, too, we are treading on controversial ground. (One may doubt, for example, whether religious precepts in the United States are really that influential.) But let us take advantage of the point raised by these scholars and proceed to the institution of religion itself. From the evidence provided, we ask more specifically: What place historically and ethically could religious experiences and values occupy in an effective program of *dōtoku kyōiku?*

In the first place, although our community informants appeared on the whole to be more religiously devout than our prefectural panel, it would be quite as incorrect to imagine a horizontal bar dividing these two levels here as in the case of other institutions. Our value study once more supports this observation: impressive proportions of both higher and lower groups agreed that in the case of illness a combination of science and religion is better than either one alone (item 4); some of both groups may well have approved of praying on occasion to the Shintō god of fishermen (item 15); and some of both believed that their own children should think more seriously about religion if only the newer ones (item 8). Among these newer religions, nonetheless, the Sōkagakkai movement is clearly not included (item 14). Nor did either our higher-level or lower-level group reveal anything but the feeblest regard for the magical powers of *gyōja*, priests of folk belief (item 29).

Yet, in the second place, the impression derived from interviewees remained one of more sophistication concerning religion among our leaders than among our community panelists. Virtually none of the former respondents, so far as we were able to determine, were seriously influenced by folk rituals such as *yakudoshi* (to ward off evils threatened by "bad luck" years), whereas especially among Ebibarians such rituals are still commonly observed. Similarly, both Shintō and Buddhist ceremonials (recall the lively July festival sponsored by the Ebibara shrine) continue to be cherished events. Both the *butsudan* (Buddhist family altar) and *kamidana* (Shintō votive shelf) are likewise commonplace in Ebibara and Kawabara households. Among our leaders, however, only a few still maintain a *kamidana*, and whereas most of them perpetuate *hōji* (ancestral commemoration) most regard orthodox Buddhist tenets such as personal immortality with far more of a perfunctory air than do many of our lower-status friends. But it is also true that several leaders lamented what they considered a deterioration of religious faith—a deterioration which, as our always admirably frank Jichikai Secretary Kamada confessed about himself, often levels off during the closing years of life.

As in the case of sexual ethics, the question of how religious concepts and practices of the kind just reviewed could throw light upon the moral life is almost entirely avoided by *dōtoku kyōiku*. Admirable, to be sure, is the senior high school course that studies great thinkers in the history of Western and Eastern ethics, some of whom are religious figures. Admirable, too, is the recognition accorded in certain courses to the tremendous roles that Buddhism, Shintoism, and Confucianism have played in Japanese history. But the question we are raising is of a different order—a question anticipated by, among others, both Priest Azuma on the leader level and Social Director Ueno on the community level when they proposed that comparative religion be taught in the public schools. This proposal, not without precedent, would enable young people to learn of the great religions of the world without presupposing that any one is the "right" religion, hence without jeopardizing in any way the separation of "church and state" guaranteed by Japan's postwar Constitution.

What significance might effectively taught comparative religion have, in turn, for moral education? Granting that the criterion of "effectively taught" is exceedingly difficult to practice, one may properly inquire whether this does not mean the same kind of conscientious study of varying religious positions, conflicting values, and above all direct involvement of learners, that has already been considered for economic and political experiences. Thereby the affiliations of, say, Ebibarians and Kawabarians with

Zenshū, Nichirenshū, Jōdoshinshū, Shingonshū, or any other sect could become direct resources not only for clearer understanding of their own cultural heritage but for throwing light upon those moral controversies of the pesent day (the values of *on* and *giri* as compared with egalitarian values, to choose one example) that are often traceable at least partly to religious sources.

As in the earlier case of pilot projects in consumer co-operatives for the public schools, we realize that here we are extending beyond the direct evidence provided by our principal informant groups. Yet, recalling how some informants have lamented the sterility of both *dōtoku kyōiku* and older religious faiths, it would seem appropriate to encourage critical, comparative, down-to-earth rapprochements between both.

This is not to suggest that customary religious institutions and faiths can or should become merely revivals from the past. That large numbers of citizens now incline to repudiate such a heritage appears so well demonstrated that any prospect of genuine revival would seem quite as unplausible as would any prospect of an upsurge of Christianity in Japan. What we have in mind is rather the more elusive, more existential meaning of common human purposes that emanate surely in part from this heritage, yet that become transcended in much larger part by prospects and hopes of the modern age. To apply a term that seems just as applicable to Eastern cultures as to those of the West, what we are trying to convey is the quest of contemporary Japanese culture for what Paul Tillich calls "ultimate concern"—that is, for an ethos of indigenous character that is magnetized by half-expressed goals drawn from the past and present but directed, above all, toward man's future.

Nor is this to suggest that *dōtoku kyōiku* should merely become absorbed into and diffused through other fields of study. Rather this is to suggest that the concept of the core curriculum, and thus of integrated learning, would have to be redesigned. With Chairman Natsui of the prefectural school board, we agree that moral education has a distinct place in the curriculum—a place, however, that requires constant attention to and relations with a great variety of issues, including spiritual issues, that should also be studied elsewhere in the curriculum.

Whether such revitalization would help, in turn, to revitalize and modernize the role of religion reconceived in nondoctrinaire and ethical connotations no one can predict. No one can predict, either, whether the rampant symptoms of corrupt moral conduct that we have discovered in Ebibara fishing practices, in Kawabara habits of social parasitism, or in the machinations of Yoneshima-ken political campaigns[20] would be drastically

---

[20] For evidence, cf. pp. 31–34 and pp. 133–134, 206.

reduced were a moral-religious period of renewal to occur. What one can predict more assuredly is that a stimulating and realistic program of moral education could contribute abundantly to the search for those ubiquitous human meanings that serve as goals of "ultimate concern," goals without which twentieth-century and twenty-first-century Japan can hardly hope to rise to heights of greatness.

VI

Dōtoku kyōiku and its potential amenability to comparative religious experience opens a pathway to the fourth large educational issue that we have chosen for this culminating synthesis. For to inquire into the *goals of education* is also, of course, to compel us once more to face the vexatious question of values and thus the purposes of Japanese culture viewed in its totality.

This question has permeated many preceding pages, such as the value patterns of Ebibara and Kawabara (Chapters 3 and 6), and certainly if also implicitly at times our discussion of the three preceding issues of this chapter. One cannot move very far into the meaning of *educational control*, without realizing that control itself often becomes a moral concept. In behalf of what human values, after all, and hence for what kind of human order is control of any kind (political, economic, religious or educational) to be justified? The *learning-teaching process*, too, leads quickly to the cultural goals of that process. In familiar ethical terms, for what ends are the means of teaching and learning to be exercised? A comparable question may be asked of the *curriculum*: If courses of study are not means in themselves, then for what purposes of life, of personal and social fulfillment, are they warranted at all?

Such questions as these are not in the least unique to education in Japan. But neither are they any less appropriate or simpler to answer by virtue of that fact. Following our rule of strict selectivity we propose to delineate only a few of many aspects of this climactic issue.

The issue is climactic, moreover, not merely for its relevance to our grassroots communities nor, for that matter, even to the overarching purposes of the whole of education. It reminds us of our need to view education once more within the larger setting of cultural evolution, or, if one prefers, within the dialectic of Japanese history characterized especially in the last hundred years by extraordinary turbulence. The goals of Japanese culture and education become, we reiterate, deeply meaningful only in such a setting.

How, then, shall these goals be delineated? That they cannot be compressed into simplistic formulae has become evident; "variations in value orientations" have been proved to be far too conspicuous for that. Even so, these variations themselves provide one clue to our guiding question; they imply that the goals of contemporary Japanese culture, certainly so far as our evidence justifies that implication, are much more viable and pluralistic than they are rigid and uniform.

As suggested earlier, the virtue of this situation is that the Moderative mood emerges emphatically stronger than does either the Transmissive or Innovative mood, a conclusion that follows not only from our value study but, by and large, from the more penetrating although impressionistic evidence provided by our clusters of informants.[21] In terms of the immediate issue before us, this conclusion may be very significant indeed. It challenges the policymakers of education to consider much more seriously than they have thus far at least three other prescriptive generalizations to the effect that: (1) the system of administrative control, although still within a national framework, needs to be revised to allow substantially more flexibility and decentralization than is currently the case; (2) whereas high standards remain a desirable objective, the teaching-learning process can attain this objective far more meaningfully and fruitfully through functional and cooperative methods of study, instruction, and examination-taking than through those that are now typical; (3) the curriculum, granting that language, mathematics, and science continue to hold a legitimate position, should also provide much more adequate time and attention to: (a) both the traditional and modern arts; (b) community-oriented enculturation; (c) controversial examination of basic institutions, including politics and economics; and (d) moral education integrated with a wide range of such controversy, including family and religion.

These inclusive goals were no more acceptable to all our informants, let us re-emphasize, than were other educational proposals. They were, nevertheless, acceptable to some on both the community and prefectural levels who discussed them with us, while to still others (especially if of Moderative or Innovative preference) they may well have been acceptable. As for the minority of informants on both levels whose value preference leaned toward the Transmissive oftener than it did for the majority, even they, we believe, would usually agree that the majority has a constitutional

---

[21] Cf. pp. 184–188 and pp. 227–228. This is not to overlook the fact that our images of the "dominant value orientation" and "modal personality" in Yoneshima-ken are not necessarily prototypes of Japanese culture as a whole. (Cf. pp. 218–219 for a contrasting image of the Ōyama-ken "modal personality.") Therefore we reiterate that the applicability of any generalizations to spheres of education beyond those circumscribed by our own research can be advanced only with this qualification constantly in mind.

right to encourage and endorse new educational policies, so long as the right of free minority dissent is equally guaranteed.

What may these objectives augur for the directions toward which culture and education ought now to be pointing? One of the most urgent tasks, certainly, is the need for both Monbushō and Nikkyōso to reassess their policies. The cleavage between them, for too long a time, has prevented education from functioning as an institution guided by any clearly formulated national conception of either its means or ends. Their vituperative struggles, moreover, are surely responsible in some unmeasured way for a rate of national advancement in education decidedly disproportional to the rate of advancement in technology. Monbushō, in persistently accusing Nikkyōso of trying to inject a socialist ideology into the schools, has sought to support its accusations with a long docket of charges. Nikkyōso, in attacking Monbushō even more abrasively, has tried to prove that the public school curriculum is already the vehicle for imposing another ideology—that of the conservative power structure.[22]

It is not possible for us to assess the accuracy of these charges and countercharges. That some zealous Nikkyōso teachers have at times utilized classrooms as forums to advance their own beliefs is doubtless true. That local school boards during the brief postwar period of decentralization sometimes came under the control of left-oriented citizens is also probably true (a chief reason offered, at any rate, for the political liquidation of these boards). What appears to be at least equally true (whether or not prescribed programs of study are also at times slanted in directions congenial to doctrines of the Liberal Democratic party) is the effectiveness with which Monbushō succeeds in minimizing controversial studies of any kind. It accomplishes this, as we have seen, primarily by weighting the curriculum with science, mathematics, and languages, and secondarily by treating most remaining courses, such as social studies, as objective bodies of information that must be learned much in the same way that major subjects are learned.

The result is disastrous to public and democratic education. It fails to recognize that biased teaching in behalf of either socialist or capitalist ideas, on the one hand, and circumvention of great human issues, on the other hand, are by no means mutually exclusive alternatives. Neither Nikkyōso nor Monbushō, so far as we have been able to determine, has paid sufficient attention to *a third and far more tenable alternative*. This is the alternative

[22] Typical of polemical documents on both sides: *Nikkyōso to Kaikyūtōsō* (Japan Teachers' Union and Class Struggle), (Tokyo: Department of Primary and Secondary Education, Monbushō, 1963); *Nikkyōso Dai-nijū-hachi-kai Teiki Taikai Keika Hōkoku* (Japan Teachers' Union 28th Annual Conference Process Report for 1964), (Tokyo: Nippon Kyōshokuin Kumiai, 1964).

of comprehensive and scrupulous interpretation, from the earliest years of
schooling upward, to all kinds of personal and social problems germane to
learners—always with opportunities to experience community involvement,
always with abundant classroom dialogue, always with honest airing of
beliefs by both teachers and students, always with the privilege of attaining
together whatever agreements or disagreements any or all participants then
see fit to reach.

To recall the "dominant value orientation," $M > I > T$, we are trying
to suggest, in short, that both Monbushō and Nikkyōso have failed to appreciate the great significance of this orientation for their own major policies.
Monbushō appears to have reverted to a stronger reinforcement of the
Transmissive value preference than is warranted by prevailing attitudes, just
as Nikkyōso appears to have supported a more extreme Innovative value
preference than is presently warranted by these attitudes.

Not that either organization is completely insensitive to attitudes and
orientations other than its own. In human experience, value preferences
rarely if ever prove as discrete as academic analyses tempt us to suppose;
rather they occur invariably on a continuum. This guiding principle is just
as appropriate to Monbushō and Nikkyōso as it is to personality types—a
principle exemplified by certain Moderative and even occasionally Innovative tendencies already noted on the part of Monbushō; and comparably by
Moderative and even occasionally Transmissive tendencies on the part of
Nikkyōso.[23] In the light of such evidence it is not too surprising if both
organizations have at least begun to explore avenues of possible rapprochement, a possibility that could lead not only to productive communication
but eventually even to the kind of collective, professional negotiation and
bargaining that becomes a prime essential if present blockages are to be
surmounted.

These observations deserve one further pertinent example—the program which we have come to know as *dōwa kyōiku* (education for integration) and which nominally at any rate is endorsed by both organizations.
To be sure, what Monbushō means by the concept may depart at various
points from what Nikkyōso means. But just as in the case of our two *burakumin* organizations, Dōwakai and Kaihōdōmei,[24] where differences are

[23] To cite an instance representative of Nikkyōso's Transmissive propensities, careful perusal of recent reports of national study conferences fails to uncover any clear
awareness, much less advocacy, of the conception of cooperative and functional learning implied by our discussion above of the teaching-learning process as a "third alternative" to traditional forms of that process. Cf. *Nippon no Kyōiku* (Japanese Education—
Report of 15th National Educational Study Conference) (Tokyo: Nippon Kyōshokuin
Kumiai, 1966).

[24] Cf. pp. 118–120 and pp. 155–156.

not absolute (both agree, for example, that the goal of *dōwa kyōiku* is the integration and assimilation of *burakumin* into the larger culture), so, too, both major educational organizations formally endorse a similar goal. Where the dispute still remains acute is, of course, on the issue of means. Dōwakai (like Monbushō) prefers a strategy of gradual conciliation; Kaihōdōmei (like Nikkyōso) prefers militant, forthright action.

Granting that such disunities as these are scarcely easier to resolve than they are between hostile political camps, nevertheless so far at least as education is concerned they still remain, we believe, viable. Is it not possible that education for integration could itself provide an arena within which to test out the cultural capacity for resilience that has been repeatedly discerned in the "dominant value orientation" of everyday people?

Consider, then, how the key educational issue in *dōwa kyōiku* may be expressed in two further questions. Shall the severities from which *burakumin* suffer be dealt with in the curriculum of the public schools with utmost frankness and thoroughness? Or are they better approached through the wider, more diffused framework of democratic human relations, a framework that includes not only *burakumin* and other minority groups (aboriginal Ainu and North Korean immigrants perhaps most prominently) but all other citizens as well? We have termed these choices respectively the "direct" and "indirect" ways of *dōwa kyōiku*, but they apply equally well to all controversial areas of the curriculum including, of course, *dōtoku kyōiku* (moral education).

But are they really as dichotomous as they frequently seem? The M $>$ I $>$ T value orientation suggests that they are not. Instead of an approach so indirect that it all too easily eventuates in little more than an escape from responsibility (remember *fure-nai*—"don't touch") or an approach so direct that it boomerangs into counter-hostilities and thus into greater public resistance to assimilation than prevailed before (remember the Suiheisha movement of the 1920s) the urgent need may well be a synthesis of both approaches.

Let us underscore this contention. Any curriculum formerly based upon a philosophy of democratic values (and the Fundemental Law of Education declares that it is) ought to pay close attention to the inclusive meaning of every kind of human transaction. Simultaneously, however, the curriculum should equally provide intensive opportunities to perceive this meaning in the milieu of specific living situations. Such situations embrace prejudice, segregation, and all the concomitants of *burakumin* life that continue to negate the fulfillment of democratic values.

In urging a common meeting ground we are not unmindful that a frequent criticism made of the early postwar, progressively oriented program was that students did not learn as much or as systematically through problem-centered learning or the core curriculum as they had learned under the traditional system. Let us assume the partial truth of this contention as willingly as another one to the effect that teachers simply could not switch "overnight" from centuries-old habits of teaching-learning to what for most of them were unprecedented ways.

Thus, when the American educational sociologist, George S. Counts, a member of the 1946 Educational Mission, opposed the majority report of his colleagues on the ground that they were altogether too eager to superimpose American conceptions of education on a foreign culture and a defeated people, he was reacting as any well-informed sociologist or anthropologist ought to have reacted.[25] Yet, as Dr. Counts would also agree, to contend that the Japanese system was simply unprepared for extreme innovations is not at all to prove that it was therefore right in perpetuating its own inherited, Tokugawa-influenced educational philosophy.

Where the American missions most tragically failed was, we are convinced, in neglecting to plan step by step for *at least a three-decade program of systematic and modifiable transition from older to newer patterns.* This program should have provided not only for the careful evolution of modern teaching-learning processes but equally for modern administrative structures and curriculum designs. It should have sensitized teachers (through exposure to such fruitful concepts as modal personality) to *variations* in cultural and hence student patterns of habitual behavior. It should have demonstrated how students may learn far more richly and thoroughly by means of an integrated and functional curriculum than they could ever learn in merely traditional or routine ways. Yet it should have incorporated such strengths of customary ways of life as profound respect for learning, for pervasive values of mutual responsibility, and for the beauty of esthetic simplicity.

At any rate, that no such plan was ever carefully developed surely helps to explain the severe reactions of the 1950s, and thus the phenomenon of Monbushō appearing to move considerably closer to the Transmissive end of our value continuum than have our rank-and-file citizens. But that Monbushō was more heavily responsible for this anachronism than were the United States Educational Missions themselves is not, we think, a demonstrated fact of recent history.

It is worth remembering the clairvoyant welcoming speech delivered by the Minister of Education to the 1946 mission. A few excerpts deserve quoting:

[25] In a letter to the author, Dr. Counts has confirmed our understanding of his opposition.

In a mad reaction against the war-time hardships and restraints placed upon freedom, the people are . . . rushing from one extreme to another . . . It is my conviction that democracy is to be the basis . . . of education. . . . But the characteristics of a tradition that is still alive among the people should be respected. Thus I would like to ask America not to deal with us simply from an American point of view. . . . America, as a victorious country, is in a position to do anything it pleases with Japan. . . . If this is . . . the case . . . I fear that we shall never . . . have a true Japanese education . . . firmly rooted in our soil. . . . [For] democratic education cannot be carried out in our country in exactly the same way as it is in yours. . . .[26]

But errors of the past are not irremediable errors, certainly not in a culture as resilient as Japan. In the decades that have passed since the Minister's speech, is it reasonable to argue that teachers are just as ill-prepared as they were assumed to be in the arduous years after 1946? Are national leaders of education, when they caution us to wait until most teachers attain some mythical state of perfect proficiency, just as legitimately protective of the sort of unilateral and rigidified policies and programs that still remain more endemic than not?

Much of our evidence and judgments do not warrant, we believe, discouraging replies to these rhetorical questions. Let the professional preparation of teachers emphasize much more vigorously than heretofore a teaching-learning process that encourages participative and experiential learning, that welcomes and critically appraises every sort of evidence germane to the problems of people, and that cultivates educational goals vastly more significant to human growth and maturity than the ability to pass examinations. In the meantime, let those teachers be encouraged and supported who, with only limited in-service training and guidance, are already eager to break through the lock-step system and to demonstrate that they as well as their students may benefit enormously both from what they learn and how effectively they learn it.

And what of the future? Recent history, after all, hardly provides a reliable base from which to generalize about history still unborn, certainly not in the case of a nation so scarred with battles of a long and hectic past. Meanwhile, we should not fail to record the progress that education has achieved and is achieving even under Monbushō's frequently restrictive regulations. We are reminded of the contributions, for example, that vocational learning has been making to industrial expansion; of the considerable attention paid to the meaning of democratic concepts in family and com-

---

[26] Quoted in Passin, *op.cit.*, pp. 275 ff.

munity; of the prediction that some three-fourths or more of all students are planning to attend upper secondary schools (we hope tuition free as recommended by the original United States Educational Mission); of the record of accomplishment in disciplines such as mathematics where Japanese students are said to excel over those of most other countries (although it must be added that this achievement in our view is also partly responsible for the circumvention of what could have been much more significant achievements); and of the considerable success with which faculties of some colleges and universities have resisted the Transmissive value preference and pressed for Moderative, even sometimes audaciously for Innovative, theory and practice.

And yet in the light of our investigation, the most promising of all anticipations of the future lies less, we think, in such instances as these than in the qualities of ordinary people—in the capacity for cultural survival and experimentation discovered in our *gyomin* friends; in the deep indignation with which *burakumin* have fought for their rights as human beings and fellow citizens; above all, in the lively intelligence that we have come to respect in both our grassroots and leader informants.

Indeed, people such as these may cause one to wonder whether, recalling once more our favorite terminology, the Moderative value preference is a sufficiently mature and admirable goal. To be sure, one may well come to understand how in the postwar period of renewed search for cultural identity (a search that has fascinated scholars[27]), the qualities of flexibility and receptivity that we have earlier discussed seem plausible enough. Equally plausible are the compromises and concessions, the frequently opportunistic fluctuations in political, educational, and other processes that one expects of a period characterized by severe cultural mutations. Even so, no less in the case of Japan than of other cultures where the Moderative posture is conspicuous, one may suggest (but *only* suggest: more than this would carry us far beyond the boundaries established for the present work) that *this posture is deficient.* It is deficient in certain other qualities which elements both of the Transmissive and Innovative value preferences, were they broadly enough conceived, could help to rectify.

This conjecture may be rephrased in terms of the dialectical design that has encompassed this chapter. Unlike so relatively young a civilization as the United States, the civilization of Japan reaches back some two millenia. Culmination in the feudal Tokugawa era solidified the nation not only socially and militarily but also philosophically—philosophically at once in the formal sense and on the less articulate plane of its underlying ethos. Here such virtues as personal and collective loyalty, expressed and taught often

[27] Cf. Appendix IV, Bibliographical Notes.

as mandates (Confucianist, Buddhist and Shintoist in many combinations), were powerful indeed. They were virtues rooted so firmly that they continue to be revered to this day both in, say, Ebibara's pattern of the family and surely in deposits of influence even upon the burgeoning urban population.

Nor is the family alone among institutions drawn by the invisible magnetism of the Transmissive value preference. In business likewise it remains very influential—a subject that we have only been able to touch upon.[28] So, too, in religion, in art, in recreation, and by no means least in education itself.

What then of the Innovative mood? Its forerunners, too, are discernible in the Tokugawa era, certainly in its declining stages. Throughout much of the succeeding Meiji era, moreover, the attraction of deviant ways of thought and action has been compelling. Although at times forcefully suppressed, this attraction has never been destroyed, not even during the prewar years of ruthless totalitarianism. On the contrary, the Innovative preference has been much more persistently and vigorously expressed in political and intellectual circles, we believe, than in countries such as the United States where no full-fledged feudal, autocratic culture has ever prevailed, and where accordingly the thrust of antithetical ideas (Marxian, most potently) has never made the impact that it has in certain other countries such as Japan. The distribution of political power helps to punctuate this argument: roughly one-third of all seats in the two houses of the national Diet are of leftist orientation, an impressive opposition to the predominantly rightist power structure. Such opposition must surely help to account in turn for the fact that the policies of Monbushō are sometimes more conciliatory and liberal than they would be otherwise.[29]

The question that still arises is whether the dialectical emergence toward synthesis that we have been implying will ever occur. Since any theory of historic inevitability is, we contend, outmoded, the question is unanswerable. All that can be said is that this kind of emergence is, at best, altogether possible—nay, more, eminently worth the struggle to achieve. Were it to occur, such values as we have observed in the Japanese heritage could be reawakened—not, of course, in their original forms but in organic fusion with the goals of a democratic order where control and full sharing of *all* major institutions rest in the hands of the great body of citizens.

[28] Cf. Appendix IV, Bibliographical Notes.

[29] One further instance of Monbushō's amenability has recently been reported to us: a growing numbers of prefectures are now allowed to admit qualified graduates of junior high schools into senior high schools without special entrance examinations. Cf. also footnote 6, Chapter 8, p. 210, but compare footnote 18, above, p. 249.

In some respects the phenomenon of the Sōkagakkai[30] suggests to us a kind of search for just this needed fusion. Grounded as it is in one venerable if relatively small Buddhist sect, it reveals in this respect a Transmissive orientation. Yet in its this-worldly concerns and international-mindedness, the mood is clearly Innovative. We agree with informants in much of their criticisms of the Sōkagakkai; yet we cannot agree that in its undercurrent of expectations it is wholly without merit. With two or three other informants, we find the movement to be symptomatic of the half-expressed groping of millions of citizens (alienated as they have been from the simpler rural order of yesterday) for a way of life commensurate with the complex industrialized and urbanized world order of today and tomorrow. The hope of Japan, in short, is that of a philosophy of humanity and existence—a modern philosophy as yet unfulfilled which neither the devious coalitions of the political and economic right nor the often clumsy and still too largely superimposed ideologies of the Japanese left are themselves able to provide.

But perhaps a less opaque and more promising example than the Sōkagakkai can be discovered immediately within our two communities and their adjacent municipalities. We mean the community, neighborhood-based organization known as *jichikai*.[31] Stemming originally from the feudal system of political control with orders emanating always from above, it is now a social-political instrument with control largely from below. Through it almost any citizen, if he so wishes, may help to shape the policies both of his neighborhood and of the community at large. In practice, *jichikai* operates far from perfectly, so imperfectly, in fact, that Secretary Kamada sometimes wondered whether the people of Yamada-shi would ever realize their still mainly latent capacity to direct their own affairs. Nonetheless, its often unverbalized assumption appears to be a potent one: the still vital collective loyalties expressed in family and neighborhood groupings (*kumi*) can be syncretized at first with grassroots decision-making and then more and more inclusively with democratic power and control.

Jichikai is also an apt symbol of education at work as an agency of culture—not, to be sure, so much in the formal sense as in the inclusive sense of what we have termed enculturation. Yet it exemplifies how by its limitations still another fusion must occur if the Moderative mood is ever to be transcended. This is the fusion of school and community, of exciting education for adults (recall the program of the municipal workers' union) as well as for children—in short, of education as the crucial enterprise of culture engaged simultaneously in perpetuation and renewal of the life of its people.

[30] Cf. pp. 65–67, 145, and pp. 200–202.
[31] Cf. pp. 10–11 and pp. 87–88.

In this comprehensive sense, Japanese education, allied to be sure with other democratic forces, could and should become a vastly greater institution than ever before in its history.

Return for a final moment to our principal authorities. Do some informants themselves envisage the cultural syncretism that we have been seeking to express? We find that they do. Recall, for example, how Superintendent Fuji of Utsumi-shi hoped for a new unity of customary and democratic ethics in the family itself, a unity that would continue to respect the core of such venerated values as *giri* and *on,* yet would endeavor to harmonize these with the democratic rights of both young and old members. On the leader panel several of our friends, among them School Board Chairman Natsui, Welfare Director Sumida, and Priest Azuma, expressed comparable hope. Not a single one of these spokesmen could be termed defeatists; each, on the contrary, perceived his culture as involved in healthful but often agonizingly swift growth toward higher, still elusive moral and spiritual goals.

Most poignantly our artist informant, Nagashi-san, again and again urged creative synthesis. Traditional forms of art provide, as he put it, essential "nourishment," yet these are far from enough. Appealing to his favorite metaphor of the growing plant, he viewed such fine arts as lacquer, painting, and sculpture as the richest fruits both of the national heritage and of all that it has borrowed from outside, yet forever seeking forms of expression both refreshing and unique. An esthetic renascence, Artist Nagashi maintained, could very well arise, indeed its seeds are already stirring. As and if it does arise, education itself could become a work of art—a true testimonial to the wondrous capacity of Japanese culture to mold its future as it builds anew.

Appendix

I

RESEARCH
METHODOLOGIES:
EBIBARA
AND KAWABARA

This work evolved in three large stages. The first stage began in 1962 when the author was invited by the U.S. Department of State to serve in Japan as a "Visiting Specialist" for several months. During this period, he had the opportunity to lecture in a number of institutions of higher learning all the way from Nagasaki and Kyushu Universities in the southwest to Hokkaido University in the north. These trips also provided initial exposure to different types of communities—for example, the large *burakumin* ghetto in Fukuoka. Several weeks were spent in the latter city as a guest lecturer of Kyushu University, and a briefer period in Kyoto as faculty participant in the annual seminar on American civilization conducted by Kyoto and Doshisha Universities. With the encouragement of many new Japanese colleagues, the plan for this study germinated at that time and gradually took shape with the assistance of the pioneering Research Institute of Comparative Education and Culture at Kyushu University.

The second stage was a somewhat more systematic introduction to the culture in 1963. One of its aims was to search for the most promising areas in which to concentrate research; another was to develop initial orientation toward cultural and educational patterns by direct contact with people and institutions of many sorts. Therefore brief periods were spent in a small industrial city near Fukuoka and in a seaside village at the extreme southwest end of Kyushu (one of the four principal islands of Japan); in a city slum area, a rural village near Nara, and a suburban city near Osaka (all on the major island of Honshu); and finally in various communities of the smallest of the four islands, Shikoku.

267

From these experiences the research design was sketched sufficiently so that by the fall of 1964 it was possible to return to Japan with a fairly clear formulation of methods and objectives. In preparation, the Research Institute of Comparative Education and Culture and the author had reached agreement that what we have named Yoneshima-ken would constitute a fertile territory for our study. An advisory committee of academicians and other experts who laid out preliminary plans was then organized in that prefecture. Upon our arrival, these plans were thoroughly reviewed. The Institute was also represented. It was decided to investigate two or three *burakumin* and *gyomin* subcultures with a view to selecting one of each that would appear to offer the most promise according to such measures as their amenability to cultural change and their potentialities for cooperation. Following visits to several likely communities with prefectural guides, the advisory committee and research team agreed that Ebibara and Kawabara should constitute our foci, provided that these communities were themselves agreeable.

A full year of intensive field research followed, mostly in Yoneshima-ken, but also with brief excursions to other Asian cultures (South Korea, the Philippines, and Hong Kong).

Subsequent periods in America were devoted to compilation, interpretation, and continued association both by personal contact and correspondence with a number of those closely involved in the study and who are named in the Acknowledgments.

A general design of research is one thing, of course, and its implementation is quite another. From the outset, complex problems arose which in some cases were never fully resolved. It had been our original intention, for example, to include a third area of concentration along with *gyomin* and *burakumin* communities, thus further paralleling the research design of *The Remaking of a Culture: Life and Education in Puerto Rico*.[1] This third community hopefully would also be lower-middle class but would concentrate on the Sōkagakkai movement, in which the author had become fascinated during his second trip to Japan. It is worth recording here that our expectation was completely thwarted by the refusal of top echelons of the organization to permit rank-and-file members to participate without close official supervision—a condition unacceptable to us. Despite our assurances that the study would be submitted to officers for criticism and that strict rules of anonymity would prevail, official permission was never granted. Nevertheless, as our frequent references to the Sōkagakkai indicate, interest

[1] Theodore Brameld, *The Remaking of a Culture: Life and Education in Puerto Rico* (New York: Harper and Row, Publishers, 1959; New York: John Wiley and Sons, 1966). Cf. especially Chapter 2 and Appendix I.

in and contacts with the movement have not been unrewarding. In one way, moreover, this modification in our plans proved fortunate: it enabled the research team to concentrate more fully upon the two other selected subcultures, as well as the leader panel described in Appendix III.

Certainly there were problems enough even without the Sōkagakkai. Thus in planning our work with the *burakumin* village of Kawabara, we immediately confronted another kind of suspiciousness. (The Sōkagakkai has rightfully resented much of the biased reporting on the movement in the American press.) *Burakumin*, too, are suspicious of attempts to investigate them, particularly if the investigator happens to be an American. For, from the point of view of the radical ideology that pervades *burakumin* communities, Americans are easily stereotyped as advocates of imperialism and even (according to one rumor circulated in Kawabara about the author) secret agents of the State Department.

In our own case, the problem was compounded by our wish to involve *burakumin* (and *gyomin*) not only as informants but as participants in planning our study. Unlike many conventional research works in the social sciences it was not our purpose to superimpose our project; rather we wished to elicit the active cooperation of the communities themselves. This procedure is familiar to anthropologists, of course, and even to some sociologists, but is carried further than usual in our study by virtue of a theory developed at length in the author's anthropological philosophy of education and most concisely characterized by his term, *anthropotherapy*. This term connotes a process of community diagnosis and prognosis through which participants learn with guidance and stimulation to confront their own intra- and intercultural problems and act upon them with greater vigor and deliberation than they would otherwise. Education in the inclusive sense of enculturation is conceived as anthropotherapy at work.[2]

In the case of Kawabara, such a participative venture was more difficult than usual because of the community's severe internal troubles. We believe that Part II demonstrates that the difficulties were not insurmountable. Nevertheless, our strategy of approach deserves brief recapitulation. An introductory meeting of local *burakumin* and educational leaders of Yamada-shi was convened on our arrival to permit the author to outline his research rationale. One of those who came late and left before eating the lunch provided for all guests was openly hostile. (He, it turned out, was also the most vehement Communist in Kawabara.) Most others either seemed mildly amenable or maintained a discreet silence.

Thus began a whole series of discussions with various citizens on how

[2] Cf. Theodore Brameld, "Anthropotherapy—Toward Theory and Practice," *Human Organization*, vol. 24 (1965), pp. 288 ff.

it might be possible to motivate genuine community interest and cooperation. A long dinner meeting was held with one of the most influential Kawabara citizens, a slipper maker, with the hope of winning his confidence and
support. Most crucially, a conference was held in Kawabara with chairmen
of the seven *kumi* (neighborhood groups of households) affiliated with
jichikai, the grassroots community organization embracing all of Yamada-
shi. At these meetings the methods and purposes of our study were patiently
and simply explained, invariably with stress upon our wish for maximum
involvement of citizens. Thus assurance was reiterated that no information
or opinions conveyed to us would be revealed to city officials, that neither
the community nor any participants would be identified, but that the people
themselves would have complete access to our findings with the expectation
that these would prove useful to their efforts at community improvement.

All but one of the subchairmen agreed (after another session limited
only to themselves) to support the study. This dissenter, although he became
an excellent informant and privately favored our efforts, maintained that he
might endanger his family were he to do so openly, since several households
in his Kawabara *kumi* were headed by hard-core Communists. Repeated
efforts of other Kawabarians were made to persuade him to endorse the
study, even to the extent of a late night meeting at the home of the slipper
maker mentioned above, in which the author discussed our proposal freely
with the same Communist who had expressed hostility at the initial conference. But, although personally courteous, the latter gentleman could not
be persuaded. The study was therefore publicly endorsed by six of the seven
subchairmen.

One of the most distinctive and certainly debatable features of our
research methodology was the method of selecting informants.[3] The most
important assumption of this method is that by involving the community at
the earliest possible moment one is able to establish much stronger rapport
than by more orthodox anthropological procedures, and that the strengths
to be gained thereby more than offset obvious weaknesses.

In the case of Kawabara, we therefore requested opportunity to meet
with the household members of each cooperating *kumi*. These evening meetings in the homes of citizens were invariably friendly, and the modest
rooms were usually crowded with as many men, women, and children as
space would allow. *Kumi* leaders were present also. Always the theme of
involvement was stressed, with the immediate target being that of selecting
one informant from each *kumi* by the group itself. Our only specification
was that informants be persons in whom their neighbors had confidence and

---

[3] Interested readers are invited to consult our Puerto Rican study for a comparable
rationale. Cf. *The Remaking of a Culture, op. cit.,* pp. 426 ff.

who not only knew the problems of Kawabara intimately but would be willing to discuss them freely and critically.

The extent to which a democratic process prevailed in the final choice of each informant remains unclear. What did seem clear was that many members of the community became personally acquainted with the author and his research associates, and that in some cases the subchairman probably discussed the choice of an informant with others in his neighborhood group. At any rate, however accomplished, informants were finally named, of whom one was an elderly woman, another was one of the very few non-*burakumin* males who lived in Kawabara (it was pointed out by his *kumi* chairman that he might therefore hold a more impartial outlook), and the rest were *burakumin* males. Three of this group did not continue as informants after the second interview with each, but since the seventh *kumi* leader volunteered to serve privately, as did both the slipper maker and the *burakumin* city councilman, the panel consisted of seven fairly regular informants and three of brief duration.

It would be misleading to leave any impression that difficulties did not arise intermittently as we became more and more immersed. To recall one instance, early in our Kawabara work we were invited by a group of Dōwakai members (headed by the councilman and prefectural chairman of this "conciliatory" *burakumin* organization) to spend a late evening in the small amusement section of Yamada-shi. There we were seen by members of the opposing, more militant *burakumin* organization, Kaihōdōmei. Immediately we were suspected of favoritism. It was only after further prolonged discussion with *jichikai* and other influential Kawabarians that they were persuaded of our aim to understand the problems besetting Kawabara as fully and impartially as possible, and that we would just as gladly fraternize with Kaihōdōmei as with Dōwakai members. Many such opportunities gradually followed.

Further difficulties developed in carrying out our design to administer two objective surveys in Kawabara. The first was a sociological, strictly fact-finding inventory of household information (e.g., number and age of family members, size of residence, education, employment, and recreational habits), which we have not reproduced in this book but have drawn upon in various chapters. The second was the value study described in Appendixes II and III. After several months of association, we felt that Kawabara would be ready to support these further steps involving all residents. The forms we had prepared for both ventures were submitted to the *jichikai* subchairmen for suggestions, with the renewed guarantee of individual anonymity. In the case of the sociological survey, one or two improvements were incorporated by these grassroots leaders; otherwise it was accepted. In the case of the value study, one of our informants, a *jichikai* subchairman, objected to it on the ground that it dealt with sensitive issues which, if the results became known, could damage Kawabara's reputation. A long discussion with him followed, in which we reiterated our wish to submit the evidence to him and his associates confidentially in order for them to determine whether or not it could be useful to their own efforts to improve community life. He finally agreed that he would not voice his objections publicly, although he would not cooperate personally. (Other members of his own family did so.)

How we prepared and administered both surveys is likewise indicated in subsequent Appendixes. Here it is appropriate to note only that one reason given by two *jichikai* subchairmen for some reluctance in endorsing these surveys—namely, that they wished to protect us from being rebuffed by residents—proved unwarranted. Not only did six of the seven subchairmen sign a letter that was mailed to all Kawabara residents urging coopera- tion, but the number of respondents actually increased in the second study. In both, a majority of households responded. And this despite continued opposition by the small Communist group which went so far as to drive a sound truck through the main street of Kawabara early one morning urging citizens not to cooperate with the American. (Our slipper maker ally, inci- dentally, told us that he blocked further attempts of this kind by warning this hard-core group that he would no longer support the one Communist city councilman unless the sound truck was withdrawn.)

One final problem arose toward the culmination of our work. In ac- cordance with our earlier promise, we asked the *jichikai* leaders whether it would be desirable to share the findings of both the sociological survey and value study with the people of Kawabara. Again, some reluctance was shown, this time by the chairman of the group: although personally friendly, he feared that the meeting would be picketed if not disrupted by the oppos- ing minority. Our answer was that citizens have a perfect right to picket and to dissent, although naturally we hoped to be able to present our evi- dence. After various delays the meeting was held in the community center on a late summer evening. To our disappointment, however, it had hardly been publicized. One somewhat inebriated resident arrived to heckle us but left the meeting early. Six *jichikai* leaders attended at different moments and the chairman himself was tardy. Altogether, 23 persons convened, about half of them women. Neither the city councilman nor the slipper maker was present. Nevertheless, except for the one heckler, everyone was courte- ous and several bid us a friendly farewell.

Besides our involvement in Kawabara itself we wished to understand its relations to the surrounding municipality, Yamada-shi. This involved various forms of participation in the life of the city, including many festive occasions, talks before various groups, interviews with leading citizens such as the mayor, and above all meetings with the faculties of the elementary and junior high schools enrolling the most *burakumin* children. As far as practicable, the same procedure of democratic selection of Yamada-shi informants was followed. The extent to which the two principals influenced the choice of teacher informants we again are unable to say. Nor can we say with certainty how far they influenced the choice of parent spokesmen for the PTAs. We are reasonably certain, however, that the junior high school student who became our informant was chosen by his 300 or so classmates. After our presentation of the cooperative role we hoped that students would play in our study, his class subdivided into eight "home rooms" where one candidate was picked from each; then the final selection was made by the eight nominees themselves.

Yet in carrying through the educational aspects of our work we confronted further obstacles. Particularly in the junior high school, where previous principals had experienced severe encounters with aggressive *burakumin* (at least one had been dismissed), it soon became evident that the present principal was extremely insecure. Selection of parent and student informants was so repeatedly postponed that we finally decided to become "aggressive" ourselves. A meeting was therefore requested with the principal and superintendent of schools at which, once more, our purposes and operating procedures were reviewed. In asking permission to address both parents and students we tried to assuage the principal's concern: no explicit reference would be made to *burakumin*, rather our theme would be the desirability of parent and student participation in this school and community venture. The addresses were given, and thereafter the principal and superintendent seemed somewhat more ameliorative.

In Ebibara, the procedures leading to involvement were similar in principle but quite different in practice from those of Kawabara. Three orientation meetings preceded the launching of our actual research. The first was a dinner with several leaders of the fishing co-operative and its women's auxiliary in which we tried to impress upon our guests our wish to have them actively participate, but they were not to reach a decision until they had thoroughly discussed the proposal among themselves. A few days later we were notified that the decision was unanimously favorable. A second meeting occurred with *jichikai* subchairmen in Ebibara where again the democratic procedure for selecting informants was reviewed. Our third orientation was another dinner meeting with fishing co-operative and educational leaders of both Ebibara and Utsumi-shi as guests. This meeting was attended by the mayor, vice-mayor, superintendent of schools, and other officials. At all of these sessions, the author and his colleagues expressed their eagerness both to learn from others and to share their work with the community.

One *jichikai* district chairman, for reasons never made clear, refused to participate, but all others did so. So far as we could tell, informants were not selected according to strictly democratic rules. Rather, the most likely persons seemed to be more or less handpicked by *jichikai* subchairmen. However this might be, selections were made and our primary Ebibara informants totaled eight: four were active or retired fishermen, one was the wife of a fisherman, and three were Ebibarians in other occupations.

Educational informants, similar to Kawabara, consisted of two teachers, a junior high school student, the two principals of the elementary and junior high schools enrolling, in this case, the most *gyomin* children, and PTA officers. Here, too, we spoke to the faculties and to the third-year class of the junior high school on the nature of our study and urged that strong informants be chosen. Our impression was that the process of actual selection operated much as it did in Kawabara.

One interesting difference did develop in our methods of studying the two communities. At an initial conference with staff members of the Research Institute of Comparative Education and Culture, the suggestion had been advanced that schedules of interviews be structured in such a way that the author and his associate, Professor Inai, would meet parallel types of informants. Since it is often contended that foreign researchers are unable to perceive a culture as sensitively or accurately as native ones, the hypothesis that this is indeed the case might be partially tested. Professor Inai's comparable informants consisted of a teacher, a principal, a co-op official, and two wives of fishermen. In addition, he interviewed at length the leader of the co-op youth section, the Utsumi-shi director of adult education, and a kindergarten director. We have incorporated his own evidence at numerous points in Part I.

This venture demonstrated that although we had agreed on similar themes for our interviews no pronounced incongruities emerged. The most that might be contended is that informants appeared to be franker with one or the other of the interviewers depending on the nature of the topic. Thus Professor Inai's data included virtually no information on illegal fishing practices, but whether or not this omission was due to reluctance on the part of informants to speak as frankly to a fellow Japanese as to a foreigner about these practices we cannot prove.

The most striking difference between our association with Ebibara and Kawabara has already been implied: the relative ease with which arrangements and schedules were carried out in the former as compared with the latter. This difference is consistent with some of our evidence concerning modal personality, in particular with what we have termed a tendency on the part of Kawabarians toward introversion and of Ebibarians toward extroversion. One of many illustrations of the latter was the invitation extended to us by officers of the women's auxiliary to join them during a cherry blossom festival in Utsumi-shi—a delightful occasion of temple-visiting, feasting, and general merrymaking, during which the author was the only male guest. On other occasions, such as our participation in the summer Shintō festival, rapport appeared exuberant indeed. This is not to overlook the warm hospitality also extended to us by Kawabarians: we shall never forget a most convivial New Year's party at the home of the *burakumin* councilman, or the many dinners with other *burakumin* both in their homes and ours.

Nevertheless, fairly distinct differences in the quality of rapprochement prevailed to the end. For example, we detected no hesitation by Ebibarians in accepting our proposal to administer the sociological survey and value study. Moreover, when we proposed (as we had in Kawabara) that a concluding session be held at the fishing co-operative during which we would share the findings of these two studies with the community, the meeting was carefully planned in advance. Virtually all of our informants appeared at this session, in addition to co-op officers, leading educators of Utsumi-shi, and the mayor. We only regretted that no active fishermen were present, even though this was unavoidable: the fleet was out on its night trawling schedule.

Overviewing our research methodology, it may be estimated that the approximately 300 community interviews conducted by Professor Inai, Dr. Shimahara, and the author have seemed to complement each other more than to reveal glaring inconsistencies. The primary informants to whom the author will always be indebted totaled 15 in both subcultures. In addition, 17 primary informants with close educational associations were interviewed chiefly by Dr. Shimahara, and 8 primary informants in Ebibara and Utsumi-shi were interviewed by Professor Inai—a total of 40, not counting many additional single interviews by all three.

The average time involved with each primary informant varied considerably. Five to eight or more separate interviews per informant were typical and each interview occupied two to four hours. This does not include innumerable opportunities to socialize in homes or to visit schools, factories, bars, temples, shrines, theaters, museums, and other typical institutions both in our focal areas and in other parts of Japan. One week, for example, was spent in Kyoto temples with the generous assistance of a leader informant.

In the author's case, an interpreter was also present at every interview. Dr. Shimahara was chief interpreter, although Professor Matsuura served for two members of our leader panel and Miss Matsuyama for the wife of a fisherman. We are aware of the pitfalls of misinterpretation that can result from any kind of translation; undoubtedly this has resulted in misunderstandings at various points in the present work. Comparing our Puerto Rican and Japanese experience in this regard we are nevertheless convinced that skillful interpretation by a native person familiar with idioms and dialects is a far more reliable technique, generally speaking, than dependence upon one's own secondary knowledge of a foreign language. The author was fortunate in having chief interpreters in both cultures who were completely at home in the linguistic idiosyncracies of rural areas, as well as in the governing theory of our investigations. It should also be added that interviews were recorded in notes, although tape recorders were sometimes also used. In all cases, findings were shared in duplicate among all three interviewers.

Research techniques differed partially from those of the Puerto Rican study in several respects, however. One was made possible by our primary research team of four Japanese. Although the design was provided principally by the author, every important step of implementation was taken only in consultation with this team and, in many instances, evidence and interpretation were collaborative. Our prefectural advisory committee was also frequently consulted. Another difference was a more open-ended approach to our informants; that is, interviews were less structured and hence tended to produce a wider and more diverse range of responses. (One weakness in this approach may also be noted: the unevenness with which informants sometimes reacted to issues.) A third major departure was in our more intensive as well as extensive involvement in the culture. Limiting ourselves primarily to two communities while studying them concurrently enabled us, we believe, to penetrate somewhat more deeply into the Japanese than into the Puerto Rican culture. Finally, our attempt to develop and administer a study of values has given us an additional stance from which to compare and evaluate both quantitative and qualitative evidence relating to cultural goals.

But we are not unmindful of many limitations, especially of unintentional distortions resulting from insufficient skills, sensitivities, and time.[4] Interdisciplinary studies such as ours can never be judged by the criteria of an exact science—in this case, even by whatever may be meant by the standard criteria of anthropological research. To the extent that they may be called successful, studies at all comparable to the present one may be regarded at least as fairly as works of art as works of science. They depend upon the impressionistic and affective as well as upon the exact and cognitive. They can never be considered strictly finished, for the life with which they deal is never finished. And, like Japanese culture itself, they are involved in a continuous process of emergence at the same time that they reveal semblances both of order and of goals.

Much the same kind of judgments may be made of our very modest

---

[4] Some of the limitations noted in our Puerto Rican study are equally apropos of the present one. Cf. *The Remaking of a Culture, op. cit.,* p. 437ff.

attempts to practice anthropotherapy. Just as psychotherapy is justifiably considered art as well as science, so anthropotherapy, although as yet far from an adequately formulated or tested methodology, attempts to stimulate subcultural groupings to deal creatively with their particular tensions and disturbances. In this work, no claim could possibly be made that a single outstanding innovation has resulted from our all too brief participation. To be sure, a few changes may be said to have gotten under way—most conspicuously, perhaps, the study group on family problems sponsored by the Ebibara women's auxiliary. But only first steps have been taken.

Far more important, in any case, are the elusive and quite unmeasurable consequences that could have followed the heightened awareness that develops from continuing face-to-face dialogue with representative citizens. Conceivably, such a dialogue could have produced a double consequence: not only has it enlightened us in literally hundreds of respects, but it may have enabled our informants to look upon themselves, their communities, and their schools somewhat more searchingly and hopefully than they did before. Moreover, as some if not all of our informants came to understand that their concerns were ours as well as theirs, it is not too much to claim, we believe, that their sense of personal significance and, above all, their capacity to direct their own futures were in some degree enhanced.

II

THE VALUE STUDY:
MODEL
AND FINDINGS

Planning and execution of the value study were accomplished in several steps.

1. *Preparation of the instrument.* After approximately six months of close relationship with our two subcultures, the author drew up a rough draft of the instrument reproduced below. This was then carefully examined by his four Japanese colleagues who discarded some items and added others in the light of their greater familiarity with the culture. Only after complete consensus had been reached was translation into Japanese effected. This translation was also carefully reviewed until all three associates were satisfied with its accuracy and simplicity. (In retrospect, the author remains dissatisfied with the final form of the instrument at several points. The number of items by institutions is too unevenly distributed, and the I-M-T alternatives are by no means always precisely enough distinguished. The reader should remember, however, that the value study is regarded as a subordinate feature of this entire study.)

2. *Community approval of instrument.* As described in Appendix I, *jichikai* or other grassroots associates were invited to review and amend the forms before implementation.

3. *Training of student teams.* Two teams of college undergraduates (about a dozen in each team) were trained in techniques of approaching individual households—one group was from Yoneshima University, the other from Yamada College. These teams were paid travel expenses and stipends, and many of the same students were employed for both the sociological survey and value study. The rationale of the entire

project was explained in preliminary meetings and some background on the nature of the *gyomin* and *burakumin* communities was provided. Since few students had ever associated with people of these subcultures, effort was made to sensitize them to the meaning of prejudice, segregation, and other phenomena common to minority group relations. The need of a cordial manner and a patient willingness to assist respondents with the printed material was stressed, especially in the case of those with meager education. Every worker was cautioned against influencing responses. Role-playing was also utilized by simulating interviews before actual involvement.

4. *Canvass of households.* Every household was visited within Ebibara and Kawabara. Return visits were often made by the canvassers in cases of absence or where skepticism was indicated. Frequently a team worker would spend an hour or more with one respondent to explain the rationale of the study. Rudeness was reported in only one instance, whereas in a number of cases team workers were welcomed as guests and served refreshments. (It may be added that partly as a result of this experience further associations between Yamada College students and Kawabara citizens have continued.)

5. *Compilation of data.* Both student teams helped to compile the data immediately after completion of the canvasses. This work was accomplished under close supervision by the research staff.

6. *Random-sample surveys.* For the purpose of comparing the value orientations of our subcultures with those of their surrounding municipalities it was decided to submit the same instrument to a random sample of households throughout both Utsumi-shi and Yamada-shi. In order to accomplish this it was essential to obtain the cooperation of city officials such as the mayor and superintendent of schools. Partly because we wished to test their amenability to our work, we requested small investments (about $85) from each city, which we would match with equal sums, to cover the costs of preparation and canvassing. It was pointed out that these investigations could help improve the life of citizens by making them more aware of their own values, hence that our proposal should be regarded as a venture in community education. Since superintendents of schools have almost no control over budgets, the mayor cordially agreed in each city to cooperate and to provide the necessary funds (the *jichikai* chairman in Utsumi-shi made a voluntary addition of $28). These canvasses took place after the author had left. Some members of the same student teams participated under the direction of Professors Inai and Matsuura.

7. *Submission of findings.* How this step was accomplished in Ebibara and Kawabara is reported in Appendix I. In addition, we offered to submit confidentially the findings of our two random-sample studies to the two mayors, together with our interpretation of their significance.

VALUE STUDY

Directions to respondents:

Please check whichever of the three choices comes nearest to expressing your own belief, even though in some cases none of the three choices may do so to your complete satisfaction.

You are free to discuss these items with other members of your family, but please indicate in the space provided whether you did discuss them or not.

1. Shoko-san, age 22, has fallen in love with Yoshimi-san, a young man she met at the factory where she works. They want to marry, but her father strongly opposes. He says he has selected another young man for her to marry who comes from a better family.

   _____ a. Shoko-san should marry Yoshimi-san.
   _____ b. Shoko-san should discuss the question fully with her family (including her father, mother, two brothers, and married sister).
   _____ c. Shoko-san should respect her father's wishes.

2. The PTA of Takashima junior high school holds a meeting to discuss the teaching of Japanese traditional arts, such as the tea ceremony and calligraphy. Three teachers present a panel discussion.

   _____ a. The first teacher urges much more class time to study these traditional arts.
   _____ b. The second teacher insists that the present tasks of Japan are much more important to study than these traditional arts.
   _____ c. The third teacher argues that the children need a little of both but not too much of either.

3. Kosaka-san and his wife have reached the age of 65 and wish to retire. They have saved enough money to live comfortably.

   _____ a. They should live with their oldest son and his wife.
   _____ b. They should live separately.
   _____ c. They should move to a center where many retired people are living together.

4. Hanako-chan, three years old, is sickly and her parents are afraid she may not live long.

   _____ a. Her father believes that the best hope is for the family to pray to Buddha and Shintō gods every morning.
   _____ b. Her mother believes that only medical science can save her.
   _____ c. Her brother, a senior high school student, believes that prayers and medical science are equally necessary.

Column: (1) Question number. (2) Institutions: F, family; R, religion; P, politics; E, economics; Re, recreation; Ed, education. (3) Choices. (4) Value preference: I, innovative; M, moderative; T, transmissive. (5) Ebibara percentages. (6) Kawabara percentages. (7) Utsumi-shi percentages. (8) Yamada-shi percentages. (9) Average percentage, four communities. (10) Average rank of preference, four communities: 1, strongest; 2, next strongest; 3, weakest. (11) Leader percentages.

(1)	(2)	(3)	(4)	(5) Eb	(6) Ka	(7) Ut	(8) Ya	(9) Av.	(10) Av. R	(11) L
1.	F									
		a	I	42.9	47	40.0	30	40.0	2	46.2
		b	M	48.0	44	57.5	68	54.4	1	53.9
		c	T	9.2	8	2.5	2	5.4	3	0
2.	Re									
		a	T	32.7	29	29.4	36	31.8	2	53.9
		b	I	35.7	48	46.2	32	40.5	1	38.5
		c	M	31.6	23	24.4	32	27.8	3	7.7
3.	F									
		a	T	69.4	36	45.0	38	47.1	2	15.4
		b	M	27.6	58	49.1	60	48.7	1	76.9
		c	I	3.1	4	5.9	1	3.5	3	7.7
4.	R									
		a	T	1.0	3	1.7	2	1.9	3	0
		b	I	27.6	31	35.2	24	29.5	2	46.2
		c	M	71.4	66	63.1	73	68.4	1	53.9

5. Women who work in small factories around here receive about 400 yen to 500 yen per day. Three are talking about it.

_____ a. Yasue-san: We should organize into unions and go on strike if necessary for higher wages.

_____ b. Sachiko-san: We have to organize a committee and talk with the boss in a friendly way to pay us a little more.

_____ c. Asako-san: We have to be satisfied with what we are getting and not make trouble or we'll lose our jobs.

6. Professor Itagaki from a certain university gives a public lecture in the community center, in which he urges Japan to give up her national independence and join a strong world federation of nation. The audience is asked to react to his proposal.

_____ a. Some favor it.

_____ b. Some oppose it.

_____ c. Some say it is all right in theory but impossible in practice.

7. Yoneshima-ken has been ranked high among all Japanese prefectures in national achievement tests. Three fathers of children who took the tests are talking.

_____ a. Noda-san is proud of Yoneshima's success because he says it proves education here is superior.

_____ b. Obata-san does not like the tests but believes they are necessary to improve learning of required subjects.

_____ c. Kosaka-san is against the tests because he says they stress memory ability and not other kinds of learning, such as critical thinking.

8. It is often said that most young Japanese are no longer religious. Suzuki-san, a parent, has been thinking about this and can't decide whether:

_____ a. He should teach his children to respect religious traditions.

_____ b. To do nothing about it.

_____ c. To ask his children to think seriously about religion and consider whether some new religious movements would be better than the old ones.

9. The Kuichi family of fishermen is in serious trouble because its fishing boat was lost in a storm.

_____ a. It is up to the family itself to find a solution.

_____ b. Officers of the fishing co-op should offer to lend money from the credit union for a new boat.

_____ c. Kuichi-san, being the head of the main house, should expect the branch houses of the family to provide labor and money for a new boat for him.

(1)	(2)	(3)	(4)	(5) Eb	(6) Ka	(7) Ut	(8) Ya	(9) Av.	(10) Av. R	(11) L
5.	E									
		a	I	11.2	20	10.1	5	11.6	3	30.8
		b	M	64.3	59	83.2	86	73.1	1	61.5
		c	T	24.5	20	6.7	9	15.1	2	7.7
6.	P									
		a	I	8.2	18	16.0	7	12.3	3	7.7
		b	T	22.4	17	21.8	30	22.8	2	23.1
		c	M	68.4	64	62.2	62	64.2	1	69.2
7.	Ed									
		a	T	21.4	19	12.6	11	16.0	3	15.4
		b	M	55.1	47	66.4	68	59.1	1	46.2
		c	I	21.4	32	21.0	20	23.6	2	38.5
8.	R									
		a	T	26.5	46	36.1	26	33.7	2	38.5
		b	I	28.6	12	9.2	15	16.2	3	23.1
		c	M	43.9	40	54.7	58	49.2	1	38.5
9.	F									
		a	I	18.4	12	23.5	16	17.5	2	15.4
		b	M	74.5	79	72.3	84	77.5	1	76.9
		c	T	7.1	8	4.2	0	4.8	3	0

10. Three candidates for Senator in the House of Councillors are speaking at a political rally.

_____ a. Nohara-san urges voters to support his party because it wants all big industries to be owned and run by society as a whole rather than by private, individual owners.

_____ b. Obata-san says voters should support his party because it advocates a mixture of both kinds of ownership—some industries should be owned and run by society, some by private individuals.

_____ c. Muto-san asks the voters to elect him Senator because he supports an economic system in which all big industries are owned and run by private individuals.

11. Three elementary school teachers are drinking tea and talking about Nikkyōso (Japan Teachers' Union).

_____ a. Ikemae-sensei: I do not like Nikkyōso and refuse to belong because it's too radical.

_____ b. Fukuda-sensei: Yes, it is radical and that's just why I do belong.

_____ c. Ishimoto-sensei: I belong but I think Nikkyōso should become more moderate because then it would be more influential.

12. Japanese newspapers recently carried a series of letters by readers about student political demonstrations.

_____ a. One writer said that demonstrations should be forbidden by law.

_____ b. A second writer said that the demonstrations are a good thing.

_____ c. A third writer said it is all right to demonstrate provided that there is advance approval from school and city authorities.

13. Fusako-san is pregnant. She already has three children and prefers to have no more.

_____ a. Fusako-san should have an abortion at the city hospital.

_____ b. She should have the child, but from then on strictly practice birth control or be sterilized.

_____ c. She should have as many children as Divine Nature intends her to have.

14. A member of Sōkagakkai (Buddhist lay organization) is trying to persuade some friends to join.

_____ a. Eda-san: You can't persuade me; I don't like your pressure method, for one thing.

_____ b. Inoki-san: I will join because I think you make Buddhism vital again in Japan.

_____ c. Kimura-san: I admire your enthusiasm, but the Buddhist sect I belong to now is good enough for me.

(1)	(2)	(3)	(4)	(5) Eb	(6) Ka	(7) Ut	(8) Ya	(9) Av.	(10) Av. R	(11) L
10.	E									
		a	I	35.7	48	26.9	35	36.4	2	7.7
		b	M	39.8	38	65.5	49	48.1	1	69.2
		c	T	19.4	10	7.6	11	12.0	3	15.4
11.	Ed									
		a	T	10.2	6	13.5	18	11.9	2	38.5
		b	I	3.1	17	8.4	2	7.6	3	7.7
		c	M	79.6	73	78.1	79	77.4	1	46.2
12.	P									
		a	T	20.4	13	34.6	32	25.0	2	15.4
		b	I	12.2	15	15.1	5	11.8	3	7.7
		c	M	64.2	71	50.3	61	61.6	1	69.2
13.	F									
		a	I	7.1	9	11.8	10	9.5	3	7.7
		b	M	73.5	70	79.0	77	74.9	1	84.6
		c	T	19.5	18	9.2	13	14.9	2	7.7
14.	R									
		a	T	20.4	8	14.3	10	13.2	2	23.1
		b	I	3.1	1	2.5	5	2.1	3	0
		c	M	76.5	91	83.2	85	83.9	1	76.9

15. Fishermen are chatting on the wharf before they start out for the night work.

_____ a. I never pray to *Ryūōjin* (Shintō God of fishermen) or to any other god before I go out to sea.

_____ b. Honda-san: I pray to *Ryūōjin* every time I go out.

_____ c. Kato-san: I think it's good to pray once in a while if the weather looks bad—maybe once a month.

16. Okusa-san, director of social education, invites several chairmen of local neighborhood groups to lunch.

_____ a. Chairman #1: Nowadays neighborhood organizations should be more important to people than their families.

_____ b. Okusa-san: Families should always be more important to people than neighborhood organizations.

_____ c. Chairman #2: People should move to big cities so that they don't have to join neighborhood organizations unless they want to.

17. Girls in their early twenties are talking about the idea of marriage with a man from another nation.

_____ a. Nobuko-san: I wouldn't care what nation he belonged to, as long as we loved each other deeply.

_____ b. Hisako-san: I think I could only love a Japanese man enough to marry him.

_____ c. Mieko-san: It would depend on which other nation the man belonged to.

18. At a Takamatsu meeting of prefectural PTA officers, an American educator tells his audience there is no Ministry of Education in America. Control of the schools rests with states and local communities. Afterward people talk about his speech.

_____ a. PTA president: I think the American system is much better.

_____ b. PTA secretary: The American system would be impractical in Japan.

_____ c. PTA vice-president: What Japan needs is less centralized control and more decentralized control in combination.

19. A Japanese philosopher is lecturing on television about the future goals of Japan. "We have to choose one of three roads to travel," he says:

_____ a. We should strengthen traditional patriotism of the people to the Japanese nation.

_____ b. We should reject national patriotism as no longer suitable to the age we live in.

_____ c. We should develop a new ideal of patriotism in which the Japanese nation is united with mankind as a whole.

(1)	(2)	(3)	(4)	(5) Eb	(6) Ka	(7) Ut	(8) Ya	(9) Av.	(10) Av. R	(11) L
15.	R									
		a	I	17.3	9	10.1	6	10.6	3	23.1
		b	T	33.7	71	66.3	70	60.3	1	38.5
		c	M	48.0	20	22.7	24	28.7	2	38.5
16.	F									
		a	I	25.5	17	10.1	14	16.7	2	0
		b	T	71.4	75	87.4	83	79.0	1	100.0
		c	M	3.1	6	2.5	2	3.4	3	0
17.	F									
		a	I	50.0	72	48.7	53	55.9	1	61.5
		b	T	42.9	19	46.2	41	37.3	2	30.8
		c	M	7.1	9	5.1	5	6.6	3	7.7
18.	Ed									
		a	I	7.1	16	9.2	6	9.6	3	30.8
		b	T	50.0	33	71.5	70	56.1	1	53.9
		c	M	37.8	48	16.8	20	30.7	2	15.4
19.	P									
		a	T	26.5	14	16.8	20	19.3	2	30.8
		b	I	3.1	0	6.0	0	2.3	3	0
		c	M	67.3	86	77.2	79	77.4	1	69.2

20. The cost of medical care through national health insurance has been rising. People differ as to what should be done about it:
    _____ a. Some say that there is no need to change the present system because most people can afford to pay more than they used to.
    _____ b. Some say that the government should provide completely free medical care to all citizens.
    _____ c. Some say the whole present system of public medical care should be abolished in favor of private medical care, in which every patient pays his own doctors or hospital personally for the service received.

21. Local community associations such as co-ops and young people's clubs have recently become strong in Japan. But some social scientists are critical of these associations because they are said to be run usually by a few leaders who control the program and restrict democratic participation by the members. Three mayors of Japanese towns are asked whether they agree with the social scientists.
    _____ a. First mayor: This is the way organizations have to be run if they are to be efficient and active.
    _____ b. Second mayor: It would be a shame if the social scientists are correct.
    _____ c. Third mayor: Let us not be impatient. Democracy in Japan can only develop slowly.

22. The curriculum of the elementary school is being discussed by three teachers as they are riding home on a bus after school.
    _____ a. Koga-sensei: We spend too much time drilling children in reading, writing, arithmetic.
    _____ b. Noda-sensei: I think we do all right now.
    _____ c. Kase-sensei: The trouble is that we don't spend enough time drilling the children.

23. Many companies in Japan provide bonuses, pensions, and other benefits to loyal workers. Union leaders, however, often disapprove because they say this system makes workers over-dependent and complacent.
    _____ a. Some workers agree with union leaders who make this criticism.
    _____ b. Some workers say they like the present system.
    _____ c. Some workers say it doesn't make any difference what the system is as long as it provides fair wages and good working conditions.

(1)	(2)	(3)	(4)	(5) Eb	(6) Ka	(7) Ut	(8) Ya	(9) Av.	(10) Av. R	(11) L
20.	E									
		a	M	32.7	18	26.1	26	25.7	2	53.8
		b	I	56.1	73	69.8	68	66.7	1	38.5
		c	T	9.2	9	4.1	5	6.8	3	7.7
21.	P									
		a	T	37.8	31	44.5	46	39.8	2	0
		b	I	38.8	48	44.5	32	40.8	1	46.2
		c	M	21.6	18	11.0	18	17.2	3	53.9
22.	Ed									
		a	I	16.3	14	19.3	19	17.2	3	53.8
		b	M	40.8	39	26.1	40	36.3	2	0
		c	T	40.8	42	54.6	40	46.9	1	38.5
23.	E									
		a	I	21.6	10	8.4	8	12.0	3	7.7
		b	T	25.5	32	40.3	37	33.7	2	53.8
		c	M	52.0	53	50.4	54	52.4	1	38.5

24. After supper, adult members of the Noda family (parents and grandparents) are discussing their children's behavior:

_____ a. Chiyoko-san: Nowadays children do not understand *on* (obligation) and *oya kōkō* (filial piety) at all. It makes me sad to see traditional family relations collapsing.

_____ b. Taro-san: *on* and *oya kōkō* should be discarded.

_____ c. Yuki-san: Japanese people should not ignore *on* and *oya kōkō* but they should combine them with the democratic idea that all family members should discuss and reach decisions together.

25. Taro-san just graduated from junior high school. He lives in a rural community of *burakumin* (minority people). His uncle, a shoemaker, urges Taro-san to work for him.

_____ a. Taro-san should seek a job in Osaka but tell no one where he is from.

_____ b. He should stay in his community where he feels secure among friends and relatives.

_____ c. He should seek a job in Osaka but struggle proudly with other *burakumin* for full emancipation.

26. Yoko-san, age 20, has a boyfriend who wants her to go dancing with him. She has never done this and is not sure whether it would be right or not.

_____ a. She should decide for herself, whatever others think.

_____ b. She should refuse to go because neighbors and relatives might gossip.

_____ c. She should follow the judgment of her parents.

27. A reporter from *Asahi Shinbun* calls at the door of Endo-san's home and asks him how he would enjoy spending a gift of money:

_____ a. By taking an excursion trip to a famous shrine.

_____ b. By going to the amusement section of a nearby city.

_____ c. By attending a national *sumō* tournament.

28. Three young men, third-year students in junior high school, are studying at night in the home of Akita-san, the father of one. He enters the room and asks: "Why are you studying so hard?"

_____ a. Jiro-san: Because I like to study.

_____ b. Saburo-san: Because my parents have always expected me to go to senior high school and I want their approval more than anything.

_____ c. Santa-san: Because I want to become a man who will be completely independent of my parents.

(1)	(2)	(3)	(4)	(5) Eb	(6) Ka	(7) Ut	(8) Ya	(9) Av.	(10) Av. R	(11) L
24.	F									
		a	T	10.2	8	4.2	7	7.4	2	7.7
		b	I	0	2	2.5	0	1.1	3	7.7
		c	M	88.8	89	93.3	92	90.8	1	84.6
25.	P									
		a	M	8.2	7	8.4	7	7.7	3	30.8
		b	T	27.6	4	27.7	27	21.6	2	0
		c	I	64.3	87	63.0	66	70.1	1	61.5
26.	F									
		a	I	58.2	69	53.7	54	58.7	1	53.8
		b	M	5.1	1	1.7	0	2.0	3	0
		c	T	36.7	28	44.6	46	38.6	2	38.5
27.	Re									
		a	T	67.3	56	57.9	57	59.6	1	61.5
		b	I	20.4	33	21.9	32	26.8	2	7.7
		c	M	10.2	5	18.5	10	10.9	3	15.4
28.	Ed									
		a	M	13.3	15	26.9	20	18.8	2	38.5
		b	T	9.2	8	20.2	13	12.6	3	15.4
		c	I	77.6	75	52.9	66	67.9	1	38.5

29. Last month Ono-san hid a fishing net on the beach but now cannot find it after searching.

_____ a. He should expect his relatives to help him replace the net.

_____ b. He should ask the *gyōjasama, uranaishi, aragamisama* (fortune tellers) to tell him where it can be found.

_____ c. He should stop searching and buy a new net.

30. A parent study group is discussing sex education.

_____ a. One parent says that the junior and senior high school should have units of study on sex problems.

_____ b. A second parent says that such units are unnecessary because today young people learn all about sex from magazines and movies.

_____ c. A third parent believes that sex instruction should be given entirely by the mother to her daughters and by the father to his sons.

31. Three wives are chatting in their backyards about the ways they like to spend their spare time.

_____ a. Ota-san: I like best to spend it with my family watching TV.

_____ b. Haswgawa-san: I like best to go to *ikebana* (flower arrangement) school.

_____ c. Yoda-san: I like best to go to meetings of the community women's association.

32. Different Japanese newspapers publish articles by staff writers who differ with each other on political principles.

_____ a. Maiasa Shinbun: The people should not trust their national political leaders.

_____ b. Yogi Shinbun: The people have to trust their national political leaders to do what is best, but they should watch them carefully and change them often.

_____ c. Chikyu Shinbun: It is best to trust important decisions of policy to national political leaders because most people don't understand enough to make good decisions themselves.

(1)	(2)	(3)	(4)	(5) Eb	(6) Ka	(7) Ut	(8) Ya	(9) Av.	(10) Av. R	(11) L
29.	R									
		a	M	3.1	8	1.7	3	4.0	3	0
		b	T	10.2	6	6.7	8	7.7	2	0
		c	I	85.7	84	91.7	88	87.4	1	92.3
30.	Ed									
		a	I	61.2	59	65.4	69	63.7	1	69.2
		b	M	15.3	19	18.2	14	16.6	3	7.7
		c	T	21.4	20	15.9	17	18.6	2	15.4
31.	Re									
		a	M	46.9	23	43.7	36	37.4	2	38.5
		b	T	19.4	22	15.9	16	18.3	3	15.4
		c	I	31.6	50	39.7	47	42.1	1	38.5
32.	P									
		a	I	5.1	2	4.2	8	4.8	3	0
		b	M	71.4	78	82.3	78	77.4	1	92.3
		c	T	20.4	17	13.5	12	15.7	2	0

Further Explanations

A. Percentages do not total 100 in some cases because of no choice. (For Kawabara and Yamada-shi, exactly 100 respondents were tabulated, hence no decimals.)

B. Strength of preferential agreement between Ebibara and Kawabara was determined by adding together the percentages of the first choice of each of the 19 items in which the sequence of choices was the same. Then these were ranked in order of strength of preferential agreement. The same procedure was followed in comparing Ebibara and Utsumi-shi for the 26 items in which the sequence of choices was the same, and in comparing Kawabara and Yamada-shi for the 21 items. The remaining items, in which the sequence of choices was in disagreement, were ranked in decreasing strength of disagreement by the widest difference in percentages between one or another of the three alternative choices.

C. Rankings of agreement by strength of first preference, and rankings of disagreement, according to B, above:

Ebibara and Kawabara

AGREEMENT		DISAGREEMENT	
Rank	*Item no.*	*Rank*	*Item no.*
1	24	1	15
2	14	2	3
3	9	3a	25
4a	19	3b	31
4b	28	4	8
5	32	5	18
6	16	6	11
7	13	7	10
8	4	8	6
9	20	9	12
10	26	10	29
11a	5	11	1
11b	27	12	22
12	17		
13	30		
14	23		
15	7		
16	21		
17	2		

Ebibara and Utsumi-shi

Rank	Item no.	Rank	Item no.		Rank	Item no.
	AGREEMENT				DISAGREEMENT	
1	24	13	27		1	15
2	29	14	18		2	3
3	14	15	7		3	8
4a	16	16	12		4	5
4b	11	17	26		5	13
5	32	18a	10		6	30
6	9	18b	1			
7	19	19	23			
8	4	20	17			
9	28	21	22			
10	6	22	31			
11	25	23	21			
12	20	24	2			

Kawabara and Yamada-shi

Rank	Item no.	Rank	Item no.		Rank	Item no.
	AGREEMENT				DISAGREEMENT	
1	24	10	4		1	18
2	14	11	30		2	1
3	19	12	17		3	25
4	9	13	26		4	12
5	16	14	3		5	8
6	32	15	7		6a	2
7	13	16	27		6b	21
8	5	17	23		7	11
9a	28	18	31		8a	6
9b	20	19	22		8b	10
9c	15				9	29

D. Comparison in value orientations of four communities by institutions (F, family; R, religion; E, economics; P, politics; Re, recreation; Ed, education). (° Indicates all four agree on sequence of choices.)

	Item no.	EBIBARA	UTSUMI-SHI	KAWABARA	YAMADA-SHI
F	1	M > I > T	M > I > T	I > M > T	M > I > T
	3	T > M > I	M > T > I	M > T > I	M > T > I
	9°	M > I > T	M > I > T	M > I > T	M > I > T
	13	M > T > I	M > I > T	M > T > I	M > T > I
	16°	T > I > M	T > I > M	T > I > M	T > I > M
	17°	I > T > M	I > T > M	I > T > M	I > T > M
	24°	M > T > I	M > T > I	M > T > I	M > T > I
	26°	I > T > M	I > T > M	I > T > M	I > T > M
R	4°	M > I > T	M > I > T	M > I > T	M > I > T
	8	M > I > T	M > I > T	T > M > I	M > T > I
	14°	M > T > I	M > T > I	M > T > I	M > T > I
	15	M > T > I	T > M > I	T > M > I	T > M > I
	29	I > T > M	I > T > M	I > M > T	I > T > M
E	5	M > T > I	M > I > T	M > I > T	M > T > I
	10	M > I > T	M > I > T	I > M > T	M > I > T
	20°	I > M > T	I > M > T	I > M > T	I > M > T
	23°	M > T > I	M > T > I	M > T > I	M > T > I
P	6	M > T > I	M > T > I	M > I > T	M > T > I
	12	M > T > I	M > T > I	M > I > T	M > T > I
	19°	M > T > I	M > T > I	M > T > I	M > T > I
	21	I > T > M	$\frac{I}{T}$ > M	I > T > M	T > I > M
	25	I > T > M	I > T > M	I > M > T	I > T > M
	32°	M > T > I	M > T > I	M > T > I	M > T > I
Re	2	I > T > M	I > T > M	I > T > M	$T\frac{>I}{>M}$
	27°	T > I > M	T > I > M	T > I > M	T > I > M
	31	M > I > T	M > I > T	I > M > T	I > M > T
Ed	7	$M\frac{>I}{>T}$	M > I > T	M > I > T	M > I > T
	11	M > T > I	M > T > I	M > I > T	M > T > I
	18	T > M > I	T > M > I	M > T > I	T > M > I
	22	$\frac{M}{T}$ > I	T > M > I	T > M > I	$\frac{M}{T}$ > I
	28°	I > M > T	I > M > T	I > M > T	I > M > T
	30	I > T > M	I > M > T	I > T > M	I > T > M

E. Total sequences: "Dominant value orientation"

	EBIBARA	UTSUMI-SHI	KAWABARA	YAMADA-SHI	Average
F	$M{\small{>I \atop >T}}$	M > I > T	M > I > T	M > I > T	M > I > T
R	M > I > O	$M{\small{>I \atop >T}}$	$T\!\!\!\!\underset{M}{}{>I}$	$M{\small{>I \atop >T}}$	$M{\small{>I \atop >T}}$
E	M > I > O	M > I > O	$\underset{I}{M}>O$	M > I > O	M > I > O
P	M > I > O	M > I > T	M > I > O	$M{\small{>I \atop >T}}$	M > I > T
Re	I – M – T	I – M – T	I > T > O	T > I > O	$\underset{T}{I}>M$
Ed	M > I > T	I – M – T	M > I > T	M > I > T	M > I > T

F. Distribution of first preferences by institutions:

	EBIBARA			UTSUMI-SHI			KAWABARA			YAMADA-SHI			TOTAL		
	I	M	T	I	M	T	I	M	T	I	M	T	I	M	T
F	2	4	2	2	5	1	3	4	1	2	5	1	9	18	5
R	1	4	0	1	3	1	1	2	2	1	3	1	4	12	4
E	1	3	0	1	3	0	2	2	0	1	3	0	5	11	0
P	2	4	0	1½	4	½	2	4	0	1	4	1	6½	16	1½
Re	1	1	1	1	1	1	2	0	1	1	0	2	5	2	5
Ed	2	2½	1½	2	2	2	2	3	1	2	2½	1½	8	10	6
Total	9	18½	4½	8½	18	5½	12	15	5	8	17½	6½	37½	69	21½

G. Total sequences in all six institutions ("dominant value orientation"):

EBIBARA

$$
\begin{array}{ll}
\text{I} & 9 \\
\text{M} & 18½ \\
\text{T} & 4½
\end{array}
\Bigg\} \quad M > I > T
$$

UTSUMI-SHI

$$
\begin{array}{ll}
\text{I} & 8½ \\
\text{M} & 18 \\
\text{T} & 5½
\end{array}
\Bigg\} \quad M > I > T
$$

KAWABARA

$$
\begin{array}{ll}
\text{I} & 12 \\
\text{M} & 15 \\
\text{T} & 5
\end{array}
\Bigg\} \quad M > I > T
$$

YAMADA-SHI

$$
\begin{array}{ll}
\text{I} & 8 \\
\text{M} & 17½ \\
\text{T} & 6½
\end{array}
\Bigg\} \quad M > I > T
$$

M > I > T
(69) (37½) (21½)

53.9%; 29.3%; 16.8%

H. Combined comparisons of value orientations between larger and smaller communities in terms of the frequency of first choices:

	EBIBARA AND KAWABARA		UTSUMI-SHI AND YAMADA-SHI		Difference of percentages
I	21	(56.0%)	16½	(44.0%)	12.0%
M	33½	(48.6%)	35½	(51.4%)	2.8%
T	9½	(44.2%)	12	(55.8%)	11.6%

III

RESEARCH
METHODOLOGIES:
THE LEADER PANEL

Research at the leader level required a major and a minor operation.

As reported in Chapter 8, the former consisted of a prolonged series of interviews with each of 16 leaders at the prefectural level. Following the somewhat similar procedure utilized in our Puerto Rican study (although we think more successfully in Japan) this panel was selected only after detailed discussion between the research staff and members of our prefectural advisory committee. The author's principal role was that of suggesting categories and criteria of leadership representing the several major institutions of culture included in our investigation. The same qualifications, such as frankness, were suggested for leaders as for the community panels. Final nominees were made by the advisory committee.

After these nominees were agreed upon, the author visited each and reviewed the purposes and methods of the project. Anonymity was once more assured. No one was asked to make an immediate decision. Only two nominees, one a top political official and the other an artist, decided not to participate. These were replaced with second choices.

Interviews took place in homes, restaurants, offices, prefectural headquarters, parks, and elsewhere. Each session averaged over two hours, some even longer. The number of interviews ranged from two to nine, the average being about seven. Over 200 hours thus were devoted, exclusive of the much larger total at the grassroots level or of single interviews with several other leaders.

Open-endedness and flexibility were standard procedures as in our community interviews. Both "participant observation" and "observant participation" were attempted. All interviews were conducted in Japanese with translation, although two or three informants knew a limited amount of English.

The minor research involving our leaders was our value study. The same form utilized at the community levels was submitted to each leader by mail with an anonymous return envelope and a request for cooperation. The forms were to be unsigned. Thirteen of our leaders returned them. Their responses may be compared with community responses by consulting column 11, pp. 280–293. Further data as to how results were computed are indicated below, but again we urge the reader to be cognizant of limitations —in this case the added limitation of an extremely small number of returns by comparison with those at the community level. The two levels are not therefore comparable in any exact statistical sense. This point is particularly relevant in view of the fact that the above-average education and sophistication of the leader panel may well have resulted in more precise understanding of some items in the instrument than was true of the community panels.

Further Explanations

A. Percentages do not total 100 in some cases because of no choice. All comparisons between community level and leader level are based on the average percentages of all four communities [column (9)] and percentages of leaders [column (11)] in Appendix II.

B. Strength of preferential agreements and disagreements between the leader group and community group was determined in the same way as B, in Appendix II.

C. Rankings of agreement by strength of first preference and rankings of disagreement according to B:

Leader Level and Community Level

AGREEMENT		DISAGREEMENT	
Rank	Item no.	Rank	Item no.
1a	16	1	21
1b	29	2	22
2	24	3a	20
3	32	3b	10
4	14	4	25
5	13	5	2

Leader Level and Community Level (continued)

AGREEMENT			DISAGREEMENT	
Rank	*Item no.*		*Rank*	*Item no.*
6	9		6	18
7	19		7	23
8a	30		8a	27
8b	6		8b	5
9	12			
10	3			
11	11			
12	4			
13	17			
14	26			
15	1			
16	28			
17	7			
18	15			
19	8			
20	31			

D. Comparison in value orientations of leader and community levels by institutions (F, family; R, religion; E, economics; P, politics; Re, recreation; Ed, education):

	Item no.	Leader Level	Community Level
F	1	M > I > O	M > I > T
	3	M > T > I	M > T > I
	9	M > I > O	M > I > T
	13	M $\begin{smallmatrix}> I \\ > T\end{smallmatrix}$	M > T > I
	16	T $\begin{smallmatrix}> O \\ > O\end{smallmatrix}$	T > I > M
	17	I > T > M	I > T > M
	24	M $\begin{smallmatrix}> I \\ > T\end{smallmatrix}$	M > T > I
	26	I > T > O	I > T > M
Re	2	T > I > M	I > T > M
	27	T > M > I	T > I > M
	31	$\begin{smallmatrix}M \\ I\end{smallmatrix}$ > T	I > M > T

	Item no.	Leader Level	Community Level
R	4	M > I > O	M > I > T
	8	$\frac{M}{T}$ > I	M > T > I
	14	M > T > O	M > T > I
	15	$\frac{T}{M}$ > I	T > M > I
	29	I $\begin{smallmatrix} > O \\ > O \end{smallmatrix}$	I > T > M
E	5	M > I > T	M > T > I
	10	M > T > I	M > I > T
	20	M > I > T	I > M > T
	23	T > M > I	M > T > I
P	6	M > T > I	M > T > I
	12	M > T > I	M > T > I
	19	M > T > O	M > T > I
	21	M > I > O	I > T > M
	25	I > M > O	I > T > M
	32	M $\begin{smallmatrix} > O \\ > O \end{smallmatrix}$	M > T > I
Ed	7	M > I > T	M > I > T
	11	M > T > I	M > T > I
	18	T > I > M	T > M > I
	22	I > T > O	T > M > I
	28	$\frac{I}{M}$ > T	I > M > T
	30	I > T > M	I > T > M

E. Total sequence in all six institutions ("dominant value orientation"):

Leader Level

I	7
M	19
T	6

M > I > T
(59.4%) (21.9%) (18.8%)

Community Level

I	10
M	17
T	5

M > I > T
(53.1%) (31.3%) (15.6%)

IV

BIBLIOGRAPHICAL NOTES

General. Since excellent bibliographies on Japanese culture are available, the following Notes are limited only to items that have direct bearing upon particular sections of this book. With few exceptions, references in footnotes are not repeated here.

The best available annotated bibliography of English and European sources is Bernard S. Silberman, *Japan and Korea: A Critical Bibliography* (Tucson: University of Arizona Press, 1962). Sources include land and people, language, history, religion and philosophy, art, literature, political patterns, social organization and structure, education, economic patterns, and population.

For general background, consult Edwin O. Reischauer, *Japan: Past and Present*, 3rd ed. (New York: Alfred A. Knopf, Inc., 1964). Other important sources are George Sansom, *Japan: A Short Cultural History*, rev. ed. (New York: Appleton-Century-Crofts, 1952); Esler Dening, *Japan* (New York: Frederick A. Praeger, Inc., 1961); and especially John W. Hall and Richard K. Beardsley, *Twelve Doors to Japan* (New York: McGraw-Hill, Inc., 1965). The latter contains a fine bibliography.

Probably the most relevant periodical in English is the *Journal of Social and Political Ideas in Japan* (Tokyo: Center for Japanese Social and Political Studies). A most useful issue is "Education in Japan, 1945–1963," vol. 1 (1963).

For information on all major aspects of the country, see the one-volume encyclopedia, *Japan: Its Land, People and Culture*, revised ed., prepared by the Japanese National Commission for UNESCO (Tokyo: Ministry of Education, 1964). Quantitative data published annually are found in *Nippon, A Charted Survey of Japan* (Tokyo: Kokusei-sha, 1936 ff.).

Introduction. The author's educational philosophy that underlies this work is developed in two introductory volumes: Theodore Brameld, *Education for the Emerging Age* (New York: Harper & Row, Publishers, 1965), or the Japanese edition translated by S. Matsuura, *Kitaru-beki Jidai no Kyōiku* (Tokyo: Keiō Tsūshinsha, 1966): and Theodore Brameld, *Education as Power* (New York, Holt, Rinehart and Winston, Inc., 1965), or the Japanese edition translated by J. Kataoka, *Nijūisseiki no Kyōiku* (Tokyo: Bunkyō Shoin, 1967). For more thorough treatments, consult his *Philosophies of Education in Cultural Perspective* (New York: Holt, Rinehart and Winston, Inc., 1955) and *Toward a Reconstructed Philosophy of Education* (New York: Holt, Rinehart and Winston, Inc., 1956). His concern for and research in minority group relations extends back to *Minority Problems in the Public Schools* (New York: Harper & Row, Publishers, 1946).

The two companion volumes upon which the present one rests most squarely are Theodore Brameld, *Cultural Foundations of Education: An Interdisciplinary Exploration* (New York; Harper & Row, Publishers, 1957) and *The Remaking of a Culture: Life and Education in Puerto Rico* (New York: Harper & Row, Publishers, 1959; New York: John Wiley & Sons, Inc., 1966). The triumvirate of organizing concepts—order, process, and goals—is developed in the former of the two volumes and applied in detail in the latter. The present volume derives from the theory and operations provided by these works, but not in strict form. Education, particularly, is treated here less as an institution *parallel to* than *encompassed by* other major institutions.

Part I: A Community of Fishing People. The best study in English of a fishing culture is Edward Norbeck, *Takashima: A Japanese Fishing Community* (Salt Lake City: University of Utah Press, 1954). Although extreme changes have since occurred, its interpretation and bibliography are most helpful. In Japanese, the work on which we have depended most is Hirokichi Inai, *Gyoson Kyōiku Shakaigaku* (Educational Sociology of a Fishing Village) (Tokyo: Tōyōkan, 1957). Other sources in Japanese that were utilized in both our *gyomin* and *burakumin* research may be found in Nobuo Shimahara, *A Study of the Enculturative Roles of Japanese Education.* Unpublished doctoral dissertation (Boston: Boston University Libraries, 1967).

Anthropological studies by foreign scholars of Japanese villages were pioneered by John F. Embree, *Suye Mura: A Japanese Village* (Chicago: University of Chicago Press, 1939). Probably the most thorough interpretation thus far is Richard K. Beardsley, John W. Hall, and Robert E. Ward, *Village Japan* (Chicago: University of Chicago Press, 1959). Two other important but non-comparative studies are contained in one volume: John B. Cornell and Robert J. Smith, *Two Japanese Villages* (Ann Arbor: University of Michigan Press, 1956). All of these works, however, are primarily of agricultural communities. Many other research studies deal with particular aspects of this Part; cf., for example, Edward Norbeck, "Pollution and Taboo in Contemporary Japan," *Southwestern Journal of Anthropology*, vol. 8 (1952), pp. 269 ff; and Teigo Yoshida, "Cultural Integration and Change in Japanese Villages," *American Anthropologist*, vol. 65 (1963), pp. 102 ff.

Ruth Benedict's classic *Chrysanthemum and the Sword* (Boston: Houghton Mifflin Company, 1946) may be compared with Jean Stoetzel, *Without the Chrysanthemum and the Sword: A Study of the Attitudes of Youth in Post War Japan* (New York: Columbia University Press, 1955).

Part II: A Community of Segregated People. The most comprehensive treatment of *burakumin* in either Japanese or English was published after this section of our work was completed: George De Vos and Hiroshi Wagatsuma, *Japan's Invisible Race: Caste in Culture and Personality* (Berkeley: University of California Press, 1966), to which eight other experts have contributed. It contains an extensive bibliography. (For a review of this book by the present author, see *The New York Times Book Review*, Feb. 19, 1967, p. 14.) The historical section relies heavily upon the same excellent source from which we have borrowed: Shigeaki Ninomiya, "An Inquiry Concerning the Origin, Development, and Present Situation of the Eta in Relation to the History of Social Classes in Japan." *Transactions of the Asiatic Society of Japan*, sec. ser., vol. 10 (1933), pp. 47 ff. Ninomiya's epithetical term *eta* may have been more excusable at the time of his study than in subsequent decades when *burakumin* have repeatedly objected to its use. But note John D. Donoghue, "An Eta Community in Japan: The Social Persistence of Outcaste Groups." *American Anthropologist*, vol. 59 (1957), pp. 100 ff; Hugh Smythe and Yoshimasa Naitoh, "The Eta Caste in Japan." *Phylon*, vol. 14 (1953), pp. 19 ff; and John B. Cornell, "Outcaste Relations in a Japanese Village." *American Anthropologist*, vol. 63 (1961), pp. 282 ff.

The most important Japanese source utilized in this Part was Kiyoshi Inoue, *Buraku Mondai no Kenkyū: Sono Rekishi to Kaihō Riron* (The Study of Buraku Problems: History and Theory of Emancipation), rev. ed. (Kyoto: Buraku Mondai Kenkyūsho, 1964). It is interesting to note that *Japan's Invisible Race* also borrows freely from this outstanding authority, although it appears unfriendly oftener than not to the radical orientation of the Research Institute on Buraku Problems in which Professor Inoue has been a leading figure. Toshio Fujiwara and Yoshio Nakanishi, *Buraku no Rekishi* (History of Buraku), vol. 2 (Kyoto: San-itsu Shobō, 1960) has been another helpful source.

Part III: Perspectives. Philosophic implications of the value study are discussed in the author's paper, "The Descriptive-Normative Dilemma Reconsidered in Educational Perspective." *Philosophy of Education 1966, Proceedings of the Twenty-second Annual Meeting* (Philosophy of Education Society), pp. 59 ff. For provocative comparisons between the value orientations revealed by our study and a much more comprehensive survey, see Y. Scott Matsumoto, "Contemporary Japan: The Individual and the Group." *Transactions of the American Philosophical Society,* new ser., vol. 50, Part 1, (1960), pp. 5 ff.

A primary influence upon our sketch of educational history was R. P. Dore, *Education in Tokugawa Japan* (Berkeley: University of California Press, 1965), together with Ronald S. Anderson, *Japan: Three Epochs of Modern Education* (Washington: U.S. Dept. of Health, Education and Welfare, 1959) and Herbert Passin, *Society and Education in Japan* (New York: Bureau of Publications, Teachers College, Columbia University, 1965). All three works are helpful bibliographically. Also helpful has been the Ministry of Education's *Education in Japan: A Graphic Presentation* (Tokyo: Ministry of Education, published annually). John Singleton, *Nichū: A Japanese School* (New York: Holt, Rinehart and Winston, Inc., 1967) richly supplements our own material on education, particularly at the community level.

Dōtoku kyōiku (moral education) and *dōwa kyōiku* (education for integration) have rarely been examined in English. One partial exception is Mamoru Oshiba, "Moral Education in Japan." *School Review,* vol. 69, (1961), pp. 227 ff. A great deal of discussion is, however, constantly under way in Japan. Some useful examples are Buraku Mondai Kenkyūsho, *Dōwa Kyōiku no Tebiki* (Manual of Dowa Education) (Kyoto: Buraku Mondai Kenkyūsho, 1962); Katsuo Kaigo, *Atarashii Nippon no Dōtoku Kyōiku* (New Japanese Moral Education) (Tokyo: Seibundō Shinkōsha, 1957); Tomitarō Karasawa, *Atarashii Dōtoku no Sōzō* (Creation of New Moral Education) (Tokyo: Tōyōkan, 1958); Ministry of Education, *Gakkō ni Okeru Dōwa Kyōiku no Jissai* (The Real Situation of Dowa Education in Schools) (Tokyo: Ministry of Education, 1965); and Masunori Hiratsuka, *Nippon no Yukue to*

Dōtoku Kyōiku (The Future of Japan and Moral Education), rev. ed. (Tokyo: Fukumura Shoten, 1964).

No better example of the fermentation that pervades the issue of moral education could easily be discovered than the Report of the Central Council for Education, *On the Expansion and Development of Upper Secondary Education* (Tokyo: Ministry of Education, 1967, mimeographed). This report reveals again the considerable resilience of the Ministry toward educational change, but especially controversial is its publication of the widely discussed document, "The Image of the Ideal Japanese." Among the "educational objectives" advocated as essential to this "image" are "national consciousness," the "virtue of labor," and the value of "being an independent individual with a strong will." But "democracy has not yet taken sufficient root in the minds of the Japanese people," that is, "respect for individual freedom and responsibilities and the adherence of law and order and the progressive establishment of the happiness of the masses." Although "Japanese society seems to be open and liberalistic, the aspects of a closed society remain strongly rooted."

Considerable attention has also been paid in the present volume to concepts and institutions other than those of education. Thus in attempting to operate with the difficult concept of modal personality we have been assisted not only by references already cited but particularly by Robert J. Smith and Richard K. Beardsley, eds., *Japanese Culture: Its Development and Characteristic* (Chicago: Aldine Publishing Company, 1962); Bernard S. Silberman, ed., *Japanese Character and Culture* (Tucson: University of Arizona Press, 1962); and Tadashi Fukutake, *Man and Society in Japan* (Tokyo: University of Tokyo Press, 1962).

Of hundreds of references on religion that could be cited, we select only Robert Bellah, *Tokugawa Religion: The Values of Pre-Industrial Japan* (New York: The Free Press, 1957); Philip Kapleau, *The Three Pillars of Zen* (Tokyo: John Weatherhill, Inc., 1965); Floyd H. Ross, *Shinto: The Way of Japan* (Boston: The Beacon Press, 1965); Harry Thomsen, *The New Religions of Japan* (Rutland: Charles E. Tuttle Co., Inc, 1963); and Ichiro Hori, *Folk Religion in Japan*, Joseph Kitagawa and Allen Miller, eds. (Chicago: University of Chicago Press, 1968).

On political, economic, and urban institutions, one should not overlook two other works by R. P. Dore: *City Life in Japan* (London: Routledge & Kegan Ltd., 1958) and *Land Reform in Japan* (London: Oxford University Press, 1959). Others of special pertinence are James C. Abegglen, *The Japanese Factory: Aspects of Its Social Organization* (New York: The Free Press, 1958); Ezra F. Vogel, *Japan's New Middle Class* (Berkeley: University of California Press, 1963); John M. Maki, *Government and Politics in Japan* (New York: Frederick A. Praeger, Inc., 1962); David W. Plath, *The After Hours:*

Modern Japan and the Search for Enjoyment (Berkeley: University of California Press, 1963); Robert A. Scalapino and Junnosuke Masumi, *Parties and Politics in Contemporary Japan* (Berkeley: University of California Press, 1962); and Langdon Warner, *The Enduring Art of Japan* (New York: Grove Press, Inc., 1957).

V

GLOSSARY
OF JAPANESE TERMS

amazake   homemade brew of rice
amimoto   net-owner
apaato   apartment
arai   rough
arayashiki   foundation of life—esoteric
   Buddhist term

baka   fool
Benzaiten   Goddess of Music
bon   festival of ancestor commemoration
bosu   boss
bunke   satellite family
burakumin   "outcaste" Japanese minority
Buraku Kaihōdōmei   Alliance for Burakumin Emancipation
burōkā   broker
butsudan   Buddhist family altar

chūgakkō   junior high school

daimyō   feudal lord
Dōkō Undō   Buddhist movement mean-
   ing "going together"
Dōmei   Japan   Federation   of   Labor
   Unions

dōtoku kyōiku   moral education
Dōwakai   Society for Integration
dōwa kyōiku   education for integration
   and emancipation

Ebibara-mono   man of Ebibara
Ebisu   God of Riches
Edo   term   for   Tokugawa   era   (1603–
   1867); old name of Tokyo
eta   pejorative term for *burakumin*
eto   corruption of *etori*
etori   occupation of food catchers

fujin gakkyū   women's study group
fure-nai   "do not touch"
futon   Japanese quilt and bedclothes

gakkyū-kai   classroom meeting
geisha   professional singing and dancing
   girl
giri   sense of duty; whole range of reciprocal obligations
gyōja   cult priest of folk beliefs
gyomin   fishermen

Hakai   "Transgression" (novel)

hanafuda   flower cards
hanami   cherry-blossom watching
hibachi   brazier
hinin   criminals
hiyori-moshi   informal discussion meeting; literally, "talk about weather"
hōbiki   gambling game
hobo   "teaching mothers" in nursing schools
hōgi   sacred wooden block
hōji   ceremonial to commemorate death of close kin at stipulated intervals
hōmuruumu   homeroom
Honganji   Jōdoshinshū temple in Kyoto
honke   main family

ichijōkogi   illegal one-net fishing
ihai   memorial plaque to departed relatives
ikebana   flower arrangement
inari   shrine which honors the fox *kami*
in-nen   cause-effect
ita-mandara   sacred plaque of Nichirenshōshū

jichikai   self-governing meeting
jidōkai   student council in elementary schools
Jirō   All-Japan Free Labor Union
Jōdoshinshū   Buddhist sect

kabuki   classic Japanese drama
kagikko   key children
kaikōban   heavy planks utilized in *ichijōkogi* illegal trawling
kamaboko   fish paste
kami   Shintō word nearest to "God"; honorific for noble, sacred spirits
kamidana   votive shelf honoring Shintō spirits
kamofuraaju   camouflage
kawaramono   people who live at the edge of rivers
keimō   enlightenment

Kōbō Daishi   founder of Shingon Buddhist sect
kodomokai   children's society
kogi kumiai   fishermen's protective association
kōju   local word for neighborhood mutual-aid group
Kōmeitō   Clean Government Party
koseki   family record
kumi   team; neighborhood group of about five families
Kurushii toki no kami-danomi   "When people suffer they turn to supernatural powers."
kyō   scripture
kyōkai   church
Kyōshikai   Japan Teachers' Association

mi-ai kekkon   arranged marriage
mikoshi   portable shrine
Monbushō   Ministry of Education
mōshi-awase   reaching agreement
muko-yoshi   adopted-son-bridegroom
musume yado   Kazaki-shima tradition of "house visiting"
Mutsumi   Mutual Friendship (school magazine)

Nakayama-no-wakashū   young men of Nakayama's house
nakōdo   go-between
nam myōhō renge kyō   sacred chant of Nichiren Buddhist sect
Neta ko o okosuna   "Sleeping children should not be awakened"
neyado   young men's sleeping club
Nichiren Shōnin   founder of Nichiren Buddhist sect
Nichirenshōshū   Buddhist sect of Sōkagakkai
Nichirenshū   Buddhist sect
nigō, sangō   second, third "wives"
Nikkyōso   Japan Teachers' Union
nō   classic Japanese drama

odō miniature Shintō shrine
ofuda sacred strip of paper with name of *kami*
okyū ancient folk remedy made of herbs and burned in a cube on bare skin
on kindness, favor, obligation
oyabun-kobun ritual father-ritual sons
oyakokai meeting of children and parents
oya kōkō filial piety

pachinko pinball gambling machine
pii-chii-ei PTA.

ren-ai kekkon love marriage
Ryūōjin God of the Sea

sadō tea ceremony
sake Japanese wine
samurai warrior lord
sarariiman salaried man
seitokai student council in junior and senior high schools
senmin lowly people
senshakogi legal method of trawling
serai konjō jealousy (local dialect)
shakubuku aggressive effort to proselytize, associated with Sōkagakkai
Shichō-san Mr. Mayor
Shikata ga nai "It cannot be helped"
shiken jigoku "examination hell"
Shingonshū Buddhist sect
shin-heimin new citizens
Shintō Shintoism—indigenous Japanese religion
shitsugei lacquer art
shittai unemployed workers on public construction projects
shōgakkō elementary school
shūshin prewar term for moral education
Sōhyō General Council of Trade Unions
Sōkagakkai Value Creating Society

sokobiki legal method of trawling
soroban-geta illegal method of trawling
Suiheisha Organization of Levellers
suisen "daffodil"
sumō Japanese wrestling
sutorippu strip tease

tai sea bream
Taisekiji head temple of Nichirenshōshū
Tamagawa Gakuen famous private school near Tokyo
tatakai fight
tatami straw mat
Tendaishū Buddhist sect
tempura deep-fried food
Tokugawa, Ieyasu feudal ruler who with successors ruled Japan (see Edo)
tokushu burakumin residents of special hamlets
toruko (-buro) Turkish bath
tōsō struggle

wabi Zen concept connoting simplicity and quietness
wakashūgumi group of young people

yakudoshi bad-luck year
yen 0.28 cent
yobai old custom of nocturnal courting; literally, night-crawling
yoboshigo ritualistic adoption (local dialect)
yūwa-shugi conciliationism

Zendōkyō National Integration Study Conference
Zengakuren National Federation of Students Self-Government Associations
zenjin kyōiku whole-man education
Zenshū Buddhist sect

INDEX